TECHNOLOGY DIFFUSION

FEDERAL PROGRAMS & PROCEDURES

by

GRANVILLE W. HOUGH

Lomond Books
Mt. Airy, Maryland
1975

LC Catalog Number: 73-88035

ISBN 0-912-338-05-9 (hard copy)
ISBN 0-912-338-06-7 (microfiche)

LOMOND SYSTEMS, INC.
Mt. Airy, Maryland 21771

FOREWORD

This systematic study of the technology diffusion process contributes significantly to conceptualizing, classifying and evaluating programs to extend the benefits of technology.

Knowledge about the diffusion, or transfer, process is fragmentary and limited. Conditions vary widely from one situation to another and generalized rules are not available.

Professor Hough's book provides a good general description of the problem, presents case examples and develops a set of models which should be generally useful for evaluating ongoing programs and for program planning.

The well-documented case examples of technology diffusion are a uniquely useful contribution. No similar collection is available for illustration and comparative analysis. These case examples are impressive testimony to the thoroughness of Hough's research. The selection is representative and extensive from screw worm fly control to numerically controlled machine tools. Obviously, the author did not select examples to prove any points — they represent varied patterns of success, failure, methodology, significance and transferability.

The graphic clarity of analysis of the case examples facilitates their usefulness. For each, Hough provides a capsule summary followed by a chronology of the major elements in the diffusion process: basic research and investigation, inventing and informing, innovating, and integrating. Concluding comments provide Hough's own succinct interpretation of the significance of the case experience.

The conclusions and recommendations in the final chapter could be used as a check list for policy makers of the National Science Foundation, other Federal agencies, the Congress and large industrial organizations.

The manuscript was originally submitted as a doctoral dissertation in the Science, Technology and Government program at The American University. It has been revised and updated for book publication.

Lowell H. Hattery

CHAPTER I

TECHNOLOGY POTENTIAL

Technology has increasingly affected the activities and relationships of business, government and the individual. Public funds for research and development are the main source for the technological explosion. With half and more of the national research and development budget spent by Federal agencies, the pay-out is an important question. In answer to this question, "technology diffusion," "technology assessment," "technology transfer," and "technology utilization," have entered the vocabulary.

The process of technology diffusion begins with applied research which generates a technology to satisfy a need or to exploit an opportunity, and continues through the adoption and application of the technology. Both the direct and the indirect effects of this diffusion are gaining in importance. Administrators recognize that research and development results must be translated into useful products, processes, or programs which satisfy public and private needs.

No longer is research and development (R&D) an acceptable end in itself.

This study endeavors to describe, classify, compare, and evaluate operational activities in selected Federal agencies for promoting the general diffusion and utilization of technological developments resulting from Federal applied research and development.

The findings presented in this book should be useful to all who are concerned with questions of innovation, technology diffusion and transfer, and the benefits of research and development; to engineers, business and government administrators, legislators, and other policy makers. The models in this study will aid administrators in conceptualizing the technology diffusion process, and in allocating resources for diffusing new technology. Federal agency administrators should be able to view technology diffusion programs as cybernetic systems, in dynamic equilibrium with other agencies and social processes. The analysis presented provides guidelines for measuring and evaluating feedback from programs.

Importance of the Problem

Technology diffusion relates to Federal expenditures of about $15 billion annually or to 1½% of the Gross National Product. If properly focused, these expenditures can be the cutting edge of national power. If frittered away, opportunities are lost.

The analysis was carried out between Jan. 1, 1968, and Oct. 4, 1969, then reviewed and updated during the summer of 1973. The level of concern in 1967 can be compared with the level of concern in 1972. In 1967, the Science Policy Research Division, Legislative Reference Service, Library of Congress, reported to the Subcommittee on Science and Technology, Senate Select Committee on Small Business, that:

1. Public funds generate about two-thirds of the available technology and the government has a responsibility to get full benefits from this knowledge.

2. Federally derived technology has appreciable utility to industry and to other public programs at all levels of government. . . .

3. Therefore, Federal government efforts are warranted in devising and operating programs to make this technology readily available to all users. . . .

4. The private sector innovation rate is affected by a "climate" of which the availability of technology is an important part. . . .

5. Reeducation and counseling as to the technological needs of industry are necessary before strong demands for new information will arise. . . .

6. At the present time, there is no uniform policy or practice among Federal agencies as to technology transfer. The NASA and AEC pursue a central-agency concept of collecting and disseminating technology. The DOD makes no special effort for the transfer of its majority share of government-sponsored technology. . . .

7. Additional public discussions and formulation of opinion from both private and public sectors is necessary before detailed policy planning can proceed. . . . Ongoing Federal programs should be examined more intensively for evidence of acceptance and efficiency.[1]

These conclusions, adopted by the Senate Subcommittee, reflected the emerging dissatisfaction of the time.

Five years later, this dissatisfaction had caused action at higher levels. Dr. M. Frank Hersman, Director of the National Science Foundation's Office of Intergovernmental Science and Research Utilization, outlined four of these actions in 1972:

> 1. The President's Message to Congress on Science and Technology (March 16, 1972) stated: "Federal research and development activities generate a great deal of new technology which could be applied in ways which go well beyond the immediate mission of the supporting agency. In such cases, I believe, the Government has a responsibility to transfer the results of its research and development activities to wider use in the private sector.

> 2. The report of the Committee on Intergovernmental Science Relations to the Federal Council on Science and Technology (May, 1972), which urges policies and mechanisms to increase the capacity of state and local governments for the task of utilizing Federally developed technology and to participate in formulating national R&D priorities. . . .

> 3. The policy recommendation of the Federal Council on Science and Technology for Expanded Interagency Cooperation in the use of Federal laboratories which received general support from the Office of Management and Budget. This proposed policy would charge existing Federal R&D agencies with utilizing their resources to define and solve technological problems. . . .

> 4. The General Accounting Office (GAO) (March 2, 1972) which recommended (a) a Government-wide policy for technology transfer with guidelines issued to Federal agencies to implement a formal, active technology transfer process, (b) the Secretary of Defense establish policy and procedures to encourage more extensive application of existing defense technology to civilian problems, and (c) the establishment of a technology transfer consulting team as a central focus to assist Federal agencies in the matching of technological resources with pressing national needs.

> Despite these manifestations of executive branch and congressional interest in the development of technology transfer policy, the efforts of Federal agencies in this field are still tailored to the basic mission of each agency, the nature of the technology it develops, its perceptions of the identity and needs of the client users, and the resources available.[2]

The importance of the problem has been recognized. As more and more Americans utilize the superior or more economical technology of foreign countries, we come to recognize our foregone opportunities. We have become non-competitive where we were once world leaders.

If we are going to spend up to 1½% of our GNP in Federal R&D, we must get more out of it.

Definitions

We define **technology diffusion** as publicizing, adapting, adopting, and ingesting a new item of **technology**,[3] which may be a product, process, technique, procedure, or other application of available science or technology. **Vertical diffusion** occurs between Federal agencies or any other agents of society and the economic sectors with which they normally interact. **Horizontal diffusion** occurs from agency to agency, economic sector to economic sector, and discipline to discipline. In the form of horizontal diffusion called **technology transfer,** an item serves a purpose other than the one for which it was developed. Technology transfer generally refers to disseminating information, matching technology with needs, and creative adapting of items to new uses.

In recent usage, technology transfer has come to be associated with specific, limited programs in Federal agencies. A more useful term is **technology utilization,** the process by which existing R&D results are translated operationally into useful programs, processes, or products which fulfill actual or potential public or private needs.[4]

Inventing or inventive work is the creating of ideas and their recording in professional symbologies of working models, blueprints, sketches, equations, formulas, or technical descriptions. Inventive work is embodied in applied research, exploratory development, prototype design and development, and originator test and evaluation. **Technologists** invent or create new uses for available science and technology during applied research and development.[5]

Through **secondary invention (improvement invention, derivative invention,** and **creative adaptation),** an item of technology is improved for a present application or modified for a new one. All secondary inventions result from creative adapting, but not all creative adaptations can legally qualify to be patented as improved or derivative inventions.

Informing, as used in this study, is disclosing new technology, publicizing its characteristics and availability, and training others in its use. It includes **information science,** the systematic handling of information to transfer it in time and space from originators to users.

Innovation is the application of new technology, particularly a unit's adoption of it. A **change agent** is a person whose role, office, or inclination causes him to support the adoption of a new technology.

Integration of a technology item is social and economic accepting, adjusting to, and ingesting the item. It is the spread of new technology into other parts of the industry and into other industries where that technology is unknown.

A **system** is "an array of components designed to accomplish a particular objective according to plan."[6] Thus defined, a system embodies the concept of **cybernetics,** or automatic control (through feedback and adjustment) of inputs (energy, materials, and information) which are being processed through components and procedures arranged to accomplish an agreed goal or objective. A system in technology diffusion denotes a group of interrelated procedures of an activity such as informing, innovating, and integrating.

Other terms are defined in Appendix A.

Methodology and Sequence

At the outset of this study technology diffusion literature was reviewed to answer these questions: (1) What are the traditional and historical activities of technology diffusion, particularly in the United States? (2) How do activities of technology diffusion "group" in terms of identifiable programs? Once these questions had been tentatively answered, predictive models could be developed which suggested operational approaches.

The second phase consisted to reviewing Federal agency programs and selecting those for intensive study. The agency size, importance to the economy, and type of procedures were considered in the selection. The three agencies selected for detailed study were the Department of Agriculture (USDA), the Public Health Service (PHS), and the Department of Defense (DOD). Four other agencies were also included: Department of Commerce (DOC), National Aeronautics and Space Administration (NASA), Atomic Energy Commission (AEC), and Small Business Administration (SBA). Only the more significant programs of these four agencies were reported.

The third phase of the study comprised model synthesis. Clearly four subprocesses were involved: inventing, informing, innovating, and integrating. Inventing is of course an essential and related antecedent. Technology diffusion, as we generally accept it, includes the subprocesses of informing, innovating, and integrating. The fourth phase was initial comparison of selected agencies. It provides a check on the predictive models and tentative comparisons of Federal agencies in the total process of technology diffusion.

During the fifth phase, detailed comparisons were made of the selected Federal agencies to determine: (1) which of the four subprocesses could be identified in each agency; (2) which agencies diffused technology more effectively; (3) what *de facto* procedures were used in each agency; and (4) what goals were accomplished by each agency's diffusion of technology.

In order to test further the predictive models and basic comparisons, 22 case examples of technology diffusion were studied from over 100 originally reviewed. Criteria for selecting the examples were: (1) general information available, (2) ease of understanding the example, (3) availability of data, (4) representativeness of typical technology, (5) representativeness of agency programs and procedures, and (6) transferability of the principles of the example to the process of technology diffusion.

In order to maintain independence of thought and effort, no support for this study was sought from any agency, public or private. This independence may have provided an advantage over funded studies of technology utilization.

This study does have limitations which the author recognizes. The predictive models which emerge from both Federal and non-Federal experience are verbal rather than quantitative. Where operational recommendations are made, they derive from logical analysis rather than mathematical proof. It would be advantageous to study more Federal agencies diffusing technology. Nevertheless, the author is confident that the main thrust of the operational recommendations would remain the same.

Organization of the Book

Chapter II develops the conceptual and predictive diffusion models of inventing (generation of new technology), informing, (information transfer), innovating (adopting), and integrating (ingesting). Chapter

III presents a background review of technology diffusion in the United States and draws conclusions which apply to any diffusion situation. Chapters IV, V, and VI treat technology diffusion programs of the United States Department of Agriculture, the Public Health Service and the Department of Defense. Chapter VII summarizes the most pertinent aspects of programs of the Department of Commerce, the National Aeronautics and Space Administration, Atomic Energy Commission and the Small Business Administration. Chapter VIII compares the agency programs and Chapter IX summarizes the study, draws conclusions, and recommends improvements for diffusing technologies resulting from Federal applied research and development.

FOOTNOTES

[1] Science Policy Research Division, Legislative Reference Service, Library of Congress, *Policy Planning for Technology Transfer, A Report to the Subcommittee on Science and Technology to the Select Committee on Small Business,* U.S. Senate, 90th Cong., 1st Sess. (Washington, D.C.: U.S. Government Printing Office, 1969), p. 4.

[2] M. Frank Hersman, "Parlaying the Benefits of Federal R&D," *Science Policy Reviews,* vol. 5, no. 4, 1972, pp. 19-20.

[3] Adapted from Everett M. Rogers, *Diffusion of Innovations* (New York: Free Press of Glencoe, 1962), pp. 19-20. The more general definition of diffusion for any new concept is given in Appendix A.

[4] Adapted from M. Frank Hersman, *op. cit.,* p. 18.

[5] It is recognized that a scientist doing pure basic research may encounter a barrier where he needs a new technique, instrument, manipulating device, or material. The scientist consumes time and resources to break this barrier within basic research; but, while doing so, he acts as a technologist doing necessary inventive work. If breakthrough activity is small, relative to the overall project, it is usually funded as basic research.

[6] Richard A. Johnson, Fremont E. Kast, and James E. Rosenzweig, *The Theory and Management of Systems,* 3rd ed. (New York: McGraw-Hill Book Co., 1973), p. 117.

CHAPTER II

CONCEPTUAL MODELS FOR DIFFUSING TECHNOLOGY

I. INTRODUCTION

This chapter groups activities of U. S. technology generation and diffusion into conceptual and predictive models which represent operating systems and programs. U. S. technology diffusion has been going on long enough to be, in some economic sectors and Federal agencies, standardized and institutionalized. Farmers, soldiers, doctors, and manufacturers use widely different technologies to achieve different results; yet they all express a need that causes technology to be generated; they get information about technology so they can adopt or use it; they consider its effects on operations; and they adjust other activities to it. These activity groupings resemble open-ended social systems with feedback provided by persons who evaluate, both objectively and subjectively, output versus input needs and resources. We can organize experience in these activities into conceptual models for inventing new technology; and then diffuse it through informing, innovating, and integrating. Furthermore, these models can have predictive and operational meaning to others concerned with technology and its diffusion.

The systems approach. One can define "systems" of technology diffusion as arrays of components designed to accomplish particular objectives according to plan. The basic system of Figure 1 processes input (information, energy, and material) by approved procedures into output goods or services.[1]

According to the mathematical theory of closed-loop systems, feedback automatically adjusts the input or process, if the output is not within tolerance compared to the standard. A sensor measures the output and a comparator compares it with the objective or standard. A control balances the system by correcting input or process, so that the output moves back into tolerance. When humans perform the feedback, the system is open-looped.

A system concept for use with technology has been described by R. E. Gibson to be a network of elements, each with inputs and out-

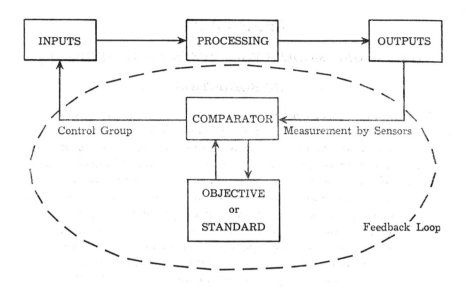

Figure 1. A basic system.

puts, each input having all the necessary ingredients to make the element function, each contributing to the other in terms of the overall objective or goal, and each having cybernetic links called feedback to adjust or reinforce the inputs. Feedback must be timely to contribute usefully. The system blocks may be machines, people, ideas, and ongoing effort.[2] If the output is in phase with the input, feedback is positive and technology grows. If output cancels the input, feedback is negative and uncertainty grows. Applying these descriptions, a government agency, business enterprise, or technology-associated organizational "system" can be discussed from Figure 2.

Information, material, ideas, and energy are assigned to different human activities to produce desired outputs. Some activities (or systems) are more efficient than others, but the goal is to allocate resources in a manner that will provide maximum utility to the concern. If the customer changes his mind about the product he wants, or if the goal changes in some other way, planning information must take this into account. Program managers provide the correct reference base of planning information, allocate the resources, and guide the functioning of the system.

Based on U. S. technology generation and diffusion experience, activities which group on inventing (development), informing (information transfer), innovating (application), and integration (ingestion and adjustment), can be treated as activities or subprocesses similar to operational systems. This makes it possible to:

1. Identify programs and procedures which group as subprocesses to achieve intermediate objectives of technology generation and diffu-

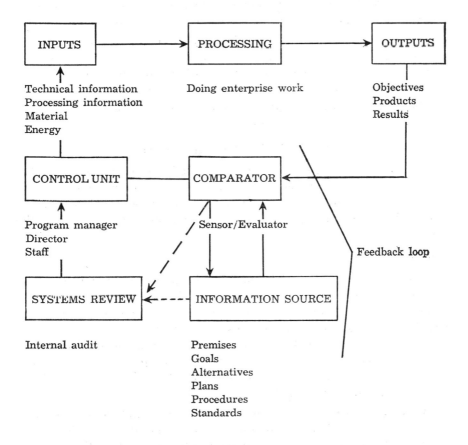

Figure 2. An operating system.[3]

sion. Each subprocess requires a network of elements, including inputs and outputs, with the inputs being adequate for the subprocess function.

2. Simplify, understand, and maintain boundaries between the intermediate subprocesses. Choose objectives for each subprocess within the boundaries.

3. Clarify relationships among the subprocess programs and the contributions each makes toward the total process. Pay attention to the amount and phases of feedback and how it enters the system.

4. Enable deliberate and coordinated suboptimization toward intermediate goals. Make most effective use of time and resources.

5. Enable Federal agencies to focus attention on the total process and all its sources of feedback, to influence the total process by balancing effort among the antecedent inventing and technology diffusion subprocesses, or to selectively support inputs which are not in balance.

The subprocesses are outlined below, then combined into the total process to show interrelationships.

II. THE INVENTING MODEL

Institutionalized inventive work as modeled in Figure 3 is the antecedent of most technology diffusion in process today and is closely allied to it. The institution has inputs which it processes into outputs. Feedback is obtained by comparing output satisfactions against the input needs.

Inputs

The inventing model may represent the combined applied research and development effort of the public and private sector, or it may represent a single inventor. Inventive work is a deliberate, intentional activity to change the status quo, using available inputs and processes in a continually adjusted effort to reach an output goal of changing the environment to satisfy the need. Thus inventive work is the antecedent of technology diffusion, though not all inventive work satisfies a need well enough to be diffused.

Mission. The mission of the inventor or the applied research and development organization, whether specific, general, or implied, gives work its direction and scope. Steel developers work with steel, not hybrid corn. Agricultural crop specialists do not develop ways of handling steel. Generation of new technology must contribute to the organizational mission to gain support and approval. If the mission is specific, the inventive activity and its boundaries must also be specific. If the mission is general, as in some corporations, support may be minimal except for the most promising items. The self-employed inventor generally infers his mission from market needs, technical opportunity, or innate curiosity.

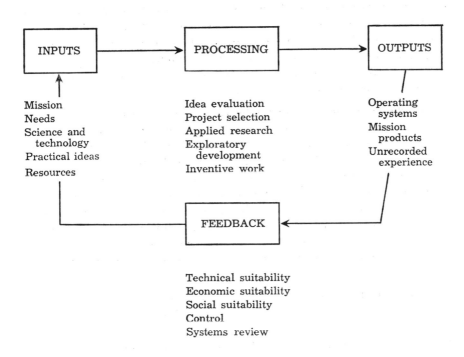

Figure 3. Inventing (applied research and development) model.

Needs. Within a mission, specific needs of economic, social or psychological origin develop. If social, development may be stimulated by an artificial economic need, such as a market for placing men on the moon. The social need in this case is national prestige, and the artificial economic need is created through lucrative contracts. In the U. S., most inventive work is clearly supported by, or follows, the perception or delineation of an economic need, either actual or artificial. These needs are defined as requirements, needed products, or corporate aims. This does not mean that new technologies satisfy only the specific need toward which the work was directed. Economic need stimulates invention; but new technology may find no market at all if it does not also satisfy some unrelated need.

Inventors who invent to satisfy innate psychological needs share with scientists the desire of knowledge for its own sake. They invent on their own time and in their own areas of interest, but do not turn down support. However, **need** as an input to inventive institutions, is largely under society's control and can be changed to satisfy society's demands. Mission and need determine which enterprise goals will dominate inventing activities.

Available science and technology. Inventive work bases in either available science, available technology, or both. The developer's academic or practical training gives him an appreciation of certain principles and equipment. Either by experience or through literature he has access to past and on-going work in the area of his interest. He may develop something he understands completely, or by trial and error solve a problem in a way he does not fully understand. If the developer has access to the store of science and technology information (current literature, proprietary information, and available raw inventions and improvements), he can focus directly on the need from an established base.

Practical ideas. Inventive work is both the development and trial of ideas generated for satisfying a need. Though frequently termed "creativity," this hardly describes the trial and error present in most inventive work. Practical ideas develop by: observation, innate understanding of science and technology, drawing analogies, adaptation, transference, lonely meditation, or group stimulation. The inventor may originate the idea himself, or he may be the integrator, but the idea remains an intellectually new input to inventive effort.

Resources. Money is the common denominator of support which provides a tangible and measurable input to the process of inventing. Scientists, non-scientist inventors, engineers, technologists, technical aids, clerical aids, and administrators can be measured by number, man-hours, and size of payroll. Laboratories, materials and power are quantifiable by total, as well as per man outlay. Tangible resources manifest the preferences of the existing culture.

Processing

Idea evaluation and project selection. Technologists process inputs in order to produce a preferred output which satisfies the need. Practical ideas are examined in terms of other inputs (available materials, people, technology, mission, and needs), and the more promising are selected for detailed paper analysis. The paper analysis uses all available information, including handbooks, technical literature, patent files, and known activities of competitors. Additional assistance may be sought by employing operations analysis, formal or informal.

Applied research and exploratory development. After paper analysis further defines the most promising approaches, applied research and exploratory development (trial and error inventive work) complete the necessary experimentation. Finally, still fewer approaches will be reduced to prototype form, sketches, engineering designs, or technical description. At this stage, the original practical idea has been advanced to a stage where it may be patentable; or, if not, it may be usable in further work.

Inventive work. These activities are inventive work as defined for this study. The process for many development programs continues through the production of an operational system. The Apollo program was destined to produce only a few copies of its system, but inventive work continued through development of the complete communication satellite system. Measurement of inputs indirectly measures the process of inventive work. As work on practical ideas transforms them into useful end products, processing becomes more costly; consequently, economy forces all except the most promising items to be discarded.

Outputs

Inventive outputs are the technologies and technical information made available for diffusion. Government agencies have recently sponsored unique whole systems such as the Space Control Center at Houston, Texas. Items available for diffusion range from a development of this size to simple technical procedures. Outputs are in hardware, technical literature, files of inventive units, and in the unrecorded experience of the people who did the work.

Operating systems. Jet transports, nuclear power reactors, computers, titanium metallurgy, and communication satellites are examples of operating systems which have been produced in the development or inventing programs and then diffused as integral units for both mission and non-mission uses. Millions of blueprints and technical documents have been diffused as a corollary to operating systems. Operators have also been trained in the systems development programs, and they are available to facilitate diffusion.

Mission products. Mission products lesser than operating systems are technological recipes for a particular function. These may be patented inventions, patent applications, technical publications of both proprietary and non-proprietary information, and unpublished minor improvements in agency or company records. The number of these is measurable or can be roughly estimated. These lesser mission products may certainly be used for their design function (vertical diffusion), or they may be used for analogous functions in quite different activities or disciplines (horizontal diffusion).

Non-mission products. In the course of development, many items are tried which fail to satisfy the mission need, but which may satisfy the need of another unit. These may take the same form as mission products, but are less well developed. They may be filed in technical papers or memoranda rather than carried through to application. These failures and near misses, R&D by-products, are at least as numerous as the successful end-products. There is, of course, much duplication among these products because many technologists may fail using the same approach. Non-failure by-products are improvements in techniques, procedures, or processes, which do not improve the mission product but do make it cheaper or easier to handle. These may be documented or they may exist only in the knowledge of those who use them.

Unrecorded experience. Product developers are recognized as uniquely interested in carrying through activities to achieve integration of their products into the market place. In corporations, they are sometimes moved from R&D to production and marketing as a short-cut to informing and innovating. This human experience output of inventing activities can support either directly usable output or by-products. Developers may have practical ideas for solving problems or new technical hunches which they can develop only by continued association with the product.

Feedback

This section relates to the feedback loops shown in Figures 2 and 3.

Technical suitability. The basic test for a product is that of technical suitability or performance against the need. Though technical suitability should logically be determined during processing, this cannot always be done. Reliability, maintainability, and reaction to environmental change can be predicted only to reasonable limits of testing time and cost. Thus, technical suitability tested through the life of the technology is a necessary feedback.

Economic suitability. No feedback is more specific than that of economic suitability, which is measured by the number of units adopting the results of inventive work. A patent or patentable item is evidence of legal suitability, and gives the inventive unit certain rights which are exploitable, if the items are economically and socially suitable.

Cost is a special type of suitability. New technology may satisfy a market or a social need, but not fall within the means of prospective users; or it may fail in economic suitability. Cost is an internal comparison, where the values of inputs are measured against the values of outputs. Economically, technology generating activities should support themselves — outputs should be worth more than inputs. Similarly, successful outputs must also support unsuccessful approaches.

Social suitability. Attributes of social suitability are continued adoption, timeliness of new technology, and absence of undesired side effects. Society is incapable of supporting technologies for which it is not ready, regardless of their patentability, technical feasibility, and economic efficiency. Leonardo da Vinci invented profusely, but there was little relationship between his inventions and ability of the society in which he lived to use them. Acceptance by society changes; for example, birth control devices were received differently in 1973 than they were in 1963 or 1943.

Timeliness also depends on the pace of other technologists. In the U. S. mass market, being six months slower than a competitor may lose patent rights, access to the market, and results of inventive work. Social acceptance is affected by information transfer programs in which marketing is a major subdiscipline. Stronger inputs into the informing program is one way to increase acceptance and to offset adverse feedback within the inventing activity.

Control. After evaluating output versus input, the administrator or program controller makes changes to increase efficiency. Beyond this, administrators normally focus inventing work by allocating resources according to need priorities within the mission. Even the independent inventor works on something he believes will have value. As needs change, priorities change. Suitability evaluations are used by administrators to modify inputs or to guide processing toward current as well as original needs.

Systems review. Self-appraisal of the inventing activity by persons associated with the enterprise is distinct from the continuing control process. Sometimes called management audit, systems review questions continuation of the inventing activity, its pertinence to enterprise goals, its priorities, and its approach to processing. When no other mechanism is available to perform the system review function, the marketing organization or buying public may force it on top management. Inventing activity outputs become inputs into technology diffusion informing programs. One secondary output has been identified as a marketing feedforward[4] to offset feedback on adverse suitability within the inventing activity. The most common form of marketing feedforward is advertising, but educational programs are more subtle forms of influence on potential adopters.

III. THE INFORMING MODEL

Informing programs, modeled in Figure 4, purvey technical information to potential users, either present or future. They encompass: (1) marketing; (2) information storage, retrieval, and analysis; (3) the technical press; (4) many types of technical training; (5) some professional and trade association activities; and (6) government-sponsored conferences, demonstrations, publications, and movements of knowledgeable people.

New technical information flows from inventing into the information transfer and dissemination programs. When received, the new information may be embodied in hardware or in knowledgeable people, but is more frequently in documentary form.

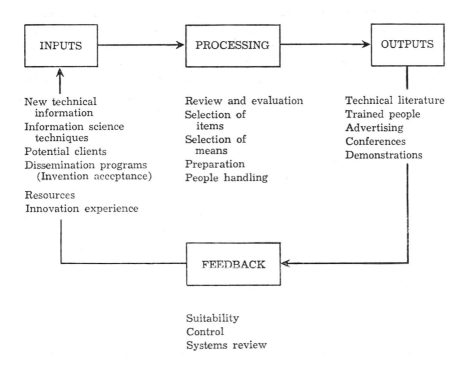

Figure 4. Informing (information transfer) model.

Information science techniques have expanded greatly since **1950,** giving information transfer great flexibility in matching the new information to needs of clients. There are many channels, several types of media, and numerous ways the information content can be formed and slanted. Every citizen can be reached in most areas of his interest; however, it becomes very expensive to reach all potential clients in a short time.

Potential clients may be individual consumers or producers, industrial firms, government agencies, engineers in training or future students. The needs and preferences of these clients are influential inputs into information transfer programs. Some clients can be reached only via television.

Dissemination programs. Information transfer is partly standardized by previous practice and regulations. Mission products, sometimes handled in the patent system, but more frequently out of it, follow formalized procedures. Within Federal agencies, for example, these procedures are funded and directed in specific directions. Clients help set up these programs and attune themselves to them. By-product or non-mission product information generally has no such standard program, and a new one must be devised for each case. For more general dissemination, standard text development for technical instruction also follows a known program; time lags in this program, however, sometimes cripple output effectiveness for rapidly changing technologies.

Invention acceptance. A feedforward from the inventing program is the need to establish acceptance for new technology — a market. When this feedforward is incorporated in the dissemination program, it gives program guidance and identifies requirements.

Resources. The level of effort is an input that is almost always more restrictive than others. It generally determines techniques used and clients approached and is measurable in terms of funds, manpower, man-hours, and materials.

Innovation experience. One feedback input into information transfer is rejects from innovation. These may have failed because information went to the wrong client, or was not in a readily understandable form, or simply was not timely. Innovation rejection may not be a function of the information program, but in each case, may occur.

Processing

Review and evaluation. Information processing includes searching the environment for material, reviewing material coming into the system, evaluating it, selecting the means of dissemination, and preparing material for dissemination. Processing has become highly specialized in recent years as clients have grown more demanding; yet it remains a significant bottleneck in technology diffusion. Volume, bulk, cost, and complexity of materials to be processed are examples of some problems faced. Special processing centers have been developed in the last few years to cope with rising input. These centers are able to repackage information into special formats for users.

Selection of items. Not all technologies can be published in complete detail. Some must be summarized, some only indexed, and some may not be published at all. Selection is generally done on the basis of items that have previously been successful for potential clients. In the feedforward case, the selection is generally on the basis of the amount of funds pushing the item. Processing of advertising is different from processing of technical presentations, though both are part of the trade and technical media.

Selection of means. Variables are channels to be used, presentation forms, and presentation content. Habits of expected customers, time period of contacts, and cost are major considerations. Some means are more timely; some are highly standardized, as are reports of granted patents and of patent processing; and some require a high level of intellectual understanding, as do preparation of textbooks, state-of-art reviews, and classroom instruction.

Media/channel mix. While one channel or one media means may be used, experience indicates that U.S. audiences are more apt to respond when a mix of channels or means is used. Further, because of variation of adoption interests among innovators, a mix is more likely to gain attention of clients than a single channel or means. Commercial radio, for example, is effective in achieving awareness about technology, but professionally approved blueprints are more helpful to engineers.

Preparation is the mass production portion of information handling. It divides into intellectual work of copy or content preparation and manual work of duplication for distribution. Recently, computers have been programmed to do some routine intellectual work and part of the preparation for mass production.

People-handling for information transfer. Processing of people for information transfer is formalized in educational systems, where instructors and students make their choices in a definite institutional environment. In some corporations, technologists are moved into production, marketing, and servicing as technologies are innovated and integrated.

For society as a whole, information transfer via people is relatively unplanned. It takes place when government agencies change contractors: engineers and technicians move, carrying their know-how with them. A cutback in major programs, such as a $1 billion cutback in NASA funds, changes the technology application of at least 20,000 technical people. They take their unrecorded experience into other work. This information transfer may lessen losses to society which result from job changes.

Outputs

Informing program outputs appear in almost every conceivable form. Traditional forms are: published patents, proprietary technical data, textbooks, movement of people with information, conventional libraries, technical and trade journals, advertisements, abstracts, indexes, and instructions. More recent output forms include adaptations to communications media of radio, television, and film. Microforms, technical briefs, conferences, computer tapes, and demonstrations are increasingly used. Another output form is the exhibition or exposition, a derivative of the English country fair of the Middle Ages.

Feedback

Suitability. Information transfer outputs are generally measured by sales, favorable reviews, and continuing requests for items. Movement of knowledgeable people transfers technical information and procedures to new units or activities. The economics of information transfer compare easily, and pragmatic information scientists look for sales versus costs in an information product. Technical suitability of means can be evaluated from customer comments. Means, or mixes of means, are almost always a compromise in processing. In feedback, an evaluation can be made of which medium or form generated most responses. Many customers register feedback comments through sales and servicing organizations which deal with aspects of products not up to customer expectations. Timeliness will be reflected in sales for items economically and socially desired at the time.

Control. Using evaluations, the administrator can adjust inputs or processing to satisfy client needs or program requirements Administrators particularly desire to exploit success and correct any processing which caused failures or no-takers. The informing administrator works between inventor and innovator and must be sensitive to pressure from both. Inventing activities may exert influence to have information focused toward certain clients. Innovator clients may need different forms of information as they go through the adoption sequence. Control is normally limited in the resources it can influence and has to resort to priorities.

Systems review can help in comparing current information science techniques against those becoming available. Control administrators, occupied with everyday problems, have trouble keeping up with improvements in information science. Apart from educational, library, and advertising fields, information transfer has normally been considered a derivative function, justifiable only in terms of the larger missions of the enterprise. Systems review, however, can establish the part information transfer plays in these missions. Outputs of information transfer feed continuously into innovation programs, with some forms giving innovators awareness of the technology and others guiding them in its application.

IV. THE INNOVATING MODEL

Innovators are individuals or units advocating adoption of an invention (use of the new information), those actually adopting, and those carrying through the work after adoption. Intended outputs of innovating units are **new products** or products which are better or cheaper because of **new processes** or **new techniques**. Innovation may require adaptation, prototype construction and testing, and commitments to produce. Innovation applies new technology by the first units capable of so doing. Innovating activities are arranged conceptually in Figure 5.

Inputs

Technical information. Innovating inputs are predominantly economic; however, technical and social inputs are prerequisites. Technical information comes direct from the informing program, but the main social input, that of entrepreneurship, is a function of general culture. New technology itself has characteristics of form, divisibility, ease of being understood, feasibility, apparent cost, and side effects, all of which affect the way it is processed.

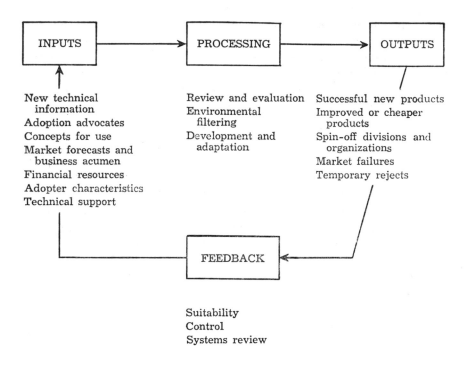

Figure 5. Innovating (application) model.

Advocates for adoption. New technical information may be considered a static input in the sense that it is available if needed, or it may be advocated by change agents. Salesmen are change agents for adoption of new products or processes. County agricultural agents are change agents for farm technology. Radical inventions frequently have champions who stake their reputations on the productiveness of a proffered change. The advocate for adoption is not the entrepreneur as often as he is the man who convinces the entrepreneur.

Concepts for use. New technical information is usually either mission or non-mission oriented; that is, a use for it may already be developed, and it is being advocated for use in that mission; or, alternatively, it is being proposed for a use different from the development mission. For mission uses, the technology is usually adequate; but organizational, procedural, and technical adjustments may be required before it is fully adopted. Technology advocated for a non-mission use may require further invention (adaptation) before it can be adopted.

Market forecasts and business acumen. Existing or potential markets are needed to entice an innovator. The market may be in the future and dependent on other advances or developments. Such markets can be forecast, but it takes considerable business acumen to properly interpret a market forecast. From another viewpoint, the adoption unit has financial, social, or technical goals which it endeavors to satisfy. These may be return on investment, provision of service, or efficiency of operation. These needs are influential inputs into the processing of new technology for adoption.

Financial resources. Innovations may be stillborn if development funds are short. In fact, new technology does not usually catch on until numerous entrepreneurs have funds available to try it out. Risk capital is a prerequisite to innovation just as are new technical information and entrepreneurship.

Adopter characteristics such as age of individuals, firms, industries, and organizations; educational level within the adoption units; and relative position of the unit in the market structure all affect the propensity of the unit to innovate. Entrepreneurs, technically or business oriented, seek the advantages of new technology and drive the innovating activity.

Technical support. As a minimum, engineers and technicians must be available to evaluate the technology. Beyond evaluation, they may adapt or further develop the new item to make it producible. The entire production process may have to be engineered.

Processing

Innovation costs more to the adoption unit than any other part of technology diffusion. In this process, high cost pilot plants, prototypes, and initial production facilities are built. Many products are filtered out after review and evaluation. The AIETA sequence is followed in some form, but particular steps may be carried out by different groups.

Review and evaluation. An adoption unit searches for new technology to satisfy needs that have not been or will not be met with current technology. Information about new technology is sought, directly or indirectly, through channels considered dependable to the adoption unit. Because of search costs, most adoption units select information channels to provide a first screening of available technology. Channels most closely aligned to the boundaries of the adoption unit's functions are selected. If additional resources are available, the adoption unit will review related technology. How the adoption unit search function is limited to specific channels by information intermediaries between adopters and technology generators is depicted in Figure 6.

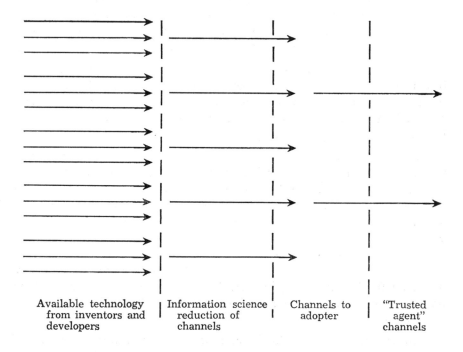

| Available technology from inventors and developers | Information science reduction of channels | Channels to adopter | "Trusted agent" channels |

Figure 6. Channels to adopters.

This is information transfer as seen by the adopter. Where he consciously chooses sources of information, he selects those he believes provide the most careful review and evaluation of the total technology applicable to the adoption unit. The information "trusted agent" intermediaries maintain awareness and interest for the adopter. Most adoption units accept the selections by their trusted agents and proceed to evaluate those selections for suitability.

Environmental filtering is one way to consider the evaluation process (Figure 5) after items receive the adopter's attention. Figure 7 abbreviates environmental filtering to an incentives/barriers submodel. If the item has more favorable than unfavorable indications, it will more likely be given a trial. Some indications can be so overriding that one can offset several which are opposing. Formal weighting of the indicators can be helpful.

FAVORABLE INDICATORS	UNFAVORABLE INDICATORS
Inexpensive	Costly
Results visible	Results not visible
Item divisible	Unit adoption
Compatibility	Requires new support
Apparent utility	Slight upgrading
Individual adopts	Group adopts
Ease of understanding	Complex

Figure 7. Environmental filtering.

Environmental filtering results in temporary rejection of items deemed unsuitable, and trial or study of those that appear applicable. For each adoption unit, the process will be somewhat different, depending on the specific environment. The selection process continues until items are finally adopted or rejected. Adopted items may be reprocessed and subsequently rejected if feedback indicates that the item will adversely affect the functions of the adopting unit.

Adaptation. Once an item is selected as applicable, it must be made suitable for production and marketing. This may require significant adaptation, and the same item may be modified differently by competing forms or adopters. The adaptations may be called production engineering, market packaging, or other terms; but they are essentially improvement inventions to adopters. Sometimes the improvements are so significant that they are patentable as derivative inventions.

Outputs

Desired innovational outputs result in successful new products and cheaper or improved products because of improved processes or techniques. There are, however, more failures than successes in innovating programs. Successful outputs may be handled by the organization as it exists, or may be developed by new divisions. Sometimes new or spin-off organizations are formed to handle the many new factors involved in the innovation. Successes go through all phases of diffusion and become a part of general culture and technology. Failures are those which are tried and rejected. Temporary rejects which do not arouse enough interest to be tried are called "no-takers". Outputs are measured in terms of gross sales, margin of profit, and in other ways familiar to enterprise managers. The economic criteria of the market place have pre-eminence.

Feedback

Suitability. To the enterprise manager, particularly the economic enterprise manager, sales and gross profit may justify cost of innovation. If costs are recovered at a reasonable rate of return, the innovation is judged suitable. The boundary condition is recovery of innovation costs. To the social or public enterprise manager, returns most offset the costs, even when he cannot directly quantify the returns. A manager whose mission is innovation may measure output by the number of successes, failures, and no-takers.

Control. The adopter evaluates relative success or failure and controls his inputs or further processing accordingly. The adopter who finds an innovation more successful than previous product lines, may choose to exploit it by changing enterprise boundaries, organization, and goals. To the innovation administrator, each technology tried must be evaluated to determine factors of success or failure. Evaluated failures and no-takers are returned to inventing programs or to informing programs for reprocessing.

Systems review is necessary to innovating because the social needs and those of the enterprise are frequently ignored by administrators. Technological forecasting of innovating effects can be made to supplement the AIETA sequence. Somewhat separate groups can do this better than processors, who normally evaluate in terms of enterprise program procedures and intermediate goals.

Systems review can disclose to administrators technologies developed in other enterprises or disciplines which may be preferable to those selected in review and environmental filtering. Systems review may also expand or change the list of "trusted agents" to include more pertinent sources of information. Finally, systems review can evaluate shifting of enterprise boundaries which result from successful innovating and can recommend long-term enterprise value maximization.

V. THE INTEGRATING MODEL

After an innovator has shown the efficacy of a new item of technology, other units of the social and economic order may adopt it. While to each of them, individually, items are new, and the process is one of innovation; to society as a whole, later adoption is imitation. Less development or adaptation of the technology is required. During this period of imitation, adjustments are forced among producers, suppliers, and markets. The "learning curve" is important while competitive forces adjust to new technology and standardize it. Figure 8 arranges these adjustments as conceptual ingestion of technology by

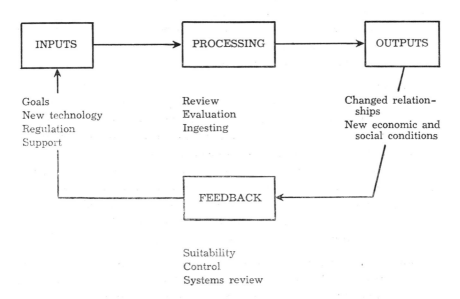

Figure 8. The integrating model.

society. The integration period may be considered as development (or adjustment) related to that technology. Cultural lag is identified and overcome. Desired and undesired effects of the technology emerge.

Inputs

Goals, missions, and needs. National goals for technology tend to be imbedded in legislation. Public and private enterprises contribute their part toward the general goals. Public enterprises have missions covering broad national goals, and private enterprises have corporate or unit goals. Within these missions, specific needs define objectives which, if fulfilled step by step, will contribute toward national goals. Corporate goals are equally useful for step by step achievement of corporate aims. Both public and private enterprise seek profit, survival, and social benefits.

New technology that innovators have shown to be acceptable and preferred is adopted by users and other producers. The degree of preference for the new item determines its rate of adoption. Diffusion or use of each new item continues until still better technology replaces it. Several such items may follow each other closely, they may compete, and they may be retarded by unwanted side effects.

Regulation. Although new technology may be welcomed into the economy, this is not always the case. New products may be retarded by forces of equilibrium established from previous integration or from incompatibility with existing regulations and social customs. Therefore, special mechanisms have been developed to speed imitation and integration. These include grants, subsidies, loans, tax incentives, and penalties for non-conformance. Finally, as imitation proceeds and adjustments are made, new products become integrated and older products or methods become harder to make, sell, or use. Thus integration gathers momentum as it progresses.

Support includes the resources and skills required by new technology. These may be new raw materials, changed finished stock, new job skills, and different work patterns. The momentum of integration forces changes in the support structure, but lack of support structure may stop innovation altogether.

Processing

Society reviews and evaluates new technology in terms of its prospective contributions. This is done in day-by-day decisions to adopt or not adopt and in continuing adjustments to adoption. Each adoption unit goes through the AIETA sequence. In a directive type activity as in the Department of Defense and most Federal agencies, ingesting new technology is through procedures similar to Planning, Programming, and Budgeting (PPB). Goals are set, plans are established to meet the goals, programs are carried out, and resources are allocated. Coordination and execution of these activities require many technical managers. In business and industry, venture capital must be available to support integration, and institutions which have venture capital help adopting units go through procedures quite similar to PPB.

Integration processing is highly iterative, or subject to reprocessing. Since effects of integration cannot be accurately forecast, adoption units have to prepare for government intervention if adoption proves a disadvantage to specific sectors of the economy or geographic areas. Intervention may take legislative, regulatory, or compensatory forms; but it affects both adopting unit and overall economy.

Outputs

Changed relationships result from integration. When new skills and new raw materials are used, prior skills are either displaced or replaced and raw materials may come from different areas of the earth. Intended changes from technology diffusion, and integrative activities within it, are: improved conditions, more readily available and better products, new jobs, and economic potential in all geographical areas. Some technology outputs call for a leap-frogging from one level of human activity to another.

Where outputs do not appear to be in balance, government makes income or opportunity transfers, directly subsidizing disadvantaged groups or areas. These adjustments or transfers may embed themselves in the culture as have tariffs, excise taxes, and welfare payments.

New economic and social conditions. Changed relationships and government adjustments complicate social and economic conditions. Some areas develop faster than others. Population shifts to advantaged areas and overcrowds them. Bypassed areas are neglected. During the changes, it takes considerable time to determine whether the new conditions are better or worse.

Feedback

Suitability. The Gross National Product (GNP) is one indicator of technology integration suitability and effectiveness, though it measures only certain aspects. Per capita income measures many of the same aspects as the GNP. Neither measures improved quality, which is also an integrating activity output. A third measure is man-hour productivity, or man-hours of labor required to obtain staples in the exchange system. This can be influenced by subsidies to areas and industries. Another gross measurement is life expectancy, which indirectly measures quality of technology in such fields as food and nutrition, environmental conditions, and public health. Annual per-capita medical expenses can indicate availability of services, need or health. Other measurements indicate unwanted displacements and side effects. The unemployment index is one indicator. Another is accident and injury statistics. A third is environmental degradation from pollution, overcrowding, and depletion of resources.

Control. Adoption units must usually choose between adopting new technology or losing business to competitors. Administrators are forced to reevaluate new technology as frequently as their standard products come under criticism. Later adopters sometimes understand undesirable side effects but have little choice except to join the majority. To a considerable degree, once diffusion starts, administrators do not regain absolute control; they can only channel adoption by new regulation.

Systems review. Lack of timely systems review in integrating activities has caused much unfavorable comment about technology. Systems review groups can evaluate undesirable side effects better than administrators who strive only to satisfy enterprise needs. Such groups objectively evaluate actual results versus enterprise needs and national goals, then they suggest changes in subprocesses of technology diffusion. The main systems review work now occurs in Congressional committees, various national associations, and in a few academic institutions. Some larger corporations can review technology dispassionately, but they are too few to establish any coordinated control. In fact, they are forbidden to do so by antitrust legislation.

VI. TOTAL TECHNOLOGY DIFFUSION PROCESS

Figure 9 interrelates the inventing subprocess and the three technology diffusion subprocess models in the total process. These continu-

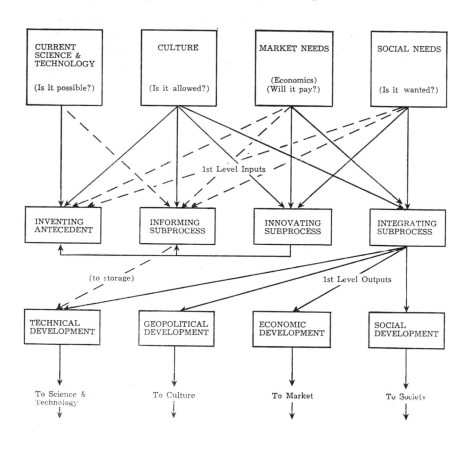

Figure 9. Overall technology diffusion process.

ing subprocesses, as well as the total activity, constantly change; and outputs of technology diffusion become new inputs. Rather than being circular, the total process moves from one level to the next with only temporary stability or equilibrium. Many items are being processed at any time.

The following chapter provides a Federal historical perspective on the total technology diffusion process. It shows that Federal agency programs and procedures are an integral part of U. S. technology diffusion. These Federal agency programs influence the subprocess and total process models developed in this chapter. In subsequent chapters, selected Federal agencies are studied and compared against the models set forth in this chapter.

FOOTNOTES

¹ Richard A. Johnson, Fremont E. Kast, and James E. Rosenzweig, *The Theory and Management of Systems,* 2d ed. (New York: McGraw-Hill, 1967), p. 77.

² R. E. Gibson, "A Systems Approach to Research Management," *Research Management,* vol. V, no. 4 (1962), p. 215.

³ Richard A. Johnson, Fremont E. Kast, and James E. Rosenzweig, . . . 2d ed., *op. cit.,* pp. 117-121. Text figures from the reference have been adapted and combined for ease in presentation.

⁴ Feedforward is analogous to feedback and is adopted from Marshall Mc-Luhan and Quentin Fiore, *War and Peace in the Global Village* (New York: Bantam Books, 1968), p. 3.

CHAPTER III

U. S. TECHNOLOGY DIFFUSION ACTIVITIES: BACKGROUND

I. INTRODUCTION

The effects of technology diffusion begin with applied research — that research which is directed to satisfy a need or exploit an opportunity; and they continue through the adoption and use of the resulting technology. Federal agencies contribute to, and are a part of, the process. U. S. technology diffusion focuses on new products, new processes, new techniques, and new programs for organizing technical activity. Relevant literature includes contributions from economics, politics, anthropology, industrial history, marketing, sociology, communications, information science, and direct studies of technology diffusion. For example, economic aspects of technology emerge as companies compete to place new products on the market, which, if successfully introduced, make a profit and sustain free enterprise. Similarly, governments compete to develop and apply new technology for strategic advantage. Sociological effects arise from new technological programs like automotive and air travel, radio and television, and mechanized farms and factories. Inevitably, there are political effects, for cultural changes cause people to change their preferences about government and the way they accept regulation. Finally, an item of technology carries certain implications which may affect its chances of adoption; society, at a given time, will accept the technology items supporting its dominant values.

Whereas a literature, written from the viewpoint of a parent science, generally addresses only questions of interest to that science, here a more extensive, cross-science literature search addressed questions of special interest to this study: What is the origin of diffusible technology? How, and through what institutions, do people learn about technology? What causes, supports, or retards innovation? What are the results of technology integration? What national technology goals can be identified?

II. ORIGIN OF DIFFUSIBLE TECHNOLOGY

The U. S. spends about 2% to 2½% of its GNP on applied research and development; activities which generate new technology through various forms of inventive work. Over half of the funds are spent by Federal agencies. Most of the half-million plus scientists and engineers in R&D and perhaps 200,000 self-employed inventors are engaged in applied research and development activities. The National Science Foundation has developed information on scientists and engineers who could generate new technology in R&D units of structured organizations. Recapped in Table I, the information shows more than doubling of R&D professionals from 1954 to 1968. In 1954 R&D employed nearly thirty-one percent of all scientists and engineers. That figure rose to thirty-seven percent in 1965. From 1965 to 1971 the proportion dropped to thirty-five percent.[1] Of the 1,412,500 scientists and engineers in the U.S. work-force in 1965, seventy-one

TABLE I

SCIENTISTS AND ENGINEERS IN R&D[2]
(in thousands)

SECTOR	1954	1961	1968	1971
Total	236.8	425.2	550.6	519.4
Federal Agencies	37.4	50.6	68.3	68.5
Industry*	164.1	312.0	381.9	350.0
Universities and Colleges	25.0	42.4	66.0	68.4
Associated FFRDC's	5.0	9.1	11.2	11.5
Other Nonprofits	5.3	11.1	23.2	21.0

*Includes associated Federally Funded Research and Development Centers (FFRDC's)

percent were engineers. Scientists and engineers increased from about one percent of the work-force in 1950 to nearly two percent in 1966.[3] In 1971, a study performed for the Atomic Energy Commission showed that one technician was in support of every two scientists and engineers.[4] Table I shows the predominance of industry in R&D professionals employed. The national average expenditure in constant dollars (1971=100) per R&D scientist and engineer was $46,300 in 1961, $52,600 in 1965, and $51,700 in 1971.[5] Privately employed inventors are not included in Table I, nor a small number of scientists and engineers in state and local governments.

Fund Sources and Performers

Federal government resources (manpower and facilities) in inventive work can be calculated through its annual expenditures. The National Science Foundation estimated the extent of corporate, state, and university and college resources. Table II shows that Federal agencies are the predominant funders, but that industry is the predominant performer in generating new technologies.

The massive funding by Federal government for generating new technology is a phenomenon of the current society. Annual Federal R&D expenditures rose from $74 million in 1940 to $2 billion in 1952 to $17 billion in 1968. The total dollar expenditures then held relatively constant through 1973. R&D took 2.8 percent of the Federal budget in 1951, but jumped to 12.6 percent by 1965.[6] Though dollar expenditures held relatively constant, percentage of total expenditures dropped to 7 percent. From 1957 through 1966, more than half the expenditures were for national security. Appendix B-1 shows the dominance of DOD, NASA, and AEC expenditures compared to those of other agencies.

This study treats applied research and development, those portions of R&D which do the inventive work and generate the new technology which can further national goals. Applied research and development expenditures in the Federal government were about one-fifth to one-fourth, and two-thirds to three-fifths, respectively, of all R&D in recent years. Expenditures have totaled over $13 billion since 1966. During the 1960's, the applied research and development expenditures have ranged from ninety-three to eight-five percent of Federal R&D expenditures.[7]

Considered another way, more than ten percent of the Federal budget for the decade 1960 was allocated for generating new technology; now the annual proportion is about seven percent. Appendix B-2 shows how DOD, NASA, and D/HEW have led in applied research, and Appendix B-3 shows how DOD, NASA, and AEC have led in development. Table II shows that corporations supplied forty-four percent of all funds used in generating new technology for a 1971 total of $10 billion. In 1966 industry supplied only thirty-five percent. The third and fourth fund sources are the universities, colleges and non-profit organizations; less than two percent of the 1971 total, as indicated in Table II. Part of the funds for these two sources originate from

TABLE II

ESTIMATED FUNDS AND PERFORMERS FOR APPLIED RESEARCH AND DEVELOPMENT, 1971
(in millions of dollars)[8]

SOURCES	PERFORMERS						
	Federal Agencies	Industry*	Univs. & Colleges	FFRDC's	Non-Profits*	Total	%s, Sources
Federal Agencies	3,260	7,590	370	470	520	12,210	54+
Industry	–	10,065	22	–	75	10,162	44+
Univs. & Colleges	–	–	227	–	–	277	1
Associated FFRDC's	–	–	–	–	–	–	–
Other Non-profits	–	–	56	–	145	151	1
Total	3,260	17,655	675	470	740	22,800	100
%	14+	77–	3	2+	3+	100	

*Includes Federally Funded Research and Development Centers run by the performer.

state governments, which in FY 1968 supplied about $57 million to applied research and development.[9]

These four sources gave a 1971 sum of about $22 billion for work toward new technology. To this must be added the efforts of private inventors and developers who receive about thirty percent of the new patents each year.[10] Although resources which independent inventors represent may be small, the results are significant. In total, the U.S spends 2 to 2½ percent of its GNP on applied research and development each year. That figure will probably not lessen over the next decade. These funds support: (1) individuals working alone, (2) independent research organizations, (3) private corporate research organizations, (4) government laboratories, (5) government contract corporate research organizations, (6) universities and colleges, and (7) federally funded research and development centers. To these domestic performers must be added the foreign performers who contribute to U.S. technology—they are treated in this study only as sources of technical information.

Individuals working alone. Despite predictions and conditions to the contrary, the individual inventor still adds many useful end products to technology. According to Stacy V. Jones, patent writer for the *New York Times*, there were 225,000 self-employed inventors in 1966, and nearly half of the developments they patented are actuallly used.[11]

Inventors can dispose of their inventions in three ways. They can sell them to others, manufacture or exploit them themselves, or work through research organizations.

There has been a gradual shift away from the individual inventor as a source of new technology. In 1900, eighty percent of all patents were issued to individuals; in 1957, about forty percent; and in 1967 about twenty-eight percent. Edwin Mansfield, Professor of Economics at the University of Pennsylvania, has concluded that this shift is caused by technology's increasing complexity, more division of labor among specialists to synthesize a new product, and higher cost of experimental equipment and instruments.[12]

Independent Research Organizations (other Non-Profits). The independent research institutes, such as the Mellon Institute, band together inventors and managers of innovation. Because of tax advantages and other considerations, this form of research organization has recently proliferated and now covers nearly all disciplines. Gale Research Company, in 1969, identified 4,508 of these private centers, including 272 in engineering and technology, 205 in business, economics, and transportation, 512 in agriculture, home economics, and nutrition, and 299 in education and educational technology. Two thousand new units developed between 1965 and 1969. Older private research institutes were listed under eighty-four multidisciplinary groups.[13]

In the U. S., the research organization approach evolved after 1900 into the present nonprofit and profit forms with the establishment of the Mellon Institute at the University of Pittsburgh in 1927, the Battelle Memorial Institute at Columbus, Ohio in 1929, and the Illinois Institute of Technology Research Institute at Chicago in 1936. Tables I and II show that these independents, listed as nonprofits, performed $740 million of work and employed about 21,000 professionals in 1971. Local industry and state government groups supported the older research institutes until after 1952, when the Federal agencies began to emphasize applied research.[14]   In 1971, Federal agencies furnished nearly seventy percent of their support, as shown in Table II.

Corporate Funded R&D. Privately funded corporate applied research and development remains a current key to development of technology. This inventive work is normally done in about 12,000 commercial R&D units in industrial firms. Twenty companies did forty-two percent of the company sponsored work in 1970. The amounts shown in Table II result from industry furnishing forty percent of total U. S. funds in applied research and forty-six percent in development.   Sixty-four percent of the industrial scientists and engineers, about 229,700, were working on company funded projects in January 1971. Industries leading in R&D support were electrical equipment and communications chemical and allied products, machinery, and transportation. Commercial R&D is concentrated in the Northeast and North Central states. The leading states or areas were Michigan (12%), Pacific States (13%), New Jersey (9%), Pennsylvania (7%), and New England (9%). Area and industry distribution vary distinctly from Federally funded industrial R&D.[15]

Corporate research and development has shown increasing vitality in recent years.   As Federal expenditures have stabilized (actually reduced in constant dollars), corporate R&D has taken up the slack. The National Science Foundation predicts that corporate spending will increase. Ninety-five percent of this R&D will continue to be in applied research and development.   Gross expenditures for applied research and development are predicted to reach $13.3 billion in 1975. This corporate work is expected to emphasize product safety, compliance with government regulations, and contribution to company objectives.   R&D employment on industry funded work is expected to be fairly stable, increasing to 260,000 scientists and engineers by 1975.[16]

Government Laboratories. As reported in Table I, 68,500 scientists and engineers worked for Federal agencies in 1971; Table II shows that they performed at a $3,260 million level in applied research and development. These figures have been relatively stable since 1966.[17] The specific number of civil service government laboratories varies according to the arbitrary division of the units, but in 1969 the Federal Council for Science and Technology identified 723, including FFRDC's (Federally Funded Research and Development Centers) but excluding research vessels.[18] Government laboratories have contributed to agency missions through agricultural, medical, mineral, nuclear, military, and space applied research and development. Their contributions are discussed in subsequent chapters.

Corporate Research Organizations (Government Contract). Federal agencies contracted out $7,590 million of applied research and development to industry in 1971 (see Table II). About eighty-six percent of this was development. In January 1971, about 129,600 of the scientists and engineers in industry R&D worked on Federal projects, for a total of thirty-six percent. In 1970, the top 40 companies did eighty-five percent of the Federal R&D work. Two-thirds of the funds were furnished by DOD, about twenty percent by NASA, and about thirteen percent by all other Federal agencies. Federal funds were supplied to industry in the Pacific States (39%), New York (10%), Massachusetts (7%), New Jersey (5%), Pennsylvania (5%), and Florida (4%).[19]

Industry performed seventy-seven percent of Federal agency applied research and development. Federal funding of applied research and development in industry reached a plateau about 1967 and has held fairly constant since then, though with internal adjustments. Defense and aerospace R&D were particularly reduced while other areas gained. In 1973 Federal funding was set at about $8 billion of the $20 billion spent in industy, about 40 percent rather than the 44 percent in 1971.[20]

Universities and Colleges. Federally and privately funded support for applied research and development in the universities and colleges are together less than $1 billion annually. In carrying out R&D,

68,400 collegiate scientists and engineers educate students, create knowledge, and develop some technology. The amount of technology from this source is not great, and the university or college functions more effectively in information transfer and in fostering integration of new technology into society.

Faced with reluctant funding sources, universities have begun to market the results of their research more actively. In April 1973 a conference was held at Illinois Institute of Technology Research Institute in Chicago to promote the use of university work through patent procedures, licensing, and marketing. Addressing "Availability of Technology to Industry from American Universities and Technological Institutes," the conference featured such past successes as Vitamin D irradiation, Warfarin — the anti-coagulant and rat poison, and the toothpaste additive, stannous fluoride.[21] Whether universities will attain more success in this direction than in the past remains to be seen.

Federally Funded Research and Development Centers have developed since 1950 to handle special technical and social R&D problems of national concern. In 1971 such centers employed 11,500 scientists and engineers.[22] Some are run by industrial firms using government facilities, primarily for AEC and DOD. Universities run some for DOD, NASA, and AEC, and independent research organizations for AEC and DOD. In 1971, ninety-one of these accounted for $236 million in applied research and $892 million in development. DOD used thirteen FFRDC's including RAND, Institute of Defense Analysis (IDA), and Research Analysis Corporation (RAC).[23] The early centers focused on hardware-type problems of DOD, NASA, and AEC. More recently, D/HEW has developed centers to solve non-hardware problems.

Motivation for Technology Development

New technology is generated by trained people from available resources to satisfy identifiable needs.

How do people generate new technology? Homer G. Barnett, Professor of Anthropology, University of Oregon, is representative of those anthropologists and sociologists who have investigated aspects of inventive thinking and activity. He concluded that the individual applying some facet of technical knowledge to new uses has a cultural inventory plus non-artificial elements of his experience. The idea or proposed application itself commingles perception, cognition, re-call, and effect. Concepts are recombined, built up, transferred, or projected until a useful new concept or model emerges. People think this way to: (1) bring order from chaos, (2) relieve monotony, (3) remove some restraint, (4) purge an undesirable characteristic or get more out of a valued input or output, (5) simplify the process, (6) please others, or (7) simply make a change. With respect to the society, Barnett believed that some societies provide more opportunity for idea concentration than do others and, consequently, a more stimulating climate for change. When cultural or natural barriers rise against exchange of ideas, less opportunity occurs for their mixing and remodeling. Real advance requires decrystallizing of sys-tems of organization and thought.[24] In U. S. society, individuals, cor-porations, research enterprises, or government agencies may set up environments for generating technology. They provide facilities, focus on a need, and encourage interested individuals to visualize new relationships.

A clear statement of the problem in reaching a particular objective seems to be a significant input to the inventive work process for U. S. participants. Cases studied by the Committee on Principles of Re-search Engineering Interaction of the National Academy of Sciences-National Research Council, pinpointed recognition of an important need as a principal factor in stimulating research-engineering inter-actions. Frequently, available technical approaches were dormant be-cause no one recognized their pertinence to the need.[25]

How Much New Technology is Available?

Significant numbers of technical items are available for diffusion in unused patents, in agency and corporate files for products de-veloped but not used, in the technical literature, and in the experiences of investigators working on more pressing problems.

Lawrence W. Bass, retired Vice-President of Arthur D. Little, Inc., quoted the following commercial R&D figure: of 540 ideas initially screened, ninety-two were evaluated in laboratories, seven were re-duced to models, and one final product resulted.[26] The Small Busi-ness Administration has reported that less than two percent of the proposals originated in twenty large companies were forwarded for development.[27]   Robert Charpie, Director of Technology, Union Carbide Corporation, stated in 1966:

> Union Carbide's staff considers perhaps ten concepts per week.   Out of roughly five hundred received each year, we may take up as few as two totally new ideas.   One in a hundred seems to be average among groups who look at such opportunities routinely, I am told.   My experience is more typically one in two hundred.[28]

The marketed product from commercial R&D results directly from the sequence; applied research, exploratory development, design, test, evaluation, and commercialization.   The products additionally completed, but not marketed, are research and development by-products, possibly exploitable.   The developing company may not exploit them because of financial requirements, limited market aims or territory, or inadequate staff and facilities.   Inventive work must be broader than the eventual product line for defensive purposes; it will result in some products just outside company scope, and others differing radically from the company line.   The company may spin off a new division to exploit the off-line product, or it may license or sell it outright.   Companies also have products and processes which have served their usefulness in the company.   Among these are the technical successes which fail in the company market.   In 1968, Booz, Allen & Hamilton, management consultants, reported that in the two hundred best run companies, two of three new products failed.[29]   Another company may want these discontinued items, perhaps for noncompetitive work. All 12,000 industrial concerns with R&D thus may provide potentially diffusible technology in patents or proprietary knowledge.

In the past five years, the internationalization of business has developed channels for technology diffusion between countries which have not been previously significant.   Some academicians now consider that ten percent of the world's GNP is developed by international companies.   Through transfer of people as well as technology, the international companies may cause sigificant breakthroughs in technology diffusion.   Protectionist viewpoints have already come to the fore.

How effectively do government laboratories develop technology? One measurable form of inventive work output from government laboratories is a patentable invention, disclosed to establish precedence and to prevent others from interfering with laboratory work. It may be patented, published, or filed. Table III summarizes recent Federal agency work. Civil service laboratories dominate patentable inventive work disclosures in USDA, Interior, and DOC, all fairly small in funding. Contractors dominate in D/HEW, NASA, AEC, and in DOD, where the proportion is similar to NASA. The government averaged 11,800 disclosures each year. Agencies differ in whether they take title or allow contractors to have it. At the end of FY 1970, USDA held 1,337 unexpired patents, NASA 1,176, AEC 4,259, DOD 12,891, INT 328, D/HEW 151, and DOC 255. The Federal government held 21,000 in all. Table III also shows that some agencies choose to publish rather than patent inventive work. Publishing precludes future patenting.

TABLE III

GOVERNMENT AGENCY PARTICIPATION IN PATENT PROGRAMS FY 1963-70[30]

	USDA	D/HEW	DOD	DOC	NASA	AEC	INT
Employee Disclosure	1,546	223	16,855	504	3,433	166	682
Contractor Disclosure	594	2,099	34,720	42	18,434	11,155	460
Patent Applications	1,071	148	11,580	64	1,827	2,294	402
Published	726	1,222	0	84	0	359	1
No Protection (filed)	183	256	22,852	271	17,817	8,203	535

Smaller government laboratories have made historic contributions. Those in the departments of Agriculture, Interior, and the regulatory agencies have been accepted as leaders in specific fields; nevertheless, they have been attacked recently. Less flexible than industrial laboratories, they have fewer outstanding leaders and tend to become political pawns; but they contribute in fields generally unattractive to business and industry and unserved by other sources.

Government agencies develop technologies which await use. In 1966 Congress evaluated the routine Bureau of Mines R&D program with results as shown in Appendix C. Seven percent of expenditures for the decade 1953-1962, and six percent of the projects, failed in R&D

or did not reach their technical goals. Twenty-four percent of funds were spent on projects which achieved technical solutions later rejected as economically unfeasible. Thirty-three percent of the funds resulted in useful by-products or items with forseeable commercial use. This left thirty-six percent of the inventing effort giving results which were applied. Over a thousand projects had been conducted in Bureau of Mines facilities with total expenditures of $78.3 million.[31] Later, scarcity of precious metals and petroleum supplies may cause these discarded solutions to be profitable. Those solutions set aside for future use should surely be reconsidered. Two-thirds of the work done over this 1952-62 period is available for review and use. While Bureau of Mines work may be only a small sample, it does show that developed technologies very often await use for extended periods of time.

How effectively do large laboratories generate new technology? Both the large interdisciplinary industrial laboratory working under contract and its FFRDC counterpart were reviewed by the 1966-67 National Acadamy of Sciences Panel on Applied Sciences, which stated:

> In fact, modern applied science can hardly be discussed without reference to these homes of applicable science. These institutions derive their power from three sources: (1) their interdisciplinarity and the close interaction between basic research and application; (2) their methodology for precipitating and organizing coherent effort around big problems; (3) their ability to adapt their goals to the requirements of their sponsors. The industrial laboratories in particular have been remarkably successful in adapting the requirements for a vital scientific environment to the profit motivations of business enterprise, demonstrating that first-rate science and corporate profitability are mutually supporting rather than incompatible goals. Many of the suggestions for exploitation of science in the solution of applied problems therefore amount to suggestions as to how to maintain the vitality and spirit and sense of mission of those government or industrial institutions in which most of our applied research is done.[32]

Contract applied research and development has successfully generated the technology packages of jet transports, nuclear power plants, communication satellites, desalination plants, numerical control, computer technology, and the techniques of PPBS and PERT. Package developments have apparently succeeded more than patentable individual items. In FY 1965 when all Federal contractors reported only

8,000 patent disclosures, seventy percent of the total national R&D was spent in programs sponsored by the Federal government, with about nine billion dollars of contracted applied research and development from DOD, NASA, and AEC. About 90,000 patents were filed that calendar year and 66,401 were issued. From such data as that of Tables I, II, and III, and uses of government versus company financed patents, the Department of Commerce estimated that ten man-years of industrial R&D produce a commercializable patent, but that it takes a thousand man-years to produce such a patent from either in-house or contract R&D work from DOD or NASA.[33] Increased Federal applied research and development clearly do not increase patents directly. These funds do increase technical papers, trained people, and technology packages or programs to accomplish Federal agency missions.

Can the amount of diffusible new technology from Federal agencies be measured? Over $200 billion of inputs can be measured in applied research and developments between 1953 and 1973. Writers have assumed that outputs are represented in the most current end-products, in technical literature of Federal agencies, and in the experience of those who spent the Federal funds. In 1963 the Weinberg Committee calculated that about 100,000 informal government technical reports are prepared yearly, with about 75,000 unclassified.[34] These reports carry the results of the large outlays of Federal expenditures of funds.

III. HOW, AND THROUGH WHAT INSTITUTIONS, DO PEOPLE LEARN ABOUT TECHNOLOGY?

Information about technology is not always separated from scientific information in the available statistics. Technical information is embodied in items of technology themselves, in the people who designed or built them, and in papers. Technical papers and other documents have received attention because their exponential increase has given birth to information science and records management as professional fields.

Information Science. During World War II, scientists and technologists developed and applied radar, nuclear science, synthetic products, antibiotics, and advanced weapons. After the war these people dispersed, carrying with them technical know-how. Within a few years, technology, technical information, and R&D exploded. The U. S. underwent a wave of technology diffusion, underwritten by the availability of technical information in the minds, working habits, and inclinations of people with wartime experience. Libraries and commercial publishers could not handle the influx of information. Slowly, information science was developed to cope with the new sources and kinds of technical and scientific information.

Problems of information transfer include volume, number of objects, papers, or persons containing technical information, dispersed consumers, rapidly changing information science techniques, and the cost to stay up with or gain on the backlog of technical information. Two groups exist, those technology generators with technical information to sell, apply, or distribute, and those who can use the information in their ongoing enterprises. The information scientist, the technical educator, the marketeer, and the technical press are middlemen or couplers. Information scientists are concerned with the most effective channels and content of recorded forms of information. During the sixties they made major advances in providing technical information to potential users. (See Appendix D-1 for chronology.) In 1971, Dr. Morton V. Malin, of the Institute for Scientific Information in Philadelphia, was able to say, "We're certainly way ahead of where we were. We have a good handle on controlling the (information) explosion."[35] Numerous specialized information systems such as the National Technical Information Service (NTIS) have been established. In the aggregate, these specialized systems form a decentralized but de facto national system for handling documented information.

Information Transfer as Communication or Coupling. The transfer of information about technology is a communication process which couples performers (those who produce technology) and users (those who react or use the technical information). Table IV shows that performers are also users; that is, those who generate new technology need and use available science and technology. Both scientists and technologists are directed by the final user's needs, preferences, and financial support. Technologists tune in to other scientists and technologists for solutions to specific problems or to stay abreast of advances. Technical press writers and editors, as well as librarians subscribing to journals, couple the technologist to potential external changes which may satisfy his needs. When these couplers choose articles to publish or journals to store, they screen available science and technology for applicability. Trade associations particularly study changes for opportunities or threats to trade needs. A new patent is a special coupler of technology which must be evaluated by organizations it may affect. The passing on of accumulated preferences, values, and information is done through education, both formal and on-the-job. People hold many of these preferences in their working viewpoints and procedures. Other, more formal information is stored in libraries, information centers, and school curricula.

Two forms of technology information coupling appear in Table IV. One, the informal or active form, generally occurs orally and visually, person-to-person, or object to person. The traditional form, it retains vitality through the many channels that depend on person-to-person contact. The communications specialist works with this form.

The other, the passive or impersonal form, operates through the system of recording in media, storing and retrieving. This passive or impersonal form, moving technical information in time and space, has especially concerned information scientists. Some of the great variety of U. S. programs in these fields are discussed below.

Scientific and Technical Education. Formal transfer of technical information is provided by colleges and universities. Two-year technical institutes, community colleges, and some high schools also directly transmit technical information. Frequently underestimated are Federal in-service technical training programs, of which DOD supports the largest. In fields such as electronics, airlines, and aerospace weapons manufacturing and servicing, many technicians received their initial training in the Armed Services.

Textbook, Handbook, Translating, Abstracting, and Indexing Industry. These secondary and tertiary publication fields directly support educational programs. Traditionally private enterprises, their biggest customers are state and college educational systems. Typical representatives are Chemical Abstracts Services and Biological Abstracts, Inc. More recent entries include computer companies and government indexing services such as those in NASA, the Defense Documentation Center, and the National Library of Medicine. NASA officials estimated in 1965 that there were 100,000 collated volumes of bibliographies and 365 abstracting/indexing groups in U. S. science

TABLE IV
PERFORMER-TO-USER INFORMATION COUPLING

Performers	Users		
	SCIENTISTS (Basic research)	TECHNOLOGISTS (Applied research & development)	FINAL USERS (Practical uses & innovations)
SCIENTISTS (Body of knowledge or available science)	XXX* (Scientific journals, professional associations, conferences, educational systems, libraries, information centers)	X (Reference data, textbooks, education, information centers, moving people)	X (Public media, discoveries)
TECHNOLO- GISTS (State of the art or available technology)	XX (Instruments, techniques, technical literature)	XX (Technical literature, design manuals, patents, proprietary information, consultants, technology firms, training, libraries, information centers, moving people)	XX (New products, processes, techniques, use manuals, public media, training, moving people)
FINAL USERS (Needs & opportunities)	X (Perceived and traditional needs, financial support)	XXX (Expressed needs, buyer preferences, acquiring technology companies)	XX (Competition, advertising, salesmen, trade associations)

*The number of X's compares coupling intensity from the performer to the user. Specific couplers are in parentheses.

and technology.[36] These forms of information handling are important aids to future information retrievers.

Primary Journals, Technical Magazines, and Popular Media. Primary journals are the main reporting media for scientific associations, disciplines, and professions while technical and popular magazines also support the diffusion process. **Science** and "Applied Physics Letters" exemplify the first, while **Aviation Week** and **Research and Development** represent the second. Christopher Scott, Central Office of Information, The Social Survey, London, concluded that periodical literature was most helpful in supplying "useful information which is not being deliberately sought."[37] In reviewing problems of updating education in new technology, the Subcommittee on Economic Progress of the Joint Economic Committee of Congress accepted the estimate of weekly production of technical papers at 25,000, in addition to 400 books and 3,500 separate articles.[38]

Professional Societies, Trade Associations, and Conferences. Behind most successful journals and technical magazines are professional societies and trade associations. Moreover, these organizations without publications engage in technical exchange through conferences and social contacts. Personal contacts seem more critical to technology diffusion, which usually involves transfer of property rights, than to absorbing scientific information, which is public. Conferences sponsored by government, societies, or trade associations, have become important to such information transfer activities as hiring, marketing, and determining competitors' views and trends.

Libraries, Technical Libraries, and Information Centers. Libraries continuously handle more technical items. Specialized users have pressured them to set up technical divisions devoted to local technology needs. The purely technical library has also developed to serve professionals in closely related disciplines or applications. Most industrial company libraries are of this type. Adding reproduction and research functions to technical libraries creates information centers. Large industrial information centers like those of American Telephone and Telegraph and Du Pont approach the scope of national systems in dispersion and scale of operation. Their operations deserve study as examples of specialized, partial national systems. There were 300 of these operating in 1965.[39]

Information Analysis Centers. When an information center collates and evaluates information, it moves into information analysis and the creation of new information syntheses or compendiums. To do this, the center must employ highly trained subject specialists who can understand and assimilate the literature for others working in the field. Information analysis centers may presently apply better to science than to technology; nonetheless, the development of weekly fact sheets by some analysis centers has moved them toward technology diffusion.

Federal Agency Centers. Important information science developments have resulted from Federal programs, some with unique forms. In 1966 DOD and AEC operated thirty-six major information analysis centers on subjects of national technical interest.[40] DOD departments (Army, Navy, and Air Force) also operated specialized centers. The centers review, evaluate, and synthesize. The Nuclear Data Center of AEC, for example, contributed to the shell model of the nucleus, a major underpinning of moder nuclear physics.[41] The U. S. Office of Education in 1973 operated twenty-five FFRDC's on aspects of national concern about education, including application of new technologies to educational problems.

Other special libraries or information centers which collect, process, and distribute information or citations to sources include the National Library of Medicine, the National Agricultural Library, NTIS, the Library of Congress National Referral Center for Science and Technology, the AEC Technical Information Division, the DOD Defense Documentation Center, and the NASA Scientific and Technical Division. NTIS is particularly responsible for publishing the monthly **Index to Federal Research and Development Reports** and the twice-monthly **Technical Translations.** The National Agricultural Library has since 1862 collected world-wide information on agricultural developments. According to the National Science Foundation, Federal obligations for scientific and technical information rose from $75,870,000 in 1960 to $397,628,000 in 1971. Appendices D-2 through D-5 break down these expenditures by agency and type of channel or form. USDA, TVA, and the Department of the Interior foster active use of information. NASA and Commerce have also experimented with programs to couple users to information sources.

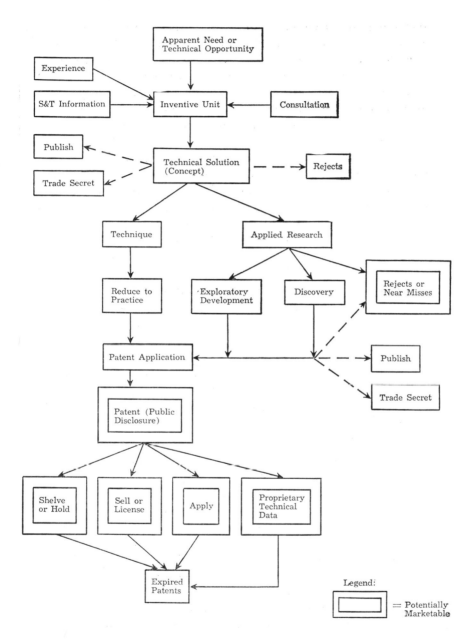

Figure 10. Marketable technical information from patents.

Marketing Organizations. Many segments of industry operate between raw materials and final consumer products. These industries take another company's output, incorporate it into their own, and sell the product to others. Much product improvement in existing product lines originates from suppliers trying to gain competitive advantages. As soon as these suppliers have a working technical development, they endeavor to capture the market through marketing organizations, which include salesmen, sample materials, vendor catalogs, and advertising in the trade media. To a lesser degree, the supplier learns about new technology and technical needs from customers. These exchanges of information are active communication about new technology. The supplier-customer technical information flow becomes one of trust and dependence in many industries. Trade association activities frequently reinforce this relationship. Industries tend to divide the external world into trusted agents (suppliers who have built up technical competence and good will) and others.

Patent and Technology Marketing Organizations. Patent and technology marketing organizations have been useful in diffusing technology. Though privately employed inventors and research associations have always marketed patents and supporting technology, industries have not taken full advantage of this source of revenue. Patents are directly negotiable as is the proprietary information or know-how which makes them useful. Figure 10 shows how various forms of technical information derive from the patent process.

The inventive unit synthesizes a technical solution from experience, consultants, or available science and technology which may be directly patentable; it may with current techniques develop or reduce the technical solution to practice in a new and useful process; it may through applied research discover unexpected results; it may through exploratory development evolve a new composition of matter or new combination of elements, which is then in turn reduced to practice. The patent application discloses the sequence, from the original concept through testing, of an embodiment of the invention capable of producing the end result. The granted patent publicly discloses the specifications of the invention; and the inventor, if not challenged, has a seventeen-year monopoly to sell or use the patented technology and to preclude others from using it. The patent rights can be used, sold, licensed, or merely held to prevent others from using them. The proprietary technical data, which are developed to apply the patent, are almost always of greater import than the patent rights. There are four potential items for sale: (1) patent specifications available for fifty cents from the Government Printing Office; (2) the patent rights protecting the technology, available from the holder for the seventeen-year period of protection; (3) the know-how which makes the patent successful and which can be sold even after the patent expires; and (4) the information on rejections from applied research and exploratory development, not often negotiated, but possibly valuable in preventing costly duplication.

When industrial firms create technology and proprietary information they cannot exploit, the patent marketing organization may assume control. For example, General Electric held 10,757 unexpired patents in 1955,[42] and some of those were not being used. GE now has a subsidiary patent marketing organization.

How effective are patent marketing activities? Hughes Aircraft Company, Culver City, California, in July 1967, held 1,115 U. S. and 583 foreign patents as well as 500 U. S. and 389 foreign patents pending. From twenty-five U. S. and seven foreign royalty agreements, it gained in nine months of 1967 $1,010,349 royalty income.[43] With patent processing costs of $500 to $5,000 each, royalty income subsidized patenting, infringement litigation, incentive awards for patenting and added to company income. Hughes has incorporated part of its technology utilization effort into its Industrial Products Division, which has six product lines. One of its recent developments in industrial automation was a laser cutter for apparel manufacture which it provided for Genesco's L. Grief and Brothers of Fredericksburg, Virginia. This laser cutter reduces some labor, but its main advantage lies in reducing inventory and order response times.[44]

Bendix Corporation is another company making a concerted effort to transfer technology. Its Advanced Products Division has a goal of cutting time from laboratory to market to seven years from the normal 12 or more. Areas of emphasis in 1972 were computer graphics, pattern recognition, and analog-digital computer interfaces. The corporation hopes to spin off one new company each year and guide it to maturity.[45]

Movement of Knowledgeable People. A historically significant diffusion of technology occurred when the Huguenot artisans, tradesmen, and small manufacturers left France for England and its American Colonies. Du Pont was started by one of these Huguenots. Even today, one of the most potent ways to obtain technical information and thus disperse technology is to hire the man who has it or understands how to use it. J. A. Morton, a Vice-President at Bell Telephone Laboratories, summed up how people with knowledge overcome barriers of space, organization, and time:

> One of the most economical ways to transmit information is in the form of a human being. It is true today, and it has been true for a long time, and I suspect it will be true for a long time.[46]

Acquisition of Knowledgeable Companies. One of the easiest ways for a big company to gain information and know-how about a new product area is simply to merge with or buy the new technology company. The business director understands rules for merger or acquisition better than for generation of technology; hence, he prefers to buy the skills and know-how of the technology entrepreneur.

Effectiveness of Information Transfer Channels

Several studies have been made in an effort to determine the effectiveness of channels of information transfer. In 1957 Herner, Meyer, and Company, an information specialist company of Washington, D. C., studied technology information acquisition in 500 smaller firms in food processing, electricity-electronics, metal fabrication, and textiles-apparel. Their findings indicated that raw material and equipment suppliers were most important.[47]

In a study made for NASA in 1966-67, the University of Denver examined sixty-two commercial firms in the industries of batteries, printing machinery and reproduction equipment, industrial controls, medical electronics, and technical education, and determined that internal sources (people, past experience, libraries, and R&D) were as important as external sources. Of seventeen external channels ranked in usefulness for current awareness and problem solving, professional journals, trade publications, meetings (including conferences and trade shows), supplier personnel, vendor catalogs, textbooks and handbooks, ranked as the top six.[48]

In 1966 Sumner Myers, Chairman of the National Planning Association, studied seventy-five innovations in six firms and found in these cases that fifty-six percent of information inputs were from sources external to the firm, thirteen percent from inside the firm, and thirty-six percent from multiple channels (possibly equivalent to library resources of some firms).[49]

The Auerbach Corporation, Philadelphia, Pa., studied the problem-solving needs of 1,375 DOD research, development, test, and evaluation (RDT&E) performers who were using scientific and technical information and found that fifty-one percent of the time, they depended on the internal environment for sources, (personal files, colleagues, and local sources). Two-thirds of the time dependence on these sources was satisfactory. Their most frequent requirements (forty two percent) were performance and characteristics data and specifications. Oral communications transferred thirty percent of the information needed. Technical reports gave sixteen percent of the information and constituted the most-used written source. From this use of information, DOD RDT&E personnel were clearly searching for specific technology to transfer to defined RDT&E problems. Sixty-seven percent felt satisfied with their ability to get the information they needed. Only half the group used the formal DOD information services and rarely as a first source.[50]

Conclusions About Sources of Information

1. Sources which couple technical information into the economy include active and informal sources or channels of the communications specialist as well as impersonal or passive sources and channels of the information scientist.

2. Some industries tend to depend on such trusted sources as trade journals, professional journals, vendor catalogs, and supplier representatives for information about new technologies.

3. People, technology-based companies, and marketing organizations diffuse technical information to a significant degree.

4. Government agencies have had some success in building de facto national information systems for accomplishing agency missions.

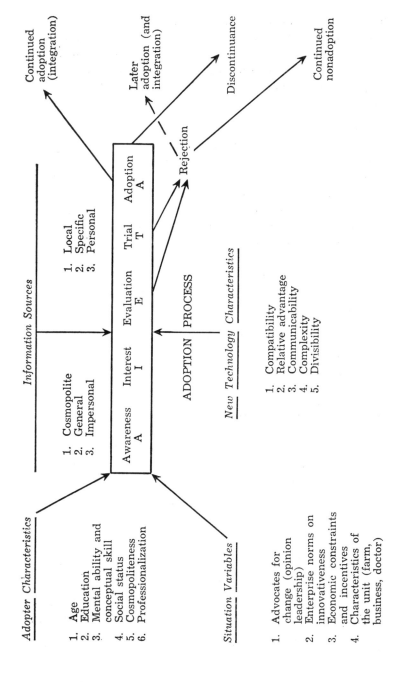

Figure 11. Technology adoption paradigm.[51]

IV. WHAT CAUSES, SUPPORTS, OR RETARDS INNOVATION?

Technology is applied when a decision unit learns about new technology and decides to adopt it. Decision units include individuals, households, firms, government units, and other organizational entities.

The application of technology occurs after its generation and continues until the application becomes accepted practice. The first part is innovation and the continuing part is integration, or imitation and adjustment. For a decision unit, technology is new if it has not been tried in that unit. It may be old in other units. The open questions are: does the user want it in preference to other items, and will it pay to produce and market?

Professor Everett M. Rogers, then of Ohio State University, developed a paradigm similar to Figure 11 to illustrate factors known to affect the adoption of new technology. Rogers divides the total environment for innovation into adopter characteristics, elements of the situation, nature of the technology, form and reliability of information sources, and the outcome of actual trials. The distribtion through time of those who adopt new technology follows the bell-shaped curve of Figure 12, which tends to approach the normal distribution curve.[52]

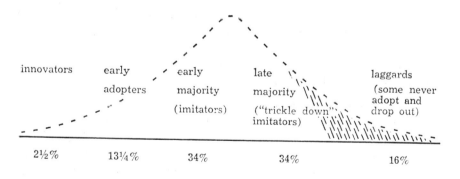

Figure 12. Adoption curve.

Each of these Figure 12 groupings has been studied in terms of the factors in the adoption paradigm. For example, each grouping tends to accept information from different sources or in different forms. Economically, the innovator may reap windfall profits before factor and market prices adjust to the new technology. The laggard must change because of adjusted prices or else drop out through failure. Findings from over 200 investigations aggregated by Professor A. Shapero, then of Stanford Research Institute, are summarized below.[53]

Adopter characteristics. Individuals are more likely to adopt new technology if they are younger, have higher than average education, high social status, high professionalization, or previous adoption experience. Though these characteristics, summarized by Shapiro, were developed by Rogers for agricultural and by Elihu Katz for medical technologies, they seem generally valid.

Earlier adopters tend to take less time from first awareness of new technology to its adoption than late adopters, and they will more likely continue using new technology over time.

Communication processes. In terms of communication processes, the model for the spread of information indicated in Figure 11 divides into five stages: Awareness/Interest/Evalaution/Trial/and Adoption (AIETA).[54] In terms of this model, it has been found that awareness occurs more rapidly than adoption. The awareness-to-trial period lasts longer than the trial-to-adoption period. Cosmopolite and impersonal sources of information create awareness and interest, but later stages in the process require more personal, specific, and local sources of information. Innovators and early adopters can use impersonal sources of information, but late adopters wait for the information to "trickle down" and be accepted by the majority before they use it.

New technology characteristics. Diffusion-related characteristics of new technology include compatibility, efficiency, communicability or associability, complexity and divisibility. The less change that new technology requires in pre-existing sociocultural values and behavioral patterns, existing facilities, equipment, and procedures, the more likely is its rapid diffusion. The higher the efficiency of new technology, the higher its superiority to existing technology, or the higher the expected profit, the more rapid the adoption. The easier it is to explain new technology, to perceive the way it functions or to associate it with other familiar objects or ideas, the more rapid is its adoption. The divisibility of new technology into parts affects the number of trials that will be made and, hence, the rate of adoption.

This principle extends into marketing, where products are tested before final adoption is tried. Early adopters perceive divisibility as more important than do later adopters. This is sometimes called the "extent of commitment" required to test out the item.

Advocates for change. Opinion leaders, champions, commercial salesmen, and professional promoters have been studied and conclusions about them made; however, there is little agreement about these conclusions. Rogers believes that opinion leaders for agricultural technology adoption: (1) conform more closely to social systems norms than average; (2) use more impersonal, technically accurate, and cosmopolite sources of information than their followers; (3) have more social participation and higher social status than their followers; (4) innovate more than their followers; and (5) do not have followers on all subjects.[55] Opinion leaders, indeed, may advocate no change if that is closer to the norm of the existing social system.

Special advocates of change (change agents) have arisen; e.g., sales forces, professional promoters, and entrepreneurs. Rogers concluded that change agents: (1) have more communication with higher status than with lower status members of a social system; (2) vary their promotional effort with the rate of adoption; (3) are more important as salesmen at the trial stage than before or later; and (4) if salesmen, are more important to early adopters than later. Rogers found that innovators (very first to adopt change) were perceived by both themselves and others as deviants from social norms.[56] Aaron Gellman, Vice-President of North American Car Company, suggested in 1966, however, that personal fulfillment from creating a new product or service will itself motivate men to run the personal risk accompanying innovation.[57]

Champions are the unusual innovators, like Lindbergh and Teller—men willing to put themselves on the line for a development of doubted success. Donald A. Schon, former Director of the Institute of Applied Technology, National Bureau of Standards, Department of Commerce, believes resistance to change is so endemic to large organizations that a champion must emerge before a change of product line will occur.[58]

Other Situation Variables. The search for new technology by private and public U. S. organizations aims at securing competitive advantages for these organizations in their respective marketplaces or at overcoming such advantages held by others. Industrial or commercial organizations secure competitive advantages by using new technologies to create new markets, to enlarge existing markets, and to improve the profitability of operations. Governmental organizations use new technologies to create new capabilities, enhance existing capabilities, and improve efficiencies in achieving them. Situation variables affecting new technology adoption include:

1. Organizations more likely to adopt new technology than others are newer ones and those which have grown rapidly relative to others in the same field.

2. Relatively new occupational fields, with boundaries still flexible, are marked by higer rates of innovation than older fields.

3. Government financial assistance to potential adopters speeds diffusion of innovations.

4. There are few conflicts of interest among agencies involved in the diffusion of new technology.

5. Lack of governmental compulsion in the adoption of new technology avoids resistance and minimizes efforts to get it withdrawn.

Mansfield studied size in innovating firms and found that larger firms have greater potential and inclination for **compatible** innovations (those using current facilities, processes, and principles organization) than smaller ones. They have greater resources, a wider range of operating conditions, and may have, at any time, some replaceable units. Estimates can be made on the differences in rates of innovation as a function of firm size.[59]

Schon found that three traditional industries (textiles, building, and machine tools), were usually innovating when invaded from outside. In characterizing the firms of the invaded industries as well as those of the invaders, he found those invaded to be fragmented and craft-oriented, focused on production and present commitments, with social systems protecting present commitments, and lacking entrepreneurial models or current champions. Invaders, science-based, with R&D an integral part of the firm, have considerable financial resources, often

Federal support, and engage in research-oriented entrepreneurial activity lacking in other firms.[60]

Economists note varied innovation with economic conditions. An expanding economy facilitates risk-taking. Within a particular industry, market expansion eases capital investment; and market retraction indicates capital saving. This applies to both long- and short-term trends. Further, individual industries tend to save labor in early life and to save capital in later life. Adoption of new technology then becomes sensitive both to the general economy and to the age of the industry. According to post-World War II trends, boom times (from pent-up demand) cause expanded production, not innovation. Limited studies for the National Science Foundation indicated a firm will more likely adopt new technology when operating at about seventy-five percent of capacity. If operating above this level, all resources are expanding production; if less, few resources remain for any new endeavors.[61]

Individual companies within an industry frequently hold different positions with respect to innovation and the market. Some can expand or innovate when others cannot. Some may prefer old equipment to new, especially when it has been written off for depreciation. Only when costs for the old factor mix exceed costs for the new factor mix will change help the corporation. With companies or larger organizations as decision units, adoption is frequently the end result of laborious procedures and discussions. Adopting major new technology puts the life of the enterprise at stake.

The AIETA process of technology evaluation by a business firm may be described as a matrix in which positive factors encourage innovating and negative factors do not. Professor Raymond Haas, West Virginia University, studied thirty firms and found that a firm becomes aware of and takes an interest in new processes or products when its present product output does not give the desired rate of return; when components of present products are in short supply or become unavailable; when customer needs and wants can be stated or forecast; and when an accidental encounter with opportunity indicates the desirability for a change. For some firms, the search for new products is continuous; for others, it is sporadic; but all have to do it eventually.[62]

Evaluation determines whether the potential adopter will make a trial. If a trial is made, then the factors for adoption must again be convincing before tentative adoption. For businesses, the initial adoption decision is never final until customers also adopt the new technology. If customers reject the technology, then the business must also reject or discontinue it. If customers adopt the technology, the business finalizes the tentative adoption. The final user of the technology thus governs whether adoption will succeed. If he does not become aware of the technology, or resists adoption for any reason, then diffusion is delayed.

Resistance to Innovation

The foregoing discussion reveals that overcoming active resistance to innovation can be as important as promoting innovation. From studying numerous cases, Bright summarized the forms of such resistance:

1. **Legal or political action** which includes litigation, taxes, or new legislation to make the change illegal or unprofitable.

2. **Business action** to block financial support or to create doubt about the feasibility of the change.

3. **Labor union action** to create strikes or new demands.

4. **Pressure group and propaganda action** to reduce the market or desirability of the change.

5. **Religious group action** to cause the change to be considered immoral.[63]

In a 1972 effort to overcome resistance to innovation, an experimental research and development incentives program was set up under the National Science Foundation. While this program focused on incentives to get technology out of the laboratory and into application, it does recognize that overcoming barriers is an important part of the effort. According to D. Raymond Bisplinghoff, Deputy Director, the governmental and institutional barriers with regard to transfer of technology include statutory (legal), financial (business), and behavioral (labor, religious, and pressure group) barriers which correspond to those found by Bright. In addition, Dr. Bisplinghoff listed informational inaccessibility, and cost and risks of new factor mixes for fragmented industries.[64]

Conclusions

1. The potential adopter is presented with new technical information which he evaluates in terms of his own activities. The results are adopted new technologies which succeed, adopted new technologies which fail, and technologies which fail in evaluation.

2. Adoption of new technology is affected by the nature of the technology, the characteristics of the adopter, the preferences of the society, and the anticipated gains of the adoption.

3. Resistance to technology may take legal, financial, social, and religious forms in an effort to make the technology illegal, unprofitable, unwanted, or immoral.

V. WHAT RESULTS FROM TECHNOLOGY INTEGRATION?

John Lear, Science Editor for **Saturday Review,** in 1967 stated then-conventional wisdom when he wrote: ". . . science provides new and fast routes to economic growth, international bridge-building, national defense, technological advance, and overcoming human problems of want and disease."[65]

Most recent writers have concentrated on the adverse effects of diffusing technology, believing that it causes premature obsolescence of capital equipment, forces management to operate in markets for which it is unprepared, reorients supplier-purchaser relationships among industries, causes job displacement and obsolescence because of new processes and automation, pollutes the environment, and endangers life. Technology diffusion may detract from economic growth by substituting new goods or services with less economic worth for old, or by social costs such as death, property damage, and environmental degradation caused, for example, by automobiles or pollution.

As one example, Frank Lynn of INTEC, Inc., Chicago, in his study for the National Commission on Technology, Automation, and Economic Progress, stated that changes from technology such as frozen foods and computers can occur so quickly that natural social and economic forces may not be able to react and adjust effectively, thus creating problems in our society.[66] This recognizes the phenomenon of cultural lag, proposed by the sociologist William F. Ogburn in 1923. Ogburn was able to show that lag in the culture's adjustment to technical change had unforeseen consequences.[67]   New methods, new products, and new pro-cesses introduce new elements which can undermine the previous systems of doing business.

To the concerned citizens, the benefits of new technology must be balanced against its costs.   For example, the agricultural sector in-creased its rate of productivity between 1955 and 1965, but at the cost of city ghettos and rural slums filled with 2.7 million workers who left agriculture.[68]   The automobile, with enormous economic and social value, kills over 50,000 people each year at an average age of thirty-one years.   The cost of these dead may be figured in terms of society's investment for thirty-one years in 50,000 people or the loss in produc-tion from 50,000 people as they age from thirty-one to sixty-five.   Any way it is calculated, the figure is significant in terms of value of the new cars built each year.   Other costs of new technology are pollution, environmental degradation, unemployment and underemployment, and job displacement and retraining.

Concern about the effects of technology has generated the expand-ing literature of technology assessment.   Leo L. Beranek, member of the National Academy of Engineering, has tentatively defined tech-nology assessment as a systematic forecasting process which yields options, costs, and benefits encompassing economic, social, and environ-mental considerations, with special focus on long-range effects, and delineating "good" and "bad."[69]   The main theme of this body of liter-ature thus far is that people should not be allowed to use technology which has been assessed as causing more harm than good.   Proposed new technology would be rigorously scrutinized to determine **all** its consequences rather than just the benefits to those who propose it. Proponents of technology assessment are indirectly recognizing the adjustments we make as our technological environment changes. Some difficulties of technology assessment lie in technological forecasting. The proposed technology must be assessed, not in the world of today, but in the technological environment of the future.   Before we can really predict our future technological and sociological environment, we must take into consideration the phenomenon of integration time lag.

The Time Lags of Technology Integration

Dr. S. C. Gilfillan, in a study for the Joint Economic Committee of the U. S. Congress, evaluated nineteen important inventions ingested between 1888 and 1913, finding time lags in all phases of diffusion. The lag between conception of the idea and patenting of the first working model averaged 176 years. Achieving practical use required twenty-four; commercial success fourteen; and generally significant application twelve more years. A second list of seventy-five inventions and a third list of 209 inventions covering different times, confirmed the lags.[70] Mansfield found that twelve major recent innovations took an average of twelve years from first use to fifty percent use, then ten more years to ninety percent use. For fifty percent use, the variation was between nine and fifteen years. Similar curves and figures were developed by Thomas F. Dornberg for television, Bryce Ryan for hybrid corn, and Harry Jerome for machine tools.[71] These are the normal curves for continued adoption of a new technology as depicted in Figure 12.

These long periods of time previously allowed society to adjust slowly, but the rate of change has accelerated. Lynn, studying the degree of acceleration for the Commission on Technology, Automation, and Economic Progress, found that the economy since WW II ingested technology faster than previously and that the ingestion rate or speed of integration has increased steadily for the past seventy years. Lynn found that a very long basic research and investigation period was usual before the technical feasibility of new technology could be visualized and attempts made at commercial application. This is the incubation or inventing period. The item is introduced commercially during the informing period and is adopted by innovators. Finally, its use grows until it is fully integrated and eventually replaced. For twenty important inventions since 1900, Lynn found an average incubation period of nineteen years and an average commercialization period of seven years, for a total development time of twenty-six years. Before WW I, this total was thirty-seven years; between WW I and WW II, it was twenty-four years; and since WW II, it has been fourteen years.

Lynn then investigated the integration or diffusion rate as a percent of GNP. He found that this has also accelerated and that consumer and industrial applications differ significantly. Between WW I and WW II, consumer applications required eighteen years to reach .2 percent of GNP. They took four years to reach .02 percent, and then fourteen more to .2 percent. Industrial applications were slower. After

WW II, however, industrial applications, though still slower in growth than consumer applications, moved faster than either had before WW II. In four years they reached .02 percent of GNP, and in five more years they reached .2 percent of GNP.

Lynn determined an overall growth rate for secondary or compatible inventions (those in existing firms for improving current product lines) twice that for inventions in new firms. Secondary inventions reached .02 percent of GNP in five years and .1 percent in a total of nine years. Primary inventions (those in new firms) reached .02 percent of GNP in six years and required twenty years to reach .1 percent of GNP.

Lynn found also that growth rates for privately funded items grew from .02 to .2 percent of GNP in twenty years while Federally funded items took only fourteen years for the same growth. Lynn's studies suggest several conclusions: (1) the time required for an invention to contribute in an economically significant way is quite long (in the order of ten to twenty years), but it is decreasing; (2) consumer applications are adopted faster than industrial applications; (3) secondary inventions (in existing companies) diffuse faster than primary inventions in new firms; and (4) Federally supported applications diffuse faster than privately supported ones.[72] From these studies of relatively slow change, one can only conclude it may be too soon to measure total impact of new technologies being integrated from U. S. R&D expenditures for the past twenty years.

Institutions for Integration

Industry and government agencies integrate new technology mostly to obtain or maintain a competitive advantage. No matter how unique or how advanced new technology may be, if it is not adopted by all potential users, possible competitive gains will be missed or smaller than they would otherwise be. The competitive advantage stems from productivity improvements which are the real basis of economic growth. To begin this growth there must be a consumer with a need that can be satisfied by buying a product, and he must be able and willing to buy. If enough consumers buy the new products and processes, they are integrated into the economy, displace older products, and affect national development.

Adoption of a new process or product results from a technical item's evaluation and reception of enough financial support to assure its competitiveness. Integration of a product or process into the economy results from the market's preference. The public (or government) forms the market with a need or willingness to buy; technology generating programs create items to satisfy the needs; companies or industries convert technologies to products; marketing organizations distribute products to customers; and financial institutions underwrite costs of technology generating, producing, and marketing.

Government Activities

Government may intervene anywhere in technology diffusion. Patent procedures, antitrust activities, support of small business policies for internal purchasing, requirements for comprehensive technology assessment, and the direction of technical education affect integration. The patent process was established in the Constitution. Antitrust laws were designed to prevent abuses of basic entrepreneurial rights. Support of small business is a recent effort to encourage competition. Most government activity continues to be mainly regulatory; but since WW II, government has often intervened directly in diffusion.

The growth in government applied research and development concerns observers because it affects directions of national development. Socialization of applied research and development constitutes government intervention in provision of markets for new products and processes. This intervention, thus far essentially unregulated, affects functions of the familiar patent system, commercial or private financial support of entrepreneurship, and economic mechanisms for maintaining markets and production. Some influences of Federal R&D policy on technology diffusion were listed by Brooks to be:

1. Support by mission-oriented agencies of basic and academic research aimed at specific technology gaps.
2. Mix of organizations and universities supported (intramural, industry, Federal contract centers, and nonprofits).
3. Types of controls used including conflict of interest, separation of government and non-government work, and report requirements.
4. Policies on making available the research reports and results.
5. Application of patent and copyright policies.

6. Geographical distribution of R&D funds and the criteria used
   in the selection of contractors and grantees.[73]

Reviewing the last hundred years, Schon found that Federal government has taken the initiative in supporting such innovations believed to be in the public interest as: (1) land grants to railroads in their westward expansion, (2) bounties for new developments like aircraft, (3) new transportation and communication systems, (4) new industry such as atomic energy and electronics, (5) development and diffusion of agricultural and medical technology, and (6) complete development of weapons and space systems.[74] At the same time, mainstreams of new products and processes in industry have continued to develop and interact with little Federal involvement.

Federal standards can freeze technology diffusion by denying new technology a market, or they can advance diffusion. Federal procurement policy amplifies the effects of Federal specifications. Federal and state governments together, with over $30 billion annual purchases of consumer goods, can uniquely stimulate the use of new technology. Overall Federal economic policy, both fiscal and monetary, enormously affects innovation, discouraging or encouraging the investments which diffuse an invention throughout the economy.

These indirect effects of government policy on innovation are less understood than any part of technology diffusion. Historically government has moved to protect invaded industry, regions hurt by technological dislocations, and small business. Government, then, for the **general** case supports innovation, but for the **specific** case tends to soften its effects or even discourage it.[75] Schon argues that this increases the costs of technology diffusion.

Conclusions

1. Integration of new technology yields both favorable and unfavorable results. Favorable results are freedom from unpleasant work, more convenient and efficient services, new and less expensive goods, and social and economic opportunity. Unfavorable results are job displacement, hazards, unequal development, degradation of the environment, and increasing government intervention.

2. The effects of new technology are difficult to assess because the technology must be assessed in a future technological environment. Each technology develops its own time lags for adoption and ingestion.

3. Federal government regulations, fund expenditures, economic policies, and support of R&D may advance or retard the integrating process.

VI. WHAT NATIONAL TECHNOLOGY GOALS CAN BE CONSIDERED?

Review of the Constitution, the Employment Act of 1946, Congressional hearings, literature on technology assessment, and on-going studies indicated that national technology goals to be considered in this study should be limited to:

1. Promoting the progress of science and the useful arts and providing technical information.
2. Providing maximum employment and purchasing power.
3. Promoting maximum production of useful goods and services.
4. Fostering free, competitive enterprise.
5. Promoting economic dispersion and equitable development of all areas of the country.
6. Maintaining national health and a healthful and sufficient physical environment.
7. Avoiding technology diffusion side effects of economic concentration, poverty pockets, and pollution.

VII. SUMMARY

One may infer from studies of technology diffusion that its activities group into technology generation or inventing, technical information transfer or informing, technology application or innovating, and technology ingestion or integrating. These activities influence, and are influenced by, the economic, social, and political institutions.

The direction of new technology generation can be changed by defining society's technical needs or goals and providing a market for items which satisfy those needs. The literature also implies the possibility of identifying or developing individuals or institutions to transfer technical knowledge. Characteristics of information systems which will support or enhance knowledge transfer and technology adoption have been developed. Certainly the literature suggests characteristics of new technology which inhibit or enhance its adoption and ingestion.

Finally, environmental and contextual variables of new technology can be controlled so that its adoption is either encouraged or inhibited.

History indicates that technology diffusion is not inevitable. It appears desirable to slow down diffusion of those forms of technology with high social costs. Indeed, it may be possible to select and diffuse preferred technologies for given industries, regions, or government organizations so as to move toward national technology goals. If preferred technologies are not now in the storehouse from past development, new developments may put them there. There are two domestic sources for these technologies: (1) commercial activities in the private sector of inventors, industry, and business; and (2) applied research and development activities in the public sector of government organizations and government-supported programs.

FOOTNOTES

[1] National Science Foundation, *National Patterns of R&D Resources—Funds and Manpower in the United States—1953-72* (Washington, D.C.: U.S. Government Printing Office, 1972), p. 9.

[2] *Ibid.*, p. 10.

[3] National Science Foundation, *Employment of Scientists and Engineers in the United States, 1950-66,* NSF 68-30 (Washington, D.C.: U.S. Government Printing Office, 1968), p. 6.

[4] Battelle Columbus Laboratories, Columbus, Ohio, *Report on 1971 National Survey of Compensation Paid Scientists and Engineers in Research and Development Activities,* (Washington, D.C.: U.S. Atomic Energy Commission, 1972), p. xvii.

[5] National Science Foundation, *National Patterns . . . op. cit.,* p. 10.

[6] National Science Foundation, *Federal Funds for Research, Development, and other Scientific Activities, Fiscal Years 1971, 1972, and 1973* (Washington, D.C.: U.S. Government Printing Office, 1972), p. 3.

[7] National Science Foundation, *Federal Funds . . . , op. cit.,* p. vi. See also Appendices B-1 and B-7.

[8] National Science Foundation, *National Patterns . . . , op cit.,* pp. 29, 31. Appendix B-1 includes expenditures for R&D plant, but Table II does not.

[9] National Science Foundation, *Research and Development in State Government Agencies,* NSF 70-22 (Washington, D.C.: U.S. Government Printing Office, 1970), p. vii.

[10] U.S. Department of Commerce, *Do You Know Your Economic ABC's—PATENTS—Spur to American Progress* (Washington, D.C.: U.S. Government Printing Office, 1965), p. 28.

[11] Stacy V. Jones, *The Inventor's Patent Handbook* (New York: The Dial Press, 1966), pp. 1-10.

[12] Edwin Mansfield, "Technological Change: Measurement, Determinants, and Diffusion," *The Employment Impact of Technological Change,* Studies Prepared for the National Commission on Technology, Automation, and Economic Progress, Appendix Vol. II of *Technology and the American Economy* (Washington, D.C.: U.S. Government Printing Office, 1966), pp. 11-109.

[13] Archie M. Palmer (ed.), *Research Centers Directory* (Detroit, Mich.: Gale Research Company, 1969), *passim.*

[14] U.S. Congress, Senate, Subcommittee on Science and Technology to the Select Committee on Small Business, *Policy Planning . . . , op. cit.,* pp. 79-81.

[15] National Science Foundation, *Research and Development in Industry, 1970,* NSF 72-209 (Washington, D.C.: U.S. Government Printing Office, 1972), pp. 52-53.

[16] "NSF Bullish on Industry R&D Funding, Jobs," *Chemical and Engineering News,* March 19, 1973, pp. 23-24.

[17] National Science Foundation, *Federal Funds . . ., op. cit.,* pp. 188-189.

[18] National Science Foundation, *Directory of Federal R&D Installations. A Report to the Federal Council for Science and Technology,* NSF 70-23 (Washington, D.C.: U.S. Government Printing Office. 1970), pp. ix, x.

[19] National Science Foundation, *R&D in Industry, 1970, op. cit.,* pp. 8, 9, 52, 53.

[20] "Rise in R&D Funding Signals Halt to Slump," *Chemical and Engineering News,* July 2, 1973, p. 13.

[21] "Universities Promote Sale of Technology," *Chemical and Engineering News,* March 12, 1973, p. 29.

[22] National Science Foundation, *Research and Development in Industry, 1970, op. cit.,* p. 8.

[23] National Science Foundation, *Federal Funds . . . , op. cit.,* pp. 46, 47, 51.

[24] Homer G. Barnett, *Innovation: The Basis of Cultural Change* (New York: McGraw-Hill Book Co., 1953), pp. 39-42, 71-72, 97-180, 181-188. Barnett used the term "innovation" for the activity herein defined as inventing. "Things," or technology, was only one of several categories treated.

[25] National Academy of Sciences—National Research Council, *Report of the Ad Hoc Committee of Research Engineering Interaction,* Report No. MAB-222-M (Springfield, Va.: Clearinghouse, 1966), p. vii.

[26] H. M. Corley, "Successful Commercial Chemical Development," a 1954 article quoted by Lawrence W. Bass, *The Management of Technical Programs* (New York: Frederick A. Praeger, 1965), p. 41.

[27] Alan A. Smith, *Technology and Your New Product,* SBA Series No. 19 (Washington, D.C.: U.S. Government Printing Office, 1956), p. 19.

[28] Robert Charpie, "The Business End of Technology Transfer," in National Science Foundation, *Proceedings of a Conference on Technology Transfer and Innovation,* NSF 67-5 (Washington, D.C.: U.S. Government Printing Office, 1967), p. 47.

[29] Booz, Allen, & Hamilton, *Management of New Products* (Chicago, Ill.: Booz, Allen, & Hamilton, 1968), p. 2.

[30] Federal Council for Science and Technology, *Annual Report on Government Patent Policy 1969 and 1970* (Washington, D.C.: U.S. Government Printing Office, 1971), pp. 100-102.

[31] U.S. Congress, Senate, *Interior Research Contracts,* Report No. 1523, 89th Cong., 2d Sess. (Washington, D.C.: U.S. Government Printing Office, 1966), pp. 1-5.

[32] National Academy of Sciences, *Applied Science and Technological Progress, A Report to the Committee on Science and Astronautics,* (Washington, D.C.: U.S. Government Printing Office, 1967), p. 3.

[33] U.S. Congress, Senate, *Policy Planning . . . , op. cit.,* p. 140.

[34] President's Science Advisory Committee, *Science, Government, and Information* (Washington, D.C.: The White House, 1963), p. 19.

[35] William F. Fallwell, "Information Explosion Closer to Control," *Chemical and Engineering News,* December 20, 1971, p. 28.

[36] Richard L. Lesher and George J. Howick, "Background Guidelines, and Recommendations for Assessing Effective Means of Channelling New Technology in Promising Directions," Draft for the Commission on Technology, Automation, and Economic Progress; Appendix Vol. V, *Applying Technology to Unmet Needs* (Washington, D.C.: NASA, 1966), pp. 37–38. Lesher and Howick were managers in NASA's Scientific and Technical Information Division.

[37] Christopher Scott, "The Use of Technical Literature by Industrial Technologists," *IRE Transactions on Engineering Management,* EM-9, June 1962, pp. 76–86.

[38] U.S. Congress, Joint Economic Committee, *Automation and Technology in Education,* Report of the Subcommittee on Economic Progress, 89th Cong., 2d Sess. (Washington, D.C.: U.S. Government Printing Office, 1966), p. 4. "Technical papers" meant those of scientific as well as technological origin. The estimate would give annually 1,250,000 papers, which means that every scientist and engineer publishes about one paper each year, which appears reasonable.

[39] Lesher and Howick, *op. cit.,* pp. 37–38.

[40] "AEC and DOD Information Centers," *Special Libraries,* 57 (no. 1): 21–34 (Jan. 1966).

[41] Allen Kent, *Specialized Information Centers* (Washington, D.C.: Spartan Books, 1965), p. 9. As Science Documentation Engineer for Battelle Memorial Institute, Kent has compared and evaluated information centers of all types.

[42] Robert Calvert (ed.), *The Encyclopedia of Patent Practice and Invention Management* (New York: Reinhold Publishing Corp., 1964), p. 313-364.

[43] Hughes Aircraft Company, Culver City, Calif., "Patent Orientation Briefing." Mimeograph, July 1967.

[44] "Aerospace Technology Infusion Aids Apparel Industry Operations," *Aviation Week and Space Technology,* March 29, 1971, pp. 48-49.

[45] Michael L. Yaffee, "Bendix Sets Technology Transfer Goals," *Aviation Week and Space Technology,* February 14, 1972, pp. 68-70.

[46] J. A. Morton, "A Model of the Innovative Process (as viewed from a science-based integrated industry)," National Science Foundation (NSF 67-5), *op. cit.,* p. 29.

[47] Saul Herner, Robert S. Meyer, and Robert H. Ramsey, "How Smaller Firms Solve Problems and Keep Abreast of Technical Developments," (Prepared for U.S. Department of Commerce, Office of Technical Services, 1957), p. ii.

[48] John S. Gilmore, *et al., The Channels of Technology Acquisition in Commercial Firms, and the NASA Dissemination Program* (Springfield, Va: Clearinghouse, June, 1967), pp. 21-29.

[49] Sumner Myers, *Industrial Innovations, Their Characteristics and Their Scientific and Technical Information Bases, A Special Report to the National Science Foundation* (Washington, D.C.: National Planning Association, 1966), p. 15.

[50] Auerbach Corporation, *DOD User Needs Study—Phase I* (Clearinghouse: AD-615-501, 1965), pp. 1-25.

[51] E. M. Rogers, *Diffusion of Innovations, op. cit.,* p. 306. Rogers' paradigm has been adapted to the accompanying discussion.

[52] *Ibid.,* pp. 28-30.

[53] A. Shapero, "Diffusion of Innovations Resulting from Research: Implications for Research Program Management," in M. C. Yovits (ed.), *Research Program Effectiveness* (New York: Gordon and Breach, 1966), pp. 371-387. Shapero used "research" for all aspects of new technology generation.

[54] The Foundation for Research on Human Behavior, *The Adoption of New Products: Process and Influence* (Ann Arbor, Michigan: The Foundation for Research on Human Behavior, 1959), pp. 4-5.

[55] Rogers, *op. cit.*, p. 314.

[56] Rogers, *op. cit.*, pp. 313-314.

[57] Aaron Gellman, "A Model of the Innovative Process (as viewed from a non-science-based fragmented industry)," National Science Foundation (NSF 67-5), *op. cit.*, p. 13.

[58] Donald A. Schon, *Technology and Change* (New York: Delacorte Press, 1967), p. 117.

[59] Edwin Mansfield, "Technological Change", *op. cit.*, p. II-125.

[60] Donald A. Schon, *op. cit.*, pp. 164-171.

[61] National Science Foundation, Office of Economic and Statistic Studies, *Inquiries into Industrial Research and Development and Innovation* (Washington, D.C.: National Science Foundation, March 1963), p. 3.

[62] Raymond M. Haas, *Long Range New Product Planning in Business* (Morgantown, W. Va: West Virginia University Foundation, 1965), pp. 43-48.

[63] James R. Bright, *Research, Development, and Technological Innovation* (Homewood, Ill: Richard D. Irwin, 1964), pp. 133-134.

[64] "Barriers to Technology Transfer Studied," *Aviation Week and Space Technology,* August 21, 1972, pp. 12-15.

[65] John Lear, "What Has Science to Say to Man," *Saturday Review,* July, 1967. Lear used "science" to mean pure science, applied science, and technology.

[66] Frank Lynn, "The Rate of Development and Diffusion of Technology," in Howard R. Bowen and Garth L. Mangum (eds.), *Automation and Economic Progress* (Englewood Cliffs, N.J.: Prentice-Hall, Inc., 1966), pp. 99-114.

[67] William F. Ogburn, *Social Change* (New York: B. W. Huebach, Inc., 1923), pp. 200-213.

[68] Gerhard Colm, "Economic Aspects of Technological Development," in National Science Foundation (NSF 67-5), *op. cit.,* p. 87.

[69] Eli Brockner, "Applying Technology to Civilian Problems," *Astronautics and Aeronautics,* March, 1971, p. 38.

[70] S.C. Gilfillan, *Invention and the Patent System,* Presented for the Consideration of the Joint Economic Committee, U.S. Congress (Washington, D.C.: U.S. Government Printing Office, Dec., 1964), p. 107. A private lecturer and writer since 1950, Gilfillan has concentrated on historical technology and patents.

[71] Richard R. Nelson, Morton J. Peck, and Edward D. Kalachek, *Technology, Economic Growth, and Public Policy* (Washington, D.C.: The Brookings Institution, 1967), p. 99.

[72] Frank Lynn, "The Rate of Development and Diffusion of Technology," in Howard R. Bowen and Garth L. Mangum, (eds.), *Automation and Economic Progress, op. cit.,* pp. 99-114.

[73] Harvey Brooks, "National Science Policy and Technology Transfer," National Science Foundation (NSF 67-5), *op. cit.,* pp. 57-58. Brooks as a scientist used the term "research" to cover all R&D. The context of his remarks focused on applied research which generates new technology.

[74] Donald A. Schon, *op. cit.,* pp. 172-178.

[75] Donald A. Schon, *ibid.*

CHAPTER IV

DEPARTMENT OF AGRICULTURE

I. INTRODUCTION

Technology diffusion in the U. S. Department of Agriculture is typical of older agencies such as the Bureau of Mines, the U. S. Geological Survey, the Bureau of Reclamation, and the Tennessee Valley Authority. Results from these government laboratories go to specific economic groups. Work has been supported by low but significant and stable funding.

This chapter describes in systems or predictive model terms how USDA diffuses technology into the agicultural sector of the economy.

Established by the Morrill Act of 1862, the Department is directed by law to acquire and diffuse useful, general, and comprehensive information on agricultural subjects. USDA fostered technical diffusion programs which made U. S. agriculture the most productive per man-hour of any nation. Rural sociologists have studied extensively the nature of mission-oriented, agricultural technology diffusion. The studies isolate many fundamental procedures of technology diffusion; these procedures may be adapted for diffusing technology to other sectors of the economy.

In technology diffusion activities, USDA dwarfs other older Federal agency programs in experience, numbers of people, channels available for use, and sheer size of individual projects. In 1971 the Department had 84,252 employees, one for every twenty-nine farms in the country. About 9.7 million people lived on farms in April 1970— one out of every twenty persons.[1] The annual appropriation was about $8 billion, of which $319 million was directed to research and development on agricultural problems. Half the R&D went into agricultural product processing industries, or agribusiness, which diffuse directly into the general economy. Farm output in 1969 was valued at over $15,700 per farm, totaling $45.7 billion from 2.9 million farms.[2] Federally funded R&D accounted for one-half percent of the gross sales of total product. USDA spent $2,800 in Federal funds per farm.

USDA programs are socially institutionalized; that is, they are politically and economically incorporated into society. Farming enterprises are capitalized at a level near that of small or medium business and many do, in fact, operate as businesses. They are in nearly perfect economic competition, and an entrepreneur with a new product or process enters freely. The agricultural sector ingests new technology faster than most economic sectors.

Activities of the USDA are described in Chapter II as generating agricultural technologies and then diffusing them by informing, innovating, and integrating.

II. ORGANIZATION

Though organized traditionally as indicated in Figure 13, USDA maintains different bureaucratic approaches in its several agencies. The decentralized Federal Extension Service works through counties

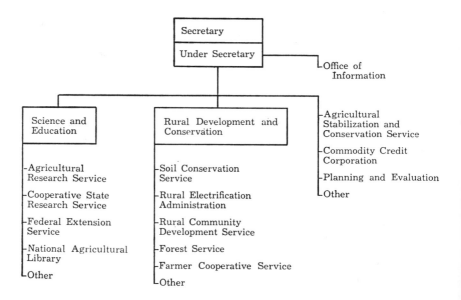

Figure 13. USDA offices of interest.

and local communities. The centralized Soil Conservation Service operates directly from USDA headquarters. Others mix public bureaucracy and private enterprise in cooperatives, like those for rural water supplies and electrification. Programs and procedures of USDA bureaus are discussed below in the context of their contributions to technology diffusion.

III. INVENTING

Inputs

With the clear, historically supported mission of developing technology for the agricultural sector of the economy, USDA has answered technical needs with the programs indicated in Figure 13. Agricultural expertise was built step-by-step, so that available science and technology both in departmental files and the National Agricultural Library give a good start on most problems. Applicable ideas come from laboratories, experiment stations, county agents, commercial firms in agribusiness, and farmers. Annual needs reflect judgment of those in the national headquarters.

Manned mostly by Federal or state employees in professional agricultural disciplines and technologies, USDA laboratories and state experiment stations support its inventing activity. With 13,784 Federal employes in FY 1971, the Agricultural Research Service was the second largest USDA agency. Stable funds have fostered a buildup of efficient, long-term development. Appendices B-1, B-2, and B-3 show that USDA received 55% of its support for applied research ($174 million in FY 1971) of which most occurs in Federal laboratories, the rest in colleges and universities. Appendices B-4 though B-6 indicate that fields of investigation were life sciences, physical properties, and, to some degree, engineering.

USDA does about one-fourth of all agricultural research, and the remaining three-fourths is done with state matching funds, state direct funds, and private research.

Examples. In this subchapter examples are discussed for each system block. In subsequent subchapters and for other agencies, examples will be discussed once only for the whole activity.

Three successful cases of development, control of the screw worm fly (Appendix F-1), natural rubber or guayule (Appendix F-2), and grain weevils (Appendix F-3), show how technology is generated in USDA.

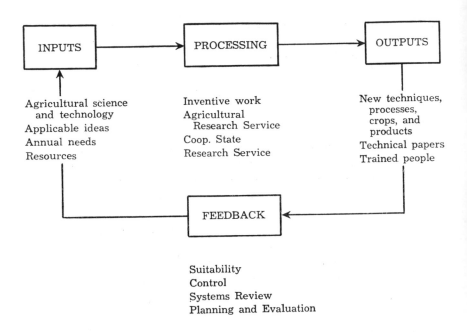

Figure 14. USDA inventing activities.

The screw worm fly in the 1930's spread north from Florida and Mexico. By the 1950's it resulted in $15 million annual losses to Southeastern cattlemen and considerably more to Southwesterners, plus uncounted losses to wildlife. Individual cattle wounds were treated directly. In the 1930's and 1940's USDA scientists developed concepts of biological control, which were put into practice in the 1950's and 1960's. Vast numbers of sterilized male flies were released in infested areas to outnumber fertile males. Development of technologies associated with this program cost $10 million. Information came from studies of X-ray sterilization of fruit flies, from nuclear energy isotope applications, and from studies of screw worm flies. Development or invention took place in USDA laboratories but required inputs from many technologies.

During World War II natural rubber became strategically important. Synthetic rubbers then required natural rubber additives.

USDA was charged with finding new natural rubber sources to satisfy defense needs. Many plants were studied, but the most promising one was the guayule shrub which grows in the Southwest and in northern Mexico. USDA learned to grow this shrub commercially, to extract its natural rubber or latex, and to use it with synthetic rubbers. Information inputs were Mexican and American techniques developed further through experiment.

Grain weevils annually damage the value of stored grain by an estimated ten percent. Conditions of damage by the well-known pests have been studied for a century. Weevils can be controlled in several ways; but the methods have been more useful to large commercial storers of grain than to small farmers, who now carry most of the annual costs.

These three examples illlustrate input needs which stimulate USDA inventing activities, the kinds of information available to it, and the resources used. None of these three examples caused political controversy during the inventing period. All took several years to show significant results.

Processing

Typical USDA inventing work is carried on by the Agricultural Research Service in four categories.

1. Plant Science and Entomology. Improve quality and yield of crops through related production technology. Control disease and insects. Reduce pesticidal residues and pollution of the environment.
2. Soils, Water, and Engineering. Mechanize crop and livestock production. Improve farm structures. Develop new uses for electrical energy.
3. Livestock. Develop superior strains. Improve feeding and management. Reduce disease and parasites. Minimize animal waste pollution.
4. Marketing and Nutrition. Develop new and improved products and processing technology. Utilize waste products to reduce pollution. Improve ways to handle products from grower to consumer.[3]

USDA also supports state agricultural experimental stations through the Cooperative State Research Service. These experimental stations do much detailed work in adapting results of USDA applied research to local areas. This frequently involves derivative inventing or development which closely associates with innovating. Within USDA inventive programs, inputs are processed straightforwardly. Project selection occurs after each processing stage but can vary with outside factors. For example, crop yields may be increased by reducing insects, irrigating, or using better fertilizers. Selection of the most useful approach may change because of side effects or of relative factor input costs. Outside factors can have considerable influence because of pressure group activity. Products are tested extensively under both laboratory and field conditions.

Examples. In the twenty year development of screw worm fly control technologies, many approaches were considered before and along with mass sterilization. Direct wound treatment methods were perfected and publicized as stopgaps. Once the biological approach was adopted, the supporting technologies for raising the flies on frozen whale meat, mass sterilization using cobalt 60, distribution over large areas, and measurement of their effectiveness had to be developed, step by step, trade-off by trade-off. In the natural rubber developments, many plants were tried along with guayule. Once adopted, guayule's specific requirements were improvements in cultivation and processing for maximum yield. Control of insects in stored grain evolved into needs for nontoxic fumigants, improved drying and storage techniques, and improved building construction.

These examples led into diverse technologies not apparent when the need was first foreseen. Yet adequate procedures were available to develop technical solutions.

Outputs

USDA inventive outputs, which include ways to produce new or old crops, process food or fiber, or do farm engineering, are embodied in public service (free) patents, technical and farmer's bulletins, trained people, and occasional items of hardware. At the beginning of FY 1971 USDA held 1.337 unexpired patents and had published about 1,000 other technological developments between 1960 and 1970.[4] The most easily measured outputs are trained people and technical papers. Only recently have outputs been developed for specific application to other economic sectors.

There are feedforward marketing outputs for department technology. In 1967, for example, strategic shortages of sugar and wool occurred. People won incentive payments for producing these items. Relevant technologies to improve production and marketing were emphasized in informing programs.

Examples. Outputs of screw worm fly control were distributed only after extensive trials showed them feasible, successful, and without side effects. USDA totally controlled procedures, workers, and sterile flies, but they were available to states and regions on a sharing basis. Technologies for biological control of insects were so successful that they have been used to control the Mexican fruit fly in the Western citrus fields and have been under development for use against the cornborer, boll weevil, European chafer, leaf roller, and tsetse fly.[5] Although control of insects in stored grain is technically feasible, different approaches are still being considered.

Feedback

As in Chapter III, discussions of feedback for Federal agency activities include comparisons with the planning information base, exercise of control over inputs and processing, and systems review of overall effectiveness. Feedback on USDA inventing programs can be evaluated against the specific need from which work was started or against national goals of technology diffusion. Out of three typical examples, only the screw worm fly control program succeeded completely. The technologies have been adopted, continued, and extended to other insects. Work on guayule ceased after natural rubber was synthesized and national need satisfied; nevertheless, the guayule technologies could still be helpful in Mexico. Control of grain weevils remains a national need despite technical successes with this program. Analysis of this failure must take into account informing, innovating, and integrating feedbacks which redefine need.

In terms of predominant goals of increasing production, conserving land, and decreasing labor, USDA inventing programs have, in the main, been timely and technically successful at a reasonable cost. From time to time, administrators question the suitability of some programs, and old research lines are dropped in favor of new ones. Secretary of Agriculture Orville L. Freeman tried valiantly to drop lines of research and close research stations for FY 1966, but he was only partly successful in getting Congressional approval. He wanted to eliminate research on food wholesaling and retailing, fibers other than cotton, fur-bearing animals, tung, sesame, bamboo, and sugar-sorghum. He wanted to consolidate other research into more efficient stations.[6] Some of the research lines he proposed to eliminate had been active for fifty years.

Secretary Freeman's concern resulted partly from a 1961 study by the President's Scientific Advisory Committee, revealing that the national research centers and regional laboratories did not cover all areas, particularly the Appalachian, deep South, and dry plains states. State centers only partially supplemented these blank areas. The Committee also noted that two hundred field research installations were too small to be efficient.[7]

USDA inventing activity funds spread through every state with the largest concentrations in Maryland and the District of Columbia which together received over \$20 million in R&D funds for FY 1971.[8]

Some inventive programs have stabilized because of nature's adaptations. New strains of rust-resistant wheat must be constantly developed to offset the more virulent natural strains of rust which emerge. USDA must find new pesticides and antibiotics to cope with new strains of insects and bacteria while reducing residual contamination.

Control. USDA controls new technology generation through priorities and allocation of resources; but because this activity is mostly internal and centralized, the control is simplified. To the extent that USDA works with all states, the work must be carefully coordinated. Suitability evaluations during the past twenty years have caused a gradual shift in priorities from increasing production to improving quality for consumers. The control function has been emphasized more following the 1965 advent of program budgeting.

Systems review. For several years, the USDA Research Program Development and Evaluation Staff functioned in both control and systems review. This staff coordinated the department's inventive activities and audited internal management. It provided a departmental Uniform Project System through which all USDA research projects were documented, coordinated, and made available for further coordination to outside Federal, state, and private research agencies.[9] Before 1965, systems review was submerged at a lower and less effective level under the Agricultural Research Service.[10] In FY 1970, systems review was again submerged.

In addition to this internal review, Congressional committees on agriculture make substantial inputs into redirecting USDA inventive efforts. Organizations such as the Farm Bureau provide political support.

IV. INFORMING

Inputs

Inventing programs produce the flow of technical information and trained people into agricultural information transfer and dissemination represented in Figure 15. Though USDA can handle information by both old and new techniques, it is equipped physically and by training more for older techniques. Clients are known by their areas of interest and response to historic information channels and means. By the dissemination plan, information reaches farm operators, agricultural product processors, and consumers.

Funds for the informing program, not including those for generally informing the public, are shown in Appendix D. USDA gets between two and three percent of Federal funds used in scientific and technical information for publication and distribution, bibliographic and reference work, symposia, and other traditional forms of information dissemination. Programs for informing the general public, via radio and television, contain general technical information designed to provide awareness and gain interest. Funds for the technical portion of the public information program cannot be separated from other information.

Support for updating the National Agricultural Library has lagged behind the two other national libraries, and it remains outdated, mostly manual, and plagued by overgrowth and crowding.

The limited USDA marketing feedforward of its R&D results may be in the form of support or preference to be given a particular development. Feedforward may be funds for publicity, to make farmers aware of new diseases and preventive measures, or it may be publicity related to a crop in short supply. Also, as items go into innovating and integrating, different packages of information are needed to support differing phases of adoption, evaluation of effects of adoption, and adjustment to it.

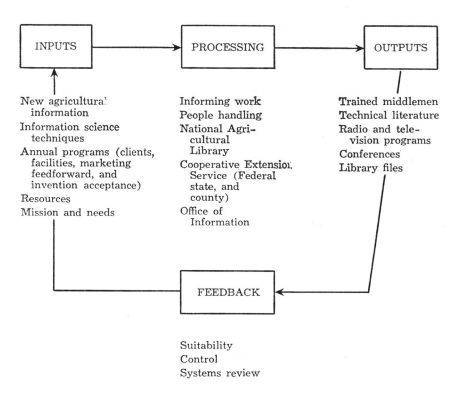

Figure 15. USDA informing activities.

For transferring information to the farmer, USDA uses the county agent system, land grant colleges, and vocational agriculture educational programs. Since 1966 funds for training these middlemen have been at about $160 million annually.[11, 12]

The importance of using trained people for transferring useful information from development to innovation has been emphasized by managers of industrial activity. C. Guy Suits, for many years Director of Research for the General Electric Company, has stated that there is no substitute for technologists working with marketing people to transfer information about new products. The transfer of the items, he states, is not sufficient, nor are oral or written exchanges of information, nor is a demonstration of technical feasibility. A face-to-face confrontation, where technical judgments juxtapose marketing judgments, seems the most effective way to transfer information.[13] USDA has incorporated this procedure in informing programs because the concept apparently works as well for farmers as for other entrepreneurs. USDA has adopted the middleman approach, but the principle of an interface between developing and marketing is not violated.

Processing

USDA informing programs pervade U. S. agriculture. The most centralized facility is the National Agricultural Library in Washington, D.C., with 1,300,000 volumes. It collects information on agriculture from worldwide sources and supports USDA research efforts, agricultural colleges and universities, industry, scientists, farmers, and the general public. The Library provides photocopies, reference services, bibliographies, and indexes. The work moves slowly and conventionally but renders substantial support. The Office of Information, a staff agency directly under the Secretary of Agriculture, processes information output which involves policy. Within the bureaus, technical writers and communications specialists convert applied research and development reports into technical bulletins, farmers' bulletins, articles for journals, radio and television programs, and training materials. Channels, media or means to be used, and the form, slant, and emphasis of information vary according to clients. Resources must be spread for maximum results. Limited interest project reports may simply be deposited in the library. The annual **Yearbook of Agriculture** once summarized the status of all projects. About 1940, this became impossible and themes like soils, insects, home economics, and rural life were selected for emphasis each year.

This selection problem continues in USDA, as well as in other Federal agencies. From available channels, USDA may choose county agents, experiment stations, symposia, county or state fairs. The actual product and the developer are often available at state fairs. Or USDA may choose farmers' bulletins distributed direct to farmers or to libraries. Agribusinesses also convey extracts of new technology through advertising.

Progress reports on agricultural research were initiated in 1889 by authority of the Hatch Act of 1887, which established state experiment stations. The Hatch Act also allowed experiment stations to mail their reports free. Availability of reports and freedom for dissemination helped diffuse research results.

The Federal Extension Service is a partner in the Cooperative Extension Service along with state land grant colleges and county governments. The Extension Service interfaces directly between the agricultural technology generator and the user at the state, county, and local levels. County agents are middlemen for change—technology couplers. Agricultural educational programs under the Department of Health, Education, and Welfare also serve to disseminate information about agricultural technologies. The programs influence young farmers and agricultural leaders through high school and college programs.

Outputs

In the late 1960's USDA annually distributed 65 million copies of bulletins and articles on its research, written and illustrated at four levels of comprehension—for scientists, other researchers, the average farmer, and the nearly illiterate farmer; published in scientific journals related to agricultural research; conducted 20 million consultations on adapting research findings to individual farms; sponsored radio and television broadcasts, and supported demonstrations and exhibits in communities, counties, regions, and states.

Technical literature is the standard, traditional, and cheapest output of the USDA informing program. This literature is designed to be used in all innovating phases. Much of it is also summarized in film, both instructive and entertaining, for television and movies. Developers are nearly always available in USDA, but middlemen trained to transfer information and help apply it are normal contacts for farmers. County agent offices and experiment stations support training in an ever-expanding wave of information from the developer to the people who apply the information.

Marketing includes advertising (to create awareness), sales agents (to foster adoption), distribution channels (to make new technology available in hardware form), and servicing (to assist in application and use). These four activities transfer technology from a unit in society which has it to another without it. USDA, as other Federal agencies, "markets" new technology. For USDA, advertising may be by associated agribusiness or through county agents. Sales agents in all Federal agencies include administrators who must engender public acceptance for their programs and specific approval by Congress and Executive Branch budget makers. Conferences and demonstrations bypass delays in preparing and distributing technical literature and frequently sponsor adoption.

The concept of a library as an information transfer channel to future users has been developed in USDA as well as in the Public Health Service. A library is also an output of informing programs. In fast moving technical fields such as pesticides, conventional libraries focused on future generations have less usefulness because of their non-specific coverage and the half-life of technical information. The Pesticides Information Center therefore supplements the Agricultural Library for this rapidly changing field.

Examples. Technical solutions for controlling screw worms, finding natural rubber sources, and controlling grain weevils generated informing programs as the information became available. USDA resources were allocated to inform customers about these projects. In processing information for controlling screw worm flies, USDA used newspapers, magazines, radio, television, and professional groups to tell cattlemen of procedures to be used and of the need for cooperation in evaluating results of the control effort. Conferences were held between developers and operational people to be sure the best available procedures were used. State farmer organizations aided in specific transfers of technical information. Information transfer on guayule remained specfic and experimental, though a few hundred people were eventually involved in planting, harvesting, processing, and studying guayule. In the control of grain weevils, most combinations of publications, channels, and media have been used.

Dramatic information outputs appeared in screw worm fly control after that project began to succeed. Statewide campaigns were developed in Texas, for example, to eliminate flies once and for all. Control of grain weevils has never engendered such outputs, though the information is readily available. The approaches for controlling grain weevils included farm bulletins, county agents. and to a lesser degree, public media.

Feedback

Suitability. Information from USDA on the screw worm fly reached the proper source for action, but grain weevil information has apparently not been suitable for all clients, and will be considered under innovating. USDA maintains a national information system for agriculture which has USDA goals, user requirements and preferences, fixed or available facilities, support, and decision points in processing. How well does it compare with theoretical national systems?

Various system models have been investigated which could apply. John S. Sayer concludes with regard to a national system that "the least expensive method of organizing a science information system network appears to be on a regional basis with centralization of acquisition input processes being undertaken in a central clearinghouse."[14] USDA's system, for agricultural science and published technology, is probably not the most economical in that it has national, state, and county centers of information with acquisition at all levels. Yet it effects its historic objectives. USDA, depending on free distribution, can evaluate immediate success by the number of requests for publications. However, total needs or missions are normally evaluated rather than success of particular outputs of its informing programs.

Technical suitability of means has been measured by follow-on requests from different audiences, applications of the technology which became known, and oral comments from users. Farmers' bulletins are useful to farmers, but not to food processors. Timeliness must also be considered. As a marketing activity, information transfer should be timely or it will not "catch on."

Control. With its mission to gather and diffuse worldwide agricultural information, USDA has studied information transfer more than other government agencies. Feedback evaluations are the basis for its Office of Information, the control agency, redirecting goal achieving efforts. This office, high in USDA organization hierarchy, has controlled informing since 1925 and has become an institution in the agricultural sector. It allocates department information resources by priorities and available facilities.

Systems review of informing is not generally separated from overall program review, which is done within agencies and at department level. Before 1965, systems review was primarily carried out by the Office of Information. The obsolescence of the National Agricultural Library may have resulted from complacency caused by past success. Lack of effectiveness in reaching disadvantaged farmer groups has caused revamping of certain farmers' bulletins. Informing problems in the changing U. S. society have been recognized, and adjustments are slowly being made.

V. INNOVATING

Inputs

The innovating activities of Figure 16 are those where agriculture-related economic units decide to adopt or innovate. The most involved

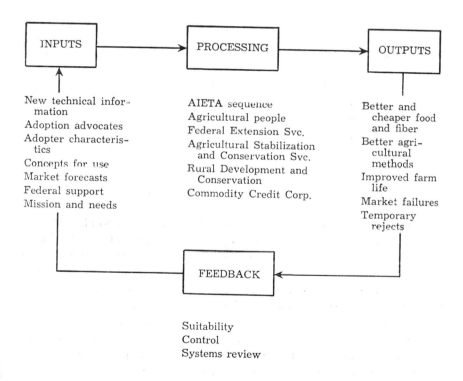

Figure 16. USDA innovating activities.

agencies are those under Processing plus their associated state, land grant college, and county offices, which help integrate Federal programs. In applying new technology, indeed, state and local experience transfer better to farms than will experience of more distant Federal installations.

Comparing USDA activities to the innovating model shows that USDA's patent-free technical information inputs are suited to farmer needs, that its advocates for adoption are close to and know the farmer, that the new technology's uses are identified, that markets are supported, and that the farmer can procure loan assistance for obtaining a farm or improving technology. As noted in Chapter III, rural sociologists have concentrated on agricultural innovation, and USDA has benefitted from their conclusions. USDA administrators understand and use the AIETA model of adoption.

Packaged technologies designed to upgrade several communities or even a few counties are now available through the combined services of USDA agencies. Rural development specialists have hoped they can end rural migration to cities by supporting packaged technologies of community land conservation, electrification, water supplies and sewage disposal, and crop planning. This is an input mission and need of the innovating process which has only recently become feasible.[15]

Processing

Federal Extension Service employees join county and state government officials to form the county agent system for diffusing information to farmers and helping them use this information. County agents are "how-to-do" people who combine local publicity (information transfer) with active demonstration, assistance, and encouragement. According to the rural sociologist Everett M. Rogers, the county agent divides his time into consulting (24%), administering public programs (24%), selling ideas and information (17%), organizing and supervising agricultural events (16%), organizing groups (7%), studying (7%), and expediting (5%). In his role as a consultant and salesman for information, the county agent gets support from Extension Service specialists (39%), Experiment Station Bulletins (27%), farm magazines (14%), agricultural technologists and scientists in USDA and state offices (9%), key farmers (7%), and Extension Service News Releases (4%).[16] Two well-known programs associated with the county agents are extension home economics agents and Youth Programs such as 4-H Clubs. In this processing by the county agents, coupling is encouraged between those who generated and those who apply new technology.

The Soil Conservation Service innovates through over 3,000 soil and water conservation districts with individual cooperating farms. Farms receive soil surveys, and owners are aided in developing and carrying out land use plans. The Rural Electrification Administration helps farmers create cooperatives for placing electricity, plumbing, and telephones in rural homes. Thirty-five year loans are provided at two percent interest, which is a real subsidy at recent interest rates. The Farmers Home Administration works through 1,726 local county offices to provide loans for family farms and both loans and grants for farm communities to develop common water supplies, recreational areas, and conservation projects. The Commodity Credit Corporation subsidizes farm income and rewards conservation of crop land. This frequently supports innovating by the individual farmer. The Agricultural Stabilization and Conservation Service (ASCS) works with the Commodity Credit Corporation in adjusting production, providing incentive payments for scarce crops (sugar and wool), and diverting acreage to conservation uses. This program invests about $300 million annually in conservation. ASCS has operated 2,865 county offices. Some of its support programs were curtailed or terminated in 1970-71.[17]

Input processing by the individual farmer follows the AIETA model of new technology adoption which was described in Chapter III. The rather sophisticated agricultural education of farmers has created a population prone to try new developments. Community projects, such as milk tank trucks rather than separate cans, have been adopted less readily than items a farmer can try himself.[18] The county agent's advice is valuable during Evaluation and Testing. Development and adaptation include the farm's adjustment to new technology as well as the reverse. The farmer sometimes follows the advice of equipment and seed companies or farm magazines when innovating.

Outputs

Results of applying technology to agricultural problems are new and cheaper food and fiber, better methods, and improved farm life. Typical of this generation are hybrid corn, soy beans, and grain sorghums; new strains of turkeys, swine, and cattle; improved methods of irrigating; increased use of inorganic and liquid fertilizers; pesticides and herbicides; more adaptable farm machinery; and new types of prefabricated farm construction. These have been adopted steadily as they became available and as farmers obtained the means to acquire them. Technology is actually available to produce the entire agricultural output with fewer people if that is a desired goal.

An indication of the farmer's propensity to innovate can be inferred from statistics on sales of farm machinery and equipment between 1945 and 1966. From 1945 through 1954, average annual sales of tractors, plows, harrows, planters, cultivators, dusters, combines, mowers, hay balers, feed grinders, and other labor saving machinery were two to ten times higher than annual sales in the decades preceding or following. Prices also rose, so that the unit cost of these items in 1966 was about five times the unit cost for the period 1945-49.[19] In effect, the American farmer mechanized in the 1945-49 period, and rising costs of machinery pinched out the laggards in adoption. These are the dropouts or forceouts shown on the adoption curve of Figure 3.

There have been some rejects in innovating as well as successes. One can find areas in the country seemingly bypassed by all agricultural progress, where the quality of life is low by any standard. The message, or perhaps the means to accept the message, has not reached these sections. All new technology offered seems to be rejected. The special programs of the Rural Development and Conservation Service are designed to help these areas.

There are also current as well as historic failures because innovators have not taken economic and local conditions into account. USDA failed quite early in innovating tea culture, silk culture, and converting sorghum plants to sugar.[20] These could not compete with foreign imports or local conditions. Wet-rice culture in the Yazoo-Mississippi basin after WW II created mosquito problems. Wool and sugar are in short supply, and new technologies have not yet been attractive enough to cause farmers to shift to the production of these scarce items.

Examples

The needs for screw worn fly control, new rubber sources, and stored grain insect control were justified inputs into the USDA innovating programs. Guayule rubber and control of grain weevils were both found uneconomical in the evaluation process. Guayule rubber simply could not compete with natural synthetic rubber. Grain weevils can be controlled economically in large stores of quality grain, but the methods were found to have too many dangerous and unpleasant drawbacks for the small farmer who needs most to control the pests. He has temporarily rejected it. The processing of information for controlling screw worm flies showed the farmer had nothing to lose and a chance to gain. The program depended on cooperation among Federal, state, local, and individual farm units. It was conducted under the normal arrangements of Federal-state matching funds. The informing and innovating programs were coordinated to a remarkable degree in keeping count of the decreasing infestations. Screw worm fly control resulted in more beef for the same effort, or a cheaper product. Flies had caused millions of dollars damage each year ($15 million in the Southeast and more in the Southwest). After 1961, resources previously used to control flies could be used to grow more beef.

Feedback

Suitability. Some USDA programs for long term gain, like watershed improvement or conservation, do not weigh heavily immediate gains; but normally, new technology either pays off in the short run or it does not. If it pays off, however, there may be undesirable side effects or excessive support requirements. Screw worm fly control had no discernible undesirable effects for the farmer. Its success resulted from carefully preparing the project to fit needs of farmers, obtaining their approval and cooperation, and using constant and near real-time feedback on the progress of the project. The main feedback for the total program was the realization that reinfestation from Mexico prevented a final solution and that the project would have to be continued as a permanent USDA activity. For USDA programs at large, feedback determines the direction of further technology generation. This is the present state of grain weevil control. Small farmers have temporarily rejected the proposed solution of periodic fumigation because of its excessive support requirements for drying grain and storing it in airtight cribs. The project now awaits new developments in these related support areas or, alternatively, new ways to destroy or control the weevils. During FY 1968, irradiation (a byproduct of DOD and AEC food irradiation) and grain storage in inert gases were tried for weevil control.[21] These approaches would most benefit the commercial storer rather than the small farmer.

Control. USDA agencies propose, and farm units dispose. If USDA proposes impractical technology, the farmer rejects it. Administrators support successes and study failures to determine what went wrong. Feedback is not always obtained for analysis in a timely manner and corrective action then comes too late.

Department agencies have developed independently, and the Department was reorganized in the 1960's for better control. For example, the Office of Rural Areas Development evolved in 1961 to coordinate the economic support efforts of USDA agencies in overall rural areas development. The Office was consolidated with other agencies by 1964 to become a new major agency of Rural Development and Conservation. The Rural Areas Development Office itself became the new and expanded Rural Community Development Services by 1965-66. These constant changes show the continuing effort to exercise some control over innovating in the changing rural environment.

Systems review. The county agent system and land grant colleges work with farm groups in giving the most direct overall review of innovational effectiveness. These develop political inputs which impact on annual planning of USDA activities. USDA planners must include or consider agricultural sector goals along with national goals, as well as departmental interests, when it submits new USDA programs or proposes to reduce old ones. Congressional committees, farm professional associations, and the Bureau of the Budget also scrutinize innovating activity. It has been historically difficult to find an unbiased group to review USDA innovating activity and also influence Congress and the public. The Bureau of the Budget has not fully compared USDA programs with other ways of accomplishing national goals.

VI. INTEGRATING

Inputs

The same agencies which promote initial adoption and application of technology also promote the continued adoption of Figure 17. As more and more units adopt, production standards adjust to new technology; and adoption accelerates, giving the well-known S-shaped imitation or logistics curve described at least seventy years ago.[22] More recently the Foundation for Research on Human Behavior has described imitation in the form of the standard deviation curve of Figure 12. When the technology is essentially diffused, the adoption rate drops off as laggards either conform or withdraw.[23]

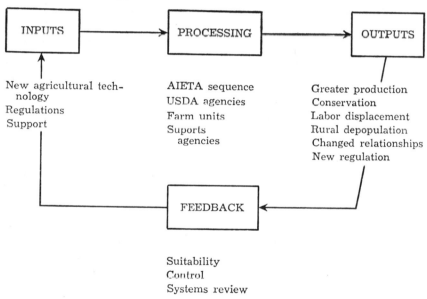

Figure 17. USDA integrating activities.

From the viewpoint of the decision unit, adoption of new technology requires adjusting the unit operation to the new technology. In shifting from animal to tractor power, grain consumption decreases, and some equivalent cash crop must be grown to provide funds for tractor fuel. When most adoption units shift to tractors, tractor repair shops replace blacksmith shops, animal sales and growth of grain crops decrease, fertilizer sources change, school instruction shifts from veterinary science to mechanical technology, and pasture land can produce beef. Laggards still using animal power find they cannot sell at a profit and that they cannot get equipment and care for their animals. In the agricultural sector, the decision unit has new technology, price support from government regulations on acreages that may be grown without penalty, and limitations of farm resources. He also has supporting community financing, marketing, and information.

Processing

The individual farm or product consumer decision unit considers new technology inputs in terms of advantages to his unit and elects to adopt or not, following the familiar AIETA sequence. Later adopters have less trouble because the community, after some lag, shifts toward new practices. Continued integration of new agricultural technology rests on support through government as well as private agencies. Regulations and standards on various meat and dairy products reflect integration of these items into consumer diets and protect the consumer in his acceptance of them. Price support through government agencies encourages efficiency in production but may discourage experimentation with completely new crops.

Labor willingness to accommodate itself to change has been a feature of U. S. agriculture which may not continue. Facilities, materials, skilled people, and technical information have been available until recently to support integration without social disruption.

Speed of integration varies with products and area. Ryan and Gross found that it took fourteen years for the majority to adopt hybrid seed corn in Iowa.[24] This was the area with most advantages and fastest adoption.

Examples. Screw worm fly control programs continue because of reinfestation from Mexico. USDA, cooperating with Southwestern ranchers and farmers, have devised procedures for sealing the Mexican border by releasing along it 300,000 sterile flies weekly during season. Work was continued in FY 1973 with the Mexican government to reduce infestation in Mexico. The total program has stabilized with $5 million costs each year in USDA's operating budget. Control of stored grain pests among large operators has tightened under pressure from consumers of grain products. These pressures have only marginally affected the small farmer who sells or uses damaged grain locally.

Outputs

USDA, through such processes and mechanisms as the county agent system, regulation, and farm support, has clearly diffused technology directly and indirectly into the economy. Agricultural production could not have advanced so much without this support. Between 1950 and 1965, only fifteen years, yields per acre in corn, cotton, oats, peanuts, rice, sorghum grain, tobacco, and wheat increased between 150 and 200 percent. Four and one-half million farm workers in 1969 supported themselves and more than 200 million additional people, over forty-four persons per worker.[25] The very recent increases in per acre production attest to the efficiency of the integration programs of the sector. The man hour production figures are even more impressive.

A second output has been improved nutrition through a better mix of foods and higher quality foods. Control of stored grain pests by large operators helps produce this output. USDA agencies enforce the regulations which support these improvements. A third output is conservation of land for future use. The application of technology simply forces marginal farms out of production so that they can be reclaimed for less destructive uses or recombined into more efficient operations. Soil erosion, already advanced in Appalachia, the Southeastern states, and the high plains, has been slowed.

In terms of the integration model, technology has reduced rather than increased jobs. With respect to the intent of the Employment Act of 1946, the agricultural technology ingestion has been dysfunctional. Though USDA studies predicted the job losses as early as 1940,[26] few programs were specifically designed to increase farm employment. Farm product processing, fertilizer, pesticides, herbicides, and machinery have increased employment off the farm.

One major integration output in agriculture is the institutionalizing of Federal agency activities in the sector. These activities have supplemented or displaced market, finance, and support forces of the economy.

Feedback

Suitability. Improvement in output per man hour input is one measure of integration of new technology. USDA support of preferred agricultural activities makes feedback on output per man hour very popular. Given the historic goals and orientation of increasing production and conserving land, this is a positive feedback. But it has a flaw, well stated in 1965 by Congressman John Brademas of Indiana, who observed that agriculture has been the most amazing phenomenon in U. S. science and technology for increasing productivity and decreasing the labor force. If science and technology were as successful in industry, he believed there would be enormous social, political, and economic problems.[27] Brademas was worried about displaced people moving from agriculture to other sectors. They were no longer being absorbed fast enough to avoid disruption in the other sectors. Economists and USDA have usually neglected social costs of technology ingestion. For example, Zvi Griliches, Professor of Economics, University of Chicago, has estimated the social rate of return on research and development of hybrid corn to be 700 percent per year.[28] Theodore W. Schultz, also a Professor of Economics, University of Chicago, extended this estimate to consider the output of U. S. agriculture using 1940 versus 1950 technologies. The difference between actual (1950) and the output had technology stagnated at 1940 levels gave a social rate of return of 35 percent on the low side and 171 percent on the high side.[29] Neither Griliches nor Schultz calculated social costs of people displaced by machines, rising welfare payments, increasing social dissension, or ghettos, nor were they criticized for not so doing. Measuring of undesirable side effects of technology integration has rarely been required.

Another more dramatic feedback caused passage in 1965 of laws to indemnify dairy farmers for destroying milk which had been contaminated from residues of chemicals registered and approved for crop-dusting by USDA. Without indemnities the farmers faced bankruptcy. The registering of crop-dusting chemicals, the testing of milk for purity and edibility, and the indemnifying of dairy farmers are all integration activities of the Secretary of Agriculture. Food contamination is thus an undesirable side effect of technology ingestion.

Erosion and land exploitation have caused farm families to find themselves on wornout soil or with too few producing units to subsist. Too poor to adopt new technologies, these families depopulated the farms and withdrew into welfare programs and big city ghettoes. Plights of tenant farmers on marginal land has been even worse. The agricultural sector has simply not captured enough gains of technology ingestion to ease the transition to urban life. USDA belatedly established Community Action programs and other procedures to help low-income groups.

Control. Individual farm units ingest new technology because of its relative advantages and the forces of competition. Individual USDA agencies influence adoption through subsidy and support programs; indeed they try to control adoption when its side effects cause national problems. USDA regulatory offices handle these cases. Once ingestion and integration start, it is generally too late for normal control measures. The effort to relate the ingestion directly to specific national goals or even to departmental goals is normally after the fact. Long term conservation goals, for example, conflict with short term support for the marginal farmer.

Systems review. A very difficult function in technology diffusion is predicting and preparing for the effects of wholesale adoption of some new item. USDA cannot predict any better than other elements of society. The Planning and Evaluation staff offices evaluate major programs in terms of goals and objectives, with some political and external inputs. The most effective external systems review of the USDA integrating subprocess takes place in congressional hearings before annual appropriations and major agricultural legislation. These hearings juxtapose, at least, national goals, USDA goals, agricultural sector goals, and USDA programs so that legislators, administrators and the public can finally compare them.

VII. USDA IN THE TOTAL PROCESS

USDA has through the years developed within a single department mission-oriented activities for generating new agricultural technologies, for disseminating information about them, for advocating their adoption by farmers and consumers, and for supporting and subsidizing diffusion of these technologies throughout the agricultural sector.

Inventing. Applied research and development effort of $187 million yearly precedes USDA technology diffusion efforts; this amount does not, however, measure the technology available to diffuse. Some programs are defensive, such as those of new strains of wheat which can resist new rust or new pesticides which do not build biological residues. Just holding the line requires significant amounts of money. Developments in other sectors may supersede such innovations as guayule rubber. Still others may be so specialized that they benefit only a few, as does bamboo culture. Many diffused successes were not expensive in applied research and development. New crops, fertilizers, machinery, new animal strains, and new techniques accumulated year by year without large appropriations for any single item. Steady funding of civil service agricultural technologists has been very productive, and the results are made freely available as public services. They are tried and adapted in experiment stations close enough to the potential adopter that he can go see the results himself. Review and control at department level are effective, but some programs have developed specialized support and outlived their usefulness.

Informing. With about $160-$170 million in training and $10 million in scientific and technical information, USDA informing effort is substantial and sustained. Though not as up-to-date as other Federal agency informing programs, USDA has been effective for the audiences it reached: the educated and literate farmers and consumers. The informing activities can handle feedforward marketing support for applied research and development through county agent and colllege channels, they can store and retrieve information for future users in the National Agricultural Library, and they can evaluate feedback demand for information outputs. Programs are characterized by conventional but multiple channels, forms, and media; and feedback moves through county agent and college channels as well as directly to the program managers. USDA effectively couples agricultural technology generators to users, but programs are normally evaluated only in terms of overall department goals and needs.

Innovating. With well-defined customers and strong and institutionalized support through the county agent and state land grant college systems, USDA agencies effectively advocate adoption of new agricultural technology. To the farmer and consumer adopter, information use and its potential market are identified so that he can go through the AIETA sequence without information gaps. For technologies considered most needed, USDA agencies support innovation through loans, agricultural facilities, and trained people. Failures and no-takers still occur, and the small farmer who most needs to adopt new technology is the one who frequently turns it down after evaluating it.

Integrating. Integrating inputs from USDA into the general economy are represented in proportion by the annual funding for the Department of $5 to $8 billion. This amount covers generating new technology as well as diffusing it, but major expenses are in supporting continued adoption or integration of new products through market support, regulation, loans, and subsidies. Adoption units evaluate new agricultural technology in terms of government support as well as its own merits as they go through the AIETA sequence. Effects have been labor saving, capital using, farm concentrating, and suboptimizing for the agricultural sectors. USDA has become a major factor in every farmer's life, and it affects the amount and quality of food and fiber for every consumer. Integrating effort has been reviewed most critically, but not unfavorably, by Congressional and farmer groups.

De Facto Procedures

In 1962, William O. Baker, Vice-President for Research, Bell Telephone Laboratories, stated that agriculture had adapted to technology changes unparalleled in any other economic sector. Nothing equivalent has been observed in automobiles, steel, or the building trades. Government agents advocated change; applied research and development improved machinery, fertilizer, crops, pest control, and herbicides; and college educational systems supported adaptivity.[30] Another scientist, Harvey Brooks, has credited this success partly to the agricultural sector's clear recognition of the marketing of technology and applications engineering in institutionalizing the innovative effort.[31] According to Sterling Hendricks, writing for the Panel, National Academy of Sciences, agricultural diffusion patterns support intensive technology generation while ensuring its use by individual producers. Unorganized producers can easily turn for advice to a readily accessible organization. The government technologist has an effective organization for putting his findings to work.[32]

In diffusing its technology, USDA has taken title to all patents and other information developed from technology it generates, and made these patents and information generally available. Public service patents are freely published in information dissemination programs, freely advocated, and freely used. USDA programs and procedures for diffusing technology comprise a *de facto* system which has developed apart from private enterprise processes of monopolistic patenting, commercial innovating, and independent educational and commercial integrating.

National Goals

USDA has clearly promoted progress of science and the useful arts, improved agricultural productivity, conserved agricultural land, upgraded the farmer's health and physical environment, given the consumer better products, and provided technical information to potential users. It has succeeded less in providing employment, encouraging family farms, and developing all areas equitably. Undesirable side effects of new technologies are becoming of greater concern.

Employment. Undesirable effects of agricultural technology diffusion have not yet been fully evaluated, although it was this activity, more directly than any other, which gave American society the urban farm, and 1960 decade reductions occurred at the same time total U. S. Department of Labor, noted in October 1967, that in the 1950's ten million people migrated from farms to cities, that this migration continued, and that two and one-half more non-whites than whites were moving.[33] Between 1960 and 1971, about 6 million more people left the farm, and 1960 decade reductions occurred at the same time total U.S. population was increasing by 24 million persons.[34] At the time the national goal from the Employment Act of 1946 was full employment of human assets, the agricultural sector, through massive ingestion of technology, was rapidly reducing employment.

Even a clearly beneficial program may displace jobs. Screw worm fly control, costing $5 million yearly in 1968, employs 250 to 300 people in the public sector. The programs prevent livestock losses from infestation and costly treatment of about $50 to $75 million yearly. If the U. S. uses the same amount of meat, then over two thousand people who formerly combatted the screw worm fly and raised additional stock are now displaced.

The family farm. Rising costs, increasing mechanization, and competition have combined to squeeze out marginal family farms. In addition, expectation of continued high price supports has been capitalized in land values, making rents and prices high.[35] The family-worked farm is slowly losing out to commercial operators.

Equitable development of all areas. In 1963, 52.9 percent of farm subsidies went to low income areas of the Southeast and Southwest, when these areas had 29.7 percent of population and 22.9 percent of national income. Only 4.6 percent of farm subsidies went to Mideast and Far West high income areas with 34 percent of population and 39.1 percent of income.[36] Yet rural sociologists have observed that the most successful farmers adopt early. Marginal farmers change slowest and are being forced out. Farm subsidies do not assure that new technology will be integrated fast enough to offset other factors.

In terms of the overall technology diffusion model (Figure 9), USDA technologies have been needed, wanted, and preferred. The steps from one level of technology to the next have come too rapidly for the sector to adjust socially and culturally. Undesirable side effects have begun to take their toll in displaced and unemployed farm workers now in big city ghettoes, reduction in numbers of family owned farms, and high prices for land and agricultural equipment. In recognition of the dangers of continued rural population movement to cities the USDA began refocusing part of its effort to give a viable life to the subsistence farmer.

FOOTNOTES

[1] U.S. Department of Commerce, *Statistical Abstract of the U.S., 1971* (Washington, D.C.: U.S. Government Printing Office, 1972), pp. 572-574.

[2] *The Budget of the United States, 1971* (Washington, D.C.: U.S. Government Printing Office, 1970), p. 265.

[3] Federal Register Division, National Archives and Records Service, General Services Administration, *United States Government Organization Manual, 1971-72* (Washington, D.C.: U.S. Government Printing Office, 1971), pp. 256-257.

[4] U.S. Federal Council for Science and Technology, *Annual Report on Government Patent Policy . . .* , *op. cit.* pp. 42 and 102.

[5] U.S. Department of Agriculture, *Imprint on Living: A Report on Progress,* Agricultural Research Service Information Bulletin No. 333 (Washington, D.C.: U.S. Government Printing Office, 1969), pp. 16 and 23.

[6] U.S. Congress, Senate, Committee on Appropriations, *Department of Agriculture Elimination of Agricultural Research Stations and Lines of Research,* Hearings before the Subcommittee on Agriculture and Related Agencies, 89th Cong., 1st Sess. (Washington, D.C.: U.S. Government Printing Office, 1965), pp. 4-6.

[7] President's Scientific Advisory Committee, *Science and Agriculture* (Washington, D.C.: The White House, Jan. 29, 1962), *passim.*

[8] NSF, *Federal Funds . . . , op. cit.,* pp. 159-168.

[9] Federal Register Division, National Archives and Records Service, General Services Administration, *United States Government Organization Manual, 1968-69, op. cit.,* p. 296.

[10] Federal Register Division, National Archives and Records Service, General Services Administration, *United States Government Organization Manual, 1963-64* (Washington, D.C.: U.S. Government Printing Office, 1963), p. 252.

[11] Bureau of the Budget, *Special Analyses, Budget of the United States FY 69* (Washington, D.C.: U.S. Government Printing Office, 1968), p. 12.

[12] Bureau of the Budget, *Special Analyses, Budget of the United States FY 71* (Washington, D.C.: U.S. Government Printing Office, 1970), p. 127.

[13] C. Guy Suits and Arthur M. Bueche, "Cases of Research and Development in a Diversified Company," in National Academy of Sciences-National Research Council, *Applied Science and Technological Progress . . . , op. cit.,* p. 346.

[14] John S. Sayer, "The Economics of a National Information System,," Vol. I of *Annual Review of Information Science and Technology,* Charles A. Cuadra, (ed.), (New York: John Wiley & Sons, 1967), p. 142.

[15] "USDA Urges End of Migration by Rural People to Big Cities," *Northern Virginia Sun* (Arlington, Virginia), January 10, 1968.

[16] Everett M. Rogers, *Social Change in Rural Society: A Textbook in Rural Sociology* (New York: Appleton-Century-Crofts, 1960), pp. 320-322.

[17] *The Budget of the U.S. Government,* FY 1971, *op. cit.,* pp. 252-253.

[18] Rogers, *op. cit.,* p. 404.

[19] U.S. Department of Agriculture, *Farm Machinery and Equipment,* Economic Research Service Statistical Bulletin No. 419 (Washington, D.C.: U.S. Government Printing Office, 1968), pp. 1-10 and 19-26.

[20] Alfred Charles True, *A History of Agricultural Experimentation and Research in the United States,* U.S. Department of Agriculture Misc. Pub. No. 251 (Washington, D.C.: U.S. Government Printing Office, 1937), p. 62.

[21] U.S. Department of Agriculture, *Imprint on Living . . . , op. cit.,* p. 13.

[22] Gabriel Tarde, *The Laws of Imitation* (New York: Holt, Rinehart, & Winston, 1903), quoted in Everett M. Rogers, *Diffusion of Innovations, op. cit.,* p. 152.

[23] The Foundation for Research on Human Behavior, *op. cit.,* p. 5.

[24] Everett M. Rogers, *Diffusion of Innovations, op. cit.,* p. 2.

[25] Department of Commerce, *Pocket Data Book, USA, 1971* (Washington, D.C.: U.S. Government Printing Office, 1971) pp. 36, 219.

[26] U.S. Department of Agriculture, *Technology on the Farm* (Washington, D.C.: Government Printing Office, 1940); and John A. Hopkins, *Changing Technology and Employment in Agriculture* (Washington, D.C.: U.S. Government Printing Office, 1941). Both these documents clearly indicated that farm employees would be displaced by mechanization.

[27] John Brademas, "Technology and Social Change: A Congressman's View," *The Impact of Science on Technology*, Aaron W. Warner, Dean Morse, and Alfred S. Eichner, eds. (New York: Columbia University Press, 1965), p. 161.

[28] Zvi Griliches, "Research Costs and Social Returns: Hybrid Corn and Related Innovations," *Journal of Political Economy*, Vol. LXVI (October, 1958), pp. 419-431.

[29] Theodore W. Schultz, *The Economic Organization of Agriculture* (New York: McGraw-Hill, 1953), pp. 114-122.

[30] William O. Baker, "The Dynamism of Technology," in Eli Ginzberg (ed.), *Technology and Social Change* (New York: Columbia University Press, 1963), pp. 102-103.

[31] Harvey Brooks, *op. cit.,* p. 62.

[32] Sterling B. Hendricks, "The Transition from Research to Useful Products in Agriculture," in National Academy of Sciences-National Research Council, *Applied Science and Technological Progress. . . , op. cit.,* p. 169.

[33] Frank H. Cassell, "The Development of Jobs; Realities and Opportunities," *Vital Speeches of the Day*, Vol. XXXIV, No. 2 (Nov. 1, 1967), pp. 59-64.

[34] Department of Commerce, *Pocket Data Book, op. cit ,* pp. 37, 218.

[35] "What Price Parity," *Barron's* (Dec. 9, 1968), p. 12.

[36] U.S. Congress, Joint Economic Committee, *U.S. Economic Growth to 1975: Potential and Problems*, 89th Cong., 2d Sess. (Washington D.C.: U.S. Government Printing Office, 1966), p. 45.

CHAPTER V

PUBLIC HEALTH SERVICE

I. INTRODUCTION

The U.S. Public Health Service diffuses technology into the public health sector of the general economy. It represents an independent bureau in a department and also exemplifies agencies which have expanded rapidly. In the 1965-69 period, Federal funds for health and medical care almost tripled, and more health legislation was enacted than during any comparable period in the nation's history.[1] With its forerunner office created in 1798, PHS is 155 years older than its current parent, the Department of Health, Education, and Welfare (D/HEW). During its long history as an independent bureau, PHS developed its procedures for technology diffusion, greatly influenced by the medical profession, medical associated industries, and medical schools.

Under current legislation, PHS is the Federal agency responsible for protecting and improving health of the people. It generates new medical technology or applicable knowledge through research, operates the National Medical Library for disseminating medical knowledge, supports research training in health and medical sciences, advocates adoption of its advances, and supports integration of medical advances through medical and hospital services. PHS spent $3.3 billion in FY 1971, but total Federal direct and indirect expenditures for medical and health-related activities were $20.6 billion, about six times this amount.[2] These related expenditures were in social security, vocational rehabilitation, veteran support, military support, and welfare.

II. ORGANIZATION

The Public Health Service, because of its tenfold expansion since 1953 in its support and activities, was reorganized twice between 1965 and 1969. Figure 18 presents 1971 offices of interest to this research, although the Food and Drug Administration will be treated less fully than NIH and HSMHA.

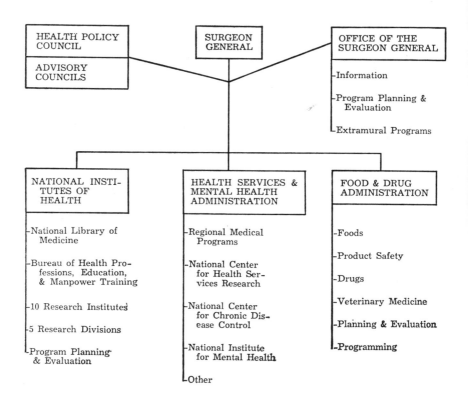

Figure 18. PHS offices of interest.

III. INVENTING

Inputs

Inventing activities of PHS (Figure 19) encompass applied research and development portions of R&D funding. This antecedent work to technology diffusion is performed partly in government laboratories of the national institutes and partly through contracts and grants to large semipublic and private hospitals or research institutes. Inventing programs reflect a changing mission, rapidly increasing support, changing clients with different needs from those of former years, and changing organization. The medicinal scientific and technical information base comes from the National Library of Medicine and separate agency files.

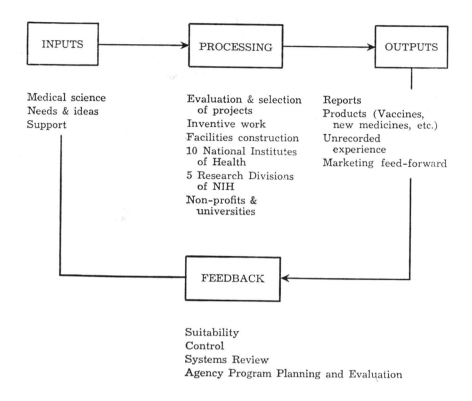

Figure 19. PHS inventing activities.

Needs and ideas. With the mission of creating technology for the express purpose of distributing it to the health and scientific community, both public and private, industrial and nonprofit, PHS must first define needs. This definition of need, however, has caused growing difficulty and partly explains reorganization Needs have shifted from traditional medicine for controlling communicable disease to newer areas of controlling injury, environmental death, and pollution. Needs and ideas are coming less frequently from professional medical groups and societies and increasingly from public administrators and aroused citizens.

Support. Cost of applied research and development in PHS has risen rapidly, from $638 million in 1966 to almost $900 million in 1971, over 6% of the Federal total. PHS represents about two-thirds of Federal expenditures on health R&D. Primary PHS institutions for applying new knowledge are the ten National Institutes of Health, researching cancer, heart disease, eyes, allergy and infectious diseases, arthritis and metabolic diseases, child health and human development, dental research, neurological disease, environmental health, and general medical science. About one-fourth of the work occurs inhouse in 33 Federal field laboratories and research centers, and three-fourths is done through grants for projects in medical non-profit organizations, hospitals, and universities.

Processing

Needs and ideas for PHS inventive work are evaluated, and applied research and development funds are targeted on specific problems by research institutes and research divisions. The 19,000 annual projects each contributes something to the total of technical and scientific information about specific problems.[3] The evaluation process in PHS results in projects going to institutions with established competence in the subject of the grant. A peer system of advisors to the National Institutes largely determines the grantees. Areas selected for medical grants and other inventive work are predominantly medical, psychological, and social science, but with small though increasing amounts in a broad spectrum of physical sciences, as indicated in Appendices B-5 and B-6. Grants are also awarded to special research laboratories for constructing or renovating very large and costly equipment for regional pools of scientists, clinical research centers, and animal study centers. PHS further provides "research support" grants to permit an institution more project flexibility than is possible through other grants.[4]

Outputs

Products of project grants are reports, new procedures and techniques, trained people in the subject of the grant, and considerable new vaccines, equipment, or medicines for performing actual medical functions. Numbers of products will be at least 19,000 per year, with numbers of trainees exceeding this figure by several times. Many outputs have considerable feedforward, or impetus, for their general use and adoption.

Examples

Development of antibiotics (Appendix F-4) was spectacular, but PHS contributed little to initial work. Serendipity, trained people, and an accepted need were instrumental in getting the earlier results. Unhindered scientific and technical information were also available. PHS has recently assumed more control of antibiotics.

Fluoridation to prevent tooth decay (Appendix F-5) represents a development in which community participation and consent were required. This program has been accepted by the majority of American people though rejected by a majority of communities. (Alternatives were developed for individuals to take part in other applications of fluoridation if the community did not.)

Rubella vaccine (Appendix F-6) is a success story in development of a public health measure, a step-by-step development in the best traditions of medical science. Serendipity played a part in several stages of work. Technical and scientific information were available without proprietary barriers to their use. The need for rubella vaccine was recognized and trained people were available, willing to work on the problem. Favorable publicity for the rubella project was a feed-forward supporting its successful adoption.

Trauma from automobile accidents (Appendix F-7) represents another public health problem where need has only recently been defined in a way that PHS staff people recognize as their responsibility. Inventions, new developments, and applications have not been made to cope with this total problem. PHS reduces death and suffering **after** the accident.

Feedback

Suitability. The project grant system has worked to produce considerable new technology, but it has also concentrated skills into places and areas where they already existed. In FY 1963 half of PHS R&D funds went into four states of Massachusetts, New York, Maryland, and California. In FY 1964, the same four states again received the same ratio, even though overall expenditures had increased by over 18%.[5]

The project grant system, with 19,000 separate outputs, is also difficult to coordinate. Large collaborative research projects are needed for newer (or more current) medical problems such as environmental control, fertility control, drug addiction, and organ transplants or re-placements.

The slow response of PHS to control of environmental degradation appears in its FY 1961, FY 1964, and FY 1968 expenditures of 10, 20, and 40 million dollars. The FY 1969 expenditures accounted for only 50 million out of $1038 million in health research.[6] The 1971 estimate for expenditures was $104 million for air pollution and $52 million for environmental control.[7]

Control. The Public Health Service, organized into several his-torical bureaus in the early fifties, made quiet, slow progress. When social and medical legislation flooded PHS with applied research and development funds, the agency could not continue with its previous procedures. The 1966 reorganization was overdue and only partially established control. The 1968 reorganization followed and brought the service more up-to-date. The National Institutes developed a Program Planning and Evaluation office for maintaining direction and comparing major tradeoffs. The normal administrative organization has controlled on-going projects.

Systems review. Program Planning and Evaluation Offices evaluate inventing activities and their relationship to agency missions and needs. These offices also receive inputs from Congress and professional groups. In fact, these external groups compare PHS inventing activities with national goals. The change of direction recently forced on PHS has resulted from these external inputs.

IV. INFORMING

Inputs

New medical information. PHS inputs identified in Figure 20 con-trast to those of the Bureau of Mines (Appendix C) which processed about 1,000 reports over the decade 1953-63. The 1971 **annual** input from its own grants was about 19,000 reports. In addition, the National Library of Medicine collects about 100,000 annual international entries. These make the informing program of PHS one of the most active in the Federal government. Clients, or users, of the information are health workers, including PHS employees and grantees, physicians in private practice, and the general public. In addition, medical li-braries of professional associations, non-profit organizations, and medical schools make extensive use of PHS library and information resources. The size of the potential user population is estimated to be 3,000,000.[8]

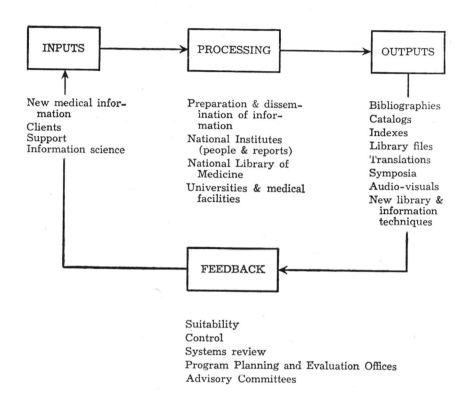

Figure 20. PHS informing activities.

Support. The institution handling this influx of materials and needs for library services is the 135-year-old National Library of Medicine. With 1,347,000 volumes, it was a principal information handling system in NIH and PHS. Formally established in PHS in 1956, it is the greatest collection of medical literature in existence; and it specializes in worldwide collection, dissemination, and exchange of information important to progress of medicine and health. Bibliographic access to current information in this collection is through an automated Medical Literature Analysis and Retrieval System (MEDLARS), a computerized information system, and catalogs, indices, and bibliographies. The MEDLARS computer file in 1971 contained 1.4 million bibliographic citations. Physical access is provided through interlibrary loans, photoduplication, and reference services. The Library is located at the National Institutes of Health at Bethesda, Md. —it became part of the Institutes in 1968. Support for the library rose from $6 million in FY 1966 to double that amount in FY 1967, then doubled again in FY 1968. Appendices D-4 and D-5 show that overall NIH expenditures run about $40 million to $50 million for scientific and technical information and that these concentrated in FY 1971 into bibliographic, R&D, publication, information center, translation, and symposia activities.

People trained in project grants represent mobile inputs which tend to stay in areas where they received training. PHS has charged NIH with teaching physicians and health professionals to put research results into practice. Annual PHS expenditures related to technical training have been as high as $1 billion.[9]

Information science. PHS disseminates new medical technology by placing it everywhere it can be used. Because of the relatively small PHS effort prior to 1960, present emphasis has made it necessary to develop wholly new dissemination capabilities. Few traditional equipments or procedures hamper PHS, and most new technologies are being used, as indicated in Appendices D-4 and D-5.

Processing

National Library of Medicine. Professional information scientists, indexers, cataloguers, and librarians complete NLM processing. Many have extensive medical training. The intent in processing is to provide timely information about medical advances. MEDLARS focuses on current journal literature and can make special searches and printouts. NLM also supports health science libraries and information science development and has led in trying new ways of processing. These include grants to improve facilities of medical libraries, to support biomedical publications, and to prepare and publish materials on new developments.

Other. The Institutes also publish results of their own projects, both for internal distribution and for public use. Other agencies of

PHS have their own informing systems which prepare items for public and professional medical use. People with medical know-how are catalogued to some degree in information processing; normally, their services are made available through symposia and information centers. Difficult or tedious procedures are prepared both in print and in audio and visual media.

Outputs

NLM in FY 1969 filled 200,000 circulation and 25,000 reference requests. Twenty-three recurring bibliographies, including **Index Medicus,** were distributed in FY 1971 to libraries and information centers. The main NLM publications are available through the U. S. Government Printing Office, and bibliographies are published through nonprofit medical organizations. Foreign medicine documents in 70 languages are made available including some translations. Consultation services and support for medical librarianship are also provided. PHS as a whole outputs all information forms, with heavier emphasis on bibliographic and reference services, information centers, and symposia. After the Department of Defense, PHS is most heavily involved in R&D in information science.

Examples

Full availability of evaluated information characterized rubella vaccine and antibiotics programs. Internal PHS resources, as well as medical professional journals, have been widely used for dissemination. Movement of trained investigators and relinquishment of property rights were key factors in each case. The rubella informing program had gained public acceptance by 1971.

Fluoridation, relationship of smoking to health, and effects of drug use are examples in which PHS competes with other information sources for audiences and credibility. Fluoridation illustrates how champions of private interests can subvert PHS efforts for their own goals. It illustrates as well as any example, how handling of information by a Federal agency can jeopardize an otherwise valuable program.

Feedback

PHS spearheads efforts to provide a national system for medical information, and it holds a good professional reputation for this work. It serves as a resource for medical education, research and service activities of Federal and private agencies, organizations, institutions, and individuals. Increasing support to the National Library of Medicine, the National Institutes, and PHS shows acceptance of this information program.

Cost of the system has not been excessive in terms of the total outlay of health funds. In general, outputs have been suitable and timely. NLM has particularly been cited as a leader in processing developments in information science.

No amount of document dissemination can offset the concentration of medical information in people and working procedures which has resulted from PHS support for applied research and development in the four states of Massachusetts, New York, Maryland, and California. The informing process as well as its antecedent R&D has been criticized for this concentration. Aid to medical libraries, medical librarians, and technical journals has reduced some of the criticism. The medical information dissemination system compares to Sayer's Model[10] even better than that of the Department of Agriculture. Acquisition is done centrally by the National Library and dissemination is through regional medical libraries.

Control and systems review. NLM offices along with NIH Offices of Program Planning and Evaluation exercise immediate control and systems review, but user demands for the information system have greatly influenced its development. Panels of physicians, editors, and librarians select the journals to be included in the **Index Medicus.** Advisory groups evaluate indexing, cataloguing, storing, retrieving, and disseminating.

The National Library of Medicine was well established before the influx of funds into PHS and has adjusted faster than the parent organization. Recognized by Congress and the professional public as the central source for the existing national biomedical system, the Library has tried since 1966 to develop a national biomedical communications network to provide biomedical information for national needs.

Congress performs part of an overall review in its Medical Library Assistance Act which added 11 regional medical libraries to the central source.

V. INNOVATING

Inputs

Mission and needs. Since 1944 PHS has gained control of grants for construction of hospitals and medical facilities, for state health services, for community health centers and facilities for the mentally retarded, for regional medical programs, and for comprehensive health planning by state and local agencies. These functions outlined in

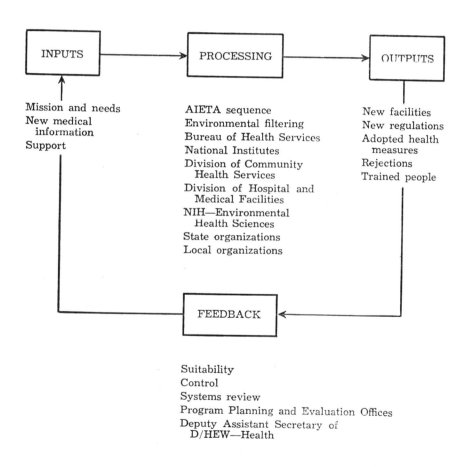

Figure 21. PHS innovating activities.

Figure 21 are PHS missions of aid to developing community health
services including hospitals, and for promoting application of new
knowledge towards disease prevention and control and towards a
healthy environment.[11] These missions and needs support innovation
at the operating level, which is fostered both internally in PHS facilities and externally through grants.

The newest agency, the **National Institute of Environmental Health
Sciences,** very directly applies the newest medical technology to
problems previously carried in other divisions such as the National
Centers for Air Pollution Control, Radiological Health, Urban and
Industrial Health; part of the National Center for Communicable
Disease Control; and the Food and Drug Administration.[12] This was
part of the continuing effort to refocus PHS toward current and
future health problems.

New medical information. Most information inputs into medical
innovating are techniques, procedures, and specialized equipment itself.
As these become available, practitioners learn to use them. Frequently
use of new equipment or techniques causes the hiring of knowledgeable people who thus become innovational inputs.

Support institutions. The Bureau of Health Services, National Institutes of Health, National Institute of Mental Health, and National
Institute of Environmental Health Sciences support PHS innovat-
ing.[13] Professional medical organizations help in some programs. The
PHS offices work directly with state organizations through the Divi-
sions of Community Health Services and Hospital and Medical Fa-
cilities. The National Institutes of Health incude the Division of
Biologics Standards, where vaccines are developed and tested, and the
Division of Regional Medical Programs. The National Institutes of
Mental Health include two psychiatric hospitals and St. Elizabeth's
Hospital, giving PHS practitioners opportunities to innovate in mental
health.

Resource support. PHS expenditures for innovating tie in with
those for integrating, or continued adoption. These innovating expenditures cannot be isolated from public health innovating expenditures
in other agencies. The July 1, 1968 reorganization was publicized as an
effort to unify $15.6 billion in Federal spending in public health
through 15 separate agencies.

Processing

Since the late 1950's, one major goal of PHS has been to use new medical knowledge as promptly and effectively as possible. This goal has stimulated information transfer between applied research and clinical practice. More recently, this relationship has been extended to environmental pollution and hazards. In terms of the innovation model, technical information goes directly from developer to user as well as through the informing program for PHS.

Evaluation of new medical technology is considerably influenced by the nature of adoption units and environmental filtering. State and community organizations, as well as doctors and patients, are adopters. PHS has had considerable success getting state and community public health installations to adopt. As noted in Chapter III, medical sociologists have concentrated on application and adoption of improved techniques by doctors. Katz, Coleman, and Menzel, reporting work for Columbia University Bureau of Applied Social Research, state that doctors go through an AIETA sequence, that they have fast and slow adopters, and that the more outwardly oriented adopted earlier than others. Greater professional association with other doctors increased the rate of innovating new antibiotics.[14] Private physicians have quickly adopted some new technologies, but not all. The American Medical Association has opposed several public health measures. It even has political action committees for influencing legislation and political appointments. Processing (environmental filtering) depends heavily on the adoption unit's cultural prejudices and concepts of advantage.

Technologies of the PHS are transferred horizontally into non-health activities primarily by investigators in identical or associated disciplines. Veterinary science extends human medicine to livestock and domestic animals. Space medical scientists adapt earth medicine to the space environment. Information scientists study operations of NLM and MEDLARS and apply the same procedures or better ones in their own agencies. The man with the need searches PHS literature or consults with PHS investigators, then adopts the technologies he finds useful.

Outputs

Outputs of public health innovating programs consist of adoption of new products such as vaccines, passage of regulations or laws which prevent environmental degradation and hazard creation, training of health people who can apply new techniques, and building of public health facilities. Other outputs are measures tried but rejected. Abortion procedures, perfected in Japan, have been only recently legally and socially acceptable in the U. S.

Examples

Adoption of antibiotics and vaccines by the public and medical profession has been phenomenal. Publicity, favorable tests, and reduced medical cost supported adoption. Fluoridation has not enjoyed complete success; and the reasons for its problems are considered to be overeager champions, opposition from private "health fad" interests, and the requirement for plebiscite adoption. The latter requirement is similar to adoption of milk tank trucks by dairying communities. When a large group has to agree to adopt simultaneously, innovation may be slower. The construction of new hospitals with modern facilities is wholesale innovation quite different from item by item adoption. PHS support for community hospital development has been successful. Reduction of trauma from automobile accidents has thus far been a relative failure in innovation. Many diverse groups and individuals must cooperate to innovate, and this is the most difficult way to adopt.

Feedback

Public reaction to new health technology is the most valuable feedback. Sales of antibiotics indicate adoption of that development. Sales of new medical equipment reflect its adoption. Hiring of newly trained specialists indicates use of their skills in new technology. Undesired side effects are also feedbacks. Overuse of certain antibiotics has reduced their effectiveness. Too rapid adoption of new drugs has caused disaster, the best known example being thalidomide. Eagerness of surgeons to transplant hearts has raised legal and moral questions. The PHS innovating program has done very well with chronic diseases or classical medicine but not with hazards and pollution. Its program, until recently, lacked an input to force an output evaluation in terms of reduced deaths from these two evils.

Control. PHS administrative offices evaluate immediate feedback and change inputs or processing. Because innovation is decentralized to the non-PHS unit, control may or may not be effective. The Program Planning and Evaluation Offices of NIH and PHS evaluate overall feedback, and they may refocus entire programs or projects to avoid failure or to reinforce success.

Systems review. Program planning offices do some overall review, but the Deputy Assistant Secretaries of D/HEW for Health Planning and for Program Systems also review. The Health Planning office was first formed in 1968 for more adequate system review. Less specific program offices in D/HEW had performed some review since 1967. Before then, a Special Assistant to the Secretary for Health and Medical Affairs advised on overall PHS programs. Systems review has changed almost annually as top administrators have tried to direct public health innovation. Congress and pressure groups of professional medical people each made inputs into systems review which have affected current organization, with its offices for program analysis and review at each echelon. PPBS also forced more correlation between national goals, agency goals, and program evaluation.

VI. INTEGRATING

Inputs

Needs. The D/HEW Secretary's report to the President on June 14, 1968 outlined the nature of health needs indicated in Figure 22 as follows:

> The health needs of this Nation are suggested by dreary statistics on mortality and morbidity rates resulting from disease and accidents, by an unnecessarily high infant mortality rate, by the incidence of ill health among the aged, the poor, and minority groups, and by the stunted lives of thousands of retarded individuals. The needs are also evident in the growing complexity and pervasiveness of environmental hazards. They are seen in millions of days of absenteeism and suffering due to disabling illness. They are reflected in the billions lost to the economy and to family income due to premature death, short term illness and chronic disabling disorders. Many of these conditions are preventable. Early care and rehabilitation could ameliorate the burden for many.[15]

Support and new technologies. The D/HEW Secretary also outlined the support and the nature of the health system of the nation:

> These health needs and the earnest desire of the American
> people to overcome them are attested to by rapidly growing
> expenditures for health and medical services. Private ex-
> penditures for health services are rising at an annual rate
> of more than 8 percent. In 1950, these expenditures amounted
> to $12.9 billion, or 4.5 percent of the Gross National Product, in
> 1966 they claimed approximately $45.5 billion, 6.1 percent of
> the Gross National Product.
>
> . . . .

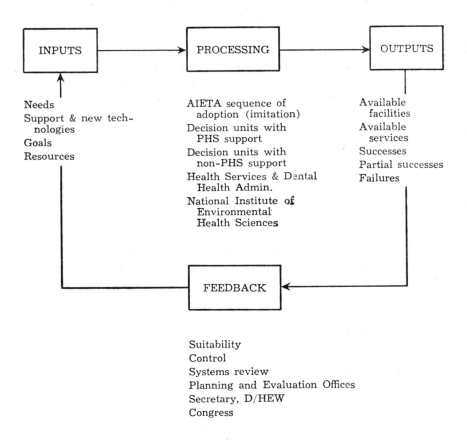

Figure 22. PHS integrating activities.

The American system of health care, research, education and disease prevention, is a mosaic of private and public efforts. Over the past twenty years it has grown and changed in response to an increasing variety of problems and an expanding body of knowledge of the causes and treatment of disease.

To serve more than 200 million Americans there are 300,000 physicians in a variety of different types of activity: research, education, individual or group practice; 700,000 nurses performing in a wide range of settings from school health services to intensive care units in general hospitals; a total of 3 million health workers providing hundreds of different kinds of services; 7,000 hospitals; 20,000 nursing homes or other long-term care facilities; 89 medical schools and hundreds of other professional and technical schools for the education and training of health workers; a multibillion dollar pharmaceutical industry; hundreds of voluntary health agencies; 55 State and Territorial health departments; a wide variety of commercial and non-profit organizations providing health insurance coverage for some of the cost of medical care for a substantial portion of the population; and a host of other agencies, institutions, and organizations.
. . . .

Federal health expenditures in the aggregate have increased almost fivefold since 1961. Yet, . . . the range of health services provided for all Americans has increased even more rapidly. Of all Federal expenditures for health in 1961, $2.4 billion, of a total of $3.5 billion, was expended for the provision of hospital and medical services for members of the military forces and their dependents, veterans and their survivors, and others: only $1.1 billion was expended for health services for all Americans. In 1969 the expenditure planned for health services to benefit the total population will exceed $11 billion, a tenfold increase.[16]

Goals. The D/HEW Secretary furthermore tried to clarify Federal goals in the total system as follows:

The part played by the Federal government in this system is that of identifying and then narrowing and closing the gap between the health protection and health services this system provides and those the American people need. It supports the various State and local governments in their efforts to prevent the spread of disease, and to develop many of the facilities required for good medical care. . . . It enforces requirements designed to improve the environment. . . . It has been increasingly responsible for protecting the interest of the consumer. Through Medicare and Medicaid it aids many Americans to meet the costs of needed medical care. . . .[17]

Resources. Expenditures have increased for developing health resources, that is, diffusing through hospitals, nursing homes, clinics and laboratories, and skilled manpower the new techniques and products from medical research. More has been spent for detection and elimination of health hazards in the environment. Medicare, in the Social Security Administration, D/HEW, consumes about $8 billion yearly for those over 65, and Medicaid, in the Welfare Administration, D/HEW, requires nearly $3 billion yearly for the needy and indigent. Military members, veterans, and other Federal beneficiaries consume over $3 billion yearly.[18] The big expenditures are thus for the aged, for the indigent, and for those entitled to care in Federal installations.

Offices of PHS most involved in integration of new technology have been discussed, except for the Food and Drug Administration. This office must maintain wholesomeness of food products and purity of drugs offered for sale by and to the public. A regulatory agency, it enforces standards for new technology and prevents new technology from introducing contaminants. The Food, Drug, and Cosmetics Act in 1962 dramatically increased this agency's responsibility to assure the public of drug effectiveness and safety. In 1971 integrating inputs included $1 billion for developing health manpower and facilities (other than research), $3 billion for medical services other than Medicare and Medicaid, $600 million for control of health problems.[19] Other inputs to integration of new public health technology were support and non-support from advocates such as the American Medical Association and other health organizations.

Processing.

Individuals, doctors, hospitals, and health services, both public and private integrate new medical technology. Citizens, as patients or users, adopt or adjust to new technologies. Some professional organizations have aroused citizens to stop or postpone health measures. Religious organizations influence integration of family planning and other hygienic measures. Other groups have opposed specific public health activities such as water fluoridation and publication of cigarette testing results. Processing is influenced by particular technology as well as its presentation. PHS administrators influence processing by their handling of technical information, funding support, and public relations. A favorable PHS image supports integration, whereas unfavorable publicity causes long-lasting skepticism. Adoption units can be divided into those with PHS support and those operating privately. Federal support has generally been cheaper for the adopter when he can obtain it. Federal support tends to speed adoption of whole groups of new medical techniques and facilities. The AIETA sequence is thus influenced by funds.

Training medical manpower through PHS programs of almost 535 million dollars annually (FY 1971 rate) also speeds integration. People are trained in the new technologies in medical schools and medical support facilities. When an individual takes a training course, he in effect adopts its technologies.

Outputs

Outputs in supporting integration of new medical technology by the public health sector are new facilities or services, new medicines and techniques in common use, trained medical people, improved public health, new protective regulations, and perhaps the countergain desire of individuals for personal, rather than Federal, medical aid. The latter could prevent private doctors from losing out to government. Increased outputs in the public health sector have created more jobs than they eliminated. Improved health correlated with decreasing death rates until about 1954. Then the trend leveled out, and rates have actually been higher since. In 1963 the rate per 100,000 for deaths from all causes was 962 versus 919 in 1954. Most disease rates continued to decrease; but the rather sharp rises in accidents, neoplasm of the respiratory system (cancer of the lung being most common), ulcer, cirrhosis of the liver, suicide, heart disease, pneumonia, and diabetes raised overall rates.[20] Relationships of several of these to modern technological conditions are well known.

Examples

Successes. PHS has succeeded significantly in pure medical development. Historical increases in longevity and relative decreases in infant mortality attest to successes sponsored in part by PHS development, and the improvements illustrate the cooperation between

PHS and private foundations working to counter specific diseases. Polio vaccines, with Salk and Sabin as the best known investigators, have been well publicized. Rubella is an example of extending to still another disease these techniques for developing vaccines. Rubella vaccine gained acceptance in health practice in 1969-70 just as its predecessor vaccines have. By Oct. 31, 1971, 30 million doses of rubella vaccine had been administered.[21]

Partial successes. Only one-third of U. S. residents now consume fluoridated water. PHS, from the record, seemed to succumb to pressures from vocal individuals favoring fluoridation. This in turn aroused violent resentment among groups opposed to fluoridation. At the height of the controversy (1952-1955), fluoridation would probably have been unacceptable in a national plebiscite. PHS has been somewhat cautious since that time; and its initial announcements on the relationship of cancer to cigarette smoking did not improve its image.

Failures. Accidents are the leading cause of death among persons aged 1 to 37; and about half of these are automobile accidents. The PHS has not assumed leadership in reducing this cause of death; and until its 1968 reorganization, its major organizational structure did not suggest it intended to do so. In fact, when the 1966 reorganizational plans hearings were held by the Senate, the name of the proposed Bureau of Disease and Injury and Control was criticized and later changed to Bureau of Disease Prevention and Environmental Control.[22] The 1968 reorganization focused on the Consumer Protection and Environmental Health Services, still not directly indicative of injuries and deaths from instruments of technology.

Feedback

Suitability. The D/HEW Secretary's report evaluated the 1968 public health system output as follows:

> This "system," relatively independent and interrelated only by a common concern with human health, possesses proven strengths. It provides great diversity, opportunities for innovation, and intense motivation rooted in the desire for professional accomplishment as much as personal gain. It has contributed persistent quality improvement and demonstrated a capacity for organizational change.
>
> But this system simultaneously has its limitations. It is weakened by a chronic shortage of trained physicians and

allied health workers. It has been characterized by persistent and substantial rises in costs and wide variations in the quality of care provided. It has failed to recognize and respond fully to the growing hazards to health in our environment. The organization for the delivery of health services to individuals is marked by serious maldistribution of physicians and facilities geographically and in relation to the poor, particularly the non-white poor. . . .

. . . .

Several conclusions emerge from a review of the scope of Federal health programs and of their changing character and size. First, the total Federal health effort includes major programs by many Departments and agencies, most of which are involved in mission-oriented activities (providing health care, for example) that represent a substantial deployment of health manpower, facilities, and other resources of the Nation. Although the Department of Health, Education, and Welfare administers some 70 percent of all Federal expenditures for health and is the sole Federal agency whose mission includes protection and promotion of the health of the American people, the Department does not exercise policy guidance over the broad Federal health effort. . . .

Second, deficiencies in coodination of the Federal health effort are apparent, deficiencies relating to the use of Federal resources to meet the health needs of the American people. . . .

Third, there does not now exist an adequate mechanism for comprehensive assessment of national health problems and needs and of the most efficient and economical approaches toward dealing with them.[23]

Problems mentioned by the Secretary for coordination were (1) DOD drafting of doctors; (2) DOD research on public health problems; (3) DOD support of retirees, veterans, and their survivors; (4) Veterans Administration support to veterans for treatments not available to the general public; (5) protecting consumers from contamination of food, water, and air; (6) proper and safe disposal of solid wastes; and (7) development of adequate urban environments. The lack of coordination was consuming scarce facilities and trained people and reducing effectiveness of the national health program.[24] Most significant changes since 1968 have been increases in Medicare and Medicaid.

The flurry of activity to focus and vitalize PHS during the Johnson Administration had great potential, but it caused a national shortage of doctors and skyrocketing medical costs for those citizens not in special groups receiving Federally supported care. Organ transplanting is currently being widely innovated. Many vital organs used for transplants come from young people killed in automobile accidents. U. S. citizens (and PHS) can choose either to save lives of young people through reducing trauma or to use their organs in transplants. Reduction of trauma is a grouping of routine, prosaic, everyday procedures and regulations which diffuse poorly to the public and which appeal little to the medical profession.

Control and systems review. PHS reorganizations and the expressed concern by the Secretary of the Department of Health, Education and Welfare show that PHS lacks adequate control and that diffusion of public health technologies has created continuing problems. Program evaluation and systems review offices of D/HEW and PHS serve some functions but not all. Moving the Food and Drug Administration under PHS was a recognition of interrelationships among public health functions from the systems point of view. Preferential treatment of population groups remains in public health activities, as well as conflicts of interest between PHS and other Federal agencies.

VII. PHS IN THE TOTAL PROCESS

Since 1950, PHS has developed within a single semi-independent agency, mission-oriented activities for generating new medical technologies, for disseminating information about them, and for supporting and subsidizing these technologies throughout the public health sector. These activities are separately identifiable in the organization and ongoing work at PHS, and they are being tightened through better feedback and evaluation within each activity grouping.

Inventing. The applied research and development effort of $750 million yearly precedes technology diffusion. PHS speeds new medical technology to the medical profession and general public as it can be made available and checked. With 19,000 separate projects, mostly requiring only one or a few investigators, PHS tends to duplicating, overlapping and piecemeal approaches to public health problems. Individual projects tend to interest medical professionals rather than public health problems. Peer group contract award procedures support this tendency. The more than tenfold increase in expenditures in the past fifteen years has not increased results more than ten times. In the short run, medical applied research and development has tied up the very people who could apply the results, making it harder to get integration.

Informing. With about $535 million in training and about $45 million in scientific and technical information, the PHS informing effort is one of the most modern and substantial in U. S. government. The information is slanted to fairly literate groups of some three million health professionals, but some publications are for families and individual citizens. The informing activities work closely with medical schools and professional medical groups, making it feasible to feed forward the results of medical applied research and development. Advisory groups help evaluate feedback so that programs and processing can be adjusted toward PHS goals. Programs are characterized by modern, computerized information dissemination, multiple services, audio and visual as well as document forms and channels, and feedback comes from professional medical as well as college and PHS channels. PHS couples medical technology directly to users, and its programs are evaluated both as information systems and as part of overall PHS goals and needs.

Innovating. With well-defined public health professional customers and strong support from these customers, PHS effectively advocates adoption of new public health advances in technology. To the doctor, the patient, and the hospital, the information input from PHS identifies uses which aid in the AIETA sequence. For aiding backward communities or to establish regional facilities, public health innovation through loans and grants is supported. Successful outputs are improved facilities, new public health regulations, and better medical technology. Failures and no-takers also occur as with the reduction of automobile accident trauma. PHS has been more successful in supporting organized and influential state and local groups than in getting mass adoption of its new technology.

Integrating. Integrating inputs from PHS into the general economy are represented in the annual funding for its operations of over $3 billion in the total annual national health care expenditures of $50 to $60 billion. The PHS share covers generation of the new medical technologies as well as diffusing them, but the big expenditures are Social Security and Welfare Administration's Medicare, Medicaid, and caring for other special groups, largely using or integrating the new technologies which have become available. Most doctors and hospitals have been affected by PHS procedures, loans, and support. Medical entrepreneurs evaluate each public health technology in terms of Federal support as well as advantages to the clients. PHS effects have been labor and resource using, with considerable suboptimizing for the public health professional. The integrating effort has been reviewed favorably by Congress and citizen groups, but rising costs caused unfavorable publicity during the late 1960's.

De Facto Procedures

The tenfold expansion of PHS since 1950 has caused it to adjust procedures to rapid changes. The National Institutes, internally and through their grant and contract systems, have greatly increased the nation's ability to find new medical technology and train people in its use, but neither the contracts and grants nor the peer group system of selecting those to receive them is in the tradition of competitive private enterprise. Nor do they follow the historic procedures of most agencies which have generated new technology. PHS has bypassed the patent system and has reduced opportunity for the medical inventor. PHS does a small amount of patenting, but it is more likely to publish in the scientific tradition. The National Library of Medicine is a strong defender of publishing as a way to gain recognition, rather than seeking remuneration through owning patents. PHS has largely captured the public health professional audience through its informing programs; hence, it is not required to participate in the Department of Commerce National Technical Information Service (NTIS) for dissemination of Federal R&D results.

Recent PHS emphasis on supporting construction and modern equipment for state and local public health activities has upgraded availability and quality of health care, but the state and local activities have come to depend on Federal funds for innovation rather than local sources. The most drastic extension of new procedures has come from Medicare and Medicaid legislation, which supports the integration of modern techniques into practice for special groups. This has to some degree reduced the opportunity for voluntary health associations to organize private enterprise health services. PHS regulation, not only from the Federal Drug Administration, but also through the PHS reporting system, pervades the public health, medical, and medically related sectors.

Federal agencies other than PHS and D/HEW have developed health care procedures which vary greatly from private enterprise, particularly in the Veterans Administation and DOD. These agencies established their programs before PHS became powerful enough to stop them; but PHS is now moving to capture the control of public health from these agencies. Medical and public health activities have socialized since 1950, changing procedures, preferences, and viewpoints. PHS has edged into new procedures through public pressures exerted through legislation and administration. Private enterprise diffusion of medical technology continues, but its importance decreases as Federal influence grows.

National Goals

PHS has promoted the progress of science and the useful arts, provided technical information to potential users, and supported maximum employment. Very recently, it has begun work to improve the physical environment, reduce pollution, and focus on national public health rather than medical profession goals. This has been less successful than for other national goals. Within the U. S., diffusion of new medical applications is probably more uniform than most other new technologies, but there is still some lack of access or availability. PHS, supporting medical buildings and services, tends to establish some uniformity for basic applications, but more advanced applications concentrate in larger medical centers. Some new medical techniques or applications have not diffused uniformly. Fluoridation, as an example, has been rejected in the technically advanced communities, for example, Orange County, California. Mass vaccination for polio moderately succeeded after much publicity. Doctors have been generally eager to apply new medicines and drugs in private practice, even over-using them, but less eager to support public health measures.

Free enterprise. The impact of Federal procedures on national health care is implied in the changes from FY 1965 to FY 1969, when expenditures from public sources increased from $5.2 billion (13 percent of the total) to $16.6 billion (28 percent of the total).[25] The big increases came from Medicare and Medicaid, new D/HEW procedures which diverge from historic private enterprise. Although PHS did not handle the major increases in funds, it did determine the lead policies. President Johnson's National Advisory Commission on Health

Facilities in 1968 stated unequivocally: "The ultimate responsibility of assuring that the total population receives health services must be borne by the public, since such care is a right."[26] With such advice to the President, private enterprise in medicine may merge with public enterprise.

National health. Is PHS gaining or losing in the battle to improve health? In 1900-1902 the life expectancy was forty-nine years. By 1959-1961 it had gained to 69.9 years. In the five years to 1965 it gained only three-tenths to 70.2 years.[27] A plateau has been reached and a downturn was recognized by 1972. The death rate per 100,000 population has reached a minimum and turned upward under the influence of technology-related deaths. This would be expected if the population averaged older. Adjusting to age shows that the minimum death rate thus far was reached in 1961, 1964, and 1965. For the white male the minimum rate was reached in 1959 and for the nonwhite male in 1961.[28] These statistics indicate that the historic public health approaches have balanced U. S. life with U. S. environment. Most U. S. adults can expect to live longer and more healthily than their parents; but their children and grandchildren may not have such expectations. Current adult health is a result of better health practices, to which PHS contributes. Most U. S. residents who become ill can find adequate medical services, and PHS contributes to this. Yet most U. S. residents live in environments increasingly degraded by pollution, noise, and lack of privacy. If degradation continues, both health (quality of life) and longevity curves will become less favorable. More U. S. residents are likely to suffer from trauma (accidents using instruments or results of technology) than ever before.

PHS expansion has come at a time when longevity, death rates, and quality of life have leveled out. Life has been balanced with environment. Deaths related to modern life and technology are rising as fast or faster than deaths are decreasing from historic killers. PHS and other public health activities have been refocused on the new problems, and they are slowly adjusting. In terms of the total process model, our culture and society are making demands for another finite step in the diffusion process. It appears that improvements in the environment are wanted and will be sought to prevent further downturn in favorable health statistics.

FOOTNOTES

[1] Wilbur J. Cohen, "Health in America—The Role of the Federal Government in Bringing High Quality Health Care to All the American People," Report to the President by Secretary, D/HEW, June 14, 1968. Mimeograph. Office of the Secretary, D/HEW, Washington, D.C., p. 2 of the forwarding letter for the report.

[2] Bureau of the Budget, *Special Analyses, Budget of the U.S., 1971, op. cit.,* p. 147.

[3] U.S.D./HEW, PHS, *National Institutes of Health 1971 Annual Report* (Washington, D.C.: U.S. Government Printing Office, 1972), p. 60.

[4] U.S. Department of Health, Education, and Welfare, Public Health Service, "The National Institutes of Health," Public Health Service Publication No. 81 (1968 Supplement) (Washington, D.C.: U.S. Government Printing Office, 1968), p. 5.

[5] U.S. Congress, House, *Obligations for Research and Development and R&D Plant, by Geographic Division and States, by Selected Federal Agencies, Fiscal Years 1961-64.* Report to the Subcommittee on Science by NSF. 88th Cong. 2d Sess. (Washington, D.C.: U.S. Government Printing Office, 1964), pp. 447-450.

[6] Wilbur J. Cohen, *op. cit.,* pp. 11 and 14.

[7] *The Budget . . . , Fiscal Year 1971, op. cit.,* pp. 309-310.

[8] Federal Council for Science and Technology, Committee on Scientific and Technical Information, (COSATI). *Selected Mechanized Scientific and Technical Information Systems,* (Washington, D.C.: U.S. Government Printing Office, 1968), p. 40.

[9] *Special Analyses, . . .* 1971, *op. cit.,* p. 109.

[10] See the previous Chapter discussion on Sayer's Model.

[11] *U.S. Government Organization Manual,* 1968-69, *op. cit.,* p. 361.

[12] See "Johnson Approves Broad Health Plan," *The Washington Post,* June 16, 1968, p. A-1; and U.S. Senate, Committee on Government Operations, *Reorganization Plan No. 3 of 1966* (Health Functions—Department of Health, Education, and Welfare). Hearing before the Subcommittee on Executive Reorganization, June 17, 1966 (Washington, D.C.: U.S. Government Printing Office, 1966), pp. 20-32.

[13] *U.S. Government Organization Manual, 1971/72 . . . op. cit.,* p. 337.

[14] James S. Coleman, Elihu Katz, and Herbert Menzel, *Medical Innovation, A Diffusion Study* (Indianapolis, Ind.: Bobbs-Merrill Co., Inc., 1966), pp. 133-138.

[15] Wilbur J. Cohen, *op. cit.,* pp. 4-5.

[16] *Ibid.,* pp. 3-11.

[17] *Ibid.,* pp. 8-9.

[18] *The Budget of the United States Government, Fiscal Year 1971, op. cit.,* pp. 155, 156, 171.

[19] Bureau of the Budget, *Budget of the United States, Fiscal Year 1971, op. cit.,* pp. 150-161.

[20] U.S. Department of Health, Education, and Welfare. National Center for Health Statistics, Public Health Service. *Mortality Trends in the United States, 1954-1962.* (Washington, D.C.: U.S. Government Printing Office, 1966), pp. 2-3 and 55-56.

[21] U.S., D/HEW, *A Common Thread to Service—An Historical Guide to HEW* (Washington, D.C.: U.S. Government Printing Office, 1972), p. 28.

[22] U.S. Congress, Senate, *Reorganizational Plan No. 3 of 1966, op. cit.* pp. 48-54.

[23] Wilbur J. Cohen, *op. cit.,* pp. 7-13.

[24] *Ibid.,* pp. 13-18.

[25] *Special Analyses, . . . FY 1971, op. cit.,* p. 147.

[26] Boisfeuillet Jones (Chairman), *National Advisory Commission on Health Facilities, A Report to the President, December, 1968* (Washington, D.C.: U.S. Government Printing Office, 1968), p. 46.

[27] U.S. Department of Health, Education, and Welfare, Public Health Service, National Center for Health Statistics, *Facts of Life and Death* (Washington, D.C.: U.S. Government Printing Office, 1967), p. 23.

[28] *Ibid.,* p. 11.

CHAPTER VI

DEPARTMENT OF DEFENSE
TECHNOLOGY DIFFUSION ACTIVITIES

I. INTRODUCTION

This chapter shows in systems or predictive model terms how the Department of Defense diffuses technology into the defense sector and indirectly into the general economy. DOD (Army, Navy, Air Force, and Marine Corps) generates new technology internally in its laboratories and supports its generation by industrial contractors; it disseminates information to each of its departments and to supporting industry; it requires that new technology be used within DOD; and it adjusts its logistics systems to integrate new technologies into common DOD use. Thus internally the Department has all subprocesses of technology diffusion. DOD merits study because its size and its consumption of national resources have greatly influenced technology diffusion both directly and indirectly.

II. ORGANIZATION

DOD organization is rather complex but the portions which contribute most to technology diffusion appear in Figure 23. The Joint Chiefs are most concerned with missions and operating needs. The Office of the Secretary is concerned with matching resources to needs, and the departments do the detailed contracting, supervision, and laboratory work.

III. INVENTING

Inputs

Mission. Clarification of the mission and development of specific military requirements or needs have become noteworthy features of DOD applied research and development. Its inventing activities are depicted in Figure 24.

The staff of the Joint Chiefs of Staff makes long, mid, and short range studies of missions and military requirements. These are con-

verted by the departments into needs of hardware, troops, and other
resources. For hardware the total system life has four phases: con-

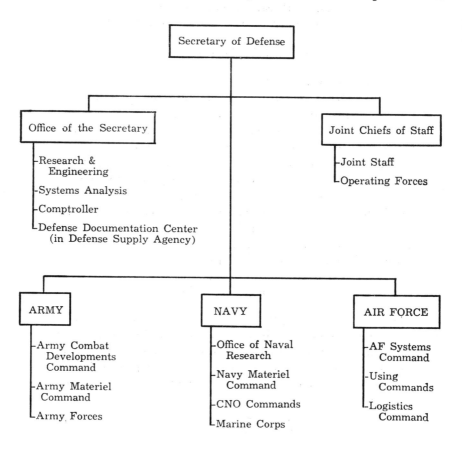

Figure 23. DOD offices of interest.

ception (determining requirements for new weapons and then by
applied research finding ways to bring them into being); definition
(working out on paper all aspects of the systems and proposing a contract for producing them); acquisition (detailed development and
design, prototype construction and testing and producing weapons);
and operation (use and maintenance of weapons by using commands).

These procedures were fairly successful, but produced vast amounts of competing paper work.

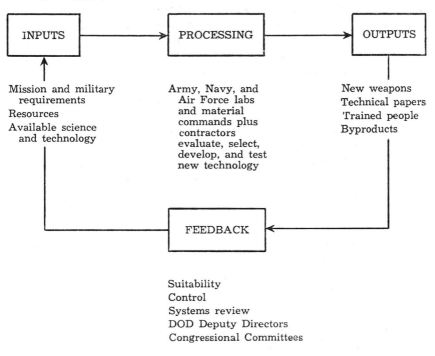

Figure 24. DOD inventing activities.

Under the impact of economic problems such as those from Lockheed's C5A, DOD began to modify some of its 1960 decade emphasis on predevelopment technical definition. More emphasis has now been given to prototype test and evaluation competition. The program manager structure has been strengthened to give better visibility on system progress. A Deputy Director of Defense Research and Engineering for Test and Evaluation was established in FY 1972 to provide policy. At the same time the Weapons System Evaluation Group was given an expanded role in operational test and evaluation.[1] DOD has tried, through the greater emphasis on hardware, to reduce difficulties in its approach to generating new technology. Broader missions of DOD have been clarified to the satisfaction of other agencies. In 1968,

DOD did 40 percent as much space work as NASA, 25 percent as much nuclear weapons work as AEC, an appreciable percentage as much work in controlling aircraft as FAA, and 1200 percent as much work as the Bureau of Mines in metallurgy and materials.[2] Applied research and development are focused on military requirements, and developments are rarely considered at the outset as potential commercial products. Contractors or Congress may consider such indirect effects.

Resources. With almost as many technology generating activities as the remainder of Federal government, DOD programs affect much of life. With funding inputs into applied research of over forty percent of Federal applied research, and development inputs of over fifty percent of Federal development, most technologies are involved. Considering only development, test and evaluation, and management (excluding all research), DOD spent about $5 billion annually for fiscal years 1961 through 1971 as shown in Appendix B-3. Institutions supporting the work are categorized in Chapter III. The caliber of technical personnel input rose rapidly while DOD was becoming the biggest spender in government. After 1960 NASA became the agency with most obtainable contracts, and now other agencies are displacing NASA. Nevertheless, DOD has through contracts employed many technicians and engineers for most of their working lives.

Available science and technology. DOD contractors, through the classified files of departments and the Defense Document Center, have access to U. S. and foreign technologies not released to industry at large. These classified items offer advantages in a few areas such as nuclear weapons, chemical and biological sprays, some forms of metallurgy, and types of precision equipment. Though there is some delay between development and publication, DOD technologists usually have up-to-date information. Exceptions are planning information (technological forecasting), and data on rapidly developing areas such as integrated circuits.

Processing

Carry-through from applied research to exploratory development to prototype testing to production models to production model acceptance is highly formalized in DOD. Procedures are incorporated in manuals and in training of service people and contractors. The Air Force through its Systems Command weapons systems development manuals, has set pace and tone. These manuals describe how to develop large, complex, technical programs (weapons systems) in a step by step, logical sequence. USAF, working with present and anticipated needs from the JCS, develops a requirement for a system and the kinds of technology which would satisfy the requirement. The Office of the Secretary of Defense, through systems analysis and engineering studies, approves or disapproves the requirement and the technical approaches. If the requirement is approved and resources appear, the department defines the system in a **Program Requirements Baseline**; then the defense industry is invited to work out concepts and overall design, using technical approaches which have been found feasible in exploratory work. The result of this phase is a **Design Requirements Baseline**, which is the guide for engineering designers. Original, adaptive, derivative, and secondary inventing enter into engineering design, which starts with a word description and ends with a prototype for testing. When a new system is put together, tested, and accepted, the **Product Baseline** is established.

In selecting contractors, there is minimal effort to maintain groups of skilled persons together. Laws on competitive bidding oppose such groups except when they are so productive that they bid lowest and make the best case. Skilled persons move from firm to firm, however, as new contracts are let.

DOD spends more money to generate new technology than any other government agency. Management and support funds exceed $1 billion each year, including operation of the Atlantic and Pacific Test Ranges. The applied research of $1.0 to $1.5 billion annually dwarfs all other agencies.

Outputs

DOD applied research and development produce weapons systems, support for weapons systems, new technologies for processing technical reports of all kinds, and byproducts of marginal use to DOD but possibly useful elsewhere. Trained people in new skills and technologies develop among contractors, but these receive no special attention. Patents are products and byproducts which usually go to the developer. Some 1968 products possibly applicable to the general economy, mentioned by Secretary McNamara in discussing the 1968 budget, were the large aperture seismic array (possible commercial use in earthquake identity and prediction); communication satellites;

navigation satellites; communications equipment; helicopters, V/STOL aircraft, and light transports; anti-malarial drugs and vaccines; insect control; deep ocean technology; reactor propulsion plants; advanced surface craft; aircraft engines; and range control technologies.[3] Secretary Laird, more concerned with DOD relationships to general welfare, established a Domestic Action Council to secure benefits to the economy of DOD use of public funds. Dr. Donald M. MacArthur suggested in August 1970, that DOD had contributed improved methods of housing construction; new and more economical hospitals; complete aircraft, radar, and communications systems; components such as integrated circuits; and improved techniques and processes like welding, plasma plating, and management systems. Dr. MacArthur believed that DOD could generate and innovate because it had a sense of need and urgency, a large scale of operations, and a built-in market.[4]

Examples

DOD activities in generation of new technologies in either primary or derivative inventing are found in integrated circuits (Appendix F-17), numerical control (Appendix F-13), titanium metal (Appendix F-12), food freeze-drying (Appendix F-14), food irradiation (Appendix F-15), and nuclear powered ships (Appendix F-22). These examples show the usefulness of stating needs specifically, making information readily available, and supporting projects adequately. Integrated circuits, numerical control, and titanium metal show that DOD's selecting and standardizing of new technology forces its adoption by defense contractors and influences the competitive structures of related industries. Nuclear powered ships, food freeze-drying, and food irradiation do not compete with current commercial alternatives.

Feedback

As noted in Chapter III, DOD has learned that a clear statement of the problem is prerequisite to planned invention. Numerical control, titanium metal and food freeze-drying examples verify this. DOD Project Hindsight showed that engineers developing weapons systems used information at hand to resolve specific problems, and that undirected research contributed little to post World War II developments. Investment in science and technology toward stated needs paid off, though frequently not for five to ten years.[5] This delay probably equated to the study and adaptation period for the new technology.

During Secretary McNamara's regime, DOD procedures for generating new technology were made considerably more specific. There was less and less concurrent development for all critical parts, and fewer parallel, alternative developments were approved. The tendency after 1960 was toward standardizing and satisfying rather than maximizing performance. Secretary McNamara repeatedly stated his determination to cull out what he termed to be marginal projects and to defer all projects for which he judged postponement would not adversely affect future capabilities.[6]

In 1968 DOD was criticized for not making technological planning information available to contractors working on advanced weapons systems.[7] This failure has been viewed as poor security procedures rather than intent not to inform industry. The most real and cogent criticisms of DOD technology generation are that it distorts national effort by area and discipline. In 1963, when DOD had 59.3 percent of all Federal R&D, its top five recipients were California (36.3%), New York (9%), Maryland (6.1%), Massachusetts (5.3%), and New Jersey (4.5%). In 1964, with 52.4% of Federal funds, the top four remained in place, but Texas had taken fifth place from New Jersey.[8] In FY 1967, the seven top firms with contracts for DOD were Lockheed Aircraft Company ($709 million), General Dynamics Corporation ($461 million), General Electric Company ($439 million), Western Electric Company ($414 million), McDonnell-Douglas Corporation ($237 million), North American-Rockwell ($236 million), and Boeing Company ($220 million).[9] These vast contracts, which concentrated economic power to firms and areas, exceeded the total budgets of many Federal agencies. By discipline, DOD effort focused heavily on engineering and the physical sciences of astronomy, chemistry, physics, and oceanography, as shown in Appendices B-5 and B-6. In disciplines such as engineering, oceanography, astronomy, solid state physics, and mathematics, DOD had the preponderant national effort.

Applied research and development programs of DOD do not focus on the general economy and have no specific input to commercial needs, but this does not mean they are without impact. Contractors, through movements of trained people, application of technology and patents, and development of company files, successfully use products of DOD applied research and development for other applications.

Control. Deputy Directors for Research and Engineering and

Systems Analysis control generation of new technology. Yet, only the most significant screening and selecting can be done at this level. More direct control is effected by the laboratories, Army Combat Developments Command, Office of Naval Research, and Air Force Systems Command. The Materiel Commands of the Army and Navy control ongoing development and procurement. Some managerial control develops in the R&D and force development staff units of Army, Navy and Air Force. The control system selects those alternatives which most promise to solve stated military needs.

Among Federal agencies, DOD has the most costly testing facilities for evaluating new technology. Annual costs for the ranges and test facilities are one and one-half billion dollars.[10] By measuring performances under a controlled environment, DOD determines whether or not the new technologies have indeed met military needs.

System review. Both internal and external groups evaluate how well DOD applied research and development has satisfied its technical needs. Internally, each higher staff group performs review of lower echelons. Deputy Directors review the complete DOD program. The Bureau of the Budget theoretically compares DOD projects with those of other agencies. Congressional committees consider economic and social implications of DOD alternatives. Interested groups such as the Committee of the Defense and Space Industries Association (CODSIA) evaluate effects on industry of DOD applied research and development procedures and policies. That no review group considers all facets of DOD activities has recently become evident as economic concentration, poor technical choices, and military surprises emerged. One redirection was accomplished in 1970 when President Nixon stopped all R&D on chemical and biological offensive weapons.[11]

IV. INFORMING

Inputs

The Defense Documentation Center operates similarly to other large government agency document distribution centers. The Center performs only a small part of the DOD informing program outlined in Figure 25 for DOD departments. Applied research and development produces inputs which feed through command headquarters to DOD. Contractors doing the work also prepare the first reports which, on approval, are distributed throughout the service and to DDC. Reports may carry either company or service designations. DDC is thus nor-

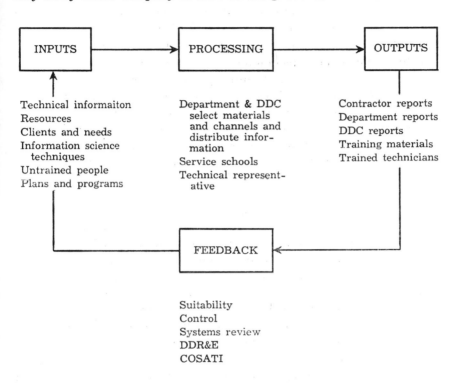

Figure 25. DOD informing activities.

mally a secondary distributor, of most use to contractors and other departments. If the applied research and development output is unclassified, it may be forwarded to NTIS for the general public.

Clients and needs. Potential clients for DOD informing programs are inservice trainees and operators as well as contractor personnel and the general public. Internal client information needs are known to a greater extent than for most government agency programs. In particular, DOD needs for technical and professional training can be predicted. In 1967, DOD needed 17,000 persons educated beyond the baccalaureate level, 13,500 replacement pilots, and replacements for 1500 separate technical specialties.   One and one half billion dollars were spent in 1967 to train people in these technologies.   For transferring information to these individuals, DOD has established training facilities shown as resource inputs in Figure 25.   The most expensive inputs are those for flight training, where many costly simulators are used.

Information science techniques mix the traditional with the very new.   More work occurs intramurally than extramurally.   DOD has used 35 to 45 percent of all Federal funds for scientific and technical information.   In 1971 it used the funds for documentation, reference, and information services ($66 million), publication and distribution ($21 million), R&D in information science ($34 million), and symposia and visual media ($18 million) as shown in Appendices D-2 through D-5.

Processing

Applied research and development results are reviewed and decisions are made on how they will be distributed and classified.   Options are: (1) to file the report without distribution; (2) to allow the contractor or laboratory to make a limited distribution without the report showing departmental approval; (3) to allow departmental distribution only; (4) to fully approve the report for interservice distribution with release to DDC; (5) to develop the report in several ways for different types of in-service clients; and (6) to release the report for distribution to the general public through NTIS.

Professional editors handle reports for general distribution without unusual procedures.   Preparation of materials for specific information transfer in training requires a network of schools and trained instructors.   Both oral and written media are used, but oral and visual media forms are emphasized.   In complex weapons systems, DOD relies on manufacturers' representatives who couple developer to user better than literature or training programs.   These representatives transfer information via people.

Outputs

DOD informing programs focus on servicemen needing specific information and on the contractor engaged in further development. Trainees get priority output.   DOD programs differ from other Federal agency programs in this emphasis.   Conferences and demonstrations are used in instruction as well as with contractors to give quick understanding and information transfer on items of vital importance. Some twenty technical information centers are outputs which are available only to DOD users. They help future Armed Forces members more than present ones. Technical reports which get to NTIS from DDC tend to contain less critical technical information. Reports describing specific technology more likely are security-classified and distributed by the originating service.

Examples

Titanium, food processing, and numerical control examples show that DOD informing programs are adequate for most contractors involved in developing and producing the end products. Only in integrated circuits was it necessary to hold regular conferences and bypass documentation channels. Integrated circuits developed so rapidly that normal information flow channels were inadequate. (The Food and Drug Administration turndown of irradiated foods shows the effects of inadequate evaluation of test information.) For informing the general public, DOD lets contractors take the initiative, as in numerical control and titanium metal. Nuclear-powered ships, at least, were publicized through Congressional hearings. The examples show the adequacy of DOD informing programs for relatively successful projects, but they do not show any direct contribution of DDC or NTIS to the general economy.

Feedback

Suitability. DOD informing program feedback indicates that the program is a costly and continuing effort to transfer changing technical information to changing people. People rotate from job to job in DOD so that they gain flexibility and learn to manage different technologies. Massive expenditures on information transfer are necessary to cope with personnel training and management policies; they do not contribute, however, as much per dollar spent as the program in USDA where a stable farmer group adds new technical information to previously integrated information.

DOD documents released through NTIS have given customers less than complete information about new defense technology. Little time has been spent packaging DOD reports and technology for commercial application, and report-editing standards have been low.

The most comprehensive feedback on DOD and DDC documentation services came from the DOD User Needs Study referenced in Chapter III. Based on this feedback, DDC began to: (1) expand the information base to include design, performance, development, production, and contractor evaluation data; (2) restructure the base to include oral and graphical forms; (3) make the base more flexible and mobile; and (4) move the informing system more into the user's environment.[12]

Control. Servicemen must be trained in weapons, procedures, and coordination with others. These imperatives guide control as it relates to part of the informing subprocess. Training receives greatest emphasis of all non-combat activities, and it is even a valued byproduct of combat. There is less emphasis on the information flow to contractors and other support elements for DOD. The Defense Documentation Center was organized only after its predecessor, the Armed Services Technical Information Agency (ASTIA), became neglected and outdated.[13] DDC originally focused on quantitative measurements of outputs; but, as noted under suitability, it has become more concerned with types of documentation needed by in-service managers as well as outside contractors. There has been minimal control over placing the results of departmental technical work into DDC distribution channels.

Systems review. Within DOD, staff elements review DDC as a system for coupling past and future R&D and innovation. The committee on Scientific and Technical Information (COSATI) of the Federal Council for Science and Technology, and information science developments in other Federal agencies have also influenced DDC development. Studies by external advisory groups like the one performed by the Auerbach Corporation influenced procedures. The informing subprocess has not generally been recognized apart from its role in R&D and innovating. Other DOD informing program outputs are evaluated in the operating and support elements of the services, and programs shift as new weapons systems are adopted. DOD has been much more detailed in reviewing training and has developed effective procedures for changing emphasis among training needs. Seldom, however, have informing programs been evaluated directly on cost benefit criteria.

V. INNOVATING

Inputs

DOD innovating activities symbolized by Figure 26 are of three

types: (1) innovation within the Department; (2) fostering innovation
in the defense industry; and (3) influencing innovation in the general

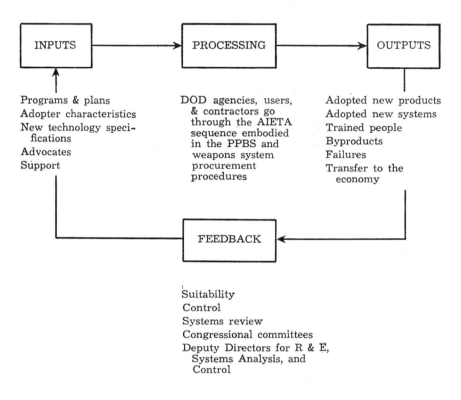

Figure 26. DOD innovating activities.

economy. Absence of a specific activity does not indicate lack of influence, because the huge amounts of DOD funds influence the whole U. S. economy. DOD specifications determine technical content of an appreciable proportion of general goods and services. Outstanding characteristics of DOD innovating are the specificity with which missions and needs are delineated, strong support compared to other programs, and visibility of the programs to administrators. Support levels produce indirect effects greater than direct effects of other agency programs.

In 1967, in contracts greater than $10,000, research, development, testing, and evaluation awards were for $6.07 billion, other services and construction expenditures were for $8.7 billion, and supplies and equipment were purchased costing $25.4 billion.[14] These expenditure proportions typify recent years. In DOD fostering of innovation in industry, development and procurement contracts seeks the best devices, processes, or weapons at lowest cost. Armed Services Procurement Regulations (ASPR) are constantly rewritten to bring procurement practice up to date. Technical specifications are used to set performance of products developed or purchased.

Adopter characteristics. With regard to internal innovating, DOD represents one pole in the centralization of government control over technology diffusion. In the agricultural sector, an operator is told in which areas he will receive incentive payments—the government takes no action. The operator may innovate or not. In DOD, the decision to innovate is made at higher levels and implemented throughout lower echelons. The operator is told what to do, and is provided the tools and training to do it. A decision to innovate, as from aircraft to guided missiles, is thus a major change causing immediate adjustments in development, training, procurement, and logistics. The adopters are high-level civilians and military officials, relatively few in number, and mostly located in Washington, D.C. Dr. MacArthur indicated three-fourths of all adoptions resulted from person-to-person contacts.[15]

Advocates for adoption. Hundreds of offices are involved in innovating programs of Army, Navy, Air Force, defense agencies, and unified and specified commands. Because of the importance of decisions to adopt new DOD technology, special programs have evolved within development and testing to emphasize all factors bearing on the decision to adopt. Life cycle costing forces the service to outline the costs of adoption all the way through to retirement of the proposed system. Contract definition aids in deciding on most effective tradeoffs in time, performance, and costs. Systems analysis as a discipline reached its present state of sophistication in groping with ways to evaluate cost and usefulness of alternative weapons systems. Contractors, offices, departments, and interested publics become advocates for adoption or against adoption.

DOD innovates in the general economy by relinquishing patent rights to companies which initiated the technology development, subject to free licenses to the government. This procedure is believed by DOD administrators to influence defense industries to innovate, both for defense use and commercial needs.

Processing

DOD embodies innovation processing in its PPBS procedures at department level and in weapons development and procurement procedures at middle management level, and in operating procedures at using unit level. Each of these three levels includes some aspects of the AIETA sequence.

Decisions to adopt new technology are pushed back as far as possible into development. Establishment of goals and the selection of those with higher priority are PPBS activities which may determine the technology to be considered. Pacification in Southeast Asia uses different technologies from missile warfare. Within pacification, overall goals can be pursued in differing ways. Determining mission needs, alternatives to meet these needs, and contributions of each alternative precedes the adoption decision. Though not different in principle from processing in other agencies, weapons system complexity and the difficulty of some DOD goals complicate processing.

PPBS deliberations continue during all phases of weapons system development, acquisition, and use. At the PPBS level during the conceptual phase, system requirements are refined and validated; an operationally suitable, technically feasible, and cost effective concept evolves; cost and performance tradeoffs are analyzed; and a system is proposed to include performance specifications. With these in hand, DOD managers and industry can define the system on paper during the Definition phase. Contract definition develops the detailed cost, schedule, and technical design requirements of the program and produces a design requirements baseline with estimated costs. Once costs are established, DOD can present to the administration and thence to Congress the request for supporting appropriations. If Congress approves adoption, funds are appropriated and the weapons system is acquired (designed, built, and tested). The acquired system is then phased into combat units of unified and specified commands. During this latter phase of acquisition, operators are trained and facilities built for using the system.[16] Trials doublecheck correctness of adoption decisions during the acquisition phase. The extensive and expensive test ranges and installations measure performance and evaluate new systems and products which have been invented and designed. When the system begins operation, integrating activities predominate. DOD does not directly process byproducts to satisfy commercial needs, although some contractors, using their patent options, may introduce useful new items to the public.

Outputs

The most direct outputs of DOD innovating efforts are adopted weapons systems. A weapons system includes hardware, facilities of support, services and supplies to maintain and operate it, people who make it perform, training of the people in the new technical skill, and software (operating procedures) which combines hardware with people and facilities. Each new weapons system indirectly produces procedures for internal adjustment of DOD practices. Byproducts include companies holding exploitable patents or other forms of technology and suppliers with experience in producing items with specified technical content. People trained to operate and maintain the new system may leave the service and continue to use their new skills in the civilian economy. The examples include output failures as well as successful transfers to the civilian economy.

Examples

Correct judgments, as well as massive mistakes, show up in DOD innovation. Even though many items are never mass-produced, their path toward tentative adoption can be costly. Carrier-based F111's, ABM developments, nuclear-powered aircraft, the B-70 bomber, the NAVAHO winged intercontinental missle, the SKYBOLT aircraft-launched strategic ballistic missile, the Manned Orbiting Laboratory, the MIDAS satellite surveillance system, and the MAULER anti-aircraft system reached far enough into adoption to consume scarce skilled manpower and materials. Adoption of first generation missile systems during the 1950's, perhaps necessary as a transition, nevertheless forced use of weapons systems so marginal in performance that a commercial company would not have marketed them. Examples which were all phased out as rapidly as possible were BOMARC I and NIKE AJAX anti-aircraft defense; TITAN, JUPITER, THOR, and ATLAS strategic missiles; and FALCON 1 aircraft armament.

Successful transfers of technology to the civilian sector include jet aircraft, helicopters, food processing, computers, titanium use, numerical control, and integrated circuits. These indicate that transfer mechanisms function effectively, however indirect they may seem. Support of the market for new technologies certainly expedited these transfers. After the market was established for military use, the civilian economy began to adopt the new items. In these examples, advantages were so apparent that DOD had to do little advocating. One can generalize from these examples that desirable technologies generate their own market and momentum. Conversely, inadequate new technologies such as irradiated food do not succeed, despite DOD support.

Feedback

DOD innovation feedback is provided by combat use, where past adoption is evaluated; from the defense industry, where on-going adoption processees are under scrutiny; and by Congress, where political and social implications of DOD innovations are studied. Battlefield or combat evaluation indicates an item's achievement of its intended function and, in addition, its impact on tactics and logistics. Industry review of current adoption gives feedback assuring that the best available technology has been applied. Congress is very sensitive to economic disruptions from DOD innovation and intervenes in adoption processing when DOD leaders are divided, when administrators are uncertain, and when members of Congress believe their expertise is greater than the executives'.

Congressmen gain feedback through testimony to their committees, visits to military installations, reports on use of appropriations, and letters from constituents.

Soaring costs of innovating were prime reasons for development of PPBS in DOD by Charles Hitch and Robert McNamara after 1961. They needed to know costs in subsequent years of adoption decisions. They set up the five year format, the budget year plus four, in dollars and the eight year format, the budget year plus seven, in numbers of weapons systems items.

Histories of 2,100 government-sponsored inventions have been studied to determine the effects of various patent policies. Of this group, including patents for DOD and AEC in 1957 and 1962, and from other agencies except NASA from 1956 to 1966, only 251, or 12.4

percent, were used commercially, and only fifty-five or 2.7 percent played a critical role in commercial products. Of the 251, 198 were DOD-sponsored where the contractor took title. Five inventions accounted for eighty-eight percent of the sales in the contractor title group, including technologies in transistors, vacuum tubes, numerical control devices, computers, and gas turbine engines. When contractors were asked why more patents were not used, over seventy percent of the first-ranked reasons were low commercial potential.[17] These returns indicate that transferable technology sometimes develops into patents in DOD or other government work; and, when it does, it is related to a use in commerce similar to its use in government.

Control. Unfavorable examples of new weapons development in DOD resulted from inadequate control of technology diffusion subprocesses. Adoption choices were not made until after vast expenditures on alternatives which could have been eliminated earlier during the inventing phase. PPBS procedures, including systems analysis and weapons systems management, were intended to reduce the erroneous choices, consider future costs of the choices considered, evaluate tradeoffs and alternatives systematically, and identify interrelationships among decisions.[18]

James R. Schlesinger predicted in 1963-64, while working with RAND Corporation, that DOD procedures would cause suppression of alternatives. This suppression would reduce rivalry but increase pressure on those at the top. Incentives at lower service levels to invent new alternatives would be reduced. He also predicted that impacts on costs and effectiveness would be neglected as well as significant uncertainties.[19] The 1964-73 Southeast Asia events indicated neglect of political uncertainties and cost impacts on military decisions. Specific cases can be found which support Schlesinger's predictions, yet there is much support for DOD's centralizing of control over its internal technology diffusion. The Deputy Directors for Systems Analysis, Research and Engineering, Controller, and the civilian secretaries of the departments have cooperated to establish this control.

Systems review. DOD is so large and its influence so pervasive that its functions are best reviewed externally. RAND Corporation, CODSIA, and similar institutions have done much to restructure the

DOD innovating procedures. Recommendations from CODSIA continually influence weapons systems management procedures. Congressional committees perform the "devil's advocate" role for analyzing on-going or proposed programs. Individual members of Congress have evaluated the total DOD impact on the economy, but they have not effectively translated their conclusions to legislation. Centralized control has made it difficult for those affected by DOD adoption processes to influence them directly. The combat commander, working with weapons in hand, can influence DOD technology only if he subsequently works in weapons development. DOD members can join professional service organizations like the Air Force Association or industrial groups like the National Security Industrial Association to advocate general or specific systems changes.

VI. INTEGRATING

Inputs

Three forms of DOD technology integration, two external and one internal, are represented in Figure 27. The first external procedure allows contractors to retain patents for commercial uses. By the other external integration procedure, DOD furnishes a market for items in the national interest. DOD markets for semiconductors supported innovating and integrating of that development into national electronics. The difference for the manufacturer who sells in this government market is that specifications for the product require that he adopt new technology. A relatively small percentage of DOD developed items are ingested into the economy through this procedure, although the number of items so ingested may be impressive compared to technology diffusion programs in other departments. The internal form of integrating new technology requires completely centralized adoption with decentralized ingestion and adjustment.

New systems from applied research and development are adopted in whole or in part and enter DOD as part of the five year force structure. Several new systems may enter the structure simultaneously. Concerned about technological obsolescence, DOD tries to keep its products and systems up to date by using military specifications, which compromise between standardization and the state of the art. Products built by "mil specs" are usually more expensive than commercial products.

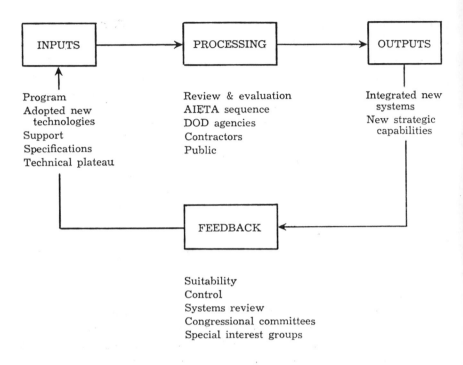

Figure 27. DOD integrating activities.

Each time a new weapons system is adopted, DOD adjusts to it from a technical plateau of existing facilities, existing training, existing organizations, and in-service people. These are usually constraints to rapid ingestion and integration of new systems. New people can be trained directly in new systems without reference to old, but this limited training may create conflict within organizations. People experienced in existing technology are usually trained along with new people.

Procurement of services and supplies includes funds considered as support for integration. The FY 1967 figure of $8.7 billion for service and construction and $25.4 billion for supplies and equipment are indicative of integration support in recent years. Constant changes in new systems, facilities, and people cause support requirements to be projected through the total system life to its retirement and replacement. DOD can support contractor integration through loans and progress payments as well as through the market support from its procurement funds.

Processing

Initial integration processing occurs during the Conceptual phase of weapons system development and procurement; in-service people propose new technology and calculate needs for logistics and training. During the Definition phase these calculations are defined further by contractor and in-service logisticians, training specialists, and tacticians. They develop system uses and technical training. Adoption actually occurs before contracts are let for the following phase of detailed development and production or acquisition. During Acquisition, contractors and in-service people work out programs to phase new technology into the inventory and to phase out the systems replaced. Actual replacement occurs during Operation, at which time adjustments are made to ingest new systems. Coordination during this phase increases when several new systems are introduced simultaneously. Because of big expenditures in replacing old with new systems, integration problems in buying, operating, and maintaining new systems are considered in decision processes at the highest government levels. During budget procedures, the President and Congress must have valid information before they can evaluate costs and benefits of alternatives. In addition there are impacts other than direct cost or performance. For example, the decision to use ICBM's rather than long range bombers changed the focus of the Air Force Strategic Air Command from mobile flyers to nonflyer technicians in underground silos.

Output

Outputs of ingestion, after many trials and adjustments, are new weapons with trained operators and adequate logistics support. When new systems are fully integrated, tactics of their use are taught and understood by members of DOD. New relationships develop among component forces which upgrade national defense, compared against the standard of former capabilities of DOD. A more meaningful comparison can be made against capabilities of potential enemy forces. Byproducts are the procedures, human skills, components, or whole systems which can be used in the general economy. Some systems and skills, like jet aircraft support, transfer easily to civilian use. ICBM technologies seem less applicable; but they have been used in commercial space applications, miniaturized electronic circuits, and metallurgy.

Examples

Food processing illustrates internal DOD integration of new technologies. DOD simply substituted freeze-dried food and irradiated food for part of the issue rations. Hungry men ate and became accustomed to the new foods. New weapons and technical procedures are substituted for old, and soldiers adjust training, support, and combat to them.

External integrating in defense industries is illustrated by titanium metal and integrated circuits. Specifications for weight, size, and reliability simply guided the contractor in integrating the new technologies. Progress payments aided in the transition. Integrating into the general economy depends on DOD training, standards, and cost benefits of the new technologies. Titanium metal and integrated circuits are well into integration. Food freeze-drying is not yet cost competitive in most applications. Food irradiation has been rejected until tested to the satisfaction of the Food and Drug Administration.

Feedback

High costs of installing new weapons systems such as ABM complexes have caused much scrutiny of the direction and impact of DOD integrating activities. Today's commitments have implications for years, conceivably even generations. There has been an increasing tendency for each proposed system to become a political issue. This tendency may be justified because of the past record of poor guesses and of contractor practices of "Buying in Low, and Forcing out High." Several programs can be started at low bids, but some will be forced out in the future when follow-on costs become more visible. Legislators and the public still remember the costly forceouts of NAVAHO, SKYBOLT, nuclear-powered aircraft, B-70, and the CHEYENNE. DOD integration indicates that efficiency increases when weapons are standardized. Technical change lowers skills until training and practice bring effectiveness to the same or higher levels. Changing technology plus changing personnel make the DOD integration program one large, continuous training exercise. The effectiveness level for a unit becomes a function of average time in training for the weapons used.

Control and systems review. Operational and logistics commanders control the integrating subprocess as they execute the innovation decisions from higher headquarters, adjusting within constraints of available facilities and resources. They can contribute to systems review, but these contributions are generally lost as they are forwarded through channels. Commanders are generally stuck with the adoption decision until the system becomes obsolete or until some overriding factor forces a reconsideration. Navy aircraft carrier commanders had such a factor in the overweight of the naval version of the F111.

The integrating subprocess among contractors or manufacturers has been controlled successfully through contract administration, technical specifications, design reviews, and product testing. Contractors must correct deficiencies at their own expense or accept penalties if the item cannot be brought to specifications. Contractors can also share in any saving in operations and maintenance which good design may bring.

The effects of DOD integrating on the general economy have been analyzed somewhat by Congressional committees; but they are more frequently assessed by external groups, more likely than not, antagonistic toward defense goals. Congressional committees have legislated DOD procedures such as small business set-asides, use of multiple source procurement, training of formerly rejected men, and awarding of contracts in depressed areas.

VII. DOD IN THE TOTAL PROCESS

With over one-third of Federal applied research and development, DOD has a primary activity in inventing new defense technology for diffusion. DOD furnishes about forty percent of the reports distributed by NTIS and does substantial technical training, providing to the general economy a secondary informing activity. DOD does costly and continuous internal innovating and integrating which indirectly affect the general economy. Internally, DOD deliberately invents to meet its mission needs, trains its service people to use the new technology, organizes new units to exploit new technology and phase out older, and adjusts its operations and logistics to the new technology. DOD can use equally effective mechanisms for working with its supporting industry in the defense sector of the economy.

Inventing. DOD expenditures in applied research and development, as well as those of NASA and AEC, are so large that their results have been considered sources of new technology waiting to be exploited. Historically, little DOD technology has been used directly, primarily because of its inapplicability and rapid obsolescence. Richard R. Nelson, researcher for the Rand Corporation, has tabulated the spillover from defense and space R&D and found it unimpressive. Few patents resulting from defense and space have been used commercially. Further, companies in both civilian and defense marketing do not benefit strikingly from defense work. Many scientists believe that emphasis on defense and space technology hinders the nation's general technological lead by preempting scientific and technical resources.[20]

Informing. With its $140 million plus in scientific and technical information and its heavy investment in technical training in 1,500 specialties, DOD led other Federal agencies in its internal programs. Primarily concerned with internal feedforward about new technology to its uniformed members, DOD training is specific and vocational. The scientific and technical information funds support NTIS outputs to the public of 20,000 reports annually as well as DDC classified and unclassified reports to the defense industry. With the main focus on its internal distribution system, DOD uses both traditional and modern information processing. Outputs are trained servicemen, contractor groups, and formal documentation. The informing effort is expensive and is evaluated only in terms of total defense needs, not in terms of economic self-sufficiency.

Innovating. Internal innovating of DOD is highly structured. Adoption of new systems and products is decided before applied research and development are completed. Then operators are trained to use the new system and older products disappear. In the supporting industry DOD uses procedures which diverge from private enterprise such as small business set-asides, progress payments, technical specifications, multiple source procurement, and government furnished facilities and equipment to gain adaptation and adoption of new technology it favors. Its support for this internal innovating stems from specific defense goals, approved annually in legislative processes. Sometimes, failures preclude alternate uses of significant resources. Effects on the general economy are indirect, with DOD allowing contractors to take title to new developments to encourage them to innovate in the general economy. This sometimes happens, particularly when a whole system is useful to the general economy such as jet aircraft, computers, or new forms of metallurgy. Constant use of new technology by servicemen and contractors eases its subsequent innovation in private enterprise.

Integrating. The indirect effect of DOD on integrating can be considered as proportional to its massive total funding of $71 million in FY 71. Much of this is procurement of material and products which are affected by new technology specifications. Internal integrating is highly structured, with DOD furnishing the market for new products, technology, and weapons systems. Individuals and contractors, trained in use of the new items, support integration in the general economy. Total effects of integrating are labor- and capital-using, concentration of the economy by area and company, and national resources focused on defense needs. The main reviews of DOD integrating and its effects on the general economy are by Congress, but pressure groups have influence.

De Facto Procedures

DOD has outwardly supported private enterprise procedures for diffusing technology by allowing a company which comes up with technical advances to patent and exploit them. Theoretically, contractors will evaluate new technology for commercial application, but there are fallacies to this theory. According to the U. S. Chamber of Commerce, most companies prominent in DOD work since 1950 have few commercial interests, or else they completely separate military and commercial work. They are under-capitalized, have little means for commercial marketing, and have little experience in production for mass consumption.[21] Patents which these companies accrue contribute little unless licensed or sold outright. In 1963, Dr. Murray

L. Weidenbaum testified before the Senate Subcommittee on Employment and Manpower that, aside from the handful of companies producing commercial aircraft (at little profit), large defense suppliers had not been producing commercially beyond one or two percent of total sales.[22] Since 1963 DOD has tried to open its business to new firms, which would result in the transfer of new technology to these firms. In FY 1967, ninety-three of the top five hundred firms, or one in five, had not been in the FY 1966 listing. Over one-third of these were small businesses. Yet top recipients were the same as for previous years.[23]

Despite some recent attention to technology transfer efforts, especially in the Navy Department, DOD lacks special programs to diffuse technology; yet, several activities transfer technology fairly effectively in the long run: training for 1,500 technical specialties, contracting policy, furnishing equipment and facilities, informing programs, and patenting policy. If these activities and procedures were coordinated and focused on benefits to the civilian economy, they might be more productive for that purpose. DOD uses private enterprise as well as **de facto** procedures in its technology diffusion; **de facto** procedures, however, predominate in the internal activities.

National Goals.

DOD focuses on national security, power, and prestige as distinct from more general national goals. DOD administrators believe the Department promotes technical progress and provides applicable information to potential users in the economy. DOD, both labor and capital using, supports full employment and purchasing power but at the expense of substituting weapons for economic growth systems. Severest criticisms of DOD have been based on its inequitable effects on free enterprise, economic and geographic concentrations, and the environment.

Through its control of contracts and government-furnished equipment and facilities, DOD can promote use of new technologies in defense industries. Low bidders on contracts tend to have past experience and known capabilities in the field; thus defense work concentrates into specific companies and areas. Resources, people, and experience for applying defense technology tend to group together, and newer technologies can be absorbed faster within these concentrations than in wholly different enterprises. California and Massachusetts have concentrations in missiles and electronics which attracted highly qualified technologists, supportive technical firms, and specialized funding institutions all during the 1960's. These California and Massachusetts concentrations developed areas not previously prominent in technology. In 1968 a Senate resolution was introduced (S Con Res 29) aimed at "promotion of a more orderly and uniform growth of population of the various states in order to minimize or avoid problems of heavy concentrations of populations so as to provide greater opportunity for wholesome living to greater numbers of people." DOD opposed the resolution because introduction of uniform geographical distribution factors "would tend to obstruct our purpose of obtaining for the armed services the best facilities, supplies, and services for the funds spent."[24]

In terms of the total technology diffusion process, defense technology is desired and needed; but much of it will not apply commercially. As the state of the art has made advanced defense technology possible, it has increased in cost and diverged from allowable commercial or cultural use. The new technologies are stored for possible future use but the steps from one technological level to the next have become less frequent. Other technologies are becoming more wanted than those DOD can provide.

FOOTNOTES

[1] John S. Foster, Jr., "Research and Development in U.S. Defense Posture," *Defense Industry Bulletin,* September, 1971, pp. 6-7.

[2] National Science Foundation, *Federal Funds . . . , op. cit.,* p. 177, and Department of Defense, *Statement of Secretary of Defense Robert S. McNamara Before a Joint Session of the Senate Armed Services Committee and the Senate Subcommittee on Department of Defense Appropriations on the Fiscal Years 1968-72 Defense Program and the 1968 Defense Budget,* January 23, 1967 (Washington, D.C.: Office of the Secretary of Defense, 1967), pp. 124-134.

[3] Department of Defense, *ibid.,* pp. 124-158.

[4] Dr. Donald M. MacArthur, "Defense Technology: Benefits to Industrial Progress," *Defense Industry Bulletin,* August, 1970, pp. 1-4.

[5] C. W. Sherwin, *et al.,* "The First Interim Report on Project Hindsight. (Summary)." Office of the Director of Defense Research and Engineering. AD 642-400. (Springfield, Va.: Clearinghouse, 1966), p. 13.

[6] Department of Defense . . . , *op. cit.,* p. 124.

[7] "Military Research: NSIA Unit Urges Improvement in DOD Transfer of Planning Data to Industry," *Federal Contracts Report* (Washington, D.C.: Bureau of National Affairs, Jan. 1, 1968), pp. A6-A7. NSIA—National Security Industries Association.

[8] U.S. Congress, House, Committee on Science and Astronautics, *Obligations . . .*, *op. cit.*, pp. 25-31.

[9] "Who Got Most Money for R&D," *Business Week* (Feb 10, 1968), p. 58.

[10] Clark M Clifford, *The Fiscal Year 1970-74 Defense Program and the 1970 Defense Budget* (Washington, D.C.: Department of Defense, 1969), pp. 122-123.

[11] "FY 1971 Research, Development, Test, and Evaluation," *Defense Industry Bulletin*, June, 1970, p. 12.

[12] Harold B. Lawson, "Defense Documentation Center Reports—User Needs Study Results," *Defense Industry Bulletin*, vol. 4, no. 7, July, 1968.

[13] The author tried to use ASTIA facilities at Arlington Hall Station, Arlington, Va., in 1961-62 and found it very difficult to determine what was available or to obtain access to it. Though in the next building, the author's organization, an Army technical agency, had no arrangements for using ASTIA facilities. ASTIA employees did not consider Army personnel to be their clients and were reluctant to service requests.

[14] DOD Directorate for Statistical Services, *Military Prime Contract Awards (Fiscal Years 1964, 1965, 1966 & 1967)* (Washington, D.C.: Department of Defense, 1967), pp. 2-10.

[15] Donald M. MacArthur, *op. cit.*, p. 3.

[16] M. S. Mitchell and C. J. Koppel, *Air Force Systems Command—Systems Management—An Introduction to Air Force Systems Management* (San Diego, Calif.: Paragon Design Co., 1964), pp. 4-11.

[17] Committee on Government Patent Policy, FCST, *Government Patent Policy Study*, Final Report Volumes I-IV. Contract Study by Harbridge House, Inc. (Washington, D.C.: U.S. Government Printing Office, 1968), pp. I-6 and I-27.

[18] James R. Schlesinger, *National Security Management—Defense Planning and Budgeting: The Issue of Centralized Control* (Washington, D.C.: Industrial College of the Armed Forces, 1968), pp. 7-9.

[19] *Ibid.*, pp. 16-24.

[20] *Federal Contracts Report* (Washington, D.C.: The Bureau of National Affairs, Inc., Jan. 15, 1968), pp. A3-A4.

[21] Chamber of Commerce of the United States, *The Economics of Defense Spending* (Washington, D.C.: Chamber of Commerce of the United States, 1965), p. 13.

[22] "The Transferability of Defense Industry Resources to Civilian Uses," Statement for the Subcommittee on Employment and Manpower of the Committee on Labor and Public Welfare of the U.S. Senate, Nov. 21, 1963, in *The Nation's Manpower Revolution*, Hearing of the Senate Subcommittee on Employment and Manpower (Washington, D.C.: U.S. Government Printing Office, 1964), Part 9, p. 3146.

[23] *Federal Contracts Report, op. cit.*, p. A-1.

[24] Bureau of National Affairs, *Daily Executive Report*, No. 104 (May 27, 1968), p. AA-2.

CHAPTER VII

TECHNOLOGY DIFFUSION ACTIVITIES OF OTHER AGENCIES

I. INTRODUCTION

This chapter reviews the most significant technology diffusion activities of the Department of Commerce, NASA, AEC, and the Small Business Administration. Commerce has a clear statutory mission to support technology diffusion. NASA has had vast amounts of national resources funneled through it into production of new technology. AEC is of particular interest because of its direct work with industry and its special relationship to applied science. SBA exemplifies small Federal agencies with specific missions but without technology diffusion as a specified mission.

II. DEPARTMENT OF COMMERCE

Organized in 1913, Commerce is intended to: (1) assure fullest use of the nation's scientific and technical resources; (2) administer the patent system—historical carrier for technology diffusion; (3) develop and publish scientific, commercial, and engineering standards; (4) operate the National Technical Information Service for Federal research and development reporting; (5) administer the Census Bureau for developing basic economic, business, scientific, and environmental information; and (6) encourage economic growth by placing findings of science in the hands of entrepreneurs. These activities, however limited in application, promote technology diffusion.

Limitations on Commerce programs are apparent from manning and funding. At the end of FY 1971, the Department had 34,359 employees and its obligations were $1,456,675,000. FY 1966 was the first year these obligations exceeded $1 billion. About 20% of the funds went to economic development in the Economic Development Administration (EDA), and nearly one-third to the merchant marine (Maritime Administration). The remainder is a substantial sum but the National Oceanic and Atmospheric Administration (NOAA) took over half of it for developing and reporting weather, oceanic, and gen-

eral scientific data. Commerce offices directly concerned with technology have budgets of about $50 million or less.[1]

Commerce offices concerned with inventing and informing include
the Patent Office, the National Technical Information Service (NTIS)
and the National Bureau of Standards (NBS).   Commerce does not
generate new technology for other than its own internal use except in
the Maritime Administration and NOAA, Commerce offices concerned with innovation include NBS, the Patent Office, and data-
distributing offices of the Department. Offices concerned with economic development contribute to integration. Commerce leads in collecting general purpose scientific data, both in natural and social
services. About forty-five percent of Federal effort has been in
Commerce, concentrated mainly in predecessor offices of NOAA for
natural science, and in the Social and Economic Statistics Administration (SESA) including the Bureau of the Census for social science.[2]
General purpose data somewhat indirectly support technology diffusion but are not detailed here.

Inventing

Commerce in FY 1971 obligated $71,897,000 for applied research and
$30,037,000 for development. The NBS, NOAA, EDA, SESA, Maritime
Administration, and Patent Office each spent funds to improve mission
operations. EDA and SESA spent funds primarily on social science
projects aimed at improving techniques or procedures for these offices.
They did not produce new technology. The Maritime Administration
and NOAA funds were for projects in physical sciences such as applications of nuclear propulsion to the merchant marine and applications
of space technology to weather data collection. These two offices conform to the model of inventive work for internal use and will not be
discussed further. The example of the N. S. Savannah, a joint project of the AEC and the Maritime Administration, is presented in
Appendix F-22 under the AEC.

Patent Office. The oldest office in Commerce, the Patent Office,
is highly autonomous. It administers patent laws as they relate to
granting of patent rights for inventions, and trademark laws as they
relate to registration of trademarks. The Patent Office has developed
its own procedures, has its own system of distributing information,
and has its own legal support through many court decisions. Com-

merce is merely the holding organization for the Patent Office. Patent Office outputs are one form of "available technology." The less than a million dollars the Patent Office obligated in FY 1971 for applied research and development was to improve its internal processing of patent applications.

National Bureau of Standards. NBS is the principal location in Federal government providing a focal point for application of physical and engineering sciences to advancement of technology in industry and commerce. It provides central national service in basic measurement standards, materials research, engineering standards, and applied technology, thus giving an underlying "available science and technology" input to all agency or individual inventive work. From $45 million operation funds in FY 1971, $14 million was for applied research and development, done almost entirely intramurally by Civil Service employees. The Institute of Basic Standards develops basic measurements and fundamental properties. Its Office of Standard Reference Data coordinates the National Standard Reference Data Program and provides a national file for evaluated data in physical sciences. The Institute for Materials Research works on basic properties of bulk materials. Its Office of Standard Reference Materials reviews reference materials for science and industry and contributes to the National Standard Reference Data Program. This program was proposed in 1963 by the President's Office of Science and Technology to reduce confusion and redundancy in U. S. inventing activities. The National Standard Reference Data Act supporting the program was passed by Congress in 1968. A Center for Radiation Research was established in FY 68 to cover basic measurements, materials research, and applied technology for applications of nuclear science. NBS has an Institute of Applied Technology to promote use of available technology and facilitate technological innovation. The NTIS was split from this Institute in 1970 and given a large mission. NBS also has a Center for Computer Sciences and Technology which is the Federal center for standardization in data processing equipment.

Commerce agencies evaluate new technical proposals and select for development those most likely to satisfy agency missions and needs. Because of limited appropriations for some agencies, selection is strict. The Patent Office procedure for granting patents is highly regulated and judiciary, and the process of obtaining protection for one's invention is done within that framework. NBS processing divides into disciplines of physical sciences or into specific problem areas.

NBS and the Patent Office services support inventive work of other agencies and people. The Patent Office issues about 1,400 patents weekly to U. S. applicants and about 200 to foreigners. Patent Office applied research and development speeds up processing and reduces the number of invalid patents. The Patent Office cannot easily check out a patent application against the file of 3,500,000 U. S. and over 7,000,000 foreign patents.

NBS outputs consist of technical standards including weights, measures, and technical literature. As of May 29, 1968, there were 4,144 subscriptions to the **Technical News Bulletin,** produced primarily for industry, and 2,155 to its **Journal of Research** (engineering and instrumentation). Another output was the program of research associates, who work at NBS for a term and then return to industry or to universities. In 1968, 65 of these were in residence.[3] NBS also furnishes updated standards to each state, and it publishes its findings and critical evaluations in non-periodicals.

Examples. In-house Commerce applied research and development continues to improve geodesy, patent processing, weather data evaluating and reporting, and standards. While vital to public service, this internal work goes unpublicized. Externally, the continuing 105,000 applications for patents per year, and the 180,000 backlog of applications awaiting processing, indicate that the private sector still considers patents helpful. Even if only a small fraction of these patents are finally adopted and used, there will be considerable technical change.

The 3,500,000 U. S. patents are examples of technically successful inventions. One example, No. 3,179,549, "Thermal Insulating Panel and Method for Making the Same," is discussed here (Appendix F-8). This example shows that new technology is rarely generated until an insightful individual states a need in a way that indicates a technical solution. Even then trial and error is involved, and the most useful information may be in the experience and informal writings of developers. Though a technical success, this invention was not adopted for general use.

Technically successful inventions are also rejected even when Federal agencies perform the work and make all information available without proprietary restraints. Chrome ore and metal processing were developed by the Bureau of Mines to exploit known and abundant ore resources to fill present and future needs for chromium. Though the project's main results have not been adopted, pure, ductile chromium wire, developed in metal processing, found an application in cancer treatment; hence a useful byproduct did result. Appendix F-9 discusses this reject and its successful byproduct. In the case of the coal carbon black process (Appendix F-10), two Federal agencies, each working with excess raw materials, developed alternative ways to strengthen rubber tires through additives. The Bureau of Mines developed technologies and economics for coal additives. USDA developed cereal starch resins for the same purpose. Industry thus can choose between two Federally derived technologies.

Most NBS outputs have been accepted and adopted in the U. S. economy. Yet there is one outstanding failure — extension of the metric system. NBS uses only the metric system, which has unusual logic and simplicity; yet the U. S. public has just begun to adopt it (Appendix F-11). In 1971, NBS completed a three-year study on how the U.S. could convert to the metric system, and passed the buck to Congress.

The automobile accident problem calls for the uninvented safe car. Until recently, Commerce had little responsibility or funds for this field, and no authority had stated the need in a way that indicated a technical solution (Appendix F-7). Patents for safety devices were available but lacked a market.

Suitability. The patent system has been attacked vigorously. The President's patent commission, appointed in 1965, recommended changes which were unsuccessful in Congress. The commission recognized criticisms of invalid patenting and expenses of litigation and delay; but it concluded the system has encouraged applied research, promoted international exchange of technology, and provided a means for public disclosure.[4]

Patent applications reached a plateau after World War II. Subsequent increases in Federal applied research and development affected work little in the Patent Office until 1971. There was a seeming resurgence of interest in 1971 and 1972.

NBS, though a highly regarded Federal activity, receives marginal support for some of its offices with large missions. Subscriptions to its journals seem too small to reach those who need the information. The 1968 establishment of the National Standard Data Reference System and the Center for Radiation Research reflects past disparity between output and mission needs.

Control and program review. With its specialized services, Commerce has had little central focus for its inventing activities. The Assistant Secretary for Science and Technology supervised applied research and development of all offices. This Assistant Secretary, set up in a 1961-62 reorganization of Commerce scientific and technical effort, has used non-government advisory groups for systems review. One of these, the Commerce Technical Advisory Board (CTAB) of 20 knowledgeable leaders, meets monthly to recommend measures to increase value to industry and business of the department's scientific and technological activities. CTAB itself reviews specific subjects with specialized panels, including the Panels on Invention and Innovation, Supersonic Transport Environment, Automotive Fuels and Air Pollution, Science and Technology, Noise Abatement, and Commodity Standards.[5] These panels indicate CTAB concern with the direction of technical effort, and their reports aid the general public and Congress in choosing among technical development alternatives. Congress has performed control and review functions by relating the National Bureau of Standards work to current problems in standardizing technology. The 1969 and 1970 legislation confirming and strengthening national information service and data banks helps all inventive efforts obtain available technology as well as standard and recognized physical science information inputs.

Informing

Informing programs about new technology are the Department's strongest support for technology diffusion. The Patent Office, NBS and NTIS, all have informing programs which, together, cover most new technology. These operate as separate systems.

The Patent Office in FY 1971 had inputs of 2,632 employees, 110,217 patent and design applications, 32,803 trademark applications, and support funds of $56,073,000, which it processed into 73,783 patents issued; and 36,400 applications abandoned. The Patent Office backlog of applications decreased slightly from 187,439 to 184,127. During the year, an Office of Technology Assessment and Forecast was established to help pinpoint areas where inventions were most needed. Applied research and development continued on devices to do mechanized search for the patent examiners. As shown in Appendix D-4, the majority of the Patent Office funds was spent on scientific and technical information. Available to the public were 11 million U.S. and foreign patents, and over 200,000 volumes of technical literature. The office prepared the weekly **Official Gazette** which describes all new patents issued during the week.

NTIS, established in 1964, as the Clearinghouse for Scientific and Technical Information, collects unclassified reports of Federal research and development from 250 agencies and distributes them at low cost, either in hard copy or in microfiche. It does not evaluate reports, but does some screening in its form of announcement. NTIS was revamped in 1970 to simplify and improve public access to Federal results of unclassified research and development in defense, space, atomic energy, and other national programs. In 1971, there were more than 600,000 documents in store; 45,000 new Federal reports were received, and 3,500,000 orders were handled. About two-thirds of the stored documents were U. S. government and one-third were foreign. In 1966 there were 6,500 subscribers to **Fast Announcement** and **Announcement of Translations:** NTIS operates eleven regional centers, which also carry 16mm films of the Patent Office **Official Gazette.**

These NTIS and Patent Office programs together cover unclassified inventive publications of individuals, industrial firms, government organizations, and some foreign groups. Both sell outputs directly to individuals or firms. Both offices are changing their outputs in an effort to improve their appeal and acceptability.

NBS as a whole received $12.3 million in FY 1971 for scientific and technical information. NBS Institutes of Basic Standards, Materials Research, Applied Technology, and the Center for Computer Sciences and Technology each coordinates and manages in its field. In addition, the Bureau has several special offices reporting to the Director. During FY 1966, a typical year, NBS published about 1,100 original papers and documents, 500 in-house and 600 in the journals of professional groups. It conducted 27 conferences during FY 1966.

Examples. Patent information was significant in development of titanium (Appendix F-12), numerical control (Appendix F-13), synthetic rubber (Appendix F-14), and highway grooving (Appendix F-18). These inventions all had considerable time lags, indicating that availability of information is a necessary, but not sufficient, condition for its use. Patent information on automotive safety devices has also been available but again with little appeal. Chrome ore and metal processing information is freely available but not used. Even with government support and available information, a new technology may have no takers.

NTIS has existed for such a short time that few diffusion examples have developed from its information. In fact, it does not directly develop statistics on the use of its reports. Some of its reports were available in time to be used in selected examples of radioisotopes, nuclear power, integrated circuits, nuclear powered merchant ships, use of microfiche, and food preservation. Because most NTIS publications are non-proprietary, the information may be used freely.

Suitability. Commerce informing activities are generally lightly funded, intramural, and focused primarily on publication and distribution (70%) and document referencing and information service (20%).[6] These activities suggest themselves as basic services rather than instruments for change. Commerce's various information outputs seem scattered, but combining NTIS and Patent Office distribution points has partly corrected this. The Patent Office, particularly, has not made its files equally available to all citizens. NBS Institute information is more fully accepted than other department outputs. There is no direct way to compare the value of 45,000 annual technical reports made available by NTIS and some 70,000 patents published annually by the Patent Office. Technical reports from government agencies, distributed through NTIS, can duplicate patents pertaining to the same technologies.

Control and program review. Because of its focus on furnishing information to the general consumer, control groups rely heavily on gross quantitative responses. Effects of the activities in the totality of technology diffusion have been little assessed. CTAB and its technical panels influence overall informing programs through studying specific problems. Better availability of patent information resulted specifically from their work. External systems review of Commerce informing programs has been conducted by the Committee for Scientific and Technical Information (COSATI) of the Federal Council for Science and Technology. The Clearinghouse predecessor of NTIS was established after COSATI recommended it.

Innovating

Innovating activities of the Department of Commerce are limited and do not compete either with other agencies or with private enterprise. Commerce furnishes information, advice, standards, and regulations about new technology and thus provides inputs into innovating activities. Only EDA provides more than these inputs at a significant level.

The Patent Office, intended to be a key institution in government to encourage innovating, is actually precluded by law from advocating any one patent. The office was on an activity plateau from 1950 to 1970, each year adding relatively less to the total number of items made available for diffusion. Patents, however, remain significant for small firms or individuals because they protect original technology proprietary rights. Though these rights are only a small portion of the average investment in innovation, they are important in obtaining private support for it. In 1970 and 1971 patents surged, probably as a result of reducing the backlog.

NBS provides technical regulation and standards for innovation and may give specific advice and assistance in selected areas such as computer applications.

Private enterprise, government agencies, or individual citizens decide to adopt new technology made known through Commerce activities after following the AIETA sequence. The market place provides criteria for making adoption decisions by producers, and advantages in cost or performance help users of new items decide on adoption. EDA contributes to the process through its technical assistance program but appears to focus little toward application of new technology. Its program, according to a Commerce official, provides specific answers to individual businesses and communities on industrial feasibility analysis, management, and financial assistance.[7] These help the businessman who is considering technology new to him but old elsewhere. In fiscal year 1965 EDA technical assistance consumed $7.1 million on 158 projects. These projects included product marketing, studies of mineral and timber resource potential, revival of fishing industries, and business counseling on how to create new jobs.[8] In 1971, 1,431 technical assistance projects cost $64.6 milion, indicating almost a ten-fold increase in projects and costs.[9]

Commerce activities each year affect innovation indirectly in thousands of new businesses, new products from old businesses, and new technical procedures. One can also think of these outputs as adopted patents, applied technical information, and rejects of patents or information. Over fifty percent of granted patents are believed to be used, meaning that this percent of the protected technology is applied during the 17-year period of the patent monopoly. Requests for technical information about an item indicate that the item is part of the AIETA process, although the extent of adoption cannot be determined directly for competitive and proprietary reasons.

Examples. Titanium metal, numerical control, synthetic rubber, highway grooving, and refrigerator insulation exemplify technologies influenced by the patent system which found their way into innovation. In the successful cases, technical information was only one of the factors which created opportunity for innovation. Government support by other agencies was the key to success of the first three examples. Highway grooving has not yet been universally adopted in spite of support by government agencies. Refrigerator insulation was rejected by its own developer, General Electric, because its use entailed a greater risk than the GE management apparently wanted to take. The metric system, adopted by several industries and most sciences, remains rejected by the average citizen. Social resistance to date has overcome logic and simplicity. Attempts at reduction of automobile accidents have met with combined economic and social resistance. No agency has assumed responsibility for the total problem.

Patent Office. The relative stagnation of the number of annual patents through 1970 may be contrasted with increases in other forms of technical literature. Innovation apparently continues despite the patent program. Technical report literature must considerably augment the patent system, particularly for innovation in government agencies and large corporations. The EDA program for technical assistance focused on business, planning, and management techniques rather than on new technology. It affects only a few communities in spite of high expenditures. Commerce does not stress technology developed from Federal programs versus that developed in commercial programs or by individuals nor do other Federal agencies stress patents. Federal agency patent files are in fact smaller than those of several big corporations. As NTIS does not evaluate nonpatent information in Federal reports, entrepreneurs use it cautiously to avoid infringement.

Control and program review. Because of limited Commerce support for innovating, as defined for this study, little program review occurs. CTAB and its panels make recommendations which only the economy or government at large can carry out. Internally, Commerce offices control and review their work with limited resources and support.

Integrating

No commerce programs focus primarily on continuing adoption of **new** technology. Statistical services of the Census Bureau and Patent Office may indicate to potential adopters needs or opportunities for new technology. NBS basic standards may support integration, particularly when these standards become regulations. Two programs deal with undesirable effects of past integration. The $479 million annual operating subsidy for the merchant marine offsets new technologies (and cheaper labor) used by foreign competitors. Economic development activities of EDA bolster those communities hurt by changing technology. Coal mining, woolen mill, and ghetto communities have received assistance. Since its inception, EDA has spent $1.5 billion in assistance for loans, technical assistance, planning grants, job training, and public works. In the long run this supports integration of technology, yet EDA would be satisfied if any job-creating enterprise moved in, even with obsolescent technology.

Commerce in the total process

The only activity in the Department of Commerce which can be called a primary technology diffusion subprocess is informing. Though logically the agency to support technology diffusion to business and industry, Commerce's activities have been specialized to specific advisory, regulatory, and administrative services. Inventive work done in applied research and development is to meet agency needs for better processing. Innovating and integrating have been indirectly supported in information services. With about $100 million annual funding in applied research and development in government facilities by civil service employees, Commerce improves its support for technology generation and diffusion going on elsewhere. The outputs are technical standards and more timely technical information in patents and reports.

Through NTIS, Patent Office, and the National Bureau of Standards, Commerce distributes technical information on most unclassified U. S. development. The patent system, only partially accounted for in national funding studies, remains strong and useful though stabilized. The store of unused and expired patents is the largest known of available and disclosed new technology. NTIS effort to make Federal reports available to the public has been widely approved. Though neither of these major informing services is funded to the level of other commerce agencies, they do couple potential users to annually available new technology in 45,000 R&D reports and 70,000 patents.

Precluded by law from advocating specific patents, and extending this concept to Federal reports, Commerce mainly provides the information input into the innovating subprocess. The Bureau of the Census and other agencies provide technical services and statistical information which aid adopters during evaluation. Once information is in hand, private enterprise adoption units negotiate privately for rights to exploit proprietary information.

The total impact of Commerce on the integrating subprocess may be proportional to its $1.5 billion annual funding when the national GNP is $1000 billion. The merchant marine receives an operating subsidy which does not necessarily advance its adjustment. EDA does concern itself with adjustment problems and has created a few thousand new jobs, but they have affected the economy little. Commerce integrating activities are marginal and have received minimal support.

De Facto Procedures. Commerce has been the support stronghold of private enterprise technology diffusion procedures and has changed more slowly than other Federal agencies reviewed. The patent system has been static compared to the actively growing technical report literature. Only with establishment of NTIS did Commerce get into the main flow of this current literature. The lower funding indicates that

Commerce administrators have not fared well in the annual scramble for funds, although Commerce has tried experimental programs such as EDA. The EDA program on public works assistance aims to offset reluctance of industry to establish new plants in underdeveloped communities by building prerequisite public works.[10] During FY 1967 EDA concluded that neediest areas benefited least from national growth but that marginally successful areas improve without EDA assistance. EDA began a "worst first" funding policy to aid areas lagging farthest behind national growth.[12]

National Technology Goals. Commerce, in the most general sense, promotes progress of science and the useful arts, distributes technical information to potential users, and promotes free enterprise. Its functions related to technology stem directly from the Constitution, and department philosophy has been to let business and industry alone. In a seemingly simple thing such as establishing a standard system of weights and measures, the Department has faltered; and the metric system, long since adopted legally, is not in everyday use. The patent system still gets new technology disclosed and helps new businesses start. Yet, year after year, the same states and areas lead in patent applications, causing concentration of new technology, primarily in areas where the markets are already developed for new technology. Problems the patent system creates in monopoly, concentration, and litigation are condemned more loudly than its real contributions. NBS, in its standardization programs, NTIS in its information dissemination, do advance "useful arts and sciences." At a fairly low and indirect level, Commerce encourages innovation and integration by providing business and census data and services. It tries to offset disadvantages of technical advances which bypass regions and communities in its EDA activities of job training, assistance, and public works. Overall, Commerce has developed into a service organization, reacting rather than guiding, and not directly focused on specific national goals.

Complacent and conventional, Commerce has lost its former importance to more aggressive Federal agencies in closer contact to business and industry needs and desires. In terms of the total process of technology diffusion, Commerce activities are not sufficient to assure diffusion, and technology may indeed diffuse into the U. S. general economy with little contact with Commerce activities.

III. NASA TECHNOLOGY DIFFUSION ACTIVITIES

NASA's generation of new technology, accomplished both through government laboratories and civilian contract centers, has been highly visible and has had good public support. Established by the National Aeronautics and Space Administration Act of 1958, NASA has missions of exploring space; developing facilities, materials, vehicles, and techniques for space technology; and disseminating resulting information. Space is explored for national prestige and to benefit mankind, and NASA was specifically given commercial use technology diffusion responsibilities in its original charter.

NASA's extensive program for several years directly employed over 30,000 people, had a $5 billion budget, and supported up to 400,000 wage earners. In FY 1971 it had 29,500 employees and expended $3.3 billion. In this program, space science applied numerous classical disciplines and techniques to solve important space problems. NASA is organized around programs shown in Figure 28.

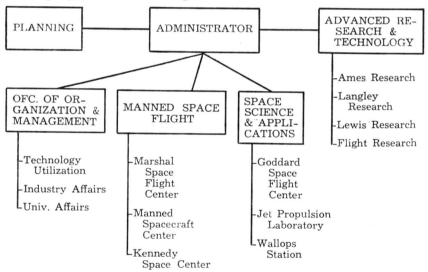

Figure 28.   NASA offices of interest.

Inventing

NASA intermediate missions and requirements are developed and justified under procedures very similar to DOD program management and will not be detailed. Resources and facilities always limit NASA missions, and much NASA support has been for R&D plant for future missions. Within a mission, NASA identification of needs varies with national prestige and public visibility. Priorities of a program's timing and execution are determined by pressures on administrators at the time of planning.

NASA funding grew by leaps and bounds, and it has been cut back almost as abruptly. Its status as a large spender, next to DOD in applied research and in development, is shown in Appendices B-2 through B-7. NASA's proportion of total R&D in Federal government increased from six percent in 1960 to thirty-two percent in 1966 while government dramatically emphasized space exploration. By 1971 it had dropped to twenty-two percent. NASA's applied research, the second largest of any Federal agency, from 1961 until 1971, is shown in Appendix B-5 to concentrate in the physical sciences and engineering. The physical sciences emphasized were earth and atmospheric, and engineering was in aeronautical, astronautical, and electrical fields, as shown in Appendix B-6. NASA resource inputs clearly concentrate in those fields supporting the main NASA mission.

NASA captivated many of the keenest engineers and technologists in the country. Employing a technical manager core, NASA depends on contractors for its inventing, as shown in Appendices B-4 and B-7. Though NASA was intended to furnish outputs of its efforts to the general economy, this mission has little influence on overall NASA planning. Less than one percent of its funds goes towards commercial technology diffusion. Every facet of science and technology which can satisfy NASA needs has been sought, making the NASA program a great enterprise in transferring and adapting technology to aerospace uses rather than the reverse.

Project offices handle the main missions, putting together equipment and procedures to explore and exploit space. New technology also differs from other agencies in that only a few copies of a particular project vehicle are made. High quality, individually engineered products are the rule. Sequential testing and parallel or backup systems assure success. More than in any other agency, technologists are apt to carry through from idea to application. Technologists thus take more personal interest in use of their ideas.

NASA procedures and project management activities are published in its project management manuals, and identification of new items of technology is important. NASA paid 94 percent of its procurement dollars to private industry in FY 1967 and FY 1968. Nearly 30 percent of these procurement dollars was in non-competitive bids, 3 percent went through formal advertising, and 67 percent was through competitive negotiation. Over 80 percent of bids to business firms were for experimental, development, or research work, essentially inventive.[12] Because of the near non-use of traditional competitive bidding, NASA administrators have considered that new technology should accrue to the government. Project offices and contractors scan available technology, develop and evaluate new approaches, select the most practicable approach, build and test, and prepare one or a few copies for use.

NASA programs produce operating systems, new products, technical literature, and identification of new items of technology. Over 500,000 technical reports are now on hand and 70,000 accrue yearly. The programs also produce people who are trained to apply new technologies. No agency has such an aggressive program for identifying new technology, and this identification program is the main support for NASA's commercial use mission. NASA systems synthesize mostly old, but some new, technology.

Benefits from NASA technology development were described in 1972 for the Committee on Science and Astronautics of the U. S. House of Representatives to include benefits to all mankind in: (1) COMSAT — international communications; (2) weather forecasting; (3) advances in technology; (4) use of computers in management; (5) ERTS — analysis of earth resources and environment; (6) advances in medical instrumentation; (7) and benefits to the home and food processing industries.[13]

In a study sponsored by NASA, two investigators identified 25 management methods which they credited to aerospace, including systems analysis, cost/effectiveness, decision theory, heuristics, modeling, forecasting, systems engineering, reliability and maintainability analyses, value engineering, matrix management, FFRDC's, procurement and evaluation systems, incentive contracting, management information systems, and PERT/LOB.[14] Though observers may agree these methods have been used by NASA, they might argue that NASA used only what was available from other sources.

Examples. The communications satellite, integrated circuits (Appendix F-17), and highway grooving (Appendix F-18), or use of microfiche (Appendix F-19) respectively point up three levels of NASA outputs: (1) a complete product application; (2) an advance in the technical state of the art; and, (3) the development of useful individual items or techniques. Both NASA and DOD fostered integrated circuits because both required smaller, lighter, and more reliable electronic components. After 1958-1959 breakthroughs in applied research, NASA and DOD assisted financially through development contracts, distributed technical information, and furnished the market for the new products.

NASA inherited from its predecessor aeronautics organization the unsatisfied need to reduce runway skidding. NASA developed a better understanding of the problem through applied research, then found a state of the art solution which commercial patented equipment could apply. NASA also used existing information science and technology for microfiche. NASA promoted standardization of this technique, and when the Educational Research Information Center (ERIC) was formed, it transferred laterally from NASA the entire set of microfiche techniques.

Suitability. NASA missions and requirements have been met successfully, but the 70,000 annual additions to NASA technical files interest primarily those applying technology to aerospace. The Patent Office annually expends about $56 million to convert about 70,000 inventions from the general public into a legal right to exploit them. Compared to this expenditure, the $3.3 billion NASA annual program publishes about 1,000 potential commercial applications as technical briefs and other descriptions of new technical items. NASA normally takes title to patents, but has no mechanism for supporting commercial adoption of the patents it accrues.

A telling example of commercial applicability and emphasis in the NASA program is that of aeronautics. Aeronautics, according to Congressional committees, was in 1968 becoming a neglected field of Federal interest. Accident rates per 100,000 passenger miles and fatalities per 100,000 departures remained on a constant level.[15] NASA shared responsibility in this area with the Department of Transportation

(FAA) and the Department of Defense. New space technologies have simply not trickled through to this in-house activity of NASA, even though aeronautics was grouped with space because of their close relationships. With round figure budgets of $5 billion, NASA carried aeronautics efforts of $82 million in FY 1964 and $168 million in FY 1966, less than 4 percent of its budget.[16] In FY 1971, the expenditures were up to $210 million.

NASA's R&D program, like DOD, is concentrated geographically. In 1963, with 23.1 percent of all Federal R&D, the five states receiving the preponderant shares were California (46.8%), Missouri (7.1%), Alabama (6.2%), Louisiana (6.0%), and Texas (5.8%). In 1964 with 30.2 percent of Federal R&D, the same five states remained on top.[17] From July to December 1969, the top five companies in NASA contract awards were North American Rockwell Corporation, Downey, CA, $277 million; Grumman Aircraft Engineering Corporation, Bethpage, NY, $176 million; Boeing Company, New Orleans, LA, $97 million; McDonnell Douglas Corporation, Santa Monica, CA, $108 million; and General Electric Company, Huntsville, AL, $65 million. The top four had not changed since 1966.[18] These were also high in DOD contracts.

Control. NASA controls its applied research and development through project experts who monitor contractual efforts, using the management methods listed above. Since organization is "projectized," each organization element is well aware of its particular objectives; and NASA's projectized accounting system helps fix financial responsibility. The expense of control has been criticized; the results obtained, however, have been generally suitable for mission products. Non-mission work can best be described as a "level of effort."

The Office of Planning reviews the totality of NASA work. This office must justify to the Executive Branch, to Congress, and to the public the mission results obtained versus the previously stated objectives. In Congress, powerful committees review the space program at least annually and compare its benefits against benefits from other programs. The National Aeronautics and Space Council of the Office of the President, chaired by the Vice President, provides overall review for aeronautics and space activities.

Informing

Inputs follow NASA's charter, which clearly entails information transfer; and by acquiring worldwide information, processing it by modern techniques, publishing and reproducing it in a variety of channels and forms, assisting in retrieval of information needed for on-going work, controlling critical aerospace data, and coordinating agency library services, NASA performs this mission.   Information is also transferred through contracting and training. The 1967 NASA Address List included 36 offices and centers, 1,300 NASA contractors and grantees, 400 government agencies, 700 non-NASA government contractors, 300 foreign organizations, and 250 aerospace affiliated private and public enterprises.[19]   In addition to these regular customers, several thousand people requested reports on particulars of NASA technology.   Potential clients may number several times those served.

The technology generating offices develop and use new information. NASA's first effort developed an efficient internal distribution of information for the 70,000 documents received or developed annually. As technology became available with non-mission applications, the information store became the backup for technology diffusion into the general economy.

The Office for Industry Affairs and Technology Utilization handles the internal disseminating program through its Scientific and Technical Information Division and the external program through the Technology Utilization Division.   The total program has resource inputs of $27 million annually, about 7 percent of the Federal total for information science.   Of this total, about $22 million goes to mission information (internal use) and about $5 million is for external or non-mission uses, as shown in Appendix D-4.   NASA has concentrated on bibliographic and reference services, publication and distribution; but Appendix D-5 shows it has also tried, more than most agencies, audio and visual means, symposia, translations, and information centers.   The Technology Utilization FY 1967 inputs were $1.265 million for identification, $0.65 million for evaluation, $2.085 million for dissemination, and $1 million for analysis.   NASA's training funds have supported advanced degree training in universities as well as training in specialized technologies such as soldering for increased reliability.   The training and research funds represent nearly direct transfer of technology internally.

The Scientific and Technical Information Division in 1969 serviced primarily aerospace audiences: contractors (22%); NASA offices (38%); academic institutions (21%); other government agencies (12%); and foreigners (7%). Its two basic output journals abstract and index through industry contract. The American Institute of Aeronautics and Astronautics abstracted and indexed worldwide published literature on aerospace subjects. About 4000 subscribed to its monthly journal, **International Aerospace Abstracts (IAA)**. The monthly journal, **Scientific and Technical Aerospace Reports (STAR)**, prepared by Documentation, Inc., abstracted and indexed world aerospace report literature and went to about 10,000 customers. NASA collected 200,000 pre-1962 documents under conventional library control, and over 300,000 post-1962 documents under computer control. The collection grows yearly by about 70,000 documents.

The documentation center searches, reproduces, and distributes literature. About 2,000 new searches begin annually and results of previous searches remain available. In reproduction and distribution, microfiche and hard copy are distributed. About 8 million microfiches are produced annually. The other major activity of the Office of Scientific and Technical Information is publication of NASA internal records (technical notes, reports, and memoranda, contractor reports and technical translations) and special publications. In one period, 118 titles resulted in a total print run of over 500,000 copies. NASA leaves master computer tape index copies at each NASA center, at key contractors, with NTIS, with the six Regional Dissemination Centers for technology diffusion, and elsewhere.

The Technology Utilization Division. All the information handling activity backs up efforts for non-mission technology diffusion, or transfer of NASA technologies to commercial aerospace and non-aerospace industries. The Technology Utilization Division couples NASA inventing and commercial innovating. Technology Utilization Officers at major NASA Program Offices identify new technology. In addition, all contractors must report new technology derived from contracted work. About 4,000 new items appear annually, of which 1,000 are finally published as NASA Technical Briefs. Three out of four of these fall in mechanical, electrical, or electronic fields.

Processing for the Regional Research Application or Dissemination Centers goes beyond this. These six centers at the University of Indiana, the University of Connecticut, the North Carolina Science and Technology Research Center, the University of New Mexico, the University of Southern California, and the University of Pittsburgh hold the entire NASA file of technical information in addition to the potential commercial products. They can thus give retrospective search, current awareness, and advocacy for adoption to companies which purchase their services. A third form of processing occurs on an even smaller scale through three biomedical teams which identify problems in biomedicine that may have been solved in NASA work. NASA performs a fourth unique service in its sales of computer programs to assist companies or agencies with computers at fractional cost. The Technology Utilization Division joins (1) AEC in identification and evaluation of new technology; (2) Government Printing Office and NTIS for publication and dissemination; (3) with SBA in providing technology for the latter to support in its innovating program.

Scientific and Technical Information Division outputs consist of abstracts, distribution of literature and microfiche, and its addition to the store of NASA's technical information. Technology Utilization Division products are Technical Briefs, Technology Utilization Reports, Technology Surveys, computer programs, and special services to selected groups.

During Calendar Year 1967, 678 Technical Briefs and 297 other compilations of new technology were issued. During the same period there were 14,742 queries from industry on the program. NTIS sold 270,000 Technical Briefs. Compilations (all forms) had cumulatively sold over 90,000 from NTIS and the Government Printing Office by December 31, 1967. 1,068 computer programs and 8,600 sets of program documentation were sold. 7,500 organizations were on the mailing list for computer program availability. Regional Dissemination Centers in 1967 had about 200 subscribers, but none had become self-sustaining. The three biomedical teams identified 240 areas for study.[20]

NASA operations trained many people, and major shifts within or from NASA programs moved these trained people from one job to another. The **Los Angeles Times** estimated in March 1969, that 200,000 people had transferred from space work between 1966 and 1969.[21] James E. Webb, when retiring in September 1968 as administrator, stated that peak employment reached 420,000 people but that it would be reduced to 200,000 by July 1, 1969.[22] Some of the people transferred their NASA-developed skills and technical know-how to other work, while others were unable to do so.

Examples. Integrated circuit information was transferred largely through conferences, contract specifications, and company exchanging of knowledgeable people. Both NASA and DOD supported information dissemination through agency information handling systems. Lucrative contracts in a new technology proffered adequate bait to stimulate industry; hence no other boosts for interest and participation were required.

NASA has widely publicized the effectiveness of highway grooving in decreasing accidents, but with few adoptions. The Bureau of Public Roads showed negligible interest until mid-1968. Only one state, California, had adopted the procedure. Yet NASA has held and promoted conferences and demonstrations, developed films and publications, and generally extolled the grooving procedure.

Suitability. Space successes indicate the effectiveness of NASA's internal transferring of technical information. In terms of Sayer's model, NASA has a centralized clearinghouse for acquisition and a projectized organization for dissemination internally. In spite of its experimental forms, NASA has not been successful in external dissemination. The work of the Technology Utilization Division is at least good public relations, and some of its activities appear nominally successful. The sale of special Technology Utilization outputs of compilations (packed-down technology) indicates continued interest and success for that program. With $5 million annual support and the information character of NASA's commercial mission, the program may be considered successful.

Industrial interest in Technology Utilization is distributed as shown in Appendix E-1. Areas interested in Tech Briefs are already developed industrially with higher populations and incomes. These same states receive more patents and rank high in R&D funds received. In other words, if industrial interest reflects potential application, NASA reinforces present concentrations of wealth and human resources.

In 1967 Richard Hayes studied a small sample of 67 electronic com-

panies to determine how they used NASA Regional Research Application Centers. Seventy percent of the firms knew about the centers
but only 27 percent used their services and believed them useful to
their firms. Most companies (61%) still preferred company R&D
for new ideas. Government sponsored technology ranked a poor third
(10%) after commercial customers (15%) as new ideas sources.[23]

The technical brief program of NASA is a shotgun approach which
appears successful in terms of the 1967 and 1968 reorders. Limited
access to the developer was added to this program to encourage coupling: person to person, inventor to innovator. NASA packs down
technical information into textbooks or state-of-the-art reports re-
sembling DOD manuals on new technology not yet in textbooks or
schoolwork.

Control and program review. NASA informing programs focus
primarily on aerospace needs and secondarily on needs of other users.
Aerospace users, contractors, and grantees feed back the most ex-
plicit information. The total program is reviewed by the Office of
Planning in terms of its contributions to missions and goals. Congressional groups have considered the work of the Technology Utilization Division and have been impressed by the availability of information on technical items of possible commercial use.
Internal Innovating

NASA innovating activities, like those of DOD, are both internal
and external, but with significant differences. The internal program
is much smaller, for NASA has only 29,500 civilian employees, while
DOD has 1,000,000 civilians and about 2.7 million uniformed members.[24] The space mission innovating program for NASA broadly resembles DOD defense innovating in defense industry. They work
with the same industries; and NASA, in fact, has borrowed Air Force
officers and civilians experienced in managing complex programs. The
same firms received most funds for both agencies. Because of these
similarities to DOD, NASA internal innovation procedures will not be
discussed in the same detail.

External Innovating

One significant difference between NASA and DOD is the handling
of patents. NASA generally takes title while DOD does not. NASA
directly advocates commercial innovation, whereas DOD normally does

not; and NASA's direct advocacy is in consonance with NASA's having patent title. Like DOD, NASA, sponsoring innovation in its supporting industry, develops performance specifications and furnishes a market for products which meet these goals. In two typical activities, weather and communications, NASA contributes to the general economy in the same way DOD contributes to food processing and AEC contributes to radioisotopes.

Unlike DOD, NASA markets new technology with a special organization. The group, the Technology Utilization Division, goes beyond information handling into advocating innovation. The Regional Research Application Centers and the Special Medical Teams try to get NASA technology adopted, and the medical teams do some creative adaptation. The missions of Technology Utilization are (1) to get maximum return on public investment in aerospace R&D by finding secondary uses for it, (2) to shorten the time gap between inventing and innovating, (3) to move new knowledge across disciplinary, regional, industrial, and market lines, and (4) to learn how to diffuse technology efficiently and effectively.[25] The $5 million annual funding of the Division has allowed it to build six contractor-operated Regional Research Application Centers which advocate change. They educate industrial management subscribers in technologies which NASA has developed or found advantageous. They help industry define its problems, search the NASA data bank for solutions to problems, and inform industry of new NASA developments. The Centers carry technology to industry as well as the reverse, carrying problems to NASA. Each Regional Center has the most significant NASA collection. As an added attraction, the Regional Centers in 1968 added index tapes of Defense Documentation Center holdings.[26] Companies subscribe to Center services at fees according to the services rendered. Of 131 companies subscribing in 1965, 89 repeated their subscriptions, 22 at higher amounts of service. The Western Research Application Center (WESRAC) organized as a non-profit, and operating at University of Southern California in Los Angeles, in 1971 offered to its customers input to nearly all Federal library sources and a number of others. Most used were Chemical Abstracts, DOD Data Bank, Computer Program Abstracts, ERIC, Engineering Index, Government Reports Abstracts, Index Medicus, NASA Data, Nuclear Science Abstracts, and U. S. Government R&D Reports.[27]

In 1971 NASA began work on a large project to transfer its technologies to city problems. Working with the International City Management Association in a Technology Applications Project, NASA proposed to tackle 15 problems:

Police command and control.
Disposal of toxic and flammable materials.
Powerline fault detection.
High voltage power transmission systems offering improvements beyond present overhead techniques.
Electronic traffic counters.
Emergency remote hospital patient monitors.
Non-emergency patient monitoring.
Communications for firemen.
Fireman's life support system.
New fire hoses and couplings.
Automatic fire hose pressure regulator.
Protective clothing for firemen.
Police body armor.
Underground pipe detection.
Pavement stripping materials.[28]

These problems have technical content which is of the type NASA has solved routinely in its space work.

The Medical Specialist Teams identify barriers to research in a medical discipline, such as bioinstrumentation, and then search the NASA store for possible solutions. If developments are available, they are forwarded to research groups for adaptation, clinical testing, and professional approval. This approach of carrying problems to NASA is again the reverse of most programs of carrying technology to industry.

Results of NASA effort to diffuse technology are difficult to determine. Inputs are relatively easy to measure in dollars, number of people, and number of technical documents disseminated. Desired outputs are adopted products or systems. By 1968 NASA had offered 8,000 technical packages or items of technology to the general economy for adoption. Of these, only 180 technical briefs and 57 technical packages were known to have been innovated by at least one firm. This may be a conservative view of the NASA effort. An optimistic view is that all 8,000 will, at some time in the future, be innovated, but even 8,000 items is not an impressive number. The indirect outputs such as the transfer of 200,000 people, each trained in some aspect of space technology, to other work after the aerospace peak may be far more significant than NASA's direct efforts to diffuse technology. Adoption of whole systems such as weather and communications satellites also integrates the technologies which go with them. In time these new technologies will diffuse into other areas without special effort. Users will in time see how they apply to other work. Ogburn noted that "the more there is to invent with, the greater will be the number of inventions."[29]

Examples. Integrated circuitry, an electronic state of the art transfer from NASA and DOD into the civilian economy, made computers and control systems economical and deeply significant to society. Neither DOD nor NASA considered this development a planned "technology transfer" program. The Office of Education use of microfiche followed NASA's example and experience. It was a horizontal transfer from one Federal agency to another within the information science discipline. The Office of Education further transferred microfiche technology horizontally when it changed its reproducer to National Cash Register Company in 1967. National Cash, in 1968, expanded its microfiche operation and won a commercial contract to put Merrill, Lynch, Pierce, Fenner, and Smith (stock brokers) research files on microfiche.[30] Originally a government agency standardized item, microfiche has now been innovated in a wholly commercial activity. NASA set the events in motion but did not plan them. The single item technical briefs, though not failures, are too small to affect the economy measurably. Even the safety grooving improvements to highways and runways have had limited acceptance. During 1968 only fifteen runways were grooved.[31]

Adoption of 8,000 potentially useful items and packages of technology identified by NASA for the general economy may be compared with over 500,000 patents granted for use in the general economy during the same decade. The NASA effort does show that adoption can be stimulated in industry by direct government advocacy. Rejects may indicate the failure of most NASA technology to meet economic criteria. The information inputs gaining the most adoption were 57 compilations (packed down processes or procedures), which averaged over 1,500 sales each.

The graduation from Technical Briefs (shotgun dissemination) to Technology Utilization Surveys and Reports (packed-down technology) to Regional Research Application Centers (where innovation is advocated) to teams of secondary inventors (who match and adapt space technology creatively to specific medical problems) is a continuing series of experiments to find the most effective way to diffuse technology by a non-trusted, non-integrated agency. Technology Utilization Reports and Surveys, which sell well, are close enough to textbook format that teachers can use them for technical training.

In 1968 Samuel I. Doctors made a searching non-NASA evaluation of the Regional Research Application Centers, then called Dissemination Centers. He found that the idea for the centers was plausible but that they had serious problems.

> . . . Finally, the RDC's, while in theory excellent linking mechanisms for transferring aerospace technology to the public sector, have not been measurably successful in transferring it to the industrial-commercial sector and have been kept from much activity outside this area. Since RDC's have been primarily limited to library functions, entrepreneurial activity and market assistance to client firms have been severely limited.[32]

Doctors found that the locations of the centers were placed to assist depressed areas, reduce R&D fund concentration, placate Congressmen, and give NASA influence over the center operation. None of these reasons supports traditional technology diffusion, which would more likely occur in highly technical areas. In fact, the locations recognized that the traditional procedures were adequate in areas of R&D concentration.[33] Doctors also found that the centers had problems with NASA in procedures and contracting. The greatest direct deficiency of the centers was, Doctors concluded, the lack of champions at the centers to push the available technologies.[34]

Control and program review. NASA has studied its successful transfer to commercial use of bioinstrumentation systems. NASA techniques transferred were: (1) determining information requirements and equipment specifications, (2) sensing and signal transmission, (3) remote monitoring and data processing, (4) manufacturing, and (5) making field measurements. These applications revealed that: (1) some NASA items or techniques transfer directly, (2) some NASA items suggest modifications for other uses or give an indirect or secondary transfer, and (3) some NASA items merely infuse understanding and sensitivity to technical opportunities. The last mode frequently crosses disciplines as from medicine to engineering.[35] NASA has also contracted with Denver Research Institute to provide continuing data on technology use by commercial and non-NASA enterprises. This is to be a continuing program review by an external organization.[36]

Integrating

NASA integrates new technology into aerospace industries by furnishing a market. This market is determined by missions approved for NASA and the numbers of needed items. Package integration of such systems as weather, communications, geodesy, and navigation satellites contribute to the general economy. The way NASA supports integrating technology into the general economy is through transfers from the aerospace sector to other economic sectors. To former Administrator James Webb NASA advances technology:

> . . . by going outside Government to build the technological muscle in industry and the scientific community while developing in-house competence to plan programs, justify them to Congress, and monitor them effectively. We have seeded scientific inventiveness in the universities to the extent of over half a billion dollars; we have added some $3 billion to an original capital base of $1 billion, for a total of $4 billion of capital plant.[37]

NASA in the Total Process

Now fifteen years old, NASA until recently enjoyed popular support and its efforts have contributed to many strategic and social needs. In terms of the total process model (Chapter II), NASA had advanced mankind through several successive levels of steps. Internally and in the aerospace industry, NASA generates new aerospace technologies, disseminates information about them, supports their adoption in aerospace work, and requires their integration or continued use. These activities are separately identifiable, with feedback within each grouping, to give visibility to NASA's program to the public as well as its administrators.

NASA's external program is limited by what NASA can do in applied research and development and information dissemination to support the general economy. NASA's innovating is a secondary program of advocacy. In integrating, NASA affects the general economy mainly through the size of its effort, its training fallout, and the economy's use of whole space systems.

Evaluation. Through FY 1971, NASA's $41 billion in Federal funds, mostly in applied research and development, had contributed to established aerospace objectives, primarily through electronics, propulsion, and control systems. Complete space systems for communications, weather observing, navigation, and geodesy have been developed and put into service for the general economy. In addition to the use of whole systems, the general economy has gained from advances in the technical state of the art, from the new management procedures for vast projects, and from specific technology items. NASA favors government patents for its contractual work, but it licenses freely. About one thousand items each year have been proposed by NASA for transfer to commercial use; but this number, however significant to NASA, has had limited significance to the U.S. economy for a decade and $3 billion annual input. The space fallout from specific technology items has been overrated, compared to real gains in whole systems and state of art advances. The disadvantage of NASA's inventive work is its concentrations of resources into narrow disciplines and technologies, reinforcing concentrations previously started by DOD.

With a statutory mission to inform, NASA uses about $27 million yearly for scientific and technical information. These funds are used internally, but some of the effects are external. About eight thousand reports go yearly to NTIS, one thousand technical briefs are issued, several hundred patents are issued, one thousand computer programs are sold, and seventy thousand aerospace documents are brought under control for future users. NASA has evolved one of the most modern document handling activities in the U. S., but it does not yet couple effectively with users in the general economy. The movements of trained people and contractors from NASA to other programs transfer far more technical know-how than has been quantified. From the viewpoint of the total process model (Figure 9, Chapter II) NASA couples plateaus of technical effort through training fallout. It also, through its formal recording of technology, establishes data bases for future generations.

The internal innovating effort is highly structured and conforms to project management procedures. The external effort is limited to advocacy of adoption and creative adaptation for special problem areas.

Where internally NASA can provide or support the market for innovating and integrating, externally NASA technology competes with other technology and with non-technology uses of resources. Some of the most successful adoptions of NASA's technology have occurred without direct NASA planning or advocacy. The advantages of whole systems like weather satellites, state of art advances like integrated circuits, and training in new technologies were so obvious that they were adopted as fast as they became available. Specific programs advocating technology use, funded at $5 million yearly, experimented with different approaches to potential adopters. These innovating activities had far more no-takers than successes or rejects. Items of space technology, taken alone, are not normally competitive with items designed for commercial use. NASA is not a "trusted agent" to most businesses. By seeking external analysis of these programs, NASA has sought to improve its record; yet the long term future of the programs remains in doubt.

NASA has integrated much new technology through furnishing a market for items of highest performance and reliability. Consideration of property rights has been secondary, with NASA usually gaining them. The multiplier effect has amplified results of NASA support for high quality products. NASA has supported integration through training many thousands of technicians, engineers, and scientists in new technologies. These people go on to non-space work using the same skills and techniques. NASA's annual funding of over $3 billion dollars uses labor and capital, precludes other national activities, and monopolizes scarce technologists. In 1969, at the moment of its greatest success, political support for NASA began to wane.

De Facto Procedures. NASA can be considered in toto as a validated special program to apply all applicable technology to space activities. Its ingredients have been clear and accepted goals, legislative and resource support, and continued attention to public relations. In order to achieve urgent goals, NASA has concentrated and institutionalized inventive work, bypassed the historic but slower education system, and spearheaded considerable development toward more progressive information handling. Though it gave lip service to patent conventions, it in fact bypassed patents in much space work. Some NASA special programs to transfer technology into the general economy have succeeded moderately while others, though highly publicized, have failed to become self-supporting.

National Goals. More rapidly than any other agency, NASA has advanced science and the useful arts, provided technical information to potential users, improved scientific and technical education, and contributed to goals of national prestige and conceived national power. It has had some effects on national health, through space medicine, but its effects on the physical environment are questionable because of its concentration of people and resources. Contracts awarded and information requested indicate that localities and industries already developed are most interested in NASA technology. Congress has deliberately placed some NASA installations in underdeveloped areas of Florida, Mississippi, Alabama, and Louisiana, yet this has not assured technical progress in these areas. The big NASA monies have gone to the same firms supported by DOD, concentrated into California, Massachusetts, and New York. Once it contracts in this way, NASA adds to the problems of pollution, attracting unemployed to ghettos in heavily populated areas, and contributing to unhealthy physical environments. Professor Raymond A. Bauer, Harvard Graduate School of Business Administration, has charged NASA with increasing minority groups' despair by demonstrating what the majority can do against the minority groups' perception of what the minority can do.[38]

NASA has provided direct employment for up to 425,000 people and continued in 1971 to employ over 100,000. If multiplier effects are considered, then several million people have gained in employment, have produced more, and have had more purchasing power than would have been the case if Federal expenditures had not included NASA funds. It has used and concentrated labor, capital, information, and entrepreneurship. NASA has in its policy statements supported free enterprise; indeed, new technology-based enterprises have thrived on NASA contracts and project subcontracts. In terms of the total process, NASA programs have been wanted and needed through several successive levels, but they are no longer competitive with other programs.

IV. AEC TECHNOLOGY DIFFUSION ACTIVITIES

Established by the Atomic Energy Acts of 1946 and 1954, AEC is intended to assure that the development, use, and control of nuclear

energy contributes optimally to general welfare as well as to common
defense and security, promotes world peace, increases the standard of
living, and strengthens free competition in private enterprise. In
discharging these responsibilities, AEC operates development and
production facilities, regulates use and handling of nuclear materials,
and disseminates scientific and technical information. Through its basic
charter, AEC generates nuclear and related technologies, disseminates
information about them, advocates their adoption and use, and regulates their integration into the economy. AEC directly employs about
7,400 people, but it contracts some 90,400.[39]

Contractual arrangements greatly interest students of technology
diffusion. By 1966, AEC had invested about $48 billion in plant,
equipment, and real estate, which cost about $2.7 billion yearly to
operate. In May 1970, the nuclear industry had 99,000 persons working
in government owned facilities, and 56,000 in those privately owned.[40]

Organization

Figure 29 shows AEC organization to be partly by project and
partly by function. Since the parent structure is a committee somewhat like a Board of Directors, a General Manager directs operations
and a Director supervises regulation. Major production facilities are
owned at Oak Ridge, TN, Richland, WA, Paducah, KY, Aiken, SC,
Fernald, OH, Burlington, IA, and Kansas City, KS. New technology
is generated and tested in the major national centers which are interdisciplinary in most of their work. In 1971 those with over $25 million
of work included:

>
Atomic Energy Laboratory, Ames, IA
Argonne National Laboratory, Chicago, IL
Bettis Atomic Power Laboratory, Pittsburgh, PA
Brookhaven National Laboratory, Upton, NY
Knolls Atomic Power Laboratory, Schenectady, NY
E. O. Lawrence Radiation Laboratory, Berkeley, CA
E. O. Lawrence Radiation Laboratory Extension at Livermore, CA
Los Alamos Scientific Laboratory Extension at Livermore, CA
Mound Laboratory, Miamisburg, OH
National Accelerator Laboratory, Batavia, IL
Oak Ridge National Laboratory, Oak Ridge, TN
Princeton Plasma Physics Laboratory, Princeton, NJ
Research Laboratory, University of Rochester, Rochester, NY
Sandia Laboratory, Albuquerque, NM
Savannah River Laboratory, Aiken, SC

National Reactor Testing Station, Idaho Falls, ID
Nevada Test Site, Las Vegas, NV[42]

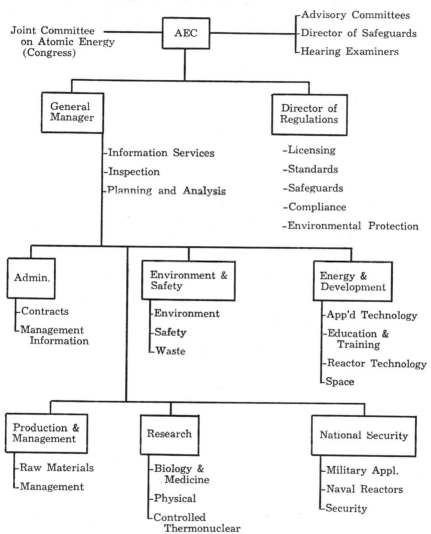

Figure 29. AEC offices of interest.[41]

Inventing

Within AEC's mission, a network of advisory groups identifies
specific needs which are developed into **plans and programs** requiring

substantial resources. In FY 1971, AEC ranked fourth among Federal
agencies in expenditures for applied research and development, with
a total of $1,026 million as outlined in Appendices B-2 and B-3. AEC,
like DOD, develops some classified products. Like NASA, AEC
shares its developments with the general economy. Like the Department of Agriculture, AEC supports selected economic sectors with
technology useful to these sectors. The interdisciplinary **facilities**
show the range and diversity of AEC work. Appendices B-4 through
B-6 show that AEC's applied research efforts are in physical sciences
of nuclear structure, chemistry, physics and chemical and metallurgical
engineering. It dominates only in its study of nuclear structure. Development funds focus toward weapons and nuclear reactors, but there
are continuing expenditures for isotopes and other applications.

Since World War II, AEC laboratories have excelled in generating
new technology, new processes, and improved procedures. Work
follows the conceptual inventing model. The scientists and engineers
screen, select, design, develop, test and produce items for AEC missions. Contractors do the processing rather than civil service technologists. Further, contractors know that the government will usually
patent their inventions. Interdisciplinary capabilities of the laboratories allow investigation of any problem from many aspects.

AEC produces new nuclear devices, nuclear material applications,
new nuclear materials, non-nuclear technology, and trained people.
Nuclear technologies are partly for the general economy (commercial
nuclear power and radioisotope industries) and partly for application
by AEC or by an AEC customer such as DOD. Non-nuclear technologies are those developments, mostly engineering, which help AEC
process difficult-to-handle and dangerous nuclear materials. Trained
people in AEC are well accounted for because Industrial Cooperation
Programs have specific needs for developers in the informing and
innovating programs, discussed subsequently. Patents are outputs in
AEC which go to the government if nuclear or nuclear associated, but
they may go to industry contractors in other cases. At the end of FY
1971, AEC held 4,525 U.S. and 3,490 foreign patents. These domestic
patents were available to the public for licensing. During the year
AEC added 319 U.S. and 384 foreign patents to its portfolio.[43]

Examples. AEC has developed competitive commercial power
nuclear reactors, and with the Navy has built 118 nuclear powered

submarines and 11 surface ships, but it has not yet produced an economically competitive merchant ship. Economic success was not the only criterion for the merchant ship, for the U.S. Savannah supported national prestige better than it moved men and materials (Appendices F-20 and F-22). AEC has successfully developed radio-isotopes for use in science, medicine, and industry. (Appendix F-21). In each of these cases, need was established and development was straightforward. The examples indicate that the conceptual model for inventing fairly represents the AEC generating of nuclear technology. Given a clear and reasonable objective, AEC facilities and contractor resources can generate required technology. Current projects include breeder reactors for commercial power by 1980, non-nuclear technology, and commercial applications for nuclear explosives.

Suitability. In the main, AEC has fared well in generating nuclear technology and contributes to government, nuclear industry, and the general economy. Favorable feedback has been steadier than for other agencies with large funding. AEC interdisciplinary national laboratories have developed reputations for competence and efficiency. The geographic origin of AEC inventive work reflects location of its facilities. In 1963, with 8.8 percent of all Federal R&D, the top five states were California (21%), New Mexico (18%), Nevada (11.4%), New York (9.3%), and Pennsylvania 8.8%).[44]

Control. Partly because of safety requirements, AEC has built into its organization control offices and checkpoint procedures. Proposals and developments are carefully screened for undesirable side effects. The international treaty limitations on nuclear testing cause more theoretical study and simulation than would otherwise be done. Undersurface testing either validates technology or indicates the need for new approaches. The thoroughness of nuclear testing has affected other AEC product testing. The General Manager has an Office for Environment and Safety. The Director of Regulation handles public innovation and integration of nuclear materials, but he receives specifications from the developing and testing divisions of the General Manager. AEC control over nuclear technology has been praised, but the costliness of AEC procedures makes them impractical to other government agencies.

Program Review. Customer needs partly determine AEC direction. For FY 1970, for example, increased AEC appropriations were earmarked for ABM nuclear weapons. AEC direction also depends on technical opportunities which emerge in development or which advisory committees propose. When changes in direction are evaluated, they are analyzed internally by the Director for Planning and Analysis and by AEC divisions which would be affected. Influential citizens such as Edward Teller, Glen Seaborg, and H. G. Rickover have made proposals which have changed applied research and development emphasis. They exerted this influence because of the audience accorded them by the Joint Committee on Atomic Energy of Congress, which acts as a permanent external systems review committee on AEC activities. AEC also has review inputs from the nuclear industries with which it works through the Director of Safeguards and other contact offices.

Informing. New technical information from the laboratories flows into the AEC informing programs, which are partly internal and partly external, serving AEC, nuclear industries, and commercial users. The plan is to provide enough information to assure safe and efficient use of nuclear materials and to support continuing and future development. The Atomic Energy Act itself provides for ". . . a program for the dissemination of unclassified scientific and technical information and the control, dissemination, and declassification of Restricted Data, . . . so as to encourage scientific and industrial programs"[45] In 1969, twenty specialized information and data centers for nuclear science and technology served as major informing facilities. Forty-six states had AEC depositories for scientific and technical information. Developers are available through the informing program to assist in innovating activities. About $5 million can be identified as annual costs of technical information in AEC. Appendix D-5 shows the uses in publication and distribution, bibliographic and reference services, symposia, translation, and R&D in information science. In FY 1970, a typical year, 23,000 students were given some aid or support in nuclear education and training.[46]

AEC processing of information is not described in detail because it follows the conceptual model and is comparable to information processing discussed already for DOD. Two more effective forms of processing are its information and data centers and the industrial training and cooperation program. The specialized data and information centers collect, critically evaluate, and compile scientific and technical information in specific fields and disseminate it in packed down form in handbooks, data tables, critical state-of-art reviews, and summaries. Evaluation of the material helps determine the means of distribution. Under the Industrial Cooperation Program, established in 1954, potential users of nuclear technology meet its developers for person to person information transfer. This form of dissemination has been used particularly to support the innovation subprocess. Offices have been at Oak Ridge, Tennessee, Argonne, Illinois, and Sandia, New Mexico.

Between 1947 and 1967, AEC brought out 500,000 items of technical literature, published 100,000 unclassified research papers, and published 25,000 articles in journals. AEC has also cooperated with NASA and SBA in joint informing programs.[47] Patent disclosure files for nonnuclear technology are open to interested clients. Developers are available to potential users at these AEC installations. Other outputs include **Nuclear Science Abstracts,** patents, engineering materials (drawings, specifications, photographs, design criteria, etc.), educational materials, motion picture files and news releases. These come from the Office of Information Services. In 1968, AEC was depositing in 97 domestic and 88 foreign depository libraries at universities, colleges, and public libraries. Through interlibrary loans, AEC information can be obtained at most U. S. public libraries. AEC also publishes in trade journals, technical journals, seminars, and through advisory committees. In FY 1971, AEC declassified 500,000 documents.

Examples. Nuclear reactor commercial power and radioisotopes show how AEC transfers information to users. Commercial power transfer was enhanced through hiring of trained scientists and technicians in power companies. AEC training courses for industry also contributed. Radioisotope information was transferred through many channels while its use gradually developed after 1946. The Isotopes Information Center was established in 1963 at Oak Ridge to collect and publish world-wide information on production and uses of isotopes. In 1969 it published four magazine issues yearly plus special interest one-time publications.[48] In these two cases, information transfer was adequately supporting application as well as inventing. In the case of the N.S. Savannah example, operating cost information has been available as well as technical information. The unfavorable operating costs have offset favorable technical information for potential users.

The Savannah example illustrates the value of non-technical (operating cost) information to potential adopters.

Feedback. Committee studies of AEC informing programs conclude it effectively provides information to nuclear-associated industries but succeeds less in transferring non-nuclear technology to industry. In 1965, a committee of industry members recommended that qualified couplers evaluate technology for marketability, determine the audience which would be interested, and develop the form in which information should be presented.[49] External feedback on the suitability of education materials has been more favorable. Users have found regulatory information adequate if not excessive. Materials for general education in the depositories have been well received. Facilities for AEC informing activities, developed after World War II, were becoming outdated by the mid-sixties, though improvements have been achieved subsequently.[50]

Control and Program Review. Control of the informing program falls within the context of overall AEC objectives and available resources. The Joint Committee on Atomic Energy hearings developed insight into the informing subprocess, and its published transcripts aid administrators in evaluating informing activities. COSATI had continuously reviewed the documentary portions of the program in its comparison of government agency informing activities. AEC has studied information science developments of other agencies to update its own procedures. In terms of Sayer's model, AEC has a centralized collecting and evaluating source and decentralized distribution points. If interlibrary loan availability is considered, AEC does quite well in terms of this model.

Innovating

New nuclear and concomitant non-nuclear technologies are inputs into the innovating program. Technical information appears in technical reports, technical briefs, and patents as well as "loose" in operating office patent disclosure and operating files. The inventor or developer is available as a feedforward to encourage innovating. Training is offered in many technologies to adopters. Technology (the actual items) and supporting equipment are also made available to adopters.

AEC sponsors innovation through its Division of Applied Technology, contractors, offices for licensing and regulation, and technologists acting as consultants to industry. AEC has subsidized innovation in fields of its interest through grants, training, and equipment. AEC support has been greater for technologies of national interest than for technologies popular in one industrial sector.

The industry working with new AEC technology can visit the originating facility or hire the developer as a consultant under Industrial Participation programs to aid in decision and evaluation steps in adoption. Licensing and regulatory offices, both state and national, assist in maintaining standards. Processing for nuclear technology differs from the non-nuclear in that the enterprise must have sufficient capital to build and maintain physical and organizational safeguards for protecting operators and the public. Further, when processing materials with nuclear methods, the production operation and sequence frequently change, creating new capital outlays. Investment requirements may thus eliminate the small or marginal operator from many nuclear applications. Government-furnished equipment, grants, and training allowances become attractive considerations in the AIETA sequence. They may even bias the sequence to favor adopting, particularly if the company management wishes to explore new fields or is short of capital. Non-nuclear technology lacks such limitations and normal AIETA sequences can be identified.

When processing of new nuclear technology indicates inadequacy, it is returned to its AEC inventing or informing facility for adaptation or repackaging. Failures after adoption are handled the same way, except that the deficiencies are better known. Breeder reactors, for example, have been returned to applied research and exploratory development. Successful innovating helps start new businesses or makes possible new processes or products in old businesses. Either AEC mission or non-mission technologies may become innovating outputs, but mission technologies have been the more frequent. The evaluation and innovating process itself produces people who understand the capabilities of new nuclear applications and can use them in subsequent adoption. When AEC changes contractors internally, whole groups of trained people become available to support adoption of nuclear applications.

Examples. Seldom does a single new technology revolutionize an existing industry or start a new one. When such a breakthrough does occur, it creates its own new markets and momentum. Nuclear power is such a new technology. Its advantages and potential have carried it well into innovation, despite some significant drawbacks. Radioisotopes, on the other hand, have many commercial applications not apparent at first. Through successive adaptation, however, some radioisotopes have been adopted generally, while others are still being evaluated. Before adoption, each firm calculates the tradeoffs which favor radioisotopes over available alternatives. Radioisotopes have continued to rise in annual sales. Other AEC generated technologies tried or evalauted in typical year 1968 included new alloy steels, small nuclear reactors, rolamite, industrial nuclear explosives, and water desalination.

Failures in innovation cannot always be predicted. The power plant for the N. S. Savannah, too small for its total cost, failed economically. The nuclear aircraft power plant worked on with the Air Force was too large and too hard to support. It was both economically and technically a failure. The irradiated food program, in which AEC was an active partner, has thus far failed to satisfy FDA safety requirements for most foods.

Feedback. To be successful, an item must show cost or use advantages over the alternatives. Weapons, commercial nuclear power, and radioisotopes certainly show these advantages. In addition, Strother found that personal contact between AEC and potential adopters contributed to successful adoption. Another useful technique in fostering adoption was to give suppliers and subcontractors enough information so that they could adapt technology for their own use.[51] Professor James W. Kuhn of Columbia University has stressed the key role of AEC in training the scientists and technicians who innovated in the commercial power field. These key people frequently had the information which made innovations successful.[52] Success in innovation then can be supported by hiring trained people or from training those who have been hired.

The operating divisions of AEC and the Director of Planning and Analysis partly **control** AEC innovating. Emphasis on the control function was indicated by the 1966-67 addition of the Director, then a Special Assistant. Internal AEC innovating is easier to control, but the mission of AEC includes fostering external innovation. The Atomic Energy Act organized **review** into AEC with its requirement for a General Advisory Committee, a Military Liaison Committee, and a

Joint Committee on Atomic Energy in Congress, balancing among scientific, military, and general economic interests. Annual hearings on AEC appropriations are public, recorded program reviews where knowledgeable witnesses are heard. Within AEC, proposals from customers and other interest groups are converted into plans by the Director for Planning and Analysis. Conservative approaches have been taken and the relatively few AEC failures have been those pushed primarily by other agencies.

Integrating

Integrating activities consist of continued adoption of AEC processes, products and materials, and adjustment of adopting industries and the public to these new technologies. Non-nuclear materials are integrated just as are technologies from other agencies, but procedures for handling nuclear items are different. By statutory requirement, AEC regulates integration of new nuclear technology into the general economy. For radioisotopes and commercial nuclear power examples, AEC support for integration resembles USDA support for the agricultural sector. The Director of Regulation is the principal office, with the offices of Military Applications and Planning and Analysis giving some support. In 1967 AEC was given expanded responsibility in national health and safety, quite apart from its historical nuclear mission.

Checking new adoptions for safety and compliance is straightforward regulation, different only in the strictness of safety precautions. Other AEC activities also contribute directly to ingestion of new technology. The first step in diffusing nuclear technology was to have contractors operate AEC facilities; the second, to change contractors after a few years to new ones not previously involved in nuclear work. A third step was to transfer production and regulatory functions to private and state agencies, respectively, as soon as they had the technical capability. A planned fourth step has been for AEC to phase down its applied research and development and merely supplement private industry. These activities are predominantly direct information exchange or specific training to help different companies or organizations apply new nuclear technology. Relatively few companies are involved, but many people in them will move into new fields with knowledge and proficiency in nuclear industry techniques. Government and industry adoption units evaluate each AEC technology in terms of the local specifics and make the adoption decision. If subsidies or grants are available, these speed adoption processes.

As AEC supported nuclear technology "integrating," year after year, new businesses formed to establish the nuclear industries which have grown in size and strength as more and more nuclear technologies became available. In addition to the nuclear industries, new products and higher quality goods have resulted from the use of nuclear technologies in other industries. Radioisotopes have contributed particularly to quality control. As nuclear materials have moved into industrial and commercial use, new regulations have been required for the safety of people and products. These have also been some failures and undesirable side effects. Nuclear energy has changed national strategic relationships as well as procedures for more mundane activities like making cigarettes or automobile tires. One output has been the realization that a government monopoly can be mixed with private enterprise to produce and diffuse new items of technology.

Examples. AEC has fostered radioisotopes so successfully that four applications in curing surface coatings, producing wood plastics, sterilizing medical supplies, and synthesizing and producing special copolymers were valued at $250 million in 1967.[53] In 1971, plans for commercial nuclear power plants continued with 23 operating, 52 under construction, and 52 contractually planned.[54] (Nuclear power plants reduce atmospheric pollution but create other forms of pollution). Other AEC technologies in commercial integration were clean rooms, liquid centrifuges, uranium exploration and processing, nuclear detecting and monitoring instrumentation, and nuclear fuel reprocessing. The most completely integrated nuclear technology is weapons, hardly useful in the general economy. Desalination and water purification technologies are still in early innovation and are in use only where need is critical, as in Kuwait. Where integration has gone far enough in a specific application, competition has caused almost complete adoption of the new technology. In cigarettes and tires the new quality control procedures with radioisotopes made possible such uniformity and standardization that old procedures could no longer compete.

Suitability. Economic criteria continue to be guiding forces during integration. Long-term side effects can be quite troublesome as adoption progresses; an example is that of disposing of nuclear wastes, which have to be buried. Even non-nuclear materials can have deleterious effects. Nuclear power plants which use water for cooling may discharge the heated water into local rivers, change the ecological balance, and kill the fish. Integration of AEC-generated commercial technology has been until recently well accepted. The gains to society in cheaper products, reduction in overall pollution, and better products are considered greater than costs.

Control and program review. The Director of Regulation was established in an AEC reorganization at the end of the 1950's when it became clear that commercial nuclear power and other commercial nuclear applications would be widespread. An office of hearing examiners was set up at the same time to perform quasi-judicial AEC functions which are not regulation, development, nor manufacture. The General Manager, the Director of Regulation, and the hearing examiners guide the integration subprocess in which individuals, institutions, industries, state agencies, and other government agencies adopt AEC outputs. The network of advisory groups at different levels and in different specialties contributes to AEC subprocesses, channeling feedback for AEC procedures and policies which affect the public. A more general feedback channel is through the Joint Committee on Atomic Energy.

AEC in the Total Process

From the AEC legislation of 1946 and 1954, AEC has developed mission-oriented activities for generating nuclear technologies, informing about them, advocating their adoption by the new nuclear industries or by the public when applicable, and supporting and regulating the diffusion of these technologies among users. With permanent channels for feedback incorporated in the enabling legislation, AEC maintains close control of each of its activities.

Evaluation. From the end of WW II until 1962, AEC was second to DOD as the largest spender of development funds; and until recently, it has been in third place, after DOD and NASA. About half of AEC development funding went into weapons and nearly half into nuclear reactors. Nuclear reactors are partly for the military, partly for space, and partly for commercial power. As a result of these allocations, a relatively small part of AEC developments has been for products or processes which apply directly to the general economy. Total applied research and development, which has exceeded $1 billion for recent years, thus overestimates AEC technologies which are applicable in the general economy Even 4,525 patents, available in 1971 for royalty free licensing, are relatively small outputs considering total expenditures. AEC applied research and development funding has been steady and increasing each year, partly from inflation and partly because AEC has developed more and more commercial applications. The work has been done successfully in government laboratories operated by contractors. Large interdisciplinary laboratories have developed which can now be used for other than nuclear work.

AEC has a substantial informing effort which uses both modern and historic ways to reach nuclear industry and general public audiences. Using depositories, information centers, and conventional publication distribution, AEC has established a national nuclear information system to carry out its statutory mission of informing the public. Evaluation indicates its informing effort is more effective with nuclear than with other industries, as would be expected.

The AEC innovating mission is much more limited than that of SBA or USDA; further, the clients are those in nuclear industry or users of the products. Internally, one of the innovating procedures is to change the contractors who operate the government owned centers. AEC does provide or support the market for internal innovating which makes it easier for new users to calculate advantages of adoption. In its external innovating, AEC works with industry in furnishing nuclear materials and training support to potential adopters during their AIETA sequence. Failures and no-takers still occur, although AEC has been cautious in its offerings. Its patent application record, for example, is the best of the large agencies.

Integrating inputs from AEC to the total economy are proportional to the total AEC annual funding of about $2.5 billion. This amount covers the generating of new technology and diffusing it, but the biggest expenses are in defense-related fields. Commercial applications have gained in importance and some special applications have completely diffused. As nuclear technologies like radioisotopes have diffused they have gained momentum, and new standards have been established for quality. New industries have formed to contribute nuclear materials and devices. Most of the commercial nuclear applications have been labor-saving and capital-using. They have required regulation and caused undesired side effects such as dangerous wastes. AEC integrating efforts have been reviewed by its internal committee and advisory system as well as by Congress.

De Facto Procedures. Established as an intentional government monopoly for national security reasons, AEC has developed government owned but contractor operated facilities for generating, producing, distributing, and using nuclear materials. No other government agency works wholly this way. One of its innovating procedures, that of changing contractors periodically, is used by other agencies but not for the direct purpose of innovating. Another procedure of turning regulation over to state agencies supports integrating in a way not found in most agencies. Furnishing government materials, equipment, and facilities to contractors is done in other agencies, but AEC also supplies these to innovators in commercial nuclear power and even helps train the technical managers and operators for the new power plants. Industrial participation and training at AEC facilities have developed as distinctive AEC features, highly effective for diffusing nuclear products into the supporting nuclear industry. AEC uses the patent system more than any other agency, partly because it must take title to basic nuclear patents and companies cannot withhold them. Though AEC uses patents, it also depends on its industrial participation and training programs to help industry package the new technology so it can be applied. In its technology generating and diffusing activities, AEC uses both historical and new, divergent procedures; but the historical procedures supplement the new ones more than the reverse.

National Goals. AEC has promoted the progress of science and the useful arts, made nuclear information widely available for potential users, and has generally supported maximum employment, production, and purchasing power. Recently, the long term effects of using nuclear materials have caused AEC to consider national goals in all AEC programs, including the second order consequences of job changes, environment degradation, and area development.

AEC investment in plant, equipment, and real estate is almost completely contractor managed, which creates the contradiction of free enterprise supporting a government monopoly. Business and industry contributed to AEC operations and development, but these have of necessity been large firms. Except in location of its enterprises,

AEC has supported concentrations of existing economic power. Even the use of nuclear materials requires resources beyond the means of most small businesses. The 1965 committee report on AEC technology diffusion stated that AEC directed its information to nuclear audiences and that little effort was made to identify and disseminate information for non-nuclear users. Since 1965, AEC joined the NTIS, NASA, and SBA in efforts to reach wider audiences. AEC-generated technology diffuses through the nuclear associated industries faster than through others, thus continuing the concentration of nuclear technologies to a select and favored group of companies which have learned to work closely with AEC.

Commercial nuclear power is an example of technical and economic success. Yet it displaces coal, the one natural fuel which the U.S. has in abundance. Nuclear waste products may not be easier to handle than coal wastes. As a testament to U. S. intent to use nuclear technology for peaceful purposes, commercial nuclear power is a psychological success. As a contributor to unemployment in Appalachia, the program deserves careful scrutiny. Radioisotopes have improved quality, but created neither jobs nor income, in their most widespread applications.

In terms of the total technology diffusion process, nuclear technologies are available, needed, and wanted more than their alternatives. Though some effects are labor-saving, capital-using, and economy-concentrating, these are offset by the desirable effects of increased national strategic capabilities, better quality products, and new industries.

V. SBA TECHNOLOGY DIFFUSION ACTIVITIES

Small Business Administration support of technology diffusion resembles the Office of Economic Opportunity, the Peace Corps, the Office of Emergency Planning, most independent regulatory agencies, the Library of Congress, and the U.S. Arms Control and Disarmament Agency. These Federal agencies receive heavy support at times and light at others. Clients generally belong either in specific economic sectors or in economic activities with long-term problems. Created by the Small Business Act of 1953, SBA aids, counsels, assists, and protects the interests of small businesses. It mostly assists financially, although it disseminates information on management techniques and new technology and helps small business obtain benefits of government-sponsored research and development.

In 1959, 99 percent of all business firms, and 99 percent of all manufacturing firms employed less than 100; but these firms only did 40 percent of the business and 20 percent of the manufacturing.[55] In FY 1971 there were 8 million small businesses in the U. S., more than 95 percent of all businesses. These employed 35 million people and did 37 percent of the business.[56] SBA aims to strengthen this group. Since October 1966, SBA has actively promoted technology diffusion through information and loans supporting innovating. SBA has always supported some integrating through its loan programs. The ongoing work is done at 80 field offices in 10 areas of the U. S. and Puerto Rico.

Inventing

From contacts with small businessmen, beginning entrepreneurs, and independent inventors, SBA feels keenly the importance of new technology to economic growth. Yet SBA does not itself support new technology generation. Its mission begins with distributing new technical information developed by others. SBA does try to assure that small business gets a fair share of Federal R&D contracts; nonetheless, large organizations have held most of these.[57]

Informing

As a nondeveloper of technology, SBA urges other agencies to study the commercial potential of new technology activities and possibly cuts costs for innovators. It must select technology items for publication and dissemination from other agencies, organizations, or individuals. Knowing the small business needs of industry and special interests, SBA can select potentially usable items. Inventors, the Patent Office, AEC, DOD, and NASA provide the most information. Items available annually include 70,000 patents, about 1,000 items from NASA's Technology Utilization Program, at least 45,000 technical reports from NTIS, technical reports from the Government Printing Office, and reports direct from government agencies. With limited funds, SBA is very selective and publishes materials free or at a nominal charge to attract the interest of small businesses.

Information handling is conventional, partly a process of selecting and partly a matter of servicing known clients. Until 1966 SBA published new inventions by independent inventors as a service, and since 1966 it has offered studies of new technology, selected and prepared to create awareness and interest. Public disclosure is the policy of SBA for technical information and even for business firm information which does not jeopardize credit and competitive position.[58] Management studies pertinent to evaluating and testing new technology are sometimes selected. The eighty field offices help small businessmen use government agency information sources other than SBA. They also help small business identify needs, frequently coupling small business clients to fruitful sources of information.

SBA efforts in Technology Utilization have resulted in publications with titles like **Technical Aids to Small Business** and **Selected Advances in Electrical Circuitry.** In years past when DOD was diffusing titanium metallurgy, SBA published information for small businesses on that technology.[59] Similarly, SBA supported AEC's diffusion of radioisotopes. Consultant services and conferences are other outputs; conferences are usually held jointly with other government agencies. During 1971, 3.5 million copies of SBA publications were sold or given away. Sixteen new publications were added to the 350 already available. Some 11,000 small firms were given answers to specific technical questions, and 18,000 data packages were mailed. 9,600 companies were counseled on technology problems.[60] Field offices have also developed trained people as outputs of the informing program. These people specialize in coupling needs to answers, clients to sources, or innovators to inventors. During 1971, 2,700 courses, conferences, and problem clinics were conducted.[61]

SBA informing indicates that small businesses see it as a "trusted agent", but that its information dissemination makes little technical impact compared to larger programs of other agencies. Because of its limited potential, SBA has combined efforts with other agencies. SBA succeeded, with AEC, in disseminating information on free patents, licensing radioisotopes, and making available Restricted Data Information. In cooperation with NASA, SBA has encouraged small business to use Regional Dissemination Centers. SBA and NASA cooperate to promote technical briefs, NASA-owned, royalty free patents, and the NASA small business set-aside program.

In Herner's 1957 study of 500 small business firms (cited in Chapter III), he found them depending largely on suppliers and to a lesser degree on trade journals for information on new products and techniques.[62] SBA has tried to supplement these channels, the trusted sources for small businessmen. SBA has continued to support studies of information sources for businessmen. In a typical study of 162 firms in Colorado, researchers found trade associations considered by 38 percent of member businessmen as their most important source of business information. These associations publish "how-to" information and basic data. Researchers cited periodical trade journals as the bulk of business information these firms received. They mentioned 538 periodicals and 12 non-periodicals. Ninety percent of the firms received one or more journals. Consultants were listed as the third most used information source.[63] SBA publications have focused on "how-to-do" information, and field offices have made consultants available.

SBA has reorganized with growth. The Technology Utilization Division was formed in 1966 as a result of feedback suggesting SBA should help small businesses more in applying new technology from Federal sources. This office and the Office of Public Information control the technical information program. Program review, to include cost benefit studies, has been done internally and supported by contractual studies on small business' use of outside information.

Innovating

SBA's mission clearly obligates the agency to work with small business in varied ways. Like the farmer in his relationship to USDA through county agents, the small businessman can work through SBA field offices with sources of new technology or with sources of financial support. The 80 field offices can advocate the use of new technology, but it is not pushed to the exclusion of other inputs. SBA helps small businesses engaged in manufacturing, wholesaling, retailing, services, and others independently owned and not dominant in their fields. Real estate, agriculture-related activities, and gambling are excluded.

In the business loan program, SBA may participate with a local bank, or it may make a 100 percent direct loan if no bank loan is available. These loans may reach $350,000. Small loans for new businesses based on new technology are available. Still another category is the pool loan to groups of small businesses to help them (1) obtain benefits of research and development; (2) buy raw materials, equipment, inventory, or supplies; and (3) build facilities to support these activities. SBA also makes low interest loans in areas designated by the Economic Development Administration as those of high unemployment.

To keep small business strong, progressive, and abreast of new technology, SBA sponsored the Service Corps of Retired Executives (SCORE), in 1964, which by 1968 had 3,200 members in 184 chapters. In 1969 SBA tried to double this number. With skill inventories running the entire gamut of small business needs, SCORE representatives frequently aid small businessmen in evaluating application of new technology.[64] SBA also sponsored the Active Corps of Executives (ACE) to help small businesses. SCORE and ACE are jointly administered by SBA and Action.[65]

The Technology Utilization Division, with several technology-oriented SCORE representatives, advocates new technology and provides counsel. This division placed its offices (eight in 1968) in Philadelphia, Boston, San Francisco, Los Angeles, Cleveland, Detroit, Minneapolis, and Atlanta. The coordinating office for the Division is in Washington, D.C.

As in agriculture, the individual small business operator goes through the AIETA sequence with respect to each new item of technology which may affect his business. During or after evaluation, he may seek an SBA loan or some other form of SBA assistance. SCORE members generally handle 1,100 problems monthly.[66] SBA review and evaluation determines that: (1) the small business is eligible for assistance in size, annual sales, and type of business; (2) problem areas which can use technological advances have been identified; (3) information and knowledgeable people are available; (4) costs and benefits of assistance can be estimated; and (5) the company has the technical and managerial capability to support the proposed program. When a program has been agreed upon, the company implements its plan, supported by SBA in one or more activities. Processing will vary for pool loans and also for the small business inventor-entrepreneur.

Regular loans are processed without regard to their technology content; but, between April and September 28, 1967, SBA made forty-seven "innovation loans" totaling more than $3 million. In the same period, with SBA assistance, one small business investment company with technical capabilities began operations in the Boston area.[67]

The SBA program has stimulated small businesses to use new technologies, produce new products, and provide new sources of employment. Small business furnished 28 percent of Federally procured materials in FY 1971.[68]

After reviewing 22,000 small firms that had received SBA loans, Administrator Robert C. Moot, in 1968, told Congress that these firms, during the 6-year period following the loans, had increased profits by 20 percent. Their assets and sales rose by 8 percent and net worth increased 6 percent. In FY 1971 SBA provided $1.3 billion in 24,286 loans. Since its inception, SBA has loaned about $10 billion to small business and collected 95 percent of it. Interest rates cannot exceed 5½ percent on SBA direct loans nor 8 percent simple interest on indirect loans.[69] These terms compete with local sources in tight money markets. SBA experience with its loan program indicates that government support indeed helps small business. Not all successes are due to taking advantage of new technology, but this is one sector. SBA's effort to get more R&D contracts into small business has not been very successful.

SBA mission and goals are embodied in the subprocess of innovating and entrepreneurship. SBA recognizes new technology as one ingredient of innovating, but it advocates other ingredients as well. The Office of Technology Utilization was intended to experiment in direct technology information transfer and subsequent innovation support. The Office of Planning, Research, and Analysis performs internal review using cumulative feedback. The office particularly looks for economic, legislative, and regulative effects on small business competitiveness. The House and Senate Select Committees on Small Business perform semi-continuous external reviews of SBA programs.

Integrating

The adoption of new technology by more and more businesses is imitation or integration of the new item into business. The Bureau of National Affairs reported in a 1967 analysis that Congressmen believe small business can provide jobs and fight poverty in the same way that supporting farmers during the Depression helped rebuild consumption.[70] Congressmen who vote funds for SBA, then, have formed a model of national goals and a view of SBA's contribution to that model. The business loan programs are to: (1) promote economic growth through innovation, expanded capacity, and improved marketing; (2) increase competition; and (3) strengthen local economies.

Later small business adopters of new technology can follow previous adopters who either succeeded on their own or received SBA loans. Loan policy requires that SBA supplement, but not compete with, private sources. With management techniques, business forecasting, and technical information equally available, judgment can be applied to extended adoption of new technologies even when Federal loan sources have been exhausted.

Because SBA specializes in private management and business support and develops no technology, while NASA, AEC, and DOD develop technology but minimally support private business or management, SBA is a natural partner for those agencies. This has been recognized and partially developed since 1966 as a way to diffuse desirable technologies.

SBA activities with new technology should help produce new businesses, create jobs, reduce economic concentration in big business, and support free enterprise. More new businesses succeed than fail. Dunn and Bradstreet estimated 287,000 new businesses started in 1971 and about 12,000 old businesses failed, leaving 257,000 additions. Other businesses cease through incorporation, sales, or consolidation. This shifting, year by year, indicates the changing business and technical opportunity. New products appear in new places and old products fade away. This is the integrating subprocess at work.

The SBA administrator is aided in his overall control and review by assistant administrators, particularly for Planning, Research, and Analysis. This assistant administrator must analyze the economic and social effects of SBA activities and prepare recommendations for long range legislative requirements. Specific SBA effects on technology diffusion are not normally considered separately from other SBA effects. Much emphasis on technology diffusion has come from the Congressional Select Committees on Small Business.

SBA in the Total Process

Since its 1953 beginning, SBA has developed into a "trusted agent" for small businesses. SBA gains new technology from private enterprise or other government agencies and then diffuses it through advice, loans, and other forms of support. Its eighty field offices can assist small businessmen in much the same way that USDA county agents can help farmers. SBA has revolving loan funds which it can use in supporting either innovating or integrating. Feedback is gained through repaid loans, requests for information, and reports on successful new businesses.

SBA can find adequate new technologies to diffuse either in the private economy or in other government agencies. Although SBA's informing effort is small compared to other agencies, it does reach an alert audience—the small entrepreneur who wants to become larger. The informing programs mix management and technical information in a way that most agencies are unable to do. SBA makes considerable use of the information sources of NASA, AEC, Patent Office, and DOD. The programs are characterized by both free and cost information, person to person instruction in conferences and workshops, and feedback direct to SBA or SCORE representatives.

SBA "customers" for innovation are defined by law, but SBA cannot reach them all with present funding. The businessman has a problem and proposes a solution which may involve new technology. SBA studies the proposal and potential market, suggests alternatives if appropriate, and works out reasonable support terms with the businessman. Loans go through normal business channels, including local financing, if possible; but they can be direct from SBA. Successful outputs are new and old businesses using new technology, stronger businesses, repaid loans, and economic dispersion.

SBA makes loans for continued adoption or integration as readily as for innovating. Its effect on integrating may be represented by its 1971 outstanding loans of $2.8 billion to 210,292 businesses. This 2.8 billion dollars does not loom large in the GNP, but it does represent a government interest in the health of small business. It disperses economic concentration, strengthens 25,000 small businesses yearly, and gives the small businessman alternatives and encouragement.

De Facto Procedures. SBA is a special program to aid a particular type of contributor to U. S. economy and culture; it clearly evolving new procedures for the general problem of supporting small business, including the specific problem of diffusing new technology to small business. In its information dissemination program, it supplements the trade association and the supplier with a trusted agent. With its management information program, it supplements the educational system. In its financial support program, it supplements local sources or replaces them under certain conditions. Through its SCORE and ACE programs, it supplements the private consultant.

National Goals. SBA efforts promote progress, provide employment and purchasing power, support free enterprise, and reduce economic concentration. However, SBA offices are located in concentrations of small businesses, and this places them in congested, already heavily developed and populated areas. The 1968 distribution of the eight Technology Utilization Offices to large cities, itself recognized that technically developed geographic areas tend to absorb new technology faster. Even the focusing within SBA on specific interest groups follows the trade association success in concentrating on technically oriented industries and clients.

SBA has responded to society's demand that free competitive enterprise be supported via the small scale entrepreneur. If SBA were several times larger, it would have greater impact and could even be dysfunctional; but at its present size, it is a dynamic alternative to local support for small businessmen.

FOOTNOTES

[1] U.S. Department of Commerce, *Annual Report of the Secretary of Commerce for the Fiscal Year Ended June 30, 1971* (Washington, D.C.: U.S. Government Printing Office, 1971), p. xii.

[2] National Science Foundation, *Federal Funds . . . 1966, op. cit.,* p. 68.

[3] J. F. Reilly, Office of Public Information, NBS, in correspondence to the author, May 29, 1968.

[4] *"To Promote the Progress of Useful Arts" In an Age of Exploding Technology, Report of the President's Commission on the Patent System* (Washington, D.C.: U.S. Government Printing Office, 1966), *passim.* The recommendations of the Commission are summarized in five charts following page 58 of the report.

[5] U.S. Department of Commerce, *Annual Report . . . 1971, op. cit.,* p. 37.

[6] National Science Foundation, *Federal Funds . . . 1971 . . . , op. cit.,* p. 197.

[7] Jonathan Lindley, Deputy Assistant Secretary for Policy Coordination, Department of Commerce, in correspondence to the author dated May 18, 1968.

[8] U.S. Department of Commerce, *Annual Report of the Secretary of Commerce for the Fiscal Year Ended June 30, 1966* (Washington, D.C.: U.S. Government Printing Office, 1966), p. 13.

[9] U.S. Department of Commerce, *Annual Report . . . 1971, op. cit.,* p. 19.

[10] U.S. Department of Commerce, *Annual Report . . . 1966, op. cit.,* p. 12.

[11] U.S. Department of Commerce, *Annual Report of the Secretary of Commerce for the Fiscal Year Ended June 30, 1967* (Washington, D.C.: U.S. Government Printing Office, 1967), p. 24.

[12] Bureau of National Affairs, *Daily Executive Report,* May 6, 1968, p. A-24.

[13] U.S. Congress, House, Committee on Science and Astronautics, *For the Benefit of All Mankind, The Practical Returns from Space Investment.* 92d Congress, 2d Sess. (Washington, D.C.: U.S. Government Printing Office, 1972), *passim.*

[14] J. Gordon Milliken and Edward J. Morrison, "Management Methods from Aerospace," *Harvard Business Review,* March-April, 1973, pp. 6-20.

[15] U.S. Congress, Senate, Committee on Aeronautical and Space Sciences. *Aeronautical Research and Development Policy,* 90th Cong., 2nd Sess. (Washington, D.C.: U.S. Government Printing Office, 1968), pp. 3-18.

[16] *Ibid.,* p. 1.

[17] U.S. Congress, House, Committee on Science and Astronautics, *Obligations . . . , op. cit.,* pp. 25-32.

[18] National Aeronautics and Space Agency, *2d Semi-Annual Report to Congress, July 1-December 31, 1969,* (Washington, D.C.: U.S. Government Printing Office, 1970), p. 183.

[19] Federal Council for Science and Technology, Committee on Scientific and Technical Information, *Selected Mechanized Scientific and Technical Information Systems, op. cit.,* p. 30.

[20] Richard L. Lesher, "Statement for the Record of Richard L. Lesher, Ass't Administrator for Technology Utilization, NASA, before the Committee on Aeronautical and Space Sciences, U.S. Senate, February 27, 1968" (mimeograph).

[21] "Time for Space Decision," (Editorial), *Los Angeles Times,* March 14, 1969, p. 6 (Part II). The Times was arguing for some ambitious new project which would keep the space skills and teams intact as an invaluable national resource.

[22] James E. Webb, "NASA, Technology, and the National Security," *Perspectives in Defense Management,* Feb. 1969, pp. 9-15.

[23] Richard J. Hayes, *A Study of the Transfer of Technology from Government Sponsored R&D to Commercial Operations in Selected Electronic Companies.* Ph.D. Dissertation, The American University, June 1967, pp. 220-221.

[24] Bureau of the Budget, *Budget of the United States: Fiscal Year 1973* (Washington, D.C.: U.S. Government Printing Offiffice, 1972) p. 84 and *Budget Appendix, Fiscal Year 1973* (Washington, D.C.: U.S. Government Printing Office, 1972), pp. 1002-1015.

[25] National Aeronautics and Space Administration, *The Technology Utilization Program,* February, 1967, Review of the Work of the NASA Office of Technology Utilization (Washington, D.C.: NASA, 1967), p. 4.

[26] Richard L. Lesher, "Innovation," *Channel 28, Los Angeles, CA,* Jan. 18, 1969. Dr. Lesher, NASA Assistant Administrator for Technology Utilization, was interviewed on progress of the Technology Utilization Division.

[27] National Aeronautics and Space Administration, WESRAC, Memo of available services, dated December 29, 1971.

[28] William H. Gregory. "Aerospace's Urban Role Debated," *Aviation Week and Space Technology.* June 7, 1971, pp. 62-66.

[29] William F. Ogburn, *op. cit.,* p. 104.

[30] "New Products—Pulling a Profit out of Left Field," *Business Week* (June 15, 1968), pp. 150-154.

[31] Richard L. Lesher, "Innovations . . . ," *op. cit.*

[32] Samuel I. Doctors, *The Role of Federal Agencies in Technology Transfer* (Cambridge, Mass. The M.I.T. Press, 1969), p. 162.

[33] *Ibid.,* pp. 96-97.

[34] *Ibid.,* pp. 104-107.

[35] National Aeronautics and Space Administration, Office of Technology Utilization, *NASA Contributions to Bioinstrumentation Systems.* NASA SP-5054 (Washington, D.C.: U.S. Government Printing Office, 1968), p. 2 and p. 87.

[36] National Aeronautics and Space Council, Executive Office of the President, *United States Aeronautics and Space Activities, 1968* (Washington, D.C.: U.S. Government Printing Office, 1969), pp. 32-33.

[37] James E. Webb, *op. cit.,* p. 13.

[38] Raymond A. Bauer, *Second Order Consequences* (Cambridge, Mass.: The M.I.T. Press, 1969), pp. 140-143.

[39] U.S. Atomic Energy Commission, *Annual Report to Congress of the AEC for 1971* (Washington, D.C.: U.S. Government Printing Office, 1972), p. 193.

[40] U.S. Atomic Energy Commission, *The Nuclear Industry—1971* (Washington, D.C.: U.S. Government Printing Office, 1972), p. 5.

[41] AEC, *Annual Report, op. cit.,* p. 199.

[42] AEC, *Annual Report . . . , op. cit.,* pp. 211-216.

[43] U.S. AEC—*Annual Report . . . , op. cit.,* p. 191.

[44] U.S. Congress, House, Committee on Science and Astronautics, *Obligations . . . , op. cit.,* p. 25-32.

[45] Federal Register Division, National Archives and Records Service, General Services Administration, *United States Government Organization Manual,* 1957-58 (Washington, D.C.: U.S. Government Printing Office, 1957), p. 346.

[46] U.S. AEC, Division of Nuclear Education and Training, *Program Statistics, July 1, 1969 to June 30, 1970* (Washington, D.C.: USAEC, 1970), p. 10.

[47] U.S. AEC, *Industrial Benefits from Nuclear Development* (Oak Ridge, Tennessee: U.S. AEC Technical Information Division, 1967), pp. 2-5 and interview with Mr. Walter Kee, AEC Division of Information, Feb. 2, 1968.

[48] U.S. AEC, Isotopes Information Center, Oak Ridge National Laboratory, *Isotopes and Radiation Technology—A Quarterly Technical Progress Review,* Vol. 6, No. 4, frontispiece. The magazine is available by subscription from the U.S. Government Printing Office, Washington, D.C.

[49] C. O. Strother, et al., *Transferrence of Non-Nuclear Technology to Industry.* Committee Report to Oak Ridge Operations Office, ORO-629 (Oak Ridge, Tenn.: U.S. Atomic Energy Commission, 1965), pp. 1 & 9.

[50] Federal Council for Science and Technology Committee on Scientific and Technical Information, "Summary Progress Report, September, 1964," reported in *The National Science Foundation—A General Review of Its First 15 Years.* Report of the Committee on Science and Astronautics, U.S. House, 89th Cong. 2nd Sess. (Washington, D.C.: U.S. Government Printing Office, 1966), p. 194.

[51] Strother, *op. cit.,* pp. 10-11.

[52] James W. Kuhn, *Scientific and Managerial Manpower in Nuclear Industry* (New York: Columbia University Press. 1966), pp. vi-ix.

[53] U.S. Atomic Energy Commission, *The Nuclear Industry—1968* (Washington, D.C.: U.S. Government Printing Office, 1968), pp. 15 & 100.

[54] U.S. AEC, *Annual Report . . . , op. cit.,* p. 221.

[55] Richard R. Nelson, *op. cit.,* p. 205.

[56] SBA, *United States Small Business Administration 1971 Annual Report* (Washington, D.C.: U.S. Government Printing Office, 1971), p. iii.

[57] Robert C. Moot, "Statement as Administrator, SBA, before the Subcommittee of Science and Technology, the Senate Select Committee on Small Business, September 28, 1967" (Washington, D.C.: Small Business Administration, 1967), mimeograph.

[58] Small Business Administration, *1967 Annual Report* (Washington, D.C.: U.S. Government Printing Office, 1968), p. 21.

[59] J. Wade Rice, *Technical Aids for Small Business* (Washington, D.C.: Small Business Administration, 1956), p. 218-227.

[60] SBA, *1971 Annual Report, op. cit.*, pp. 18-20.

[61] *Ibid.*, p. 19.

[62] Saul Herner, *op. cit.*, p. 9.

[63] L. J. Crampon and Stewart F. Schweizer, *Use of Outside Information in Small Firms* (Washington, D.C.: Small Business Administration, Feb. 1962), pp. 1-2.

[64] Robert C. Moot, *SCORE—Service Corps of Retired Executives*, SBA Brochure OPI 16 (Washington, D.C.: Small Business Administration, 1967), pp. 2-3.

[65] *U.S. Government Organization Manual, 1971/72 . . . op. cit.*, p. 385.

[66] Small Business Administration, *1967 Annual Report, op. cit.*, p. 385.

[67] Robert C. Moot, "Statement as Administrator . . . ," *op. cit.*, mimeograph.

[68] SBA, *1971 Annual Report, op. cit.*, p. 12.

[69] "Small Business: It's Big Business for Uncle Sam, This Task of Helping the Small Businessman," *Daily Executive Report* (Washington, D.C.: Bureau of National Affairs, Dec. 6, 1967), pp. AA1-AA12.

[70] *Ibid.*, p. AA1.

CHAPTER VIII

COMPARATIVE ANALYSIS OF PROGRAMS
AND PROCEDURES

I. INTRODUCTION

Federal agency programs and procedures for diffusing government-generated technology into the economy are analyzed (1) by the representative examples; (2) by agency performance in the subprocesses of inventing, informing, innovating, and integrating; and (3) by performance in the total process of technology diffusion. Summaries for each of the selected Federal agencies are shown in Appendix G.

II. EXAMPLES

The **successes** shown in Appendix F represent the current products, processes, techniques, and procedures used in the economy. Found in each Federal agency, studied successes show that technology diffusion has common features, regardless of where it occurs. These common features may be identified from the position of the technology being diffused as well as from the position of management in a particular Federal agency. Biological insect control, antibiotics, coal carbon black, rubella vaccine, titanium processing, numerical control, food freeze-drying, synthetic rubber, integrated circuits, commercial nuclear power, and use of microfiche indicate that:

1. New technologies were developed and diffused directly by Federal agencies or through Federal agency support for private enterprise developments. The examples show great variation of Federal support procedures.

2. New technology seemed to emerge to resolve current problems; it usually did not develop, however, until some insightful individual stated the problem in a way that indicated a technical solution.

3. Inventive work was preceded by careful definition of need or requirement, given enough support to focus technology on the need, proceeded from known to related areas, and allowed some freedom for exploiting breakthroughs or chance observations.

4. "Processing" divided into modestly funded, sequential work leading to such advances as antibiotics, synthetic rubber, vaccines, and biological pest control, and the heavily funded, more spectacular advances such as nuclear power, integrated circuits, numerical control, and titanium metallurgy.

5. Users had ready access to information through technical journals, movement of investigators, patents, relinquishing of proprietary rights, formal education, government contracts and reports, salesmen, newspapers, radio, conferences, television, and actual equipment. Neither security nor proprietary rights prevented the successful developing and diffusing of the items.

6. Federal agencies fostered innovating and integrating through tests and demonstrations, financial support, contract specifications, Federal-state-user cooperative programs, government furnished equipment and facilities, mobilization programs, and market support. A market was the requirement, **sine qua non,** for these subprocesses.

7. Successful examples did not cause direct social changes and did not arouse opposition. Procedures for adoption and use were tested step-by-step.

8. Final success in diffusion frequently depended on breakthroughs or advances in related fields.

9. When new technology caught on, Federal agencies reduced their support; but Federal agency regulation became mandatory when dangerous side effects appeared.

10. The most useful technologies diffused without specific Federal agency support.

11. Champions, or groups of advocates, helped to carry programs from inception through adoption.

12. Some technologies, originally diffused for prestige or emergency purposes, were later adopted on their own merits.

13. Many problems were so complex that only large, multidisciplinary organizations like Federal agencies could generate and diffuse technical solutions.

A frustrating experience for technologists is that their creations can be technically successful, but no one shows interest in adopting them. They simply do not diffuse. The study of this no-taker group, larger than either successes or failures, can show the characteristics of things which waste the energy of technologists and consume resources. All agencies have no-takers just as they have successes. Grain fumigation, refrigeration insulation, metric system, highway grooving, and water fluoridation, as well as some of the failures described in Appendix F, indicate that:

1. Technically successful technology was rejected because of its related support requirements. The technology would require a technological plateau beyond the adopter's facilities or understanding.

2. Technology items only slightly better than those in use would not have offset costs of change. This was particularly true when currently used items were standardized.

3. Technologies immediately affecting social systems were not readily innovated.

4. Innovation was delayed when large numbers of people had to approve adoption, as well as when new technology was unpleasant to use, or dangerous to the environment.

5. Innovation was slower when adoption changed relationships among suppliers and customers, as well as when the advocates were not trusted sources of information.

6. Individuals prevented adoption of new technology. They can be called negative champions.

7. Management decisions not related to technical efficiency frequently determined what was innovated and integrated.

In contrast to the no-taker, which is not even given a trial, the failure is tried and rejected or is adopted and later rejected. There are more failures than successes, and they may occur either in technology generation or diffusion. The analysis of failures can be fed back to redirect effort into more productive directions. As outlined in Appendix F, the failures of guayule rubber, prevention of automobile accident trauma, chrome-metal processing, food irradiation, and nuclear-powered merchant marine indicate that:

1. Problems for which responsibility was widely divided were not readily solved by either available or potential technology. No one thought deeply on the total problem. Neither inventors nor innovators worked on items for which they could see no market.

2. Each item of new technology competed with other new items as well as with those already in use. The more available and economically efficient was usually chosen. Many technically successful new items could not compete economically.

3. Each item competed for resources with non-technological alternative uses for such resources.

4. Overzealous Federal agencies reduced confidence in the efficacy of technologies they supported. Invention in one agency did not assure adoption in another agency.

5. Short-term economic gains concerned innovators more than long-term social gains. Neither technical feasibility nor favorable information assured adoption of an item of technology.

6. Vested interests sometimes did not support the direction and effects of inventing and innovating.

III. SUBPROCESSES

Inventing

Six of the seven Federal agencies studied generated new technology as part of their overall missions. In FY 1971, these six agencies spent 90 percent of all Federal applied research and development funds and over half of national applied research and development funds. Agency comparisons in Appendices B, G-1 and previous chapters support the following:

1. The Department of Defense has led in clearly defining need as a prerequisite to planned invention, but other agencies adopted this step under programming procedures of defining goals and evaluating alternatives. All agencies define needs in terms of their statutory missions, not in terms of the general economy.

2. Available science and technology have adequately supported inventive work in all agencies; in fact, information science has advanced largely to couple internal needs to solutions in Federal agency inventing activities.

3. Processing in all agencies with internal programs has focused on the supported sector or statutory mission. Inventive effort has remained high in a civil service environment like the U. S. Department of Agriculture, in a mixed environment as in DOD, in a contract

environment like the Atomic Energy Commission, and in a private enterprise environment as supported by the Department of Commerce. The less costly processing has been in steadily funded, long-term efforts, as in USDA and AEC.

4. Agencies have common features of evaluating ideas, selecting approaches developing prototypes, and testing them, compatible with the predictive model. Freedom to exploit breakthroughs and working from known to related areas have been applied in several agencies.

5. Inventive work led to public service patents, government patents, privately held patents, published as well as unpublished documentation, actual items, and trained people. USDA and the Public Health Service used already trained individuals while AEC deliberately trained contractor groups.

6. The most elaborate procedures for evaluating results of inventive work were those of PHS in vaccines, food contamination, and drug effects. DOD had highly formalized test procedures built into its development programs. USDA outputs were evaluated in the agricultural sector for applicability and advantage. The county agent system was the most elaborate interface between technology generators and commercial users of any Federal agency program.

7. Direction and number of an agency's new technology successes were influenced if not controlled by that agency's programs and procedures. Failures generally did not compete with available alternatives. Some inventions were not made, though need was great, as in reduction of automobile accident trauma. These were just outside the statutory missions of Federal agencies; the need was not defined in technical terms, or inventors or developers did not perceive a market.

8. Control of programs and procedures for inventing work were highly centralized in DOD, NASA, and AEC, but were increasingly less so for USDA, PHS, and Commerce. Congressional committees and special interest groups influenced control.

9. Program or systems review groups operated formally in USDA, PHS, DOD, and NASA. These were generally of post-PPB origin and reflected concern for keeping agency programs focused on timely national needs. Congressional committees and special interest groups contributed significantly to the selected agencies by channeling and evaluating feedback from general economy clients.

10. For DOD, NASA and AEC some technology developed since 1950 has been duplicative, much does not apply to peaceful pursuits, and much is obsolescent. NASA and AEC technologies were almost equally subject to obsolescence and non-applicability. These three, with up to 90 percent of the Federal applied research and development funding in recent years, simply have not directly produced civilian technologies in proportion to their expenditures. Even USDA and PHS developments since 1950 have not remained equally useful because of technical change. USDA duplicated work in adapting technologies to different areas of the country, and PHS expenditures in 19,000 projects annually included duplication through backup and parallel approaches. Even conservative inventing efforts resulted in some direct failures and no-takers. The unused patent file, mainly from privately owned inventive work, remained the largest identified reservoir of exploitable technology.

11. At the same time selected agency applied research and development increased, the percentage of patents to independent inventors gradually decreased. Numbers of technical papers, people hired, and people trained in inventive work in the agencies have increased. The U. S. inventing activity has been institutionalized and largely nationalized by Federal agencies.

12. New technology generation by Federal agencies was concentrated by program, discipline, agency, contractor, and locality. Appendix E-1 shows for two typical years that California, Maryland, Texas, Massachusetts, and the District of Columbia were favored, receiving over half the Federal R&D funds. This self-reinforcing concentration supports high knowledge content, high income, and industrialized areas.

13. Because Federal administrators have traditionally focused applied research and development toward agency rather than national goals, Federally-generated technology has generally been labor-saving with only indirect labor-using effects; despite the fact that full employment has long been a national goal.

Informing

All the selected agencies took part in informing programs and contributed to national systems for distributing information. The agencies consumed 79 percent of the Federal funds spent for scientific and technical information in FY 1966 and 74 percent in FY 1971. Comparisons from Appendices D, F, G-2, and the preceding chapters indicate that:

1. Basic ingredients of informing programs were printing, libraries, and training. Older agencies had more autonomous operations, but all had their own distribution systems for technical information. All except SBA had predominating reference libraries.

2. USDA, PHS, DOD, NASA, and AEC had strong feedforwards from their technology generating activities to internal and external clients. USDA, with the best definition of its users and how they accepted information, processed information in traditional but effective ways.

3. In processing, conventional print accounted for most information transfer, but emphasis increased on oral and visual media for developing awareness and interest.

4. Internal training programs directly transferred information supporting innovation and integration.

5. The most-evaluated technical literature items were the 70,000 annual patents of the Patent Office. PHS technical literature was more carefully screened than that of other agencies. The 45,000 annual NTIS reports were not evaluated except by the agency which released them to NTIS. NASA has released about 1,000 evaluated technical briefs each recent year for commercial use.

6. Outputs were focused information, trained people, and stored information. DOD led in training, NASA and PHS in storing, and USDA in distributing information to specific users.

7. DOD, NASA, and AEC have developed information on much new technology. Required by law to negotiate with contractors or use open bidding, these agencies transferred whole groupings of technology from one contractor to another through contract awards.

8. Most agencies separated their services to direct constituents from their services to the general public. Libraries, centers, and distribution systems focused on constituents; and the general public was served through the Government Printing Office, NTIS, or clearinghouse type information offices. Most agencies tried only minimally to determine the information needs of the general public.

9. Feedback mechanisms for informing were very well developed in USDA through the county agent system and land grant colleges. Commerce, on the other hand, had less feedback on uses of NTIS reports.

10. Agencies did not normally publish misses or near-hits dropped in reviews of applied research and development, preferring to summarize or file them for future use.

11. Obstacles to information transfer were volume, numbers of separate items, and lack of uniform significance. USDA knew best how to move evaluated information from generator to user. SBA has developed a fair continuity of clients. DOD, NASA, and AEC did well within their sectors but not in the general economy.

12. Considerable duplication existed among Federal offices of the NTIS and its 11 branches, the Patent Office and its depositories, the Government Printing Office, DDC and its branch offices, the six regional dissemination centers of NASA, the AEC centers and depositories, and the 80 contact offices of SBA.

13. The agencies have succeeded most with clients or audiences specifically concerned with agency outputs. Agency distribution systems tended to become "trusted agent" channels for these audiences.

14. The predictive model outlined in Chapter II aided in reviewing the informing programs of the agencies, yet no agency had suboptimized its informing subprocess to make it self-supporting.

15. Though still experimental, a **de facto** dissemination system has been emerging. This system has begun in national libraries and special informing programs of Federal agencies; and, in addition to these, commercial and educational outlets have been used somewhat in making Federal R&D results known.

16. Appendix E-1 exemplifies the distribution of technical literature. Technical briefs have been available equally to all areas of the U. S. They covered electrical, mechanical, and electronic advances. Patents also covered these, but included much more chemical activity. Yet there has been surprising correlation between the ranking of states in patents received and the ranking of states in the number of queries about technical briefs. The six states which made the most queries have been the six states receiving the most patents each year since 1955, and correlation by rank continued when the number of queries

seemed small. Technical information tended to move into areas already supplied with it.

17. The special informing programs of NASA, the Economic Development Administration in Commerce, and SBA provided channels to potential users who might not have considered new technology otherwise. These programs endeavored to develop into trusted sources for their consumers, and they displaced other channels when the client had to decide which services he could afford. These new channels without doubt transferred information, but they did not reach economic self-sufficiency. Yet trade associations, research institutes, and commercial information systems have long operated by subscription and made a profit. By test of the marketplace, commercial operations have been accepted and special Federal programs have not.

18. Making technical information available to all who can use it became a national goal after technical information was recognized as a factor of production. Federal agencies did not program for this goal directly; in fact, internal mission and external activities were not generally separated in the agency informing program funding so that an administrator could evaluate each part.

Innovating

USDA, PHS, and SBA sustained direct innovating programs. DOD, NASA, and AEC had mostly secondary and more indirect programs. Commerce usually approached innovating through the private sector of the economy. Funding in all agencies was less clearly delineated than for inventing and informing; hence figures indicated actual effects less directly.

Agencies labeled innovating activities as public assistance, loans and subsidies, government-furnished equipment, educational programs, multiple-source procurement, small business set-asides, mobilization programs, and public relations. DOD, NASA, and AEC internal innovating programs have been so large that the secondary effects exceeded primary effects of other agencies. Comparisons from Appendices F, G-3, and the preceding chapters show that:

1. All agencies could **advocate** innovating new technological items except the Commerce Patent Office.

2. USDA, PHS, and SBA provided business and management infor-

mation, loans and subsidies, and community support in addition to information about new technology. DOD occasionally supported the general economy through mobilization programs. AEC supported it with nuclear and nuclear-associated technology. NASA and Commerce usually stopped at advocacy.

3. Innovating required more funding than either inventing or informing. To gain funding support for innovating, the need for new technology had to be clearly recognized and accepted economically and politically.

4. The sharper the customer was defined, the more easily support was gained and institutionalized. USDA and SBA, with clearly defined clients, have received substantial and continuing resources. The USDA county agent system and the agencies supporting conservation and stabilization have helped the farmer adopt new technology and have generated support for USDA appropriations. AEC and SBA have gained similar institutionalized support. PHS, DOD, and NASA have developed vocal but more specialized group support. The steadier the resource allocation, the more readily it became institutionalized as part of an economic sector.

5. USDA, as a more successful innovating agency, gave its clients patent-free information suited to their needs through advocates the customer knew, supported adoption with loans, and subsidized the market for the new output. Success of other agencies in innovating depends on how well they performed these or equivalent activities.

6. Customers followed the AIETA sequence, but they were more prone to adopt when Federal agencies subsidized the market or reduced the risks. Agencies with authority to reduce or share risks had advantages over those without such authority.

7. In dealing with the general economy, Federal agencies did not fully recognize relationships among inventing, informing, and innovating. They rarely tried to balance these activities in order to optimize innovating. Within mission activities, effort was more balanced and proportioned.

8. Innovating was supported indirectly through training of individuals and groups. DOD led in releasing individuals trained in new technology. PHS and USDA made heavy inputs through medical

and agricultural schools. DOD, NASA, and AEC caused new groups to learn new technology by shifting contractors.

9. Innovating progressed rapidly when whole systems were transferred from mission to commercial uses as DOD and NASA have done with jet transports, computers, titanium metallurgy, numerically controlled tools, integrated circuits, and communications satellites.

10. When technical programs terminated and skilled people were shifted to new programs, innovating potential increased in new programs. Congress has supported these cutback shifts more than the Federal agencies have.

11. Feedback and control of innovating by Federal agencies depended on agency contacts with many spectrums of the using public. USDA, PHS, and SBA attained better geographical distribution and contacts than other agencies.

12. Government expenditures concentrated according to specific, mission-oriented needs for DOD, NASA, and AEC. For NASA, three-fourths of items proposed for commercial application were in electronic, electric, and mechanical fields. Forcing of these fields inflated expenditures and increased the rate of obsolescence, both reducing the value of technology awaiting innovation. DOD items have additional disadvantages of duplication from three services, multiple approaches, and commercial non-applicability of defense-oriented items. For industrial sectors, government-generated technology for other than whole systems did not compete well with company technology or with traditional commercial sources of new technology. Industrial innovators heavily discounted new Federal technology.

13. About 285,000 new businesses were formed each year and about 12,000 failed. Since most new businesses were backed by commercial financial sources, the traditional system of innovating remained strong. Government support accompanied the formation of many technology-based new businesses; nonetheless, the trend to government support did not pervade all industries. Venture capital was generally available for normal types of enterprises, either in existing companies or in financial institutions.

14. Appendix E-1 shows that not only were certain areas more interested in new technical information, but also that they ranked high in income per capita; and this attracted larger populations. The

top eight states in queries made to NASA, making nearly half the total, averaged above median income for 1965.[1]

15. Special programs in agencies without market support capabilities, such as NASA and Commerce, had limited success compared with the "normal" programs of USDA and PHS. These normal programs established agencies as "trusted agents" and supported the market for results of innovating.

16. Federally sponsored innovating increased in public health (PHS), defense (DOD), and aerospace (NASA). It remained strong in agriculture (USDA), small business (SBA), and nuclear industries (AEC). When Federal administrators urged adoption, their forecast of side effects was minimal.

Integrating

"Integrating" activities were the most costly part of technology diffusion. Selected agencies consumed over half the total Federal budget. Agencies did not normally specify their funding in terms of integration but rather in agency terms of support, regulation, and adjustment. Appendices F, G-4, and the preceding chapters indicate the following:

1. The examples showed that Federal agencies sponsoring new technology needed to support the item until it "caught on." Integration procedures for effective Federal agency support were providing or supporting a market, giving incentives or subsidies, establishing regulations or specifications, giving management assistance, providing technical information, and making direct or indirect loans and progress payments. The agency activities are compared in Table V.

2. USDA, PHS, Commerce, and SBA had the clearest legislation for supporting integration and ingestion of new technology. USDA has had general and consistent support; PHS has recently received adequate resources; SBA had effective, even growing, funding; and Commerce has received marginal support. AEC had legislation and support in nuclear areas. DOD and NASA supported integration indirectly by sheer size of their resource allocation; nonetheless, they lacked the legislation and support for integration in the general economy.

3. In indirect programs of DOD, NASA, and the weapons portion

of AEC, items were integrated into general use through market support for mission programs. The record of these agencies attested to the effectiveness of indirect procedures as well as to their costliness. Technology was used when substantial resources supported it.

4. Commerce supported inventing and innovating activities in other agencies. Though it had the clearest legislation and stated goals, its limited funding precluded it from greatly influencing diffusion of Federal technology.

TABLE V

AGENCY INTEGRATING ACTIVITIES

	USDA	PHS	DOD	COM-MERCE	NASA	AEC	SBA
Market support	E(xternal)	E	–	I(nternal)	I	I	–
Subsidies/ Incentives	E	E	L(imited)	I		I	EL	–
Regulations/ Specifications	E	E	E	I		I	E	–
Manage en- information	E	–	EL	–		–	–	E
Loans/Progress payments	E	E	EL	I		I	I	E
Technical information	E	E	E	E		E	E	EL

5. Agencies integrated more when they became part of the economic sector they supported. USDA, PHS, DOD, AEC, and SBA became parts, respectively, of the agriculture, public health, defense, nuclear energy, and small business sectors of the economy. They developed these sectors and received partisan support in return. NASA's short-lived space sector began to merge back into other sectors in 1967. Commerce identified with no specific group for support.

6. When economic and social side effects of new technology became understood, Federal agencies adjusted by regulating use of the new technology. Feedback mechanisms for controlling the new technology

were developed best in USDA and PHS. AEC developed adequate
feedback and control for most nuclear technologies which it regulated.

7. Time lags in non-mission uses between innovation and integration of new technology were not appreciated in Federal programs.
NASA in particular sought economic effects from its special programs
in one to three years. Buildup was much slower; for example, USDA
work on improved crops took up to thirty years for integration.

TABLE VI

INTEGRATION EFFECTS ON NATIONAL GOALS

	USDA	PHS	DOD	COM-MERCE	NASA	AEC	SBA
1. Promote progress and provide technical information	Yes*	Yes	Yes	Yes	Yes	Yes	Yes
2. Maximum employment and purchasing power	No**	Yes	?***	Yes	Yes	Yes	Yes
3. Maximum production	Yes	No	?	No	No	Yes	Yes
4. Free enterprise	No	No	Yes	No	No	No	Yes
5. Economic dispersion and equitable development	No	No	No	No	No	No	Yes
6. Healthy physical environment	Recent	Recent	?	?	?	Recent	?
7. Avoid undesirable side effects	No	Recent	No	No	No	No	No
8. Focus on national goals	Recent	Recent	?	?	Recent	Recent	Yes

*Yes — Results support the goal
** No — Results negate the goal
***? — Questionable results

8. NASA, DOD, and AEC activities in inventing, informing, and
internal innovating have been massive inputs into technology diffusion
for several years. Delayed effects of these efforts on the general
economy were felt in the early 1970's. Nuclear-powered aircraft, the
SKYBOLT, unmanned aerodynamic strategic missiles, and some ABM

and space programs did not contribute to agency goals and consumed national resources which might have gone into economic growth.

9. When the Federal agency became part of an economic sector, it tended to suboptimize in terms of that sector and to put less emphasis on national goals. The selected agency programs indicate that agencies did not consider all national goals equally, as shown in Table VI.

IV. OVERALL COMPARISON OF AGENCY ACTIVITIES

As summarized in Appendix G and as charted in Table VII below, each agency had technology diffusion activities contributing to national development if not to national goals.

Since 1950, the inventing antecedent process has been compared and evaluated as "R&D." Since 1960 a portion of the informing sub-

TABLE VII

COMPARISON OF AGENCY ACTIVITIES

Agency	Inventing Antecedent	Informing Subprocess	Innovating Subprocess	Integrating Subprocess
USDA	P(rimary)*	P	P	P
PHS	P	P	P	P
DOD	P	S	I(ndirect)***	I
Commerce	S(econdary)**	P	I	I
NASA	P	P	S	I
AEC	P	P	P****	P****
SBA	–	S	P	P

*A primary activity is a major effort within the agency to reach agency goals in the general economy.

**A secondary activity supports the primary activities in the general economy.

***An indirect activity is one in which the agency activity in a special economic sector affects the general economy.

****Commercial nuclear applications only.

process, scientific and technical information, has been identified for comparison and evaluation. Technical training has sometimes been delineated for comparison. Innovation has been discussed indirectly, but the agencies do not make this subprocess directly visible to the public.

Innovating activities are justified as assistance, subsidies, loans, and incentive payments; but no agency has accounting records which can be used to review innovating simply and directly. Integrating in its initial stages is continued adoption; but it later becomes ingestion and adjustment under the impact of the second order consequences of the new technology. Though most agencies regulate, provide specifications, and penalize, they do not think of these activities as corollary to technology integration.

USDA, as an example, generates new foods, fiber, and procedures in its inventive work and accounts for these in its Agricultural Research Service and Cooperative State Research Service. It informs the public through the National Agricultural Library scientific and technical information activities, through the Office of Information, and through agency publications. Its traditional innovating activities are through the Federal Extension Service and its county agent system and land grant college affiliations; but more recently innovating has shifted toward agencies of Rural Development and Conservation. USDA integrating is supported by agencies concerned with marketing, consumer services, regulation, and agricultural stabilization. USDA subprocesses are identifiable and separable, even when the time delay between getting the new technology and its full integration is many years. As each Federal agency other than USDA is studied, the divisions of effort among the subprocesses emerge, even showing gaps and excessive duplications among and within agencies. The PHS subprocesses can be identified in its offices for the public health sector and thence into the general economy. SBA directs its innovating, integrating, and limited informing into the dynamic small business part of the general economy. AEC subprocesses are mixed; but, for commercial nuclear technologies, they can be clearly identified. Though an agency may have one or two activities focused toward the general economy, they all focus on their special sector, as DOD to defense, AEC to nuclear weapons, and NASA to aerospace. Even with Commerce, all the subprocesses can be identified if the mechanisms of private enterprise are considered.

Agency effectiveness. Comparison suggests that the closer an agency works to general economy needs, the more likely it will find and diffuse technology to satisfy those needs. The more special the mission or economic sector served, the fewer the items of technology which the general economy can use. USDA, PHS, SBA, and the commercial part of AEC focus on general sectors of the economy; and, except for SBA, they also develop lower cost products which can be adopted directly and used. DOD, NASA, and the nuclear weapons part of AEC focus on special economic sectors and their available technologies tend to be inapplicable, costly or risky, obsolescent, and inaccessible. These agencies have, however, effectively transferred complete operational systems like jet transports and communication satellites. SBA has been able to mesh its innovating, integrating, and limited informing funds with inventing and informing outputs from DOD, NASA, and AEC so that it has new technology and supports the small businessman.

Without doubt, these Federal agencies diffuse some technology effectively; however, some evidence indicates that desirable technologies will diffuse whether Federally or privately generated, or even whether domestic or foreign. Specific sources of unexploited technology are in unused patents and technical data; corporate files of patented, unpatented, and unpatentable technology and accompanying technical data developed under government contract, in commercially published technical literature on government applied research and development, technical literature of Federal agencies, and in the memory and working habits of technologists. It can be argued that available technology can diffuse when a need arises for it.

De facto procedures. Have Federal agencies developed new procedures for diffusing technology? Perhaps the more meaningful de facto procedures are in agencies affecting the general economy most directly in the long and short run. USDA procedures diverging from private enterprise include: (1) developing new foods, fibers, animals, processes, and techniques in civil service laboratories, reducing the opportunity for private enterprise animal, crop, and process developers; (2) taking title to contractual work and publishing the results openly, reducing the patent incentive; (3) maintaining a national agricultural information system and providing free information to farmers, reducing opportunity for publishers; (4) providing farmers with free assistance and advice through the county agent system, reducing opportunity for free enterprise marketing; (5) controlling innovation and total production by subsidies and incentive payments, partly replacing economic procedures for adjusting supply and demand; (6) loaning to farmers, supplementing local support sources; and (7) regulating output through reports, inspection, and quality control, protecting the consumer but restricting farm output to standard products and quotas.

PHS has developed divergent procedures during its rapid expansion since 1950. Like USDA in agriculture, it has become a major component of the public health sector of the economy and draws support from the sector. Divergent PHS procedures include (1) gaining new medical technology through civil service laboratories, contracts, and grants, reducing opportunity for medical entrepreneurs; (2) using peer groups to select contractors and grantees, reducing opportunity to develop new centers of excellence; (3) taking title and publishing more frequently than patenting, weakening the patent incentive; (4) maintaining a national medical information system, reducing opportunity for publishers; (5) assisting and advising state and local public health activities, reducing opportunity for public health entrepreneurs; (6) providing policy and guidance for the subsidies and incentive payments of Medicare and Medicaid programs, reducing opportunity for voluntary health associations and groupings; and (7) regulating conduct of health professionals through reports and inspection.

SBA was formed to bolster free enterprise by giving preference to small businessmen. Its guaranteed loans have generally supplemented historical support mechanisms for innovation and continued adoption of new technology. NASA and AEC were special programs set up to accomplish national goals which Congress believed free enterprise could not reach alone. Though AEC has diffused nuclear technology and has encouraged contractors, AEC legislation established a government nuclear monopoly, institutionalized and nationalized nuclear inventing and informing, controlled innovating, and regulated integrating. NASA was established as the government agency to exploit space for the benefit of mankind, just as AEC exploited nuclear energy. AEC and NASA generally take title to proprietary information, they have developed information dissemination systems for their specialized fields, and they support the market for innovation and integration in nuclear and aerospace work. Contrary to prior procedures for exploiting new fields, private enterprise has had only secondary opportunities in either

space or nuclear effort. Since 1960 DOD has developed similarly to
AEC and NASA not only for its own defense sector, but also with its
large internal audiences of servicemen and civilians. DOD has, even
more than NASA and AEC, socialized and institutionalized inventing,
informing, innovating, and integrating through its own laboratories,
school systems, training facilities, and support and contract mechanisms. When they received only a small portion of the budget, DOD
programs and divergent procedures had little impact; but when they
reached ten percent of the GNP and forty percent of the Federal budget, they indirectly supplemented and displaced some private enterprise procedures.

All the agencies except Commerce have developed some **de facto**
procedures for one or more technology diffusion subprocesses. Yet
patents remained a potent force in commercial products, industry competed in application of new technology including patents, new business
incorporations remained at a high level, financial institutions supported
new technology enterprises, and technical education grew in importance; hence historical and private enterprise procedures remained
strong and effective.

National goals. Has diffusion of new technology by Federal agencies
moved the country toward national goals? We can note that average
income has increased by 4½ times for high income areas, by 5½ times
for the U.S. as a whole, and by 9½ times for the low income areas.
The GNP has increased fourfold since 1946. The total labor force has
continued to increase. Longevity has increased from forty years in
1860 to seventy years in 1965. Traditional diseases have been reduced
or eliminated. Agricultural land and some other natural resources
are being conserved for future generations. The educational level of
U.S. citizens is rising. Technical information has become increasingly
available to all citizens since 1960.

We can also note some continuing problem areas, such as the one
in equitable development of all parts of the country. Though the
average per capita income of the lowest income states of 1929 has
increased twice as much as the incomes of the highest income states
of the same time, the differential is still almost two to one. Although
low income states have made far greater gains, the same four states
on the bottom in 1929 (Alabama, Arkansas, Mississippi, and South
Carolina) were also low in 1970. High income states in 1970 were also

high in 1950 and in 1929 (Connecticut, Delaware, Illinois, New Jersey, New York, and California).[2] Table VIII shows the high-to-low state ratios. Special programs of USDA, PHS, and Commerce have focused on fostering development in low income and technically backward areas. These programs transferred payments to create jobs, foster new enterprises, and further development.

2. Between 1929 and 1970, population shifted from a national rural focus toward an urban concentration in high income states. Low income states held fairly static and rural populations.

TABLE VIII
INCOME EQUALIZATION

	1929	1950	1970	1970/1929 Ratio
High State	$1,159	$2,384	$4,807	4.54
Average	703	1,496	3,910	5.57
Low State	270	755	2,561	9.5
High-to-Average Ratio	1.65	1.59	1.23	
High-to-Low Ratio	4.3	3.16	1.88	

In gross terms, the population increase of these states moved to high income areas. Table VIII represented rising incomes for almost static populations in the low income states.

Federal agency technology diffusion tended to support areas already industrialized using high technology content procedures and having high incomes. Both technology-sensitive and population-sensitive programs had this effect, the former because of interest and opportunity and the latter because of population shifts to higher income areas. Concentrating heavy expenditures into a few localities conflicted with equitable goals embodied in legislation like the Public Works and Economic Development Act of 1965. Further, most new technology was labor-saving, in conflict with full employment goals of the Employment Act of 1946.

Environmental degradation continues to increase in most areas of the country. Costs of degradation in quality of life, life expectancy, and resources have not been fully determined. Technology-related deaths have increased so rapidly that the death rate from all causes per 100,000 population has begun to exceed previous years and predictions. Even when adjusted for average age, the death rates have leveled out, indicating that U.S. life and environment are in temporary equilibrium.

Feedback on technology diffusion tends to be incomplete for several years. Side effects do not tend to become pronounced until integration has begun displacing former relationships, suppliers, and jobs. Neither forecasting on side effects nor feedback on them has been adequately done by Federal agencies. Agency goals, set by legislation and indirectly adjusted each year through appropriations, constrain agency administrators.

It becomes quite clear that Federal administrators **optimize** technology diffusion efforts **toward agency goals** focused on particular economic or social sectors, and they do not fully consider consequences and impacts of their programs to other sectors. Adjusting legislation normally handles identified and major abuses which are already historical at the time of correction. Because of the feedback lag, most administrators cannot assess side effects of their programs in terms of either agency or national goals before the programs are entrenched. The systems approach which emphasizes that all related aspects of a program should be considered together has not reached full effectiveness.

Summary. Total comparison for agency activities shows that USDA and PHS programs were self-sufficient and focused strongly on agency goals. DOD, NASA, and AEC were strong where SBA was weakest. SBA programs thus complemented diffusion activities of these larger agencies. Commerce was active only in informing and generally supporting the other agencies. Even the most effective agencies had serious limitations in their programs and procedures. Cybernetic approaches of relating results to national rather than agency goals could have been used in these agencies to improve and focus their results.

To diffuse Federally-derived technology, administrators must know their own agency's strengths and weaknesses in the total process. They must compare their legislative charters against current and changing national goals and suggest adjustments which make their agencies more effective. In addition, program or systems review by external groups in Congress and the general public may be needed to recast obsolescent programs and procedures. The next chapter suggests ways improvements can be made.

FOOTNOTES

[1] U.S. Department of Commerce, Bureau of the Census, *Statistical Abstract of the U.S., 1971* (Washington, D.C.: U.S. Government Printing Office, 1972), p. 314.

[2] *Reader's Digest Almanac and Yearbook, 1967, op. cit.,* p. 417 and *U.S. Statistical Abstract, op. cit.,* p. 314.

CHAPTER IX

SUMMARY, CONCLUSIONS, AND RECOMMENDATIONS

I. SUMMARY

This chapter summarizes the study, draws conclusions from it, and suggests how Federal agencies can more effectively diffuse into the economy new technologies generated during Federal applied research and development. Summaries are developed for the subsidiary problems of: (1) developing and grouping the historical and traditional technology diffusion activities, both private enterprise and Federal; (2) synthesizing this evidence into predictive models which form the conceptual bases for operating systems; (3) comparing selected Federal agencies.

Historical and Traditional Activities

Origin of diffusible technology. The U. S. spends over $22 billion annually on applied research and development, activities which generate new technology through various types of inventive work. Over half of the funds are spent by Federal agencies. Most of the half million scientists and engineers in R&D and over 200,000 self-employed inventors are engaged in these activities. New technology is generated by trained people from available resources to satisfy identifiable needs. Results are new products, new processes, new techniques, record papers, and trained people. There are more failures than successes. Most product development occurs in private enterprise corporations, but independent inventors still contribute significantly. Appreciable numbers of technical items are available in unused patents, in the corporate files for products developed but not used, in Federal and commercial technical literature, and in the experience of investigators working on more pressing problems.

Learning about diffusible technology. Technical information available to the economy includes active and informal sources or channels of the communications specialist as well as impersonal or passive sources and channels of the information scientist. Some industries depend more on trusted sources like trade journals, professional journals, vendor catalogs, and supplier representatives for information about new technologies. Individuals, technology-based companies, and marketing organizations are significant diffusers of technical information. Informing about new technology requires resources, some concept of client needs, and knowledge of what he will use. Some government agencies have mastered these requirements and are building **de facto** national information systems.

Adoption or innovation. The potential adopter evaluates new technology in terms of advantage to his own enterprise. The new technology may fail in evaluation, it may fail after adoption, or it may succeed. Adoption is affected by the nature of the technology, the adopter characteristics, the society preferences, the support available, and the anticipated gains of adoption. Resistance to new technology may take legal, financial, social, and religious outlets to make the items illegal, unprofitable, unwanted, or immoral.

Integrating or ingesting new technology. Favorable results of widespread new technology adoption are freedom from unpleasant work, more convenient and efficient services, new and less expensive goods, and social and economic opportunity. Unfavorable results are job displacement, hazards, unequal development, degradation of the environment, and increasing government intervention. The amount of new technology useful for diffusion may be less than supposed because of its type, rapid obsolescence, and inaccessibility. The national government has the largest group of activities which advance or retard the integrating process. Market support is a prime requirement for the integrating activity.

Synthesis into Models

The historical and traditional activities related to technology and its diffusion fall into the four groupings of inventing (or generating new technology), informing (or telling people about it), innovating (or adopting it), and integrating (or adjusting the social and economic processes to the new technology). After an item of technology goes through the sequence, it is part of the culture until it is replaced by still newer technology. Technology diffusion is step-by-step from one level of technology to the next; but, at any one time, the activities do group into the four classifications. For this reason, it is feasible to group these activities in operating programs of Federal agencies as is done in summary form in Appendix G.

Federal Agencies

The U. S. Department of Agriculture closely approaches the models for generating technology and diffusing it. It is characterized by (1) nearly complete integration in the agricultural sector, (2) internal activity in inventing, informing, innovating, and integrating, (3) reliance on conventional techniques for informing, (4) use of market support subsidies for innovating and integrating, (5) historic and continuing Congressional support, (6) relatively small and slowly changing budgets, (7) labor-saving or labor-conserving effects on the economy, and (8) development efforts for all rural areas of the country. It has established regional and national development centers, information activities, the National Agricultural Library, the county agent system, and the subsidy and loan institutions which help the agricultural sector remain a leader in technology diffusion. USDA has closely associated with land grant colleges and other institutions which support diffusion subprocesses. Typical successes of USDA are biological insect control and farm mechanization, both taking place in the 1930-1960 period. A typical failure was guayule rubber which became obsolescent when natural rubber was synthesized. A typical no-taker has been insect control in stored grain, which is not competitive with alternative uses of resources. USDA is representative of older agencies which have developed relatively efficient channels for all subprocesses of technology diffusion. Feedback and feedforward channels are well developed and administrators generally understand the feedback. These agencies, though, have suboptimized in terms of agency goals which gain public approval such as maximum production per man-hour, land conservation, and efficient use of material resources.

The **Public Health Service** represents those agencies which are adjusting their position in U. S. society because of the influx of Federal aid into social programs. These agencies have programs for developing new technology, informing the public about it, and supporting innovation and integration; but their activities are inflated in cost, and feedback does not yet clearly define the results, which are population-sensitive and job-creating rather than labor-saving. Commendable features of PHS programs are inventing and informing activities in the National Institutes of Health and National Library of Medicine and the attention since 1966 to environmental degradation and hazards. Typical successes by PHS in technology diffusion are vaccines against traditional diseases, and typical failures are the reduction of trauma and deaths caused by the instruments of technology. Fluoridation of public water supplies is a public health dental measure only partially accepted.

Department of Defense programs involve: (1) heavy expenditures toward agency goals: (2) generation of much nonapplicable end item technology; (3) heavy reliance on large industrial contractors in a few geographic areas; (4) technology diffusion by providing technical specifications, supporting the market, and providing subsidies and loans; and (5) labor-using and capital-using effects on the general economy. Applied research and development activities which generate DOD mission technologies are so large that they affect the economy considerably in terms of foregone opportunities. Informing subprocess facilities within the defense sector (the military departments, DDC, and through NTIS), furnish alternatives to other information sources. DOD has supported integration for technologies deemed to be strategic necessities such as numerical control tools and titanium metal development. Mechanisms which DOD has used for supporting innovating and integrating among defense contractors have been market support, specifications, progress payments, government-furnished equipment, government-furnished facilities, tooling cost allowances, and training in new technology. Besides typical successes in diffusion such as numerical control tools and titanium metallurgy, there are typical failures such as irradiated foods, which failed for safety reasons, and typical no-takers such as freeze-dried foods, which are not economically competitive. Despite the necessary downgrading of DOD technologies, there are, from sheer numbers of projects, many products, processes, and techniques applicable to the general economy. Further, because of its $50 billion annual procurement of end items for defense goals, DOD indirectly supports innovation and integration into the general economy.

National Aeronautics and Space Administration programs originally transferred technology from other sources to aerospace applications. Gradually the technologies were adapted, new ones invented, and all made available for transfer back into the general economy. The size of the NASA effort has been considered dysfunctional, as has the large DOD effort, in terms of foregone opportunities. NASA policy for obtaining title to new technology patents may not encourage non-mission innovating among its contractors, but NASA officials believe it encourages other entrepreneurs. Other features of NASA programs are the effort to identify new technology and its Regional Research Application Centers for informing and advocating adoption of NASA applied research and development results. The amount of technology transferred back into the general economy has been small in comparison to the size of the total effort. A typical NASA diffusion success has been integrated electronic circuits, for which NASA could furnish a market. Microfiche diffused after a push from NASA, without even being part of the NASA diffusion effort. Highway grooving has been pushed for years by NASA without catching on or competing with local and state solutions to automobile skidding problems.

The **Department of Commerce** has developed as a service organization to private enterprise and other government agencies. Inventing, innovating, and integrating are carried out by private enterprise; and Commerce furnishes information on basic standards, new private enterprise technology (patents from the Patent Office), new Federal and foreign technology (reports from NTIS), and statistical information which can aid potential adopters of new technology. Commerce has actually been invaded, and it has lost many of its functions to Federal agencies which are more aggressive in meeting industry needs. The Patent System has been to some extent displaced by the technology generating and information transfer systems of USDA, PHS, DOD, NASA, and AEC.

The **Atomic Energy Commission** programs include inventing, informing, and some specialized innovating and integrating in commercial nuclear fields. National security laws require that AEC retain nuclear energy patents and nuclear process control for government. As new technology is adopted commercially, AEC drops out of production support, and licenses to users or contractors. Continued adoption is regulated and monitored as an integrating activity. In two commercial fields being diffused, nuclear power plants tend to reduce employment, and radioisotopes tend to improve quality rather than create jobs or income. The "Savannah," prototype nuclear-powered merchant ship was a typical economic failure, being non-competitive with fossil fuel powered merchant ships.

Small Business Administration programs for informing, innovating, and integrating support small business through commercial sources, or similar mechanisms. SBA can also give enterprise and management advice, and has become a trusted agent to many small businessmen. These combined features make SBA programs complementary to those of DOD, NASA, and AEC for helping small business use Federally originated technology.

II. CONCLUSIONS

This study of U. S. technology diffusion indicates that (1) most new technology originates in private enterprise organizations where a market has been established or forecast for an item, (2) Federal agencies generate some new technology to order, but mainly furnish a market for it. (3) informing activities have lagged behind availability of new technology but have begun to catch up as Federal agencies have established or supported national information systems, (4) much informing is done by people movement, changing Federal agency contractors, and acquiring technology-based companies, (5) innovating is affected by the potential adopter's calculation of advantage from the new technology to his enterprise and by the support he can get from private enterprise and Federal sources, (6) imitative or continued adoption is influenced most by success of earlier adopters but gains impetus as the economy and society shift to using the new technology, (7) Federal government agencies have many regulatory and economy-manipulative activities which affect continued adoption or integration, and (8) technology diffusion has never been a national goal per se, but goals which can be reached only by using new technology have been inherent in many national programs.

Technology diffusion activities group into identifiable programs of "informing," "innovating," and "integrating." Organizations may specialize in one or more, depending on their mission or market segment. Antecedents to these activities are establishing a need (or conceiving an opportunity) and generating or inventing the necessary technology. This inventive work is the most completely identifiable activity related to technology diffusion.

Informing activities best identified are information science, technical training, marketing, and public relations. Innovating and integrating activities are less easily separated and quantified though they are identifiable by their nature. Loans, subsidies, incentive payments, progress payments, cost allowances, depletion deductions, specifications, regulations, inspections, and reports may affect either. Each activity in the sequence is normally more expensive than the previous one.

Typical Federal agencies such as USDA and PHS diffuse technology into the general economy by using a combination of new and historical activities of technology diffusion. They develop or find technologies to satisfy their internal mission needs or the needs of their clients. They inform their clients through both modern and older methods and channels. They support innovating and integrating through advocacy, resources, and providing a market. Commerce's weaknesses and apparent lack of support are striking. Highly publicized special technology transfer programs of NASA, AEC, and Commerce show weaknesses when scrutinized against economic self-sufficiency and national technical progress. The overriding funds for DOD, NASA, and AEC for mission-oriented technology are being reduced; yet a significant opportunity remains for SBA to supplement these agencies through its more direct support of innovation and integration. All the selected agencies lack feedback on the total effects on the economy of technology which they diffuse. They program cybernetically only partially. Administrators have not recognized interrelationships of the technology diffusion subprocesses and do not provide a trail from national goals to needs to agency satisfaction of needs.

III. RECOMMENDATIONS

Operational Check Lists

Based on results of this study, Federal administrators can improve the general diffusion and exploitation of technological developments resulting from Federal applied research and development by acting within their own agencies under present frameworks of Federal legislation and procedures. These actions which embody the insights developed in the study are presented in the form of a check list which an administrator may use. Check list items 1-8 refer to the total process; items 9-17 to the antecedent activity of inventing; 18-27 to informing; 28-37 to innovating; and 38-48 to integrating.

1. What national goals does my agency support by exploiting Federal applied research and development?

2. What side effects of exploiting Federal applied research and development by my agency conflict with national goals?

3. What cost-benefit tradeoffs justify my agency's support of diffusing Federally derived technology which conflicts with national goals?

4. Are activities of inventing, informing, innovating, and integrating identified in my agency planning and organization? Could a management audit identify a trail from national goal to agency goal to need identification to invention through to the satisfaction of my agency's responsibility for the national goal?

5. Does my agency have a systems review or internal audit (management, technical, and financial) team which can use the audit trail to determine agency effectiveness in using applied research and development results to accomplish national goals?

6. Is my agency structure based on work goals with well understood and clearly stated delegations of authority for each subprocess of technology diffusion?

7. Are my agency technology diffusion activities clearly defined in planning and programming procedures?

8. Has my agency trained its people in interrelationships among subprocesses of technology diffusion? Do subordinate managers know with whom and how they must coordinate to achieve interrelated results?

9. Is the problem clearly stated? Is there access from the technology developer to the customer stating the problem?

10. Does the problem statement relate to agency and national goals? Is there a specific market for the technology? Are any other Federal agencies working on the same problem?

11. Can inventive work progress from known to related areas?

12. Is there freedom to exploit unexpected breakthroughs?

13. Do the applied research and development teams have ready access to technical information? Is there internal or external access to all disciplines which could solve the problem?

14. Is there a test and evaluation program which checks the new technology for technical, economic, and social feasibility?

15. Has forecasting been used to determine side effects of new technology? What old technologies will it replace?

16. If the technology succeeds, what groups in the general economy will benefit most? Are these groups associated with vested interests?

17. Have arrangements been made to provide data on the new technology and names of significant contributors to agency informing activities?

18. Have I obtained all available information from the inventing activities supporting my agency's technology diffusion?

19. Who are users or "customers" for my technical information?

20. What kinds of information do my customers need?

21. What channels most effectively reach my customers?

22. How can I become a more "trusted agent" to my customers?

23. Have I established reinforcing channels to my customers? Is my information packaged to give awareness and details, and to aid in evaluation after the technology is applied?

24. Can my informing activity provide access from the innovator back to the inventors?

25. Do I have feedback on my informing programs so I can adjust my efforts?

26. Is my agency's information available to all who can use it?

27. Have I considered future users of the information by storing it in readily accessible files or libraries?

28. Can I clearly identify my agency's support for innovating Federally derived technology?

29. Can my agency work with state or other Federal agencies on direct programs which it lacks?

30. Can my agency provide, either directly or indirectly, business and management information as well as technical information?

31. Can my agency provide loans and subsidies to innovators? Do other sources provide such supports?

32. Are there advocates for "adoption" in my agency with access to adoption units?

33. Does my agency exploit the adopter's AIETA sequence in its support of innovation?

34. Is the item useful enough to "catch on" and have a market without government support?

35. Can my agency provide or support a market for the outputs of adopters of new technoogy?

36. Does my agency have feedback (reports, analyses, consultations, and records) which will guide innovating activity?

37. Can innovators obtain more technical information or, if necessary, get back to the originator of new technology?

38. Can my agency provide continuing support for ingestion of Federal applied research and development results?

39. Does it have legislation and funding support for its integration activities?

40. Have I made technological forecasts of undesirable side effects from changed relationships during technology ingestion?

41. Does my agency have regulatory powers to control foreseeable undesirable side effects of new technology?

42. Does my agency alert others to side effects from its integration of Federally derived technology?

43. Do my agency's integrative activities support special interest groups within the sector?

44. Are there pressure groups supporting integration of specific technology?

45. Have feedback mechanisms been established so that effects of integration will become known?

46. Does my agency have specific programs for helping laggards in adoption?

47. Do my integrating offices and activities include cross references to other Federal supporting activities?

48. What is the cost of my agency's integrating support in terms of paper work, processing time, and additional Federal employees?

General Recommendations

The following recommendations and brief rationales apply more generally to program administrators of Federal agency technology diffusion:

1. DOD, NASA, and AEC should form a coalition with SBA to diffuse Federal applied research and development results to small and medium-sized business. This study has pinpointed SBA's capability to complement these three agencies which dominate Federal inventing and informing activities. SBA may help disperse the mission oriented economic concentration of these three to new firms, industries, and geographic areas.

2. DOD, NASA, and AEC should release as rapidly as possible to the National Technical Information Service all documents with potentially useful commercial information. This study discloses why these three agencies generate so little commercial technology; yet, the sheer amount of national resources allocated to their mission-oriented technology indicates it should be screened continuously for potentially useful information. The agency administrators will discover fewer uses than technically oriented businessmen looking for an opportunity. Information should be released to NTIS so that technology entrepreneurs have access to it.

3. Administrators should consider technology diffusion neither desirable nor undesirable in itself, but rather in terms of its usefulness in reaching national goals. They should emphasize technology from applied research and development only enough to make it competitive with equally useful results from commercial R&D or individual inventors. This research disclosed no rationale for diffusing technology for the sake of change or for treating preferentially the Federally originated technology. The rationale for diffusing any technology is that it accomplishes national goals better than not diffusing it. Administrators should select technology for diffusion according to its effectiveness in accomplishing national goals compared to other technology or to other alternatives not using technology. The origin of the technology is not a logical factor to consider.

4. Federal procurement of supplies, services, and new development should be used as a channel to support commercial innovation and integration. This research shows that market support is a requirement, **sine qua non,** for innovation and integration. With the Federal government budget over twenty percent of the Gross National Pro-

duct, its purchases frequently set the market for whatever items and services it uses. By its procurement specifications, it can support old or new technology; but by focusing specifications on performance which only new technology can produce, it can furnish market support for innovation and integration.

5. Federal agency market for technologies to absorb labor at the same time as capital should be developed. The national goal of full employment has conflicted with historical technology diffusion which has focused on labor-saving and capital-using technologies. The sixties have been characterized by excess labor, ghettoes of chronically unemployed, and scarce capital. Directing some inventing effort toward capital-saving, labor-using technologies could begin long term corrections in social and economic structures. (Recreational equipment, space devices, and tobacco are examples of labor-using but not capital-saving technologies.)

6. Procedures should be explored for making adoption and ingestion of Federal applied research and development results more attractive to less developed geographic areas and industrial segments. This study indicates that Federal agency technology diffusion gravitates to areas of economic concentration with high population densities where people have high incomes. As one sample procedure, labor-using, capital-saving technologies would support less developed areas. As another example, penalties for polluting concentrated areas could be levied, thus forcing industry into less developed areas where nature could absorb pollutants.

7. Agency programs should be arranged and budgeted so that relative costs of each subprocess of technology diffusion can be identified and compared by executives and legislators who must choose among alternatives.

Legislative

Some recommendations can be made as examples of action which Federal administrators could propose for Congressional action.

1. Recognize Federal technology diffusion activities through reorganizing and regrouping those departments, agencies, boards, and offices which now deal with it in partial forms. Consider a new Department of Technology and Industry combining the National Bureau of Standards, the Patent Office, NASA, AEC, SBA, and EDA. Several

agencies of government have developed which deal predominantly with the same aspects of technology diffusion. Now separately funded, they compete for attention and resources in the total panorama of technical change. Combination would focus the direction of the new department toward smaller economic units, more uniform geographic area development, and stronger free enterprise. This reorganization would strike a national balance difficult to achieve with present **de facto** procedures and organization.

2. Seek more technical and resource support for making Patent Office and NTIS work available sooner and disseminated more broadly. Most new technical information is released to the commercial public from these two offices. Both are required to seek economic self-sufficiency. Neither has achieved it, though both charge high prices. If a Federal goal is to maximize use of Federal technology, NTIS reports and government-owned patents could be made available sooner and more cheaply if the offices were better funded. Depositories of each system could be combined and extended to include more colleges and universities as well as Federal and state libraries.

3. Seek and encourage more high risk capital to support innovating and integrating of new technology by small business. This research revealed SBA's important role in helping small business compete with larger economic units. SBA is mainly limited by amounts of risk capital; it must loan directly or support private enterprise loan sources. Since ingestion of new technology depends on many adoptions, SBA can support diffusion through small business units if adequately funded.

V. EPILOGUE

This study has considered the total process of diffusing technology as three subprocesses of informing, innovating, and integrating, with antecedent inventing programs furnishing new technology. This way of thinking about technology diffusion, particularly the delineation of informing as a separate subprocess, is believed to contribute significantly to the subject. Each of the subprocesses is a grouping of related activities which Federal administrators can optimize by considering each as an operating system with its own objectives, inputs, processing, outputs and feedback. Once optimizing is accomplished administrators can support exploitation of Federal applied research and development more readily and effectively.

Yet the research discloses that uncritical diffusion and exploitation of Federal applied research and development results, simply because these results derive from public funds, has questionable merit. These results must be carefully analyzed to determine how much they contribute to national goals and how much their side effects detract from those goals. Federal agency administrators can logically support Federally originated technology only enough to make it competitive with equally useful technology from other sources.

BIBLIOGRAPHY

BIBLIOGRAPHY OF SOURCES CITED

A. STATE AND FEDERAL GOVERNMENT PUBLICATIONS

1. Books, Hearings, and Reports

Auerbach Corporation, *DOD User Needs Study—Phase I.* Vol. I of Contractor's Report, Advanced Research Projects Agency, Department of Defense, May 14, 1965. 2 vols. Springfield, Va.: Clearinghouse, 1965 (AD-615-501).

Bird, Kermit. *The Awakening Freeze-Drying Industry.* Washington, D.C.: U.S. Department of Agriculture, Economic Research Service, January 1965.

Cohen, Wilbur J. *Health in America—The Role of the Federal Government in Bringing High Quality Health Care to All the American People.* Report to the President by the Secretary of Health, Education, and Welfare, June 14, 1968. Washington, D.C.: Office of the Secretary, D/HEW, 1968.

Crampon, L. J., and Schweizer, Stewart F. *Use of Outside Information in Small Firms.* Washington, D.C.: Small Business Administration, February 1962.

Crawford, J. H., and others. *Scientific and Technical Communications in the Government.* Task Force Report to the President's Special Assistant for Science and Technology. Springfield, Va.: Clearinghouse, April 1962 (AD 299 545).

Gilfillan, S. C. *Invention and the Patent System.* Report to the Joint Economic Committee, U.S. Cong. Washington, D.C.: U.S. Government Printing Office, December 1964.

Gilmore, John S., and others. *The Channels of Technology Acquisition in Commercial Firms, and the NASA Dissemination Program.* Springfield, Va.: Clearinghouse, June, 1967 (N67 31477).

Hopkins, John A. *Changing Technology and Employment in Agriculture.* Washington, D.C.: U.S. Government Printing Office, 1941.

Jones, Boisfeuillet, Chairman. *National Advisory Commission on Health Facilities, A Report to the President, December 1968.* Washington, D.C.: U.S. Government Printing Office, 1968.

Knipling, E. F. "Screw Worm Eradication: Concepts and Research Leading to the Sterile Male Method," *Smithsonian Report for 1958,* pp. 409-418. Washington, D.C.: Smithsonian Institution, 1958.

Knox, William T., and others. *Recommendations for National Document Handling Systems in Science and Technology.* Report of the Committee on Scientific and Technical Information, Federal Council for Science and Technology. Springfield, Va.: Clearinghouse, 1965.

Moot, Robert C. *SCORE—Service Corps of Retired Executives.* SBA Brochure OPI 16. Washington, D.C.: Small Business Administration, 1967.

————. "Statement as Administrator, SBA, Before the Subcommittee of Science and Technology, The Senate Select Committee on Small Business, September 28, 1967." Washington, D.C.: Small Business Administration, 1967 (Mimeograph).

Myers, Sumner. *Industrial Innovations, Their Characteristics and Their Scientific and Technical Information Bases.* Special Report to the National Science Foundation. Washington, D.C.: National Planning Association, April 1966.

National Academy of Sciences-National Research Council. *Applied Science and Technological Progress, A Report to the Committee on Science and Astronautics.* Washington, D.C.: U.S. Government Printing Office, 1967.

————. *Proceedings of the International Conference on Scientific Information.* 2 vols. Washington, D.C.: NAS/NRC, 1959.

————. *Report of the Ad Hoc Committee of Research-Engineering Interaction.* Springfield, Va.: Clearinghouse, 1966 (MAB-222-M).

Panel on the Impact of the Peaceful Uses of Atomic Energy. *Peaceful Uses of Atomic Energy. Report to the Joint Committee on Atomic Energy.* 2 vols. Washington, D.C.: U.S. Government Printing Office, 1956.

President's Scientific Advisory Committee. *Science and Agriculture.* Washington, D.C.: Office of the White House, January 29, 1962.

————. *Science, Government, and Information.* Washington, D.C.: Office of the White House, 1963.

Rice, J. Wade. *Technical Aids for Small Business.* Washington, D.C.: Small Business Administration, 1956.

Schlesinger, James R. *National Security Management—Defense Planning and Budgeting: The Issue of Centralized Control.* Washington, D.C.: Industrial College of the Armed Forces, 1968.

Sherwin, C. W., and others, Office of the Director of Defense Research and Engineering. *The First Interim Report on Project Hindsight (Summary).* Springfield, Va.: Clearinghouse, 1966 (AD 642 400).

Smith, Alan A. *Technology and Your New Product.* SBA Series No. 19. Washington, D.C.: U.S. Government Printing Office, 1956.

Strother, C. O., and others. *Transferrence of Non-Nuclear Technology to Industry.* Committee Report to Oak Ridge Operations Office. Oak Ridge, Tenn.: Atomic Energy Commission, 1965 (ORO-629).

To Promote the Progress of the Useful Arts. Report of the President's Commission on the Patent System. Washington, D.C.: U.S. Government Printing Office, 1966.

True, Alfred Charles. *A History of Agricultural Experimentation and Research in the United States.* USDA Misc. Publ. 251. Washington, D.C.: U.S. Government Printing Office, 1937.

U.S. Atomic Energy Commission. *Annual Report to Congress of the AEC for 1971.* Washington, D.C.: U.S. Government Printing Office, 1972.

————. *Industrial Benefits from Nuclear Development.* Oak Ridge, Tenn.: U.S. AEC Technical Information Division, 1967.

————. *The Nuclear Industry—1968.* Washington, D.C.: U.S. Government Printing Office, 1968.

————. *The Nuclear Industry—1971.* Washington, D.C.: U.S. Government Printing Office, 1972.

————. *Radioisotopes in Science and Industry: A Special Report of the United States Atomic Energy Commission.* Washington, D.C.: Atomic Energy Commission, 1960.

————. Isotopes Information Center, Oak Ridge National Laboratory. *Isotopes and Radiation Technology—A Quarterly Technical Progress Report.* Vol. 6, No. 4. Washington, D.C.: U.S. Government Printing Office, 1969.

————. *Division of Nuclear Education and Training, Program Statistics, July 1, 1969 to June 30, 1970.* Washington, D.C.: U.S. Government Printing Office, 1970.

U.S. Bureau of the Budget. *Special Analyses: Budget of the United States: Fiscal Year 1969.* Washington, D.C.: U.S. Government Printing Office, 1968.

————. *Special Analyses: Budget of the United States: Fiscal Year 1971.* Washington, D.C.: U.S. Government Printing Office, 1970.

————. *The Budget of the U.S. Government, FY 1971.* Washington, D.C.: U.S. Government Printing Office, 1970.

————. *Budget of the United States: Fiscal Year 1973.* Washington, D.C.: U.S. Government Printing Office, 1972.

————. *Budget of the United States: Fiscal Year 1973,* Appendix. Washington, D.C.: U.S. Government Printing Office, 1972.

U.S. Congress, House, Committee on Interior and Insular Affairs. *Review of Research by the Bureau of Mines, Department of the Interior.* Committee Print No. 2. 89th Cong., 1st Sess. Washington, D.C.: U.S. Government Printing Office, 1965.

U.S. Congress, House, Committee on Science and Astronautics. *For the Benefit of All Mankind, The Practical Returns from Space Investment.* 92d Cong., 2d Sess. Washington, D.C.: U.S. Government Printing Office, 1972.

————. *The National Science Foundation—A General Review of the First Fifteen Years.* 89th Cong., 2d Sess. Washington, D.C.: U.S. Government Printing Office, 1972.

————. *Notes on Conversion to the Metric System.* 89th Cong., 1st Sess. Washington, D.C.: U.S. Government Printing Office, 1965.

————. *Obligations for Research and Development and R&D Plant, by Geographic Divisions and States, by Selected Federal Agencies, Fiscal Years 1961-1964.* Report to the Subcommittee on Science, Research, and Development by the National Science Foundation. 88th Cong., 2d Sess. Washington, D.C.: U.S. Government Printing Office, 1964.

U.S. Congress, Joint Committee on Atomic Energy. *Review of the Food Irradiation Program.* Hearing Before the Subcommittee on Research, Development, and Radiation. 89th Cong., 2d Sess., September 12, 1966. Washington, D.C.: U.S. Government Printing Office, 1966.

U.S. Congress, Joint Economic Committee. *Automation and Technology in Education, A Report of the Subcommittee on Economic Progress.* 89th Cong., 2d Sess. Washington, D.C.: U.S. Government Printing Office, August 1966.

————. *U.S. Economic Growth to 1975: Potential and Problems.* 89th Cong., 2d Sess. Washington, D.C.: U.S. Government Printing Office, 1966.

U.S. Congress, Senate, Committee on Aeronautical and Space Sciences. *Aeronautical Research and Development Policy.* 90th Cong., 2d Sess. Washington, D.C.: U.S. Government Printing Office, 1968.

U.S. Congress, Senate, Committee on Appropriations. *Department of Agriculture Elimination of Agriculture Research Stations and Lines of Research.* Hearings Before the Subcommittee on Agriculture and Related Agencies. 89th Cong., 1st Sess. Washington, D.C.: U.S. Government Printing Office, 1965.

U.S. Congress, Senate, Committee on Commerce. *Increasing the Use of the Metric System.* Hearings Before the Committee on Commerce on S. 441 and S. 2356. 90th Cong., 1st Sess., November 15, 1967. Washington, D.C.: U.S. Government Printing Office, 1967.

―――. *The Nuclear Ship Savannah.* Hearings Before the Subcommittee on Merchant Marine and Fisheries. 90th Cong., 1st Sess., June 12, 1967. Washington, D.C.: U.S. Government Printing Office, 1967.

―――. Statement of Alan S. Boyd, Secretary of Transportation, May 20, 1968, to the Subcommittee on Merchant Marine and Fisheries.

U.S. Congress, Senate, Committee on Government Operations. *Equitable Distribution of R&D Funds by Government Agencies.* Hearings Before the Subcommittee on Government Research, July 11, 17, and 18, 1967. 90th Cong., 1st Sess. Washington, D.C.: U.S. Government Printing Office, 1967.

―――. *Reorganization Plan No. 3 of 1966 (Health Functions—Department of Health, Education, and Welfare).* Hearings Before the Subcommittee on Executive Reorganization, June 17, 1966. Washington, D.C.: U.S. Government Printing Office, 1966.

U.S. Congress, Senate, Committee on Interior and Insular Affairs. *Interior Research Contracts.* Report No. 1523. 89th Cong., 2d Sess. Washington, D.C.: U.S. Government Printing Office, 1966.

U.S. Congress, Senate, Committee on Labor and Public Welfare. "The Transferability of Defense Industry Resources to Civilian Uses." A Statement Prepared for the Hearings by the Subcommittee on Employment and Manpower, Nov. 21, 1963. 88th Cong., 1st Sess. Washington, D.C.: U.S. Government Printing Office, 1964.

U.S. Congress, Senate, Select Committee on Small Business. *Machine Tool Programs: Mobilization Planning, Reserve, and Replacement Programs.* 84th Cong., 2d Sess. Washington, D.C.: U.S. Government Printing Office, 1956 (Report 2229).

―――. *Technology Transfer.* Hearings Before the Subcommittee on Science and Technology, September 20, 26-28, and October 12, 1967. Washington, D.C.: U.S. Government Printing Office, 1967.

―――. Subcommittee on Science and Technology. *Policy Planning for Technology Transfer.* 90th Cong., 1st Sess. Washington, D.C.: U.S. Government Printing Office, 1967.

U.S. Department of Agriculture. *Crops in War and Peace: The Yearbook of Agriculture, 1950-51.* Washington, D.C.: U.S. Government Printing Office, 1951.

―――. *Farm Machinery and Equipment.* Economic Research Service Statistical Bulletin No. 419. Washington, D.C.: U.S. Government Printing Office, 1968.

————. *The First 100 Years: The Yearbook of Agriculture, 1962.* Washington, D.C.: U.S. Government Printing Office, 1962.

————. *Imprint on Living: A Report on Progress.* Agricultural Research Service Information Bulletin No. 333. Washington, D.C.: U.S. Government Printing Office, 1969.

————. *Insects: The Yearbook of Agriculture, 1952.* Washington, D.C.: U.S. Government Printing Office, 1952.

————. *Protecting Our Food: The Yearbook of Agriculture, 1966.* Washington, D.C.: U.S. Government Printing Office, 1966.

————. *Technology on the Farm.* Washington, D.C.: U.S. Government Printing Office, 1940.

————. Marketing Research Service. "Insect Damage to Corn in Three Southeastern States at Time of Harvest and in Farm Storage," Marketing Research Report No. 792. Washington, D.C.: U.S. Government Printing Office, 1968.

U.S. Department of Commerce. *Annual Report of the Secretary of Commerce, Fiscal Year Ended June 30, 1966.* Washington, D.C.: U.S. Government Printing Office, 1967.

————. *Annual Report of the Secretary of Commerce, Fiscal Year Ended June 30, 1967.* Washington, D. C.: U.S. Government Printing Office, 1968.

————. *Annual Report of the Secretary of Commerce, Fiscal Year Ended June 30, 1971.* Washington, D.C.: U.S. Government Printing Office, 1972.

————. *Do You Know Your Economic ABC's—Patents—Spur to American Progress.* Washington D.C.: U.S. Government Printing Office, 1965.

————. *Pocket Data Book, USA, 1971.* Washington, D.C.: U.S. Government Printing Office, 1971.

————. *Statistical Abstract of the U.S., 1971.* Washington, D.C.: U.S. Government Printing Office, 1972.

————. Business and Defense Services Administration. *The Commercial Prospects for Selected Irradiated Foods.* Washington, D.C.: U.S. Government Printing Office, March 1968.

————. Business and Defense Services Administration. *Microforms: A Growth Industry.* Washington, D.C.: U.S. Government Printing Office, 1969.

————. Maritime Administration, Office of R&D. "Technical, Operational, and Economic Report for the Second Year of Commercial Operations: August 1966-67." Washington, D.C.: Department of Commerce, Maritime Administration, 1967.

U.S. Department of Defense. *The Fiscal Year 1970-74 Defense Program and the 1970 Defense Budget.* Statement of Clark M. Clifford. Washington, D.C.: Department of Defense, 1969.

————. *Military Prime Contract Awards (Fiscal Years 1964, 1965, 1966, and 1967).* Washington, D.C.: Office of the Secretary of Defense, December 20, 1967.

————. *Statement of Secretary of Defense Robert S. McNamara Before a Joint Session of the Senate Armed Services Committee and the Senate Subcommittee on Department of Defense Appropriations on the Fiscal Year 1968-72 Defense Program and the 1968 Defense Budget.* Washington, D.C.: Office of the Secretary of Defense, 1967.

U.S. Department of Health, Education, and Welfare, Office of Program Analysis. *Handbook on Programs of the Department of Health, Education, and Welfare.* Washington, D.C.: U.S. Government Printing Office, 1965.

————. *1971 Annual Report.* Washington, D.C.: U.S. Government Printing Office, 1972.

————. *A Common Thread to Service: An Historical Guide to HEW.* Washington, D.C.: U.S. Government Printing Office, 1972.

————. Office of Program Coordination. *Reference Facts on Health. Education, and Welfare.* Washington, D.C.: U.S. Government Printing Office, 1967.

————. Public Health Service, National Center for Health Statistics. *Facts of Life and Death.* Washington, D.C.: U.S. Government Printing Office, 1967.

————. Public Health Service, National Center for Health Statistics. *Mortality Trends in the United States, 1954-1962.* Washington, D.C.: U.S. Government Printing Office, 1966.

————. Public Health Service. *National Institutes of Health, 1971 Annual Report.* Washington, D.C.: U.S. Government Printing Office, 1972.

————. *The National Institutes of Health.* PHS Pub. no. 81. Washington, D.C.: U.S. Government Printing Office, 1968.

U.S. Federal Council for Science and Technology. *Annual Report on Government Patent Policy, 1969 and 1970.* Washington, D.C.: U.S. Government Printing Office, 1971.

————. Committee on Government Patent Policy. *Government Patent Policy Study.* Final Report Vols. I-IV, Contract Study by Harbridge House, Inc., Boston, Mass. Washington, D.C.: U.S. Government Printing Office, 1968.

————. Committee on Scientific and Technical Information (CO-SATI). *Selected Mechanized Scientific and Technical Information Systems.* Washington, D.C.: U.S. Government Printing Office, 1968.

U.S. General Services Administration, National Archives and Records Service, Federal Register Division. *United States Government Organization Manual, 1957-58.* Washington, D.C.: U.S. Government Printing Office, 1957.

————. *United States Government Organization Manual, 1963-64.* Washington, D.C.: U.S. Government Printing Office, 1963.

————. *United States Government Organization Manual, 1968-69.* Washington, D.C.: U.S. Government Printing Office, 1968.

————. *United States Government Organization Manual, 1971-72.* Washington, D.C.: U.S. Government Printing Office, 1971.

U.S. National Aeronautics and Space Administration. *2d Semi-Annual Report to Congress, July 1 - December 31, 1969.* Washington, D.C.: U.S. Government Printing Office, 1970.

————. WESRAC. Memo of available services, dated December 29, 1971.

————. Office of Technology Utilization. *NASA Contributions to Bioinstrumentation Systems.* Washington, D.C.: U.S. Government Printing Office, 1968 (NASA SP-5054).

————. *The Technology Utilization Program.* February 1967 Review of the Work of the NASA office of Technology Utilization. Washington, D.C.: NASA, 1967.

U.S. National Aeronautics and Space Council, Office of the President. *United States Aeronautics and Space Activities, 1968.* Washington, D.C.: U.S. Government Printing Office, 1969.

U.S. National Commission on Technology, Automation, and Economic Progress. *Technology and the American Economy, The Report of the Commission.* 6 vols. Washington, D.C.: U.S. Government Printing Office, 1966.

U.S. National Science Foundation. *Directory of Federal R&D Installations. A Report to the Federal Council for Science and Technology.* NSF 70-23. Washington, D.C.: U.S. Government Printing Office, 1970.

————. *Employment of Scientists and Engineers in the United States, 1950-66.* Washington, D.C.: U.S. Government Printing Office, 1968 (NSF 68-30).

————. *Federal Funds for Research, Development, and Other Scientific Activities, Fiscal Years 1971, 1972, and 1973.* Washington, D.C.: U.S. Government Printing Office, 1972.

————. *National Patterns of R&D Resources—Funds and Manpower in the United States—1953-72.* Washington, D.C.: U.S. Government Printing Office, 1972.

————. *Proceedings of a Conference on Technology Transfer and Innovation, May 15-17, 1966.* Washington, D.C.: U.S. Government Printing Office, 1967 (NSF 67-5).

————. *R&D Activities in State Government Agencies.* Washington, D.C.: U.S. Government Printing Office, 1970 (NSF 70-22).

————. *Research and Development in Industry, 1970.* Washington, D.C.: U.S. Government Printing Office, 1972 (NSF 72-209).

————. Office of Economic and Statistic Studies. *Inquiries into Industrial Research and Development and Innovation.* Washington, D.C.: National Science Foundation, 1963.

U.S. Small Business Administration. *1967 Annual Report.* Washington, D.C.: U.S. Government Printing Office, 1968.

————. 1971 Annual Report. Washington, D.C.: U.S. Government Printing Office, 1972.

————. *Small Business Applications of Radioisotopes.* Washington, D.C.: SBA, September-October, 1963.

2. Other Materials

Battelle Columbus Laboratories, Columbus, Ohio. *Report on 1971 National Survey of Compensation Paid Scientists and Engineers in Research and Development Activities.* Washington, D.C.: U.S. Atomic Energy Commission, 1972.

Burchinal, Lee G., and Harold A. Haswell. "How to Put Two and a Half Tons of Research into One Handy Little Box," Reprint from *American Education.* Washington, D.C.: U.S. Government Printing Office, 1966.

Chairman, Advisory Committee on Isotopes and Radiation Development. "Industry's Evaluation of Isotopes and Radiation." Mimeograph for AEC, April 19, 1965.

Foster, John S., Jr. "Research and Development in U.S. Defense Posture," *Defense Industry Bulletin,* September 1971.

Fowler, E. S. "Radioisotopes and Radiation Utilization by United States Industry—Growth and Trends." Presented at the Opening Session of the Sixth Japan Conference on Radiosotopes, Tokyo, Japan, November 16-19, 1964. Washington, D.C.: AEC, 1964.

"FY 1971 Research, Development, Test and Evaluation" *Defense Industry Bulletin,* June 1970.

"Intergovernmental Talent Sharing—IPA's Mobility Program is One Year Old," *Information Bulletin* No. 72-5. Washington, D.C.: Advisory Commission on Intergovernmental Relations, July 10, 1972.

Lawson, Harold B. "Defense Documentation Center Reports," *Defense Industry Bulletin,* July 1968.

Lesher, Richard L. "Statement for the Record of Richard L. Lesher, Assistant Administrator For Technology Utilization, NASA, Before the Committee on Aeronautical and Space Sciences, U.S. Senate, February 27, 1968." (Mimeograph.)

Lesher, Richard L., and George J. Howick. "Background Guidelines, and Recommendations for Assessing Effective Means of Channeling New Technology in Promising Directions." Draft for Commission on Technology, Automation, and Economic Progress, Appendix Vol. V, *Applying Technology to Unmet Needs.* Washington, D.C.: NASA, 1966.

Licklider, J. C. R., and others. "Report to Dr. Donald F. Hornig, Director, Office of Science and Technology, by the Office of Science and Technology Ad Hoc Panel on Scientific and Technical Communications." Washington, D.C.: Office of the White House, February 8, 1965.

MacArthur, Donald M. "Defense Technology: Benefits to Industrial Progress," *Defense Industry Bulletin,* August 1970.

National Institutes of Health, Division of Biologics Standards, Information Office. "Review of Rubella Research." Mimeographed Fact Sheet from Presentations by Meyer and Parkman, May 1, 1968.

Russell, G. L. "Evaluation of Minor Improvements—Pavement Serration." State of California Division of Highways, November 1967.

Webb, James E. "NASA, Technology, and the National Security," *Perspectives in Defense Management,* February 1969.

B. NON-GOVERNMENT PUBLICATIONS

1. Books

Aaron, James E., and Murland K. Strasser. *Driver and Traffic Safety Education.* New York: The Macmillan Company, 1966.

Accident Facts, 1967 Edition. Chicago: National Safety Council, 425 N. Michigan Ave., 60611, 1967.

A Select Bibliography on the Industrial Use of Radioactive Materials. Cambridge, Mass.: Arthur D. Little, Inc., 1949.

Barnett, Homer. *The Basis for Cultural Change.* New York: McGraw-Hill Book Co., 1953.

Bass, Lawrence W. *The Management of Technical Programs.* New York: Frederick A. Praeger, 1965.

Bauer, Raymond A. *Second Order Consequences.* Cambridge, Mass.: The M. I. T. Press, 1969.

Booz, Allen, & Hamilton. *Management of New Products.* Chicago: Booz, Allen, & Hamilton, 1968.

Bowen, Howard R., and Garth L. Mangum, eds. *Automation and Economic Progress.* Englewood Cliffs, N.J.: Prentice-Hall, Inc., 1966.

Bright, James R. *Research, Development, and Technical Innovation.* Homewood, Ill.: Richard D. Irwin, 1964.

Calvert, Robert. *The Encyclopedia of Patent Practice and Invention Management.* New York: Reinhold Publishing Co., 1964.

The Center for Safety Education at New York University. *Man and the Motor Car.* Englewood Cliffs, N.J.: Prentice-Hall, Inc., 1964.

Chamber of Commerce of the United States. *The Economics of Defense Spending.* Washington, D.C.: Chamber of Commerce of the United States, 1965.

Coleman, James S., Elihu Katz, and Herbert Menzel. *Medical Innovation, A Diffusion Study.* Indianapolis, Ind.: Bobbs-Merrill Co., 1966.

Doctors, Samuel I. *The Role of Federal Agencies in Technology Transfer.* Cambridge, Mass.: The M. I. T. Press, 1969.

The Foundation for Research on Human Behavior. *The Adoption of New Products: Process and Influence.* Ann Arbor, Michigan: The Foundation for Research on Human Behavior, 1959.

Haas, Raymond M. *Long Range New Product Planning in Business.* Morgantown, West Va.: West Va. University Foundation, 1965.

Johnson, Richard A., Fremont E. Kast, and James E. Rosenzweig. *The Theory and Management of Systems.* 2nd ed. New York: McGraw-Hill Book Co., 1967.

————. *The Theory and Management of Systems.* 3rd ed. New York: McGraw-Hill Book Co., 1973.

Jones, Stacy V. *The Inventor's Patent Handbook.* New York: The Dial Press, 1966.

Kent, Allen. *Specialized Information Centers.* Washington, D.C.: Spartan Books, 1965.

Kuhn, James W. *Scientific and Managerial Manpower in Nuclear Industry.* New York: Columbia University Press, 1966.

Loftness, Robert L. *Nuclear Power Plants.* New York: D. Van Nostrand Company, Inc., 1964.

McClellan, Grant S., ed. *Safety on the Road.* New York: The H. W. Wilson Co., 1966.

McLuhan, Marshal, and Quentin Fiore. *War and Peace in the Global Village.* New York: Bantam Books, 1968.

McNeil, Donald R. *The Fight for Fluoridation.* New York: Oxford University Press, 1957.

Mitchell, M.S., and C.J. Koppel. *Air Force Systems Command Systems Management: An Introduction to Air Force Systems Management.* San Diego, Calif.: Paragon Design Co., 1964.

Nelson, Richard R., Merton J. Peck, and Edward K. Kalachek. *Technology, Economic Growth, and Public Policy.* Washington, D.C.: The Brookings Institution, 1967.

Ogburn, William F. *Social Change.* New York: B. W. Huebach, Inc., 1923.

Palmer, Archie M., ed. *Research Centers Directory.* Detroit, Mich.: Gale Research Company Book Tower, 1969.

Reader's Digest Almanac and Yearbook, 1967. Pleasantville, N.Y.: The Reader's Digest Association, Inc., 1966.

Rogers, Everett M. *Diffusion of Innovations.* New York: Free Press of Glencoe, Inc., 1962.

————. *Social Change in Rural Society: A Textbook in Rural Sociology.* New York: Appleton-Century-Crofts, 1960.

Schon, Donald A. *Technology and Change.* New York: Delacorte Press, 1967.

Schultz, Theodore W. *The Economic Organization of Agriculture.* New York: McGraw-Hill Book Co., 1953.

Weiner, Norbert. *Cybernetics or Control and Communications in the Animal and the Machine.* Cambridge, Mass.: The M. I. T. Press, 1961.

2. Periodicals

"AEC and DOD Information Analysis Centers," *Special Libraries,* January 1966, pp. 21-34.

"Aerospace Technology Infusion Aids Apparel Industry Operations," *Aviation Week and Space Technology,* March 29, 1971.

Brockner, Eli. "Apply Technology to Civilian Problems," *Astronautics and Aeronautics,* March 1971.

"Barriers to Technology Transfer Studied," *Aviation Week and Space Technology,* August 21, 1972.

"Burning Up the Circuits," *Barron's,* August 9, 1965, pp. 3, 13-17.

"The Calculator Goes Electronic," *Business Week,* May 18, 1968, pp. 149-152.

Cassell, Frank H. "The Development of Jobs: Realities and Opportunities," *Vital Speeches of the Day,* XXXIV, November 1, 1967, pp. 59-64.

Dunning, James M. "Current Status of Fluoridation," *New England Journal of Medicine,* CCLXXII, January 7 and 14, 1965, pp. 30-34, 84-88.

Fallwell, William F. "Information Explosion Closer to Control," *Chemical and Engineering News,* December 20, 1971.

"From Design to Finished Product," *Business Week,* December 30, 1967, pp. 88-90.

Gibson, R.E. "A Systems Approach to Research Management," *Research Management,* Vol. 4, no. 4, 1962.

Gregory, William H. "Aerospace's Urban Role Debated," *Aviation Week and Space Technology,* June 7, 1971.

Griliches, Zvi. "Research Costs and Social Returns: Hybrid Corn and Related Innovations," *Journal of Political Economy,* Vol. LXVI, October 1958, pp. 419-431.

Hersman, M. Frank. "Parlaying the Benefits of R&D," *Science Policy Reviews,* Vol. 5, no. 4, 1972, pp. 19-20.

"Irradiated Foods Go Sour," *Business Week,* May 25, 1968, p. 160.

Johnson, G.E., and others. "Carbon Black Produced from Coal," *Rubber World,* June 1967 (reprint without page numbers).

Lear, John. "What Has Science to Say to Man," *Saturday Review,* July 1, 1967.

Milliken, J. Gordon and Edward J. Morrison. "Management Methods From Aerospace," *Harvard Business Review,* March-April 1973.

"More Fuel for New-Reactor Race," *Business Week,* January 13, 1968, pp. 46-50.

"New Products—Pulling a Profit Out of Left Field," *Business Week,* June 15, 1968, pp. 150-154.

"NSF Bullish on Industry R&D Funding, Jobs," *Chemical and Engineering News,* March 19, 1973.

"Rise in R&D Funding Signals Halt to Slump," *Chemical and Engineering News,* July 2, 1973.

Schmookler, Jacob. "Inventors Past and Present," *Review of Economics and Statistics,* Vol. 39, August 1957.

Scott, Christopher. "The Use of Technical Literature by Industrial Technical Technologists," *IRE Transactions of Engineering Management,* EM-9, June 1962, pp. 76-86.

"Tiny Computers Lead a Price Decline," *Business Week,* May 11, 1968, pp. 108-114.

"Universities Promote Sale of Technology," *Chemical and Engineering News,* March 12, 1973.

"What Price Parity?" *Barron's,* December 9, 1968, p. 12.

"Who Got Most Money for R&D," *Business Week,* February 10, 1968, p. 58.

Yaffee, Michael L. "Bendix Sets Technology Transfer Goals," *Aviation Week and Space Technology,* February 14, 1972.

3. Essays and Articles in Collections

Baker, William O. "The Dynamism of Technology," *Technology and Social Change.* Edited by Eli Ginzberg. New York: Columbia University Press, 1963, pp. 102-103.

Brademas, John. "Technology and Social Change: A Congressman's View," *The Impact of Science on Technology.* Edited by Aaron W. Warner, Dean Morse, and Alfred S. Eichner. New York: Columbia University Press, 1965, pp. 143-172.

Lynn, Frank. "The Rate of Development and Diffusion of Technology," *Automation and Economic Progress.* Edited by Howard R. Bowen and Garth L. Mangum. Englewood Cliffs, N.J.: Prentice-Hall, Inc., 1966, pp. 99-114.

Sayer, John S. "The Economics of a National Information System," Vol. I of *Annual Review of Information Science and Technology.* 2 vols. Edited by Carlos A. Cuadra. New York: John Wiley & Sons, 1967.

Shapero, A. "Diffusion of Innovations Resulting from Research: Implications for Research Program Management," *Research Program Effectiveness,* pp. 371-386. Proceedings of the Conference Sponsored by the Office of Naval Research, Washington, D.C., July 27-29, 1965. Edited by M. C. Yovits, and others. New York: Gordon and Breach, Science Publishers, Inc., 1966.

4. Unpublished Materials

Bundy, Dr. F.P. Letter to Author, May 6, 1968.

Estep, A.C., Engineer of Design, California Division of Highways. Letter to Author May 17, 1968.

Hayes, Richard J. *A Study of the Transfer of Technology from Government Sponsored R&D to Commercial Operations in Selected Electronic Companies.* Ph.D. Dissertation, The American University, June 1967.

Herner, Saul, Robert S. Meyer, and Robert H. Ramsey. "How Smaller Firms Solve Problems and Keep Abreast of Technical Developments." Unpublished Contractors' Report, U.S. Department of Commerce, Office of Technical Services, 1957.

Hughes Aircraft Company, Culver City, Calif. "Patent Orientation Briefing," July 1967. Mimeograph.

"Industry's Evaluation of Isotopes and Radiation." Mimeographed Report to the AEC by the Chairman, Advisory Committee on Isotopes and Radiation Development, April 19, 1965.

Knipling, E. F., Director, Entomology Research Division, Agricultural Research Service, U.S. Department of Agriculture. Letter to Author, May 8, 1968.

Lindley, Jonathan, Deputy Assistant Secretary for Policy Coordination, U.S. Department of Commerce. Letter to Author, May 18, 1968.

Reilly, J.F., Office of Public Information, N. B. S. Letter to Author, May 29, 1968.

Simms, Glen E., President, Concut Inc., El Monte, Calif. Letter to Author, May 3, 1968.

5. Newspapers

Northern Arlington *Virginia Sun,* January 10, 1968.

The Santa Ana, Calif. *Register,* May 15, 1968.

Washington Post, June 17, 1966, January 5, 1968, June 16, 1968, and March 3, 1968.

The Los Angeles Times, March 14, 1969.

6. Other Materials

Bureau of National Affairs. *Daily Executive Report,* December 6, 1967; March 13; April 26; May 6, 27; 1968.

——. *Federal Contracts Report,* January 1, January 15, 1968.

Lesher, Richard L., NASA Office of Technology Utilization. "Innovation," Channel 28, Los Angeles, Calif., January 18, 1969.

APPENDICES

APPENDIX A

Definitions Of Terms

DEFINITIONS OF TERMS

Technology Diffusion

The **adoption process** consists of the mental steps which an individual takes from first hearing about a new idea to finally adopting it.[1]

Adoption leaders are individuals others trust as sources of information and advice about new ideas.[2]

Anthropology deals with the effect of culture on the spread of technology and on social consequences of technology.[3]

Champions are change agents who, for personal gain, prestige, or other reasons, advocate a particular item of technology.[4]

Channels are ways to gain the potential adopter's time and interest. Agents, technical education, technical press, public press, and agency publications are typical channels.

Cosmopolites are individuals oriented outside their local communities.[5]

Coupling implies the activities of transferring information from a source to one who needs it. A handbook is a passive coupler. A champion is an active coupler.

A **cultural lag** occurs when one of two parts of culture which are correlated changes before or in greater degree than the other part does, thereby causing less adjustment between the two parts than existed previously.[6]

Diffusion research is a study of adoption of an item over time by adoption units linked by channels of communication, social structure, and a value system.[7]

The **diffusion** process itself is defined as (1) **acceptance,** (2) **over time,** (3) of some specific item—an idea or practice, (4) by individuals, groups, or other **adopting units,** linked (5) to specific **channels** of communication, (6) to a **social structure,** and (7) to a given value system or **culture.**[8]

Documentation is the presentation, location, and communication of recorded knowledge; it is also mobilization of data for computation and communication.

An **economic development** program is a formal effort, either public or private, outside of conventional lines of activity, designed to encourage an area's economic growth.

Form refers to the format or slant of the message to fit the needs of an audience or the requirements of a channel or medium.

281

Laggards are the final sixteen percent of those who adopt new technology. This group will also include the "non-adopters" if the technology is not used by everyone.[9]

A **mechanical invention** involves a device never existing before. The **chemical invention** may consist of discovering something that has always been there.

Media are the technical means for conveying the message and stem from personal contact as well as print, visual, and audio technologies.

A **new product** is any product which, regardless of the length of time it has been marketed, is unknown by name or application to over half of its potential users.

No-takers are items of technology which arouse no interest. They may be trivial or they may be beyond the technological level of understanding of the potential adopter. They are not evaluated or tried.

Reference groups are groups that influence an individual's behavior; an individual refers to these groups as he makes decisions and takes action.[10] Such groups may be local or distant, professional or social, personal or impersonal.

Second order consequences of technology diffusion are the indirect effects which occur as an item is widely adopted. Adoption of the automobile had first order consequences of road building and gasoline manufacture. Two second order consequences were changes in social habits and changes from animal to machine oriented occupations.

Social change is a continuous process over a period of time in which differences in human relationships emerge.

Sources are mechanisms, institutions, or persons who have information for others. A source is frequently associated with particular media and channels. The public press is associated with the print medium and newspaper, book, and magazine channels.

Technology is an application of science to an end useful to society. It is knowledge about the industrial arts; it is the way science is used to benefit society. In scientific and engineering activity, ideas are subjected to experiment and concepts become tested theories. Techniques and devices are developed and demonstrated. This experience and lore, ways of doing things, elements of information and experience, are part of technology. Models and procedures of the research laboratory, and inventions and imaginative solutions to problems, form bits of technology which fit into mosaics of new products, processes, and services.[11]

Horizontal transfer occurs through adaptation of a technology from one application to another, possibly unrelated to the first. It also refers to commercial use of technology developed for a mission-oriented Federal agency.

Vertical transfer refers to transfer of technology from general to specific uses. It also refers to application of specific technology to its design use.

Technological change is the movement from one level of application of science to another level. Changed techniques produce different goods, services or processes. Technological change occurs in three overlapping steps of invention (conception of the notion which will change goods, services, or processes), innovation (introduction of the new concept into the economy), and diffusion (the spread of the new concept within the industry and to other industries), according to J. Herbert Hollomon.[12] These definitions cover the generating of new technology and its diffusion as discussed in this dissertation.

Value systems refer to the distribution and patterns of wealth, power, well-being, respect, and enlightenment in organized groups.

R&D

Science is knowledge or verifiable truth gained through methodical study, analysis, synthesis, and practice.

Research is studious inquiry or examination, specifically, application of human intelligence to a problem for which a solution is not readily apparent. Used alone, it generally relates to science.

Basic research includes efforts to increase knowledge of natural phenomena and environment. **Pure** or **fundamental research** is undertaken to produce knowledge, without regard to how the knowledge might be used. **Breakthrough research** is undertaken to produce knowledge in areas where problems have been encountered or where opportunities are being sought.

Applied research focuses human knowledge and science on identified problems to produce better products or better ways of making them.

Development is technical activity concerned with nonroutine problems which are encountered in translating applied research or other general scientific knowledge into products and processes. Development covers the activities between raw invention and production. **Exploratory development** tries to solve specific technical problems. **Advanced development** includes the work in developing prototypes for experimental or operational testing. **Engineering development** includes process (or production procedure) and production model design. **Test and Evaluation** includes both routine and nonroutine testing of prototype and initial production models. Inventive activity occurs in all steps of development.

R&D exploitation means using R&D results by all those who would make net social or economic gains by such use.

The **socialization** of R&D has been its recent embodiment in large enterprises, both Federal and commercial. The **nationalization** of R&D refers to the same phenomenon but emphasizes dominant Federal funding of R&D even in commercial enterprises. R&D has been **institutionalized** as an activity of Federal agencies, meaning it has been separately identified, adopted, standardized, proceduralized, and formalized.

Public Administration

Coordination (vertical as well as horizontal) is orderly arrangement of group efforts to unify action in pursuit of common purposes.

Control is that function within the organization which provides direction in conformance to the program or holding variations from the organization objectives within allowable limits.[13]

Centralized government agencies have a direct line of authority extending from the Federal level through subsidiary levels to the action unit. Decentralized agencies are more autonomous at each level.

Cybernetics, as defined by Weiner, is control and communications in the animal and in the machine. Its major emphases are on the nature of feedback, patterns of control, and means of acquiring, using, retaining, and transmitting information.[14]

Equilibrium is that state in any system in which component variables interact without disturbance; in equilibrium no variable changes position or its relationship with other variables.

Under the **exception principle,** management's attention focuses at once on significant deviations from planned results. This helps management make prompt and effective decisions. Feedback works on the exception principle.

Government furnished equipment refers to tools and special equipment in the national stockpile which are furnished to contractors as part of a bid package. Government furnished facilities are parts of government installations furnished to contractors as part of a bid.

The **general economy** encompasses those sectors of the economy which produce for commercial as well as government customers. Most of the defense, aerospace, and nuclear sectors produce for only one customer, the Federal government, and are therefore not part of the general economy. The general economy, then, is that part of the economy on which the government does not hold a monopoly.

Institutionalization is development of formal, orderly, and stable patterns of social organization. Procedures are standardized, and change may be slowed down.

The **organization** is an assemblage of people, materials, machines, and other resources geared to task accomplishment through a series of interactions and integrated into a social system.[15]

A **predictive model** is one which foretells how it will perform in practice. A flowchart is a predictive model.

Progress payments are periodic partial payments to help a contractor meet his operating costs. They are generally made when the contractor has successfully completed part of the agreed work.

Planning is the continual review of objectives and alternative means for their accomplishment.

Long range planning is the continuous process of making entrepreneurial (risk taking) decisions systematically and with the best possible knowledge of their futurity, organizing efforts to carry out those decisions, and measuring results of those decisions against expectations through organized, systematic feedback.

A **long-range** technology plan is one which extends beyond the expected cycle of present products.

A **policy** is a general guide to action.

PPBS and **PPB** are both used to refer to the 1965 executive order installing a different form of planning, programming, and budgeting in Federal executive agencies.

Programming is translating preferred alternatives into reality. The cost of each alternative is precisely determined, but objectives are not challenged in this latter stage of planning.

Systems review is periodic review and analysis of organizational programs. After evaluation of each activity in terms of its likelihood of continuing efficiency, adjustments are made and the program is restructured into an integrated whole.

Technology forecasting is the prediction of developments in technology and of the effects of such technology on society.

Vested interests are those institutions having strong commitments to an existing technical, economic, social, or political arrangement.

Visibility is the capability of the administrator to know and understand the progress of his program towards its objectives.

FOOTNOTES

[1] Rogers, *Diffusion* . . . , *op. cit.*, p. 20.

[2] *Ibid.*, p. 169.

[3] *Ibid.*, p. 23.

[4] Definitions not credited are either in common usage or developed by the author.

[5] Rogers, *Diffusion* . . . , *op. cit.*, p. 17.

[6] Ogburn, *op. cit.*, p. 201.

[7] Rogers, *Diffusion* . . . , *op. cit.*, p. 23.

[8] Derived from *Ibid.*, pp. 12-19.

[9] The Foundation for Research on Human Behavior, *op. cit.*, p. 8.

[10] Rogers, *Diffusion* . . . , *op. cit.*, p. 302.

[11] Science Policy Research Division, *Policy Planning* . . . , *op. cit.*, p. 2.

[12] J. Herbert Hollomon, "Technology Transfer," in National Science Foundation, *Proceedings of a Conference . . . , op. cit.,* pp. 32-33.

[13] Johnson, Kast, and Rosenzweig, 2d ed., *op. cit.,* p. 72.

[14] Norbert Weiner, *Cybernetics or Control and Communication in the Animal and the Machine* (Cambridge, Mass.: The M. I. T. Press, 1961), pp. vii, 97, and 161.

[15] Johnson, Kast, and Rosenzweig, 2d ed., *op. cit.,* p. 47.

APPENDIX B

Federal R&D Expenditures In Selected Agencies

APPENDIX B-1

FEDERAL EXPENDITURES FOR R&D (IN MILLIONS OF DOLLARS)[1]

FY	USDA	D/HEW	Com-merce	DOD	NASA	AEC	Total
1940	29	3	3	26	2	–	74
1948	42	23	8	592	37	107	855
1950	53	40	12	652	54	221	1083
1952	57	64	10	1317	67	250	1816
1954	55	63	11	2487	90	383	3148
1956	88	86	20	2639	71	374	3446
1958	119	180	18	3664	89	804	4990
1960	131	324	33	5654	401	986	7744
1962	156	512	48	6812	1257	1284	10387
1964	183	793	85	7517	4171	1505	14707
1966	236	879	71	6735	5933	1462	16012
1967	270	1075	80	7680	5426	1467	16859
1968	286	1283	82	8164	4724	1594	17049
1969	284	1220	78	7868	4252	1654	16348
1970	299	1261	128	7588	3753	1616	15736
1971	319	1327	123	7706	3382	1605	15992
1972	361	1520	157	8286	3181	1580	16734
1973	361	1761	203	8442	3192	1761	17327

[1] National Science Foundation, *Federal Funds for Research, Development, and Other Scientific Activities, Fiscal Years 1971, 1972, and 1973, op. cit.*, pp. 178-179. Totals include other agencies than those listed.

APPENDIX B-2

FEDERAL OBLIGATIONS IN APPLIED RESEARCH
(IN MILLIONS OF DOLLARS)[2]

FY	USDA	D/HEW	DOD	NASA	AEC	Others	Total
1956	68	57	404	29	42	46	646
1957	76	104	361	31	44	46	662
1958	81	133	378	41	59	52	744
1959	87	165	386	95	83	71	886
1960	87	214	693	166	95	75	1331
1961	97	291	1000	263	53	92	1796
1962	101	384	1107	398	55	121	2166
1963	104	416	1374	558	62	137	2652
1964	114	497	1431	653	71	132	2898
1965	128	559	1488	762	76	151	3164
1966	134	640	1587	799	90	178	3427
1967	137	710	1307	775	90	195	3258
1968	140	750	1313	701	120	201	3293
1969	145	803	1135	618	132	240	3145
1970	156	741	1310	773	146	306	3540
1971	174	905	1351	817	152	488	4018
1972	197	1047	1429	827	157	541	4354
1973	201	1123	1514	843	171	642	4693

[2] *Ibid.*, p. 186. Appendices B-3 through B-6 amplify the FY 71 figures.

APPENDIX B-3

FEDERAL OBLIGATIONS FOR DEVELOPMENT AND INVENTIVE WORK (IN MILLIONS OF DOLLARS)[3]

FY	DOD	NASA	AEC	Other	Total development	Total applied research plus development
1956	1,786	7	324	19	2,136	2,782
1957	2,540	9	429	29	3,007	3,669
1958	2,914	11	513	52	3,490	3,934
1959	4,638	61	530	56	5,285	6,171
1960	4,850	105	563	86	5,605	6,936
1961	5,401	324	630	77	6,432	8,228
1962	5,411	725	783	89	7,008	9,174
1963	5,680	1,852	797	112	8,441	11,093
1964	5,590	3,109	928	120	9,747	12,645
1965	5,045	3,662	907	132	9,746	12,910
1966	5,174	3,692	842	325	10,033	13,460
1967	6,458	3,488	866	444	11,256	14,514
1968	6,132	3,073	967	385	10,557	13,850
1969	6,284	2,667	989	458	10,398	13,543
1970	5,804	2,390	913	621	9,728	13,268
1971	5,896	1,761	874	868	9,399	13,417
1972	6,681	1,631	881	878	10,071	14,425
1973	6,981	1,629	921	963	10,494	15,187

[3] *Ibid.*, p. 187. The total applied research plus development gives the total for Federal inventive work.

APPENDIX B-4

SELECTED FEDERAL AGENCY OBLIGATIONS FOR APPLIED RESEARCH BY PERFORMER IN FY/71 ($1000)[4]

	Intramural	Industrial	FFRDC (industry)	Universities	FFRDC (univ)	Other Non-profits	FFRDC Non-profits	Other
Total								
Federal ($4,017,859)	1,498,532	1,214,420	46,448	701,306	138,887	241,878	50,332	81,332
USDA:								
Rsch. svcs.	86,054	188	-----	2,222	-----	361	-----	-----
Coop. rsch.	1,309	-----	-----	40,513	-----	-----	-----	190
Forest Svc.	29,195	6	-----	186	-----	65	-----	8
PHS:								
Health Svcs.	30,557	551	-----	36,020	-----	17,339	-----	16,143
NIH	151,913	35,771	-----	345,393	34	97,085	894	12,478
DOD	515,450	662,515	2,568	76,083	28,732	33,033	31,076	15
Commerce:								
NBS	13,485	124	-----	8	-----	-----	-----	11
Patent ofc.	1,637	-----	-----	-----	-----	-----	-----	-----
AEC	4,174	1,978	40,669	16,584	74,830	2,962	10,418	-----
NASA	375,457	368,074	365	29,162	28,877	13,574	25	-----

[4] *Ibid.*, pp. 112–113.

APPENDIX B-5

SELECTED FEDERAL AGENCY OBLIGATIONS FOR APPLIED RESEARCH, FY/71 ($1000)[5]

	Total	Life Sciences	Psychology	Physical	Environmental	Math	Engineering	Social	Other
All agencies total	4,017,859	1,077,609	66,883	299,206	284,775	69,463	1,891,496	236,098	92,349
USDA:									
Rsch. svc.	39,776	55,387	26	18,162	801	242	14,028	1,130	-----
Coop. rsch.	42,012	28,868	-----	2,101	262	-----	1,440	9,341	-----
Forest Svc.	29,460	17,088	-----	1,768	2,652	-----	5,007	2,945	-----
Health Svcs.	115,589	83,226	17,341	-----	-----	1,199	31	13,558	234
NIH	657,400	566,983	6,610	10,147	969	13,252	18,690	5,481	35,268
DOD	1,351,410	76,483	22,044	142,177	85,431	40,426	943,046	3,649	38,154
NBS	14,159	-----	-----	5,717	-----	550	7,267	-----	625
Patent ofc.	412	-----	-----	-----	-----	-----	-----	-----	412
NASA	816,686	40,199	1,239	22,096	134,553	-----	612,816	-----	5,783
AEC	152,094	43,607	-----	71,431	10,116	-----	26,940	-----	-----

[5] *Ibid.*, pp. 119–120.

APPENDIX B-6

SELECTED FEDERAL AGENCY OBLIGATIONS FOR APPLIED RESEARCH IN ENGINEERING IN FY/71 ($1000)[6]

	Aeronaut.	Astronaut.	Chemical	Civil	Electric	Mechanic	Metallurgy and Materials	Other
Federal total ($1,891,496)	514,016	262,144	119,226	79,427	349,483	123,719	122,845	320,636
USDA:								
Rsch. svcs	-----	-----	1,816	1,820	39	572	-----	9,781
Coop. rsch.	-----	-----	-----	-----	-----	-----	-----	1,440
Forest Svc.	-----	-----	294	589	-----	589	-----	3,535
Health svcs.	-----	-----	-----	31	-----	-----	-----	-----
NIH	-----	-----	-----	-----	-----	-----	-----	18,690
DOD	216,554	81,557	40,972	18,502	245,402	53,131	66,464	220,374
NBS	-----	-----	-----	895	1,478	318	119	4,457
NASA	240,255	179,798	42,341	-----	58,753	29,651	13,777	48,241
AEC	-----	-----	4,375	-----	-----	-----	21,400	1,165

[6] *Ibid.*, pp. 130–131.

APPENDIX B-7

SELECTED FEDERAL AGENCY OBLIGATIONS FOR DEVELOPMENT BY PERFORMER IN FY/71 ($1000)[7]

	Intramural	Industrial	FFRDC's (industry)	Universities	FFRDC's (univ)	Non-profit	FFRDC's (non-profit)	Other
Federal total ($9,399,299)	2,132,427	6,003,585	404,475	148,819	329,961	171,306	157,843	10,354
USDA:								
Rsch. svcs.	10,544	79	-----	134	-----	17	-----	836
Forest Svc.	921	-----	-----	-----	-----	-----	-----	-----
Health Svcs.	7,516	4,467	-----	14,657	-----	13,318	-----	3,838
NIH	9,316	10,808	-----	25,561	214	7,398	10	1,793
DOD	1,586,474	3,998,833	4,891	14,657	113,147	50,422	119,172	509
Commerce:								
NBS	3,768	62	-----	-----	-----	-----	-----	13
Patent ofc.	165	-----	-----	-----	-----	-----	-----	-----
NASA	362,064	1,331,409	2,429	37,604	21,021	5,965	289	-----
AEC	11,892	262,573	396,057	4,257	187,563	3,683	7,785	101

[7] *Ibid.*, pp. 136–137.

APPENDIX C

Usefulness Of Bureau Of Mines Research

And Expenditures

APPENDIX C

BUREAU OF MINES RESEARCH: 1952-62 EXPENDITURES AND PERCENTAGES ($MILLIONS) [1]

Division	Economical	Future value	Uneconomical	Failure	Total
Total	$27.8/35.5%	$26.3/33.5%	$18.7/23.8%	$5.5/7.1%	$78.3/100%
Metallurgy	$12.3/40.0%	$13.3/43.0%	$ 4.8/16.0%	$ .5/2.0%	$30.8/ 39%
Mining	$ 2.2/82.0%	----------	$ .4/15.0%	$.06/3.0%	$ 2.7/ 3%
Coal	$ 5.8/19.0%	$ 8.6/28.0%	$12.0/39.0%	$4.0/13 %	$30.3/ 39%
Petroleum	$ 7.6/53.0%	$ 4.4/30.0%	$ 1.5/10.0%	$1.0/ 7 %	$14.5/ 19%

[1] U.S. Congress, House, Committee on Interior and Insular Affairs, *Review of Research by the Bureau of Mines, Department of the Interior*, Committee Print No. 2 (Washington, D.C.: U.S. Government Printing Office, 1965), p. 3.

APPENDIX D

Federal Expenditures For S&T Information

In Selected Agencies

APPENDIX D-1

CHRONOLOGY OF INFORMATION SCIENCE

1946. Documentalists began organizing and arranging captured German documents of World War II so that they could be exploited by American technologists. This project emphasized translating, interpreting, classifying, abstracting, filing for retrieval, and screening for applications.

1948. The Royal Society Scientific Information Conference, held in London, England, was attended by a few Americans who later made contributions to the development of information science.[1]

1950. The National Science Foundation was established to support basic research and education in the sciences and to foster exchanges of scientific information. Its focus has been on written records of science rather than technology; still, it has been a major contributor to technical information through its guidance of information science.

1954. The Atomic Energy Act of 1954 amended the Atomic Energy Act of 1946 so that functions of the AEC now include directing this form of energy to, among other things, "increase the standard of living and strengthen free competition in private enterprise." This includes the dissemination of scientific and technical information, which is administered through a Division of Technical Information.[2]

1958. The rising R&D expenditures continued to put pressure on information channels. The International Conference on Scientific Information was held November 16-21, 1958. The conference is considered by many to be the real birth of modern information science.[3]

Also in 1958, the Baker Panel, under W. O. Baker, Chairman, made its report to the President's Scientific Advisory Committee (PSAC), **Improving the Availability of Scientific and Technical Information in the United States.** The report recommended the establishment of a Federal science information service, with the Office of Science Information Service of the NSF as a nucleus. This Office indeed expanded to a FY 66 funded program of $12.5 million in supporting fields of primary and secondary publications, translations, and R&D in information science.

As a reaction to Soviet space exploits and as an opportunity for the U. S., the National Aeronautics and Space Act of 1958 established NASA with an included mission of disseminating information and fostering technology use.[4]

1962. The Kennedy Administration took a fresh look at Federal information handling through the Crawford Task Force. The Task Force report to the President's Special Assistant for Science and Technology recommended that each research and development agency of the Federal Government set up an office exercising agency-wide direction and control of information activities.[5]

1963. The Weinberg Panel of PSAC studied Federal information systems, and its report, **Science, Government and Information: The Responsibilities of the Technical Community and the Government in the Transfer of Information,** was approved. This was a basic advance in the concept of need for information science.

The Committee on Scientific and Technical Information (COSATI) was established under the Federal Council for Science and Technology. This has been a useful and active group and may be better known than any other committee of the parent organization.[6]

1964. The Clearinghouse for Federal Scientific and Technical Information was established in the Department of Commerce to make publicly available results of government R&D and translations of foreign R&D. This was in partial response to conditions outlined in the Weinberg Panel Report.

1965. The Ad Hoc Panel to the Office of Science and Technology, under J. C. R. Licklider, reported that a national information service system should grow out of the 1965 situation. Overall plans should be made toward a national system, and exploratory or experimental systems should begin to implement at least part of the national system.[7]

The Office of Education Educational Research Information Centers were established in response to needs for specific kinds of technical information. Information Analysis Centers of the DOD and AEC were further developed and emphasized.

The Knox Task Group on National Systems for Scientific and Technical Information of COSATI, Federal Council for Science and Technology, developed relationships between research and development and S&T information systems, and made recommendations on national document handling systems in S&T.[8] In general, incremental approaches building from the 1965 systems were preferred, although broad planning for future systems was recommended.

1966. The National Commission on Technology, Automation, and Economic Progress (the Bowen Commission appointed in 1964) reported its assessment of availability and relevance of government-generated technology and the role and obligation of (Federal) government for exploiting technology.

The National Advisory Commission on Libraries was established by the President on September 2, 1966, to appraise the role of libraries as resources for scholarly pursuits, as centers for dissemination of knowledge, and as components of the nation's communications and information exchange network.

The Committee on Scientific and Technical Communication (SATCOM) was established under the National Academy of Sciences and the National Academy of Engineering to examine how the structure, flow, and transfer of S&T information and insight fit the present and future requirements of scientists and engineers. This was the first major entry into the field by the National Academies since the 1958 International Conference. It represented a subtle shift in focus from dissemination to usability. It extended the activities worked on in Federal agencies to the non-government and professional areas.

FOOTNOTES

[1] *Proceedings of the International Conference on Scientific Information* (Washington, D.C.: National Academy of Sciences-National Research Council, 1959), 2 vols., pp. 3-4.

[2] *U.S. Government Organization Manual,* 1968/69, *op. cit.,* pp. 421-26.

[3] *Proceedings of the International Conference . . . , op. cit.* The two-volume report evaluated many of the problems of information science which continue.

[4] *U.S. Government Organization Manual,* 1968/69, *op. cit.,* p. 494.

[5] J. H. Crawford and others, *Scientific and Technical Communications in the Government,* Task Report to the President's Special Assistant for Science and Technology (Washington, D.C.: The White House, 1962), *et passim.*

[6] William T. Knox and others, *Recommendations for National Document Handling Systems in Science and Technology,* Report of the Committee on Scientific and Technical Information, Federal Council for Science and Technology, PB 168 267 (Springfield, Va.: Clearinghouse, 1965), p. 3.

[7] J. C. R. Licklider and others, "Report to Dr. Donald F. Hornig, Director, Office of Science and Technology, by the Office of Science and Technology Ad Hoc Panel on Scientific and Technical Communications," February 8, 1965 (mimeograph).

[8] William T. Knox and others, *op. cit.,* p. 17.

APPENDIX D-2

FEDERAL OBLIGATIONS FOR SCIENTIFIC AND
TECHNICAL INFORMATION ($1000)[1]

FY	Amount	Percent change
1960	75,870	--
1961	91,634	21
1962	128,506	40
1963	164,515	28
1964	203,194	24
1965	224,656	11
1966	227,747	24
1969	362,455	4
1970	386,783	6
1971	397,628	3
1972	419,020	6
1973	452,712	8

[1] National Science Foundation, *Federal Funds for Research, Development, and
Other Scientific Activities, Fiscal Years 1971, 1972, and 1973, op. cit.,* p. 34.
Seventy percent of these funds were obligated by DOD, Commerce, and D/HEW.
Funds for informing the general public were not included. Appendices D-3, D-4,
and D-5 amplify the FY 71 figures.

APPENDIX D-3

FEDERAL OBLIGATIONS, SCIENTIFIC AND TECHNICAL
INFORMATION, FY 71 ($1000)[2]

Area	Intramural	Extramural
Total ($397,628)	270,307	127,321
Publication & distribution	88,508	17,460
Document reference and information service	143,245	50,553
Symposia & audio visual media	22,914	9,912
R&D in information service	15,640	49,396

[2] *Ibid.,* p. 200.

APPENDIX D-4

FEDERAL OBLIGATIONS BY SELECTED AGENCY ($1000)[3]

Area	Actual FY 71	Est. FY 72	Est. FY 73
Total	397,628	419,020	452,712
USDA:			
Rsch. Svcs.	2,875	3,087	3,241
Forest Svc.	2,730	2,973	3,085
Library	4,007	4,188	4,061
PHS:			
NIH	41,343	46,216	51,827
Health Svcs.	7,547	8,882	9,161
DOD	141,254	145,874	152,030
Commerce:			
NBS	12,266	13,335	16,291
Patent ofc.	53,750	58,796	63,710
NASA	26,979	27,253	28,193
AEC	4,881	5,117	4,845

[3] *Ibid.,* pp. 200-202.

APPENDIX D-5

SELECTED FEDERAL AGENCY OBLIGATIONS FOR SCIENTIFIC AND TECHNICAL INFORMATION, FY 71 ($1000) [4]

	Publication & distribution	Publication support	Biblio & reference	Info. ctrs.	Trans- lations	Symposia	Audio & visual	R&D
Federal total	99,626	6,342	154,883	34,587	4,328	21,763	11,063	65,036
USDA:								
Rsch. Svcs.	938	632	620	-----	2	683	-----	-----
Forest svc.	1,323	10	435	-----	-----	856	95	-----
Library	-----	-----	3,605	-----	-----	11	-----	391
NIH	1,403	1,844	20,029	2,956	1,117	2,761	791	10,442
DOD	19,683	1,746	58,499	6,814	1,151	13,036	5,310	34,015
Commerce:								
NBS	4,445	82	1,739	4,254	22	390	255	1,079
Patent Ofc.	43,867	-----	9,145	-----	161	-----	-----	577
NASA	10,304	469	8,048	3,183	166	1,547	2,161	1,101
AEC	2,224	-----	2,594	-----	-----	63	-----	-----

[4] *Ibid.*, p. 197.

APPENDIX E

Indicators Of Technology Diffusion By State

APPENDIX E
USE OF TECHNICAL BRIEFS BY STATE

State	1967 (9 mos.) requests re tech. briefs[1]		1967 patents received[2]		1964 R&D funds[3]		1965 R&D funds[4]		Population	1965 per capita income
	Rank	No.	Rank	No.	Rank	Per-cent	Rank	Per-cent	Rank	Rank
New England										
Maine ----------	45	8			47		48		38	
N. Hampshire ----	30	56			35		35		44	
Vermont --------	42	12			51		50		47	
Mass. ----------	7	514	8		5	4	4	5	10	9
Rhode Is. ------	40	21			33		32		39	
Conn. ----------	12	262	10		22	1	20	1	24	1
Middle Atlantic										
N.Y. ----------	2	1179	2	5891	2	8	2	9	2	7
New Jersey ------	6	519	3	4577	9	3	9	3	8	6
Pa. ------------	4	883	5	3974	6	4	6	4	3	

[1] U. S. Senate, Select Committee on Small Business, *Technology Transfer*, Hearings before the Subcommittee on Science and Technology, September 20, 26, 27, 28, and October 12, 1967 (Washington, D.C.: U. S. Government Printing Office, 1967), pp. 142–43.

[2] Bureau of National Affairs, *Daily Executive Report*, March 13, 1968, p. M-1.

[3] U.S. Senate, Committee on Government Operations, *Equitable Distribution of R&D Funds by Government Agencies*, Hearings before the Subcommittee on Government Research, July 11, 17, and 18, 1967 (Washington, D.C.: U.S. Government Printing Office, 1967), pp. 761–62.

[4] *Ibid.*

APPENDIX E (continued)

State	1967 (9 mos.) requests re tech. briefs[1]		1967 patents received[2]		1964 R&D funds[3]		1965 R&D funds[4]		Population	1965 per capita income
	Rank	No.	Rank	No.	Rank	Per-cent	Rank	Per-cent	Rank	Rank
East North Central										
Ohio --------------	3	949	6	3720	13		10		6	
Ind. --------------	11	293	11		23		26		38	
Ill. --------------	5	747	4	4462	18	2	19	1	4	5
Mich. -------------	8	394	7		20	1	21	1	7	11
Wisc. -------------	18	257	12		26		23		16	
West North Central										
Minn. -------------	15	159	14		25		24		18	
Iowa --------------	28	66	23		34		34		25	
Mo. ---------------	14	212	16		11	3	15	2	13	
N. Dakota ---------	51	3			29		47		45	
S. Dakota ---------	49	6			42		51		40	
Nebraska ----------	39	24			49		44		35	
Kansas ------------	35	34			40		37		29	
South Atlantic										
Md. ---------------	10	297	13		3	5	3	6	20	10
Va. ---------------	16	153	18		17	2	14	2	14	
Washington, D. C. --	21	107			8	3	12	3		

[1] U.S. Senate, Select Committee on Small Business, *Technology Transfer, loc. cit.*
[2] *Daily Executive Report, loc. cit.*
[3] U.S. Senate, Committee on Government Operations, *Equitable Distribution of R&D Funds, loc. cit.*
[4] *Ibid.*

APPENDIX E (continued)

State	1967 (9 mos.) requests re tech. briefs[1]		1967 patents received[2]		1964 R&D funds[3]		1965 R&D funds[4]		Population	1965 per capita income
	Rank	No.	Rank	No.	Rank	Per-cent	Rank	Per-cent	Rank	Rank
W. Va.	33	41			44		39		33	
Dela.	37	31	20		48		45		49	3
N. Carolina	26	76	19		32		29		11	
S. Carolina	36	32			38		41		26	
Georgia	29	60			28		28		21	
Fla.	17	141	17		7	3	7	3	9	
East South Central										
Ky.	32	42	24		43		40		22	
Tenn.	24	95	22		21	1	18	1	17	
Ala.	19	120			12	2	18	3	21	
Miss.	41	17			39		33		31	
West South Central										
Ark.	43	12			50		46		31	
La.	27	71			14	2	11	3	19	
Okla.	25	82	15		37		36		27	
Texas	9	375	9		4	4	5	5	5	

[1] U.S. Senate, Select Committee on Small Business, *Technology Transfer, loc. cit.*

[2] *Daily Executive Report, loc. cit.*

[3] U.S. Senate, Committee on Government Operations, *Equitable Distribution of R&D Funds, loc. cit.*

[4] *Ibid.*

APPENDIX E (continued)

State	1967 (9 mos.) requests re tech. briefs[1]		1967 patents received[2]		1964 R&D funds[3]		1965 R&D funds[4]		Population	1965 per capita income
	Rank	No.	Rank	No.	Rank	Per-cent	Rank	Per-cent	Rank	Rank
Mountain										
Mont.	46	8			45		43		43	
Idaho	38	25			30		27		41	
Wyoming	48	6			31		49		49	
Colo.	20	107			15	2	17	2	30	
N. Mexico	23	99			10	3	8	3	36	
Arizona	31	56			24		25		34	
Utah	34	37			27		30		37	
Nevada	47	6			19	1	22	1	48	4
Pacific										
Wash.	18	134	21		16	2	16	2	23	
Ore.	29	59			36		38		32	
Calif.	1	1426	1	6753	1	35	1	32	1	8
Alaska	50	3			41		42		50	
Hawaii	44	11			46		31		42	2

[1] U.S. Senate, Select Committee on Small Business, *Technology Transfer, loc. cit.*

[2] *Daily Executive Report, loc. cit.*

[3] U.S. Senate, Committee on Government Operations, *Equitable Distribution of R&D Funds, loc. cit.*

[4] *Ibid.*

APPENDIX F

Technology Diffusion Examples From Selected Agencies

APPENDIX F-1

SCREW WORM FLY CONTROL

Control or eradication of the screw worm fly has long been desired for economic and human reasons. In 1940-44, annual losses of livestock were valued at $15,000,000. Loss to wildlife could not be evaluated; but it was estimated in Texas, alone, that 25 per cent of all young deer were killed by screw worms. Flies lay their eggs in open wounds of animals or in the navel just after birth. The eggs hatch and the young maggots eat the surrounding live flesh and create conditions which attract blowflies and other insects to the open sores. Once an animal in an infested area has screw worms, it is doomed unless the wounds are treated locally. By 1952, total annual losses were estimated to be $20,000,000; and, through shipment of infected animals, outbreaks had occurred as far north as Minnesota and New Jersey. According to USDA sources, current annual costs of this program are now about $5 million, and annual savings are estimated to be greater than $50 million.[1]

Basic Research and Investigation

1842. Screw worms were first reported from Texas.

Before 1930. Geneticist H. J. Muller observed that large doses of X-rays sterilized fruit flies.

1933. The first screw worm infestation in the Southeastern U.S. was reported from Boston, Georgia.

1935. Florida was completely infested with screw worms, with reports from every county. The southern counties of other southern states were also infested. Control was attempted with local treatment of wounds and insecticides.

1937. E. F. Knipling, a young entomologist with USDA, began to develop the concept of controlling the screw worm fly by breeding, sterilizing, and releasing enough males to overcome the natural population of fertile males. Since females breed only once, and normal numbers of flies are low, the procedure could be continued through several generations until the fly was eliminated. This procedure was published and discussed in agricultural and biological technical journals of the period.

1943. Annual surveys began to determine the area and incidence of infestation by year. Normally, the flies winter in Southern Florida and Southern Texas, but can survive further north in mild winters. In spring they move north as much as 25 miles in a week. They also move in infested animals shipped north.

1946. Radioisotopes became available from Oak Ridge National Laboratory for use in applied science and technology.

1952. USDA recommendation that EQ 335 Screw Worm Remedy be used locally on animal wounds. This was a three percent lindane and 35 percent pine oil solution. There was no general way to handle the problem.[2]

Inventing

1950-51. Research in sterilizing flies with X-rays at Kerrville, Texas, showed that five to ten times as many sterilized males would overcome the unsterilized ones. It was also found that sterilization had to be done on the sixth day of the eight-day pupa or rest stage.

1951-58. Successful field tests were conducted on Sanibel, an island off the Florida coast, and on Curacao, a Caribbean island.

Informing and Innovating

1958. A cooperative, matching funds program was undertaken in Florida and the other Southeastern states to eradicate screw worms. Three billion flies were grown, sterilized with radioactive cobalt as a gamma ray source, and distributed over 75,000 square miles in Southeastern states. Twenty distribution planes flew three million miles from early 1958 to mid-1959.

1959. Eighteen months after the campaign began, Southeastern U.S. was free of screw worms.

1961. Reinfestation of a small area of Florida was handled by releasing a relatively small number of sterile flies.

Integrating

1961. Texas ranchers and the state legislature raised $3 million and $2.5 million respectively to tackle the screw worm problem in the Southwest.

1962. The southwest campaign started in earnest, with a barrier along the Mexican border 1250 miles long and 100 miles deep saturated with sterile flies. Local areas which showed high incidence of the flies were also saturated. There were only 274 cases in July against a normal 50,000; however, numbers of cases began to rise during autumn.

1963. Texas citizens began an all-out effort to eradicate screw worms. All news media, radio, television, newspapers, farm journals, county agents, vocational agriculture teachers, and youth groups took part. The effort succeeded, but reinfestation continued from Mexico.[4]

1966. Mexico shared in the eradication program, but its infested area was very large. Control became the hope for the border area rather than eradication.[5]

Comments

In 1958, the screw worm fly control and eradication project was the largest example of applied zoology that man had attempted. It had been planned and field tested for several years; the total problem had been studied for twenty years. The project required cooperation of Federal, state, and local government, as well as individual farmers, whose reports provided feedback on success of the effort. Another source of feedback was in capturing flies in infested areas with bait. Existing arrangements for matching funds projects were adequate to handle the project. Later, Congress passed authorizing legislation so that control work could be pursued jointly with Mexico.

The availability of Cobalt 60 after nuclear developments of World War II reduced operational costs. There were no proprietary rights involved in the numerous developments making the project successful. In the total project, hundreds of techniques (items of technology) had to be developed before the huge number of flies could be produced, sterilized, and distributed. The sterile male technologies were applied in 1964 to control Mexican fruit flies in California and Mexico. They have been considered for many of the common pests which attack animals and crops.

Conclusions

1. Diffusion of screw worm fly control technologies was under Federal control from basic research through integration. Existing legal and organizational frameworks of government were adequate for all phases of the program.

2. Information on all the technologies used was published as they were developed and remains available to any potential user. There were no problems of either proprietary rights or security in the handling of information.

3. The decision to adopt the procedure after the Florida and Curaçao tests was made by USDA and state agencies of the Southeastern states involved. There was no public opposition. The careful testing was the key to this success.

4. Integration of the program into the annual USDA budget to reduce reinfestation from Mexico was supported through the efforts of private organizations and governmental units of the Southwest.

5. The program was a financial and technical success as well as a breakthrough in pest control.

6. Some problems are so complex that technical solutions to them can only be diffused by Federal agencies. Existing Federal agencies, furthermore, have considerable flexibility in diffusing clearly desirable technology.

FOOTNOTES

[1] Personal correspondence from E. F. Knipling, Director, Entomology Research Division, Agricultural Research Service, USDA, to author, May 8, 1968.

2 U.S. Department of Agriculture, *Insects: The Yearbook of Agriculture, 1952* (Washingotn, D.C.: U.S. Government Prniting Office, 1952) *passim.*

3 E. F. Knipling, "Screw Worm Eradication: Concepts and Research Leading to the Sterile Male Method," *Smithsonian Report for 1958* (Washington, D.C.: Smithsonian Institution, 1958), pp. 409-18.

4 U.S. Department of Agriculture: *The First 100 Years: The Yearbook of Agriculture, 1962* (Washington, D.C.: U.S. Government Printing Office, 1962), *passim.*

5 U.S. Department of Agriculture, *Protecting Our Food: The Yearbook of Agriculture, 1966* (Washington, D.C.: U.S. Government Printing Office, 1966), pp. 225-30.

APPENDIX F-2

NATURAL RUBBER (GUAYULE)

Guayule grows wild in Big Bend country of Texas and adjacent areas in Mexico, as well as in dry areas of most Southwestern states. It competes with sage and other dry area plants, but lives up to 30 years. Rubber (latex) is contained in the plant's cells, not in the sap. In order to extract rubber, the entire plant is processed. Each cell is broken to release the latex. If planted thickly, one acre gives 1000 pounds of rubber after one year, under optimum conditions. Its yield increases for several years if it is allowed to stand. The yield is about one-fourth of the dry weight. Guayule provided natural rubber for the Indians, and it has been considered as a source for the United States since 1900.

Basic Research and Investigation

1852. J. M. Bigelow found guayule near Escondido Creek, Texas, while surveying the Mexican boundary after the Mexican War.

1876. Guayule rubber was first exhibited in the Centennial Exposition of Philadelphia.

1902. Rubber production from wild guayule began in Mexico.

1905. Intercontinental Rubber Company, Salinas, California, began producing rubber from wild Mexican guayule.

1909. Texas Rubber Company, Marathon, Texas, began operations.

1910. 9,000 tons of guayule rubber were imported from Mexico, one-fifth of the national needs of the times.

1925. Cultivation of guayule began in California under the International Rubber Company, Salinas, California. The company botanist had developed several high-yielding strains.

Inventing and Informing

1941. The U.S. was consuming 775,000 long tons of natural rubber when the Japanese cut off 90 percent of the supplies from Southeast Asia.

1942. The government, under the Emergency Rubber Project (administered by USDA), bought the entire holdings of the International Rubber Company, improved the extraction process, and began plans to plant 75,000 acres of guayule. A second processing mill to the one at Salinas was added at Bakersfield, California.

1946. When the war ended and the Emergency Rubber Project was discontinued, only 1,400 tons of guayule rubber had been produced. 32,000 acres had been planted.

1941-46. During the war, Mexico had produced 9,000 tons of guayule rubber annually. This fairly well exhausted the supply of natural wild shrubs in Mexico.

1946. When reappraisal showed the continuing need for natural rubber (to mix with synthetic rubbers of the time), Stanford Research Institute and the Office of Naval Research began to work to develop the guayule rubber source.

1947. The Office of Naval Research cancelled its support and Congress brought USDA back into supervision. USDA established the Natural Rubber Research Station at Salinas, California.

1950-51. Methods for improving guayule production had included plant breeding (development of high-yielding, vigorous hybrids), better extraction and purification, and methods of cultivation which induced latex forming in the plant cells. The Natural Rubber Station was responsible for developing a domestic source of natural rubber for national security purposes. One of its proposals was to plant half a million acres of marginal land in the Southwest to guayule to grow naturally and be available for harvesting in case of war.[1]

1955. Natural rubber was synthesized for the first time. This artificial natural rubber could be added to give synthetic rubbers their desired qualities. All government rubber facilities were sold to private industry.

Comments

Technology for extracting rubber from the guayule plant was a success and was rapidly being improved in 1955 when synthetic **natural** rubbers were developed which made the whole technology obsolete. New technology was overcome by cheaper and more efficient technology. Guayule rubber was not competitive with foreign natural rubber and did not store as well; however, it did serve useful purposes as an additive to synthetic rubbers of WW II. The necessity of having the natural rubber additive spurred both guayule research and the synthesis of natural rubbers. When natural rubbers started becoming available in the 1960's, there was no reason to have the guayule source, even as a back-up.

Guayule technology is an example of many such technologies from both government and industry which are feasible, useful, and desirable, but which do not compete with others just a little better.

Conclusions

1. Guayule technology did not reach innovation, or significant application, because of better and more efficient technologies which became available.

2. Guayule technology is in the storehouse of R&D results for Mexico, the U.S., or any other interested country.

3. Neither the technical possibilities for guayule nor its use of marginal land could overcome its economic handicaps.

4. In the Federal R&D store, there is much technology that has already been superseded.

FOOTNOTES

[1] U.S. Department of Agriculture, *Crops in War and Peace: Yearbook of Agriculture, 1950-51* (Washington, D.C.: U.S. Government Printing Office, 1951), pp. 367-74. The chronology of this example was also developed from this source.

APPENDIX F-3

GRAIN WEEVILS

USDA has developed ways to control or eliminate most insects which attack food or animals; however, the solutions have not always been accepted. The rice weevil, which does its greatest damage in corn, and similar weevils still consume ten percent of the U. S. grain crop each year. In the deep South, stored corn can be destroyed at a rate of nine percent each month. Infestation occurs before the corn is harvested.

Losses vary from year to year depending on growing and harvesting conditions. Auburn University studied samples of the 1962 corn crop for USDA and found the weight of the corn dropped from fifty-five pounds per bushel to forty-two pounds after one year. Nutritive value of the corn dropped twenty-seven percent. Based on the loss in nutritive value, scientists estimated a $6 million loss of the corn's value for feeding purposes in Alabama, Georgia, and Mississippi. Insect population per pint of shelled corn grew from nineteen at harvest to 151 after a year. Rice weevils were most destructive, followed by red flour weevils, flat grain beetles, cadelles, square-necked grain beetles, and eleven other insect species.[1]

Carbon disulfide (CS_2), an effective but dangerous fumigant, has been known and used since 1854. To reduce weevil damage one must harvest early to avoid field infestation; shuck, shell, dry, and store; and fumigate periodically. CS_2 can be mixed with carbon tetrachloride (CCl_4) in one part CS_2 to four parts CCl_4 to make a safer fumigant, though still unpleasant to use. Ethylene dichloride and ethylene dibromide are also used.[2] Fumigation has been accepted as a necessity for preserving seed stock. Small airtight containers and limited amounts of seed stock are involved. Fumigation is also practiced in large granaries where significant capital is invested and storage conditions are controlled. Fumigation technology has failed on the average farm, and the damage continues each year. Weevil losses from corn alone are as great as losses from the screw worm fly.

Why do so few farms fumigate when it offers such clear advantages? Several factors are involved. In the deep South where damage is greatest, corn is not shucked and shelled, but is stored in the ear, for the simple reason that this form of storage slows weevil damage. Southern farmers have traditionally preferred corn varieties with a tight heavy shuck to reduce field infestation as well as the rate of damage when the corn is stored. In the pre-tractor, mule-farming South, corn was most needed in the spring and summer months when the animals were working. The heavy-shuck, cross-bred corn varieties generally grown before 1940 satisfied this spring and summer need better than more recent high-yielding hybrids. Corn was also stored in log cribs or some other well-ventilated building because of corn's high moisture content. This storage allowed corn to dry without molding, but made fumigation impossible. The farmer took the lesser of evils in that moldy grain would kill animals while weevils would not.

Farmers who lose corn today have inherited equipment from outmoded methods of farming. To change to more effective procedures for harvesting and storing means corn pickers, dryers, new storage units, and capital outlays beyond the means of the average farmer. Insect-proof cribs are no good without dryers. The investment is hardly worthwhile if the grain crop is small and only a subsidiary operation. Fumigation is only part of a set of applied technologies necessary to reduce damage.

This example illustrates the plight of many adoption units in agriculture, business, and industry. These units allocate fairly efficiently the resources within their means. Increasing total productivity generally requires not one but a set of new, interrelated technologies.

Conclusions

1. The farmer fails to prevent weevil damage not through ignorance of the need or of the technology but through the small scale of his operation and equipment.

2. Neither availability of the technology nor publicity about its feasibility has caused adoption in areas it could help the most.

3. Adoption and integration of fumigation techniques may come after traditional farms recombine into up-to-date units with technically oriented operating procedures.

FOOTNOTES

[1] U.S. Department of Agriculture, "Insect Damage to Corn in Three Southeastern States at Time of Harvest and in Farm Storage," Marketing Research Report No. 792 (Washington, D.C.: U.S. Government Printing Office, 1968), passim.

[2] U.S. Department of Agriculture, *Insects: The Yearbook of Agriculture, 1952* (Washington, D.C.: U.S. Government Printing Office, 1952), pp. 629-639, 345-350.

APPENDIX F-4

ANTIBIOTICS

Antibiotics come from soil microorganisms. They attack bacteria directly instead of merely killing them or hindering their growth, as do antiseptics. They are not toxic to human cells, as are antiseptics. Penicillin, dehydrostreptomycin, tetracycline, terramycin, and bacitracin are best known. There are over 500 known antibiotics, but only about ten percent are suitable for medical use. Some are specific, useful only against certain bacteria, and some have undesirable side effects. Those used by man also work on animals. In addition, poultry and livestock may be fed antibiotics with vitamin B_{12} in enriched feeds to make them grow faster.

Antibiotics are mass produced in giant closed tanks of from 5,000 to 30,000 gallons capacity. After about three days of growth, the broth is evaporated and the remaining material is the antibiotic extract. It is tested for purity and sold in tablets, liquids, or other suitable forms. There is a constant search for new antibiotics because bacteria grow resistant to them, and new types have to be introduced to stay ahead of the bacteria.

Basic Research and Investigation

1922. Alexander Fleming discovered a germ-killing substance he called lysozyme in tissues, secretions, and white blood corpuscles of the human body.

1927. Fleming discovered that after several generations, bacteria grow resistant to germ-killing substances.

1929. Fleming announced the accidental discovery of penicillin and its strong antibacterial action in the **British Journal of Experimental Pathology.**

Inventing and Informing

1930's. Rene J. Dubos discovered how a chemical from a bacillus dissolved staphylococcus. Sir Howard Florey learned of his work in 1938, and then found Fleming's paper.

1939. A group of investigators at Oxford undertook a study of penicillin to determine its possible usefulness during the war.

1940. The Oxford group, headed by Florey and Ernst Boris Chain, concentrated penicillin and demonstrated its curative powers. It attacked gram-positive bacteria, 40 percent of disease-causing germs.

Innovating

1941. After developing methods of producing and extracting, Florey induced U. S. authorities to begin production. The Rockefeller Foundation brought Florey to the U. S. to assist. USDA contributed to techniques for growing the mold.[1]

1944. Penicillin production was still experimental, with nearly all output destined for the Armed Forces.

Streptomycin was first identified from work begun by S. A. Waksman at Rutgers University in 1939. It attacked gram-negative bacteria, 30 percent of disease-causing germs.

Integrating

1945. Penicillin reached civilian markets. Streptomycin was introduced at a cost of about $30 per gram. By 1953 streptomycin cost about 35 cents per gram.

1947. Chloramphenicol, the first broad spectrum antibiotic, was tested.

1948. Chlortetracycline (aureomycin) was discovered and tested by B. M. Duggar, age 75, of Lederle Labs. It attacked both gram-negative and gram-positive bacteria.

1950. Oxytetracycline (terramycin) was discovered after 100,000 cultures were examined in 10 months by Charles Pfizer Company. It is effective against 90 percent of disease germs. Chloramphenicol was synthesized.

1953. Tetracycline (achromycin) became available, largely replacing aureomycin and terramycin in medical practice since it caused fewer side reactions.

1959. Penicillin cost 3 cents per 100,000 units compared to $20 per 100,000 units in 1943. 3,600 tons were produced yearly.

1964. Antibiotics constituted about 60 percent of the $800 million pharmaceutical industry. They cost $67 per pound compared to $301 per pound in 1950.

Comments

Federal support of antibiotic development during WW II gave industry the foundation in research and production from which it rapidly expanded. Successful use of antibiotics with patients in service hospitals and on the battlefield gained acceptance from the ten percent of the population in uniform. Later, doctors and non-military patients immediately accepted antibiotics. In 1957, four years after tetracycline was introduced, its sales reached $150 million. Antibiotics reached sales of .1 percent of GNP in ten years; however, it lost the ratio, the GNP having risen faster than the spread of disease.[2]

Conclusions

The discovery of penicillin was a classic example of serendipity, careful scientific observation, and recording of observations and results.

Fleming distributed information in technical channels, so Florey discovered it when he reviewed the field.

2. Technology diffusion to the U. S. was in the form of the individual, Florey, imported specifically to assist in production.

3. Antibiotics received impetus from Federal government because of wartime needs; hence, innovation costs and risks did not block the industry's development.

4. Public integration and acceptance followed penicillin's successful use by doctors with WW II patients. The Armed Services can foster new technology acceptance and integration.

5. Aside from wartime exigencies, support of antibiotics required no special Federal organization.

FOOTNOTES

[1] U.S. Department of Agriculture, *Crops in War* and *Peace* . . . , *op. cit.*, pp. 734-741. Part of the chronology was developed from this reference.

[2] National Commission on Technology, Automation, and Economic Progress, *The Employment Impact of Technological Change*, Appendix II, *Technology and the American Economy* . . . , *op. cit.*, pp. 1177-1179. Part of the chronology was also developed from this reference.

APPENDIX F-5

FLUORIDATION TO PREVENT TOOTH DECAY

Basic Research and Investigation [1]

1902. Dr. Frederick S. McKay, a young dentist of Colorado Springs, noted discolored teeth in area residents.

1912. Dr. W. A. Arthur of Franklin, Virginia, noted in patients the same discoloration reported in McKay's 1909 paper to the Colorado State Dental Association.

1917. McKay discovered that immigrant Portuguese from some Cape Verde Islands had discolored teeth and those from other islands did not.

1923. Residents of Oakley, Idaho, changed water supply to stop mottling of their children's teeth.

1928. McKay noted that mottled teeth had few cavities and published this in the **Journal of the American Dental Association.**

1931. H. V. Churchill, chief chemist of ALCOA, found fluoride traces in water at Bauxite, Arkansas, a mining town well-known because of the children's discolored teeth. The amount of fluorine was 13.7 parts per million of water. Analysis of water supplies in all U. S. areas with high incidence of discolored teeth showed fluorine traces of from two to thirteen parts of fluorine per million (ppm).

1930-31. Dr. Margaret Cammack Smith and others of Arizona produced mottled teeth in rats by feeding them water with fluorine content equivalent to that of some local drinking water believed to have caused discolorations.

1931. Dr. H. Trendley Dean of PHS began studies to verify the relationship between mottled teeth and fluorine content of drinking water.

T. Masaki of Japan noted infrequent caries among people with mottled teeth.

1936. Dean verified the fluorine-mottling relationship and set the threshold level between mottled and clear teeth to be about one ppm.

1937-38. Dean established the inverse relationship between mottling and caries. He suggested controlling caries by fluoridating water supplies. He began surveying 21 cities to establish the correlation between fluorine amounts and numbers of caries.

Inventing and Informing

1941. Bibby of Tufts Dental School studied direct topical application of sodium fluoride solution to adolescents' teeth.

1943. The survey of 21 cities showed the correlation between absence of fluorine and presence of caries.

1945. PHS began a controlled experiment at Grand Rapids, Michigan, of fluoridating public water supplies at one ppm. Similar ten-year experiments began at Newburgh, New York; Brantford, Ontario; Sheboygan, Wisconsin; and Marshall, Texas.

PHS published results of reducing tooth decay by direct topical application of two per cent sodium fluoride on children's teeth.

1946. Fluoridation champions in Wisconsin campaigned to get all towns to fluoridate. Madison voted to fluoridate and the campaign started to get 50 other towns to fluoridate by 1950. Champions urged PHS and national dental and medical associations to support fluoridation.

1948. PHS supported topically applied sodium fluoride but urged delay in fluoridation until the experiments could be evaluated.

1950. Fifty Wisconsin towns had fluoridated. Stevens Point voted to fluoridate and then voted to cease. The champions had aroused local opposition; fluoridation became a political issue. Opposition charged inadequate testing, statism, irreligion, outside interference in private affairs; and they charged officials with knowing some harmful effects of fluorides, intending to slander, and insidiously plotting to undermine the people's health.

1950. PHS approved fluoridation based on tentative results of the controlled experiments and on the historical evidence. The AMA and the American Dental Association followed with their approval. The opposition construed these acts as politically inspired to force fluoridation.

1952. Seattle, Washington, voted against fluoridation. The Delaney Committee in Congress began hearings on fluoridation, giving all sides equal opportunity to testify. After misgivings and suspicions were aired, adoption rates dropped off.

1953. PHS and dental and medical organizations approved fluoridation without reservation, based on the controlled experiments and the historical evidence. These organizations were attacked and vilified.

1954. A House of Representatives Committee held three days of hearings on a bill to "protect the public health against the fluoridation of water." The bill was dropped on the logic that it was no more legal to prevent fluoridation than it was to require it.

Innovating

The greatest number of adoptions of fluoridation were in 1952, before the Delaney hearings. By 1956, about six percent of public water supplies were fluoridated. In 1968 about one-third of Americans were drinking fluoridated water. The cost was 5¢ to 15¢ per person per year. Since 1965 there has been some indication that fluorides may be of positive value to bones of older persons, improving calcium metabolism and alleviating such conditions as osteoporosis.[2]

Comments

The fluoridation issue was a public defeat of the forces for medical and social improvement. Wisconsin champions for fluoridation, insistent that their state should lead, triggered intemperate opposition that became a crusade against fluoridation. Once grass roots opposition was aroused, no amount of reassurance by national authorities was acceptable. It may be significant that the period of the controversy, the Delaney hearings, and the proposed law against fluoridation were in the time period of the Senator Joseph McCarthy charges and countercharges. Though about one-third of all Americans were drinking fluoridated water in 1968, opponents to the measure were still active in California.[3]

Considering the fuss over putting one ppm of fluorine equivalent in drinking water, it is notable that, in the same time period, there was little opposition to the topical application of 20,000 ppm to children's teeth. This procedure was widely used in towns without fluoridated water.

Conclusions

1. This example illustrates the role of champions, in this case McKay and Dean, in carrying through the necessary fact-gathering, doing the applied research, and validating the results. It also shows the harmful effects that can occur from premature championing of a technology that has not yet been proved to the satisfaction of all affected by it. Wisconsin proponents could not wait for the end of the controlled experiments and probably set back the diffusion of fluoridation by several years. They caused development of champions **against** adopting the technology.

2. Literature on fluoridation is very extensive, and considerable publicity has been given continuing tests and checks by PHS. The availability of scientific information, therefore, does not assure adoption.

3. This example also shows the difficulty of adopting new technology when the numbers of those who must consent become large. Topical application did not arouse the same opposition because the family was the adoption unit, and no one was pressuring the family to try it. Availability of the topical application approach also illustrates the advantages of having alternate ways to accomplish a desired end.

4. With only a third of Americans drinking fluoridated water, the technology is still in innovation.

FOOTNOTES

[1] Donald R. McNeil, *The Fight for Fluoridation* (New York: Oxford University Press, 1957), *passim*. Most of the historical chronology was developed from this reference.

[2] James M. Dunning, "Current Status of Fluoridation," *New England Journal of Medicine,* 272:30-34, 84-88, January 7 and 14, 1965.

[3] Arthur Ribbel, "Word Fluoridation Symbol for Fighting," *The Register* (Santa Ana, California), May 15, 1968, p. D13.

APPENDIX F-6

RUBELLA VACCINE

Inoculation, deliberate development of mild forms of disease in order to produce immunity for life, has been practiced since ancient times. Edward Jenner, an English physician, in 1796 developed inoculating with cowpox to protect people from smallpox. The antibodies developed against cowpox, a mild disease, were also effective against smallpox, a very killing and disfiguring disease. The principle of inoculation, or injection of vaccines, has been developed so that many serious diseases can be controlled by using them. Vaccination is particularly effective in preventing virus diseases, including smallpox, measles, polio, mumps, and some forms of encephalitis. Some immunity can also be developed against the bacillus bacteria, such as those which cause typhoid fever, and against the rickettsias, such as those which cause typhus. One of the most publicized developments was the control of polio by the Jonas E. Salk vaccine. Dr. Salk's vaccine was effective against the three common forms of polio viruses.

Immunization records are maintained by all members of the Armed Forces, by those going into other countries with passports, by children in public schools, and by many private citizens. The development of immunization procedures has been a continuing effort of PHS, state health organizations, and private foundations. Development of vaccine to be used against rubella (German or three-day measles) did not start until the disease was recognized to cause congenital defects in children when the mother had the disease during certain periods of her pregnancy. Previously the disease was unemphasized because of its mildness and lack of residual effects.

Basic Research and Investigation

Before 1880. Rubella was defined clinically.

1941. Rubella's role in the causing of congenital defects was recognized by Dr. Norman Gregg, an Australian ophthalmologist, who traced an unprecedented number of infant cataracts to a 1940 rubella epidemic.

1949. Enders, Weller, and Robbins developed a practical cell culture technology through which viruses could be propagated in tissue cultures. This was a basic development for both polio and rubella vaccines.

1962. Rubella virus that could be related to the disease was first propagated in monkey kidney cell cultures by Parkman, Buescher, and Artenstein of Walter Reed Army Institute of Research and in human amnion cell cultures by Weller and Neva of Harvard University. Buescher, studying undiagnosed cases of respiratory illness to isolate rhino-viruses, included some rubella in the survey. These were rec-

ognized and successfully propagated, giving the first positive identity
of the rubella. Buescher was using the interference phenomenon for
virus detection which had first been applied in 1960 by Tyrrell of
England to detect the cold rhino-viruses.

Inventing and Informing

1962. Even basic investigation could not have occurred without the
1949 development of cell culture technology and the 1960 use of interference phenomena to detect viruses.

1963. Between 1941 and 1963 gamma globulin had been used em-
pirically for pregnant women exposed to rubella, particularly during
the first three months, to prevent fetus infection and damage.

The Division of Biologic Standards, National Institutes of Health,
began a comprehensive rubella research program. Cell cultures
demonstrated that gamma globulin contained rubella antibodies and
made possible selection of highly potent lots. The vaccine approach
to rubella prevention began as soon as methods of cell culture of the
virus were available. Two types of vaccine were desired — live virus
for use with children and non-pregnant adults and killed virus vaccine
for pregnant and possibly pregnant women.[1]

1964. Killed virus vaccines were tested in animals and man but
failed to provide adequate antibody response in man.[2]

The live virus program aimed for a vaccine which was safe to the
recipient, gave him immunity, and was not directly contagious to
susceptible pregnant women, and did not cause excretion which might
affect pregnant women. Tests began in animals.[3]

1965-69. Live virus tests in man began at the Arkansas Children's
Colony and were continuing in other groups in 1969.

Innovating

1964. Sever et. al. determined that the reservoir of rubella-suscep-
tible women in the U.S. was about 18 percent.

1964-65. Rubella reached epidemic proportions in 1964 and was
followed by a great increase in abortions and defective children. There
were 10,000 fetal deaths and 20,000 defective children credited to this
epidemic.

1966. Meyer and Parkman developed a quick test for rubella
immunity.

Live virus vaccines tested included monkey attenuated and grown
(Meyer and Parkman), duck embryo cell culture attenuated and grown
(Hilleman and Buynak), and diploid human cell strain attenuated and
grown (Plotkin). All vaccines produced rubella antibodies, none
caused significant illness, and all had low or no contagiousness to

susceptible children. Safety and immunogenic capacity had not been established in at least 100,000 susceptible persons with accepted vaccine strains.

Gamma globulin prophylaxis for pregnant women exposed to rubella remained in dispute. The protection afforded may not, it was argued, offset the masking of the disease.

1967. Pilot production began commercially. 10,000 persons had received vaccination and 97 percent had developed antibodies indicative of immunity. The most effective strain of rubella found for inoculation was HPV 77, the 77th one tested. It was made freely available to pharmacists and scientists both in the U. S. and abroad.

1968. Parkman stated to the California Medical Association that the vaccine tests had succeeded and that others would start that year. 30,000 persons had been vaccinated. He estimated that general use of the vaccine would start by 1970 if tests continued to succeed.[4]

Comments

This example of vaccine development illustrates work in public health which was less controversial than that of fluoridation of public water supplies. Some contributors were public servants, others were in private foundations or in the private sector. Much feedback on the applications has come from the observations of doctors in private practice. The breakthroughs were: (1) establishing rubella as a cause of congenital defects, (2) learning to grow virus in culture, (3) learning to detect virus by interference, and (4) identifying the rubella virus, the key breakthrough by Buescher and a serendipitous one. The other breakthroughs came through systematic research. The work was organized along lines already proven successful in polio and rubeola. There was adequate support from multiple sources, particularly after the 1964 epidemic. The rubella example has been a success thus far, and it represents the best in straightforward mission-oriented Federal agency development. It phased into preventive medicine with little trouble. Comparing the rubella example with those of fluoridation or trauma indicates that the public accepts technology diffusion by public health authorities only in certain areas. Car accidents, fluoridation, and cigarette smoking are in areas of only partial acceptance.

Conclusions

1. Rubella vaccine technology began with discovery of rubella virus. A perceptive public employee found something he was not looking for, the virus. Other advances have come from carefully formulated, follow-on, mission-oriented research development.

2. Technical and scientific information on rubella was available in the literature; indeed, the information was actively discussed and analyzed throughout the developments.

3. Public and private sectors have actively supported innovation because of the non-controversial expected benefits to man.

4. Acceptance of other vaccines expedited integration of rubella vaccine. Ingestion of this technology reduces numbers of defective children and saves the heartbreaking expenses of caring for them.

FOOTNOTES

[1] Maurice B. Visscher, "Applied Science and Medical Progress," in *Applied Science and Technological Progress, op. cit.,* pp. 185-206.

[2] *Ibid.*

[3] *Ibid.*

[4] "Review of Rubella Research," Mimeographed Fact Sheet Extracted from Presentations by Meyer and Parkman, Prepared by the Information Office, Division of Biologics Standards, National Institutes of Health, May 1, 1968.

APPENDIX F-7

TRAUMA   (AUTOMOBILE ACCIDENTS)

The Number One killer for the population group aged four to thirty-seven is accidents, and automobile accidents account for half these deaths.   Car accidents have killed over 1.6 million Americans and continue to kill over 50,000 annually.   During WW II, civilian deaths and injuries on highways exceeded combat casualties by three times.   The $10 billion cost of these accidents is at least half the value of new U. S. cars manufactured each year.[1]   The automobile accident problem is divided into highway, vehicle, and driver categories; but more efforts have been made in highway and driver improvement than in vehicle improvement.   From 1965 to 1968, safety that can be built into the vehicle has received more emphasis.   With 96,000,000 or more cars on the road, accidents will happen and the least that can be done is to reduce injury and death from them.

Federal government divides responsibility among administrators of public health and safety, road builders, and car manufacturers.   Federal responsibility is shared with states and local authorities.   Thus far, no focal point of responsibility has been established.   The Departments of Commerce, Transportation, and HEW can be blamed separately or as a group.   Public safety and health, however, are overriding factors, and the engineering factors of vehicle and road design merely support these.   If the Surgeon General is responsible for indirect, delayed effects of environmental pollution, then he is even more responsible for direct, immediate deaths in daily car accidents.

Anything that is the chief killer of young people must be regarded as socially significant.   If it kills more people than war does, it is even more significant.   Why, then, is not the car accident recognized as a non-contagious disease of epidemic proportions?   The answer seems to be that the problem has not been defined in terms that indicate a solution with social and technical tools at hand.   Certainly the problem has not been defined so that a systems approach is possible, nor has any segment of government or society assumed responsibility for the total problem.   Society remains in the basic research and investigation stage, with some inventive activity in partial solutions.   There was far more concerted effort to control screw worm flies.

Basic Research and Investigation[2]

1907.   Ford introduced mass production of cheap cars with the Model T, and accidents began.

1916.   Federal aid in highway improvement began.

1924.   Herbert Hoover, then Secretary of Commerce, convened the National Conference of Street and Highway Safety.

1928.   Car accidents began to cause more than $1 billion damage annually and to kill more than 30,000 annually.

1933. Neyhart of Pennsylvania State College introduced the first complete program of driver education, including both class and lab instruction, into high school at State College, Pennsylvania.[3]

1946. The President's Highway Safety Conference made recommendations on all aspects of the problem except improving safety features of automobiles. It laid the basic program followed until 1966.

1954. The White House Conference on Traffic Safety concentrated on building citizens' support for the 1946 program. South Dakota voted to require that all drivers be licensed, the last state to do so.

1956. The Federal-Aid Highway Act of 1956 established the program for upgrading the national highway system. This program, as originally envisioned, would be complete by 1972.

1962-63. Sixty percent of public high schools provided driving instruction, but less than half of eligible students took part.

1964. Congress cut research funds on highway safety for the Bureau of Public Roads and for accident prevention in PHS.

1965. The President noted in a message to Congress the absence of a safe highway program, confusion of responsibility at the Federal level, and the inadequacy of statistics on causes of accidents.

Inventing and Informing

1966. The National Traffic Safety Act of 1966 required safety equipment on automobiles. The Highway Safety Act of 1966 authorized the Secretary of Transportation to require safety precautions on highways and to sponsor R&D and coordinate functions in highway safety. PHS functions were concentrated in the Division of Accident Prevention, one of eleven divisions or offices in the Bureau of Disease Prevention and Environmental Control. The functions were upgraded in July 1968.

Conclusions

1. No adequate accident prevention program has been articulated and no effective solution has arisen **ad hoc.**

2. Responsibilities for motor vehicle, driver, highway, and other aspects of traffic safety remain divided in Federal government.

3. No within-government champion has arisen, though Ralph Nader has won fame as the citizen champion of trauma reduction.

4. The accident rate will continue until organizational, technical, and responsibility adjustments are made.

FOOTNOTES

[1] *Accident Facts, 1967 Edition* (Chicago: National Safety Council, 425 N. Michigan Ave., 60611, 1967), pp. 40-72.

[2] James E. Aaron and Murland K. Strasser, *Driver and Traffic Safety Education* (New York: Macmillan, 1966); Grant S. McClellan (ed.), *Safety on the Road* (New York: The H. W. Wilson Co., 1966); and The Center for Safety Education at New York University, *Man and the Motor Car* (Englewood Cliffs, N. J.: Prentice-Hall, Inc., 1964). The chronology for this example was developed from these three references.

[3] *Ibid.*

APPENDIX F-8

REFRIGERATOR INSULATION

Refrigerators were originally large, bulbous, and heavy because of their insulation, an outgrowth from the earlier icebox. The trim, square refrigerators of the present did not appear until the market for refrigerators became the new home with built-in kitchen. Refrigerators have a design life of 20 years, with 5-year guarantees usually given for compressors and evaporators. Insulation is not usually guaranteed, but it is not expected to fail during the design life. An insulation improvement would be expected to have a ready market. If independent inventors or government agencies had such an invention and could not exploit it, they would believe that manufacturers were prejudiced against them. Yet, the "world's best insulation," developed by one of the biggest refrigerator manufacturers, remains unexploited.[1]

Basic Research and Investigation

1920's. Langmuir studied best transfer in evacuated powders.

1945. Dr. A. W. Hull of the General Electric Research Laboratory worked on evacuated wall panels.

1947. A G.E. Refrigeration Department engineer, Mr. A. Janos, stated the problem for technical solution. He noted that since more than half a refrigerator's volume was insulation, more efficient insulation would give increased inside space without increasing exterior dimensions.

Inventing

1949. In February the G.E. Research Director assigned Dr. H. M. Strong and Dr. F. P. Bundy, both physicists in the Research and Development Center, and Mr. Nerad to work on the project. He reminded them of Dr. Hull's work. The physicists concluded after study that evacuated panels were the most feasible insulation. They isolated the technical problem in this approach to be the heat transfer through the bridgework holding the walls apart. In September experimental work began on ways to construct walls and bridgework. In December Dr. Strong hit on the idea of using glass fibers stacked like jackstraws to support the walls. This concept was developed into a test model which proved better than anything else tried.

1950-51. Detailed testing continued of the trial panels to determine leakage rates, production problems, and relative costs.

1953-54. Experimental models were constructed for refrigerators, freezers, cooking equipment, and ovens. Surveys showed, however, that the cost of home space was less than the cost of the space gained through use of the new insulation, called P-Zero.

1954. A new compressor was introduced into the G.E. refrigerator line and G.E. management decided not to introduce two changes at once. The new insulation was shelved.

Informing (Information Transfer)

1951-54. The P-Zero insulation was widely discussed in internal G.E. reports, brochures, and technical information media.

1959. The P-Zero concept was presented to the Fifth National Conference on Cryogenic Engineering and published in the proceedings, **Advanced Cryogenic Engineering** (Plenum Press, 1960).

1960. Bundy, Dr. H. P. Bovenkerk, and Strong published the results of their investigation, "Flat Panel Vacuum Thermal Insulation," **Journal of Applied Physics**, 31, No. 1, 39-50 (January, 1960).

1960-68. Trade journals have had numerous descriptions of the P-Zero concept.

1964. On June 10, Strong and Bundy applied for a patent which was issued April 20, 1965, as No. 3,179,549, "Thermal Insulating Panel and Method of Making the Same."[2]

1964-68. The G.E. Patent Sales Department actively tried to license the P-Zero insulation to other users. Inquiries came from people interested in insulating trucks, freight cars, liquid methane ships, and items as small as navigation gyros.

1968. There was no known application of the "world's best thermal insulation." In the 1960 time period, the concept may have influenced the designers of Linde's super dewar containers for transporting and storing cryogenic liquids such as nitrogen, hydrogen and helium.

Comments

P-Zero insulation is an example of useful patents that await application. Thirty to forty percent of all patents are not used commercially, and many sound as good as this one. Some may be too early or too late. Some may be less desirable alternatives. The non-application is usually traceable to cost, user preference, and/or inclinations of the times. According to Dr. Bundy, the reasons for the non-use of P-Zero have included engineering complexity, cost, weight, and lack of development facilities.[3]

The P-Zero insulation concept was not patented until the G.E. Patent Sales Department decided to sell R&D byproducts. The amount of such non-patented technology is greater than that which is patented if the ratios developed by invention investigators are correct. Each invention patent costs about $1000 if there is no interference. The work on evacuated wall panels began for the specific purpose of using it in refrigerators only after the problem of lost storage and excessive insulation volume was clearly stated by an applications engineer and the technical approach was suggested by the technical director with a knowledge of previous work. By a combination of theory with trial and error, the two physicists were able to invent a solution to the problem in a short time.

Conclusions

1. The development of a technology frequently does not start until some insightful individual states the problem in a way that indicates a technical solution.

2. The development of a technology to solve a particular problem still follows a trial and error procedure. The information is likely to be in local files or in the memory or experience of developers.

3. Neither the usefulness of a technology nor widespread publicity about it assures that it will reach the innovation stage.

4. Decisions of management not related to technical efficiency frequently determine which items are innovated and integrated.

5. An appreciable amount of useful but unused technology is available in patent files.

6. In the files and collective experiences of inventors and corporations, there are technical concepts, developments, and prototypes that are unused and unpatented.

FOOTNOTES

[1] C. Guy Suits and Arthur M. Bueche, "Cases of Research and Development in a Diversified Company," in *Applied Science and Technological Progress, op. cit.,* pp. 306-308. The chronology for this example was developed from this reference.

[2] Personal communication with Dr. F. P. Bundy, dated May 6, 1968.

[3] *Ibid.*

APPENDIX F-9

CHROME ORE AND METAL

Between 1953 and 1963, the Bureau of Mines tried to make commercial use of low-grade, high iron, chrome ore deposits in the Western U. S. $700,000 was spent at Albany Metallurgy Research Center, Albany, Ore., and $47,000 was spent at several other western centers. The Bureau learned to concentrate various low-grade ores and to produce commercial quality ferrochrome by furnace methods. The Bureau also produced superpure, ductile chromium, a material never before available, and new chromium alloys. Thirty-five scientific articles were published detailing the work. After ten years, no private industry considered the main Bureau work on ores economically attractive.

Ductile wire was a byproduct of the superpure chromium development, and this wire became useful in cancer therapy. Dr. William C. Myers of Ohio State University had found that pure chromium, when irradiated, emitted radiation lethal to cancer cells but harmless to healthy cells. The Bureau supplied Dr. Myers with the wire and later provided samples worldwide to laboratories.[1]

Comments

This example, an economic reject or item of possible future value, typifies nearly sixty percent of all Bureau of Mines projects. The Bureau divided its projects into failures (7.5%), economic (35.5%), not economically feasible (24%), and projects of future value (34%). The chrome ore and metal project stands in the third or fourth category.

Conclusions

1. Careful development of internal resources to satisfy present and future needs by a Federal agency does not assure economic successes (only 35.5%), but it can reduce absolute failures which provide only negative information (7.5%).

2. Immediate reporting and ready availability of technical information allow industry to evaluate results of R&D with relative ease. Chrome ore processes were rejected for economic reasons, but they may be more attractive in the future.

3. The use of superpure ductile chromium wire in cancer research was a true transfer of technology. Dr. Myers was able to make this transfer because of information in the technical press and continuing availability of the wire from the Bureau of Mines.

4. The chrome ore and metal technology is part of the R&D store available for future use.

FOOTNOTES

[1] U.S. Congress, House, Committee on Interior and Insular Affairs, *Review of Research by the Bureau of Mines, Department of the Interior, op. cit.,* p. 6.

APPENDIX F-10

COAL CARBON BLACK

In 1965 the U. S. produced 2,354 million pounds of carbon black and production has been rising about seven percent per year since 1949. Uses with rubber account for 94 percent and the remaining six percent is divided among ink, paper, paint, and plastics. Until 1945 all carbon black was produced from natural gas by channel, furnace, and thermal processes. In 1945, new furnace processes made possible the reduction of petroleum to carbon black. The petroleum source has replaced the natural gas source except for the finest grades produced by natural gas channel processes. The Bureau of Mines, in investigating potential new uses for coal, has been able to produce carbon black from coal which can be used with rubber. The carbon black was produced by pyrolysis of coal at 1250 degrees Centigrade. Carbon black produced in a nonoxidizing atmosphere equated to finer carbon blacks produced by natural gas channel methods. Carbon black produced in an oxidizing atmosphere equated to that used with rubber from petroleum sources. Costing with conservative procedures, the Bureau calculated that, with a $3,500,000 investment, an 18 percent gross return on total investment could be achieved. Production costs would be three to four cents per pound and market prices (1967) were 6.2 cents per pound. Details of the Bureau of Mines process are available in the open literature. To apply the process it would be necessary to engineer a full scale plant.[1]

Comments

This is a typical example of government agency inventing, informing, and advocating adoption. If industry shows no interest, the Bureau may propose a joint venture. The possibilities for an 18 percent return on a relatively small investment, however, should stimulate industry. At the same time the carbon black research was in progress, USDA chemists were investigating use of cereal starch resin as an additive to rubber. The wheat starch additive showed a greater maximum tensile strength than rubber reinforced by carbon black. The economics of this additive have not been developed.[2]

Conclusions

1. Government agency programs for inventing, informing, and innovating may carry the new technology to the point that it can be adopted by a user without significant adaptation.

2. Competition exists between the Bureau and USDA in the field of additives to rubber. This kind of competition may occur among government agencies in many fields.

3. Either new additive will displace petroleum-derived carbon black. Products may be cheaper but it is questionable whether the American economy will gain in total numbers of jobs.

FOOTNOTES

[1] G. E. Johnson, W. A. Decker, A. J. Forney, and J. H. Field, "Carbon Black Produced from Coal," *Rubber World,* (June 1967), pp. 63-68.

[2] "Government Research: Experimental Rubber Reinforced with Cereal Starch Resin Is Described by USDA Chemist," *Daily Executive Report,* April 26, 1968 (Washington, D.C.: Bureau of National Affairs).

APPENDIX F-11

THE METRIC SYSTEM

Technology diffusion faces many of the same problems that have faced the use of the metric system in the United States. The only legal system is the metric system; nevertheless, the English system continues to be used.

Investigation and Invention[1]

1781. The Articles of Confederation gave Continental Congress power to fix standards of weights and measures, but Congress never acted.

1790. Washington called on the 1st Congress to adopt a uniform system of weights and measures as suggested in the Constitution, Article I, section 8. The Congress appointed a committee which called on Jefferson for advice.

1791. Jefferson submitted two plans to the Congress, one suggesting the common usage English inch-pound system, the other proposing the metric system. Congress rejected both.

1821. John Quincy Adams prepared a 250-page treatise in an unsuccessful effort to promote a uniform system of weights and measures.

1830. Hassler of the Treasury Department collected data on European standards and forwarded them to custom houses.

1836. Congress required the Treasury to forward the Hassler standards to each state; the states adopted them by various procedures.

1866. On July 28 Congress made the metric system the official basis for weights and measures. Each state was furnished conversions from the Hassler tables to the metric system.

1875. On May 20 the U. S. and sixteen other powers in the Treaty of the Meter established the International Bureau of Weights and Measures and provided for its administration.

1878. The U. S. ratified the treaty and received Meter No. 27 and Kilogram No. 20 in 1890.

1893. All U. S. standards were based on the international prototype meter and kilogram in the Office of Weights and Standards (now the National Bureau of Standards).

Informing and Innovating

1902 and 1906. Bills to make the metric system mandatory were narrowly defeated in Congress.

1921. The National Industrial Conference Board studied the problem and reported in Research Report No. 42, "The Metric versus the English System of Weights and Measures," October, 1921.

1938. Bills to make the metric system compulsory were introduced in both Houses of the 75th Congress, but were not passed.

1947. To achieve speed and simplicity, the Army adopted metric units in its design of mapping systems.

1957. The army adopted the meter as the measurement for weapons and related equipment. The U.S. pharmaceutical industries converted to the metric system. The Organization of American States proposed that the metric system be adopted in the Western Hemisphere.

1958. The English-speaking countries of the world agreed on standard conversions from the inch-pound to the metric system.

1958-63. Studies of metric conversion were conducted by the National Bureau of Standards, Bureau of Reclamation, American Geophysical Union, American Standards Association, USAF Research and Development Command, International Civil Aviation Organization, Stanford Research Institute, General Electric, and the British Board of Trade.

1955-65. France, Japan, and India began conversion to exclusive use of the metric system.

1959-65. Several bills and resolutions were proposed in Congress for the Department to **study** the problems of conversion.

1960. The International System of Units was adopted at the Eleventh General Conference on Weights and Measures.

1965. The UK announced it would adopt the metric system over a ten-year period.

1967. Australia, Canada, and South Africa studied converting to the metric system.

Integrating

Ninety percent of the world's population uses the metric system. Over 60 percent of the world's trade is in that system. U. S. science and parts of her engineering use it. Yet common technologies remain in the inch-pound system.

Comments

The English measurement system is part of American language and customs. Adults socialized in the English system in their youth will probably refer to it for rest of their lives. Science is internationalized and effectively using the metric system, but technology and engineering trades remain predominantly in the English system. No amount of legalizing has caused the hoped-for stampede to the metric system. Yet it would not be hard to change. Government, as predominant customer in many industries, could simply state its requirements in the metric system. The General Services Administration, Post Office, USDA, and DOD could shift to the metric system and get to most industries and consumers. All Federal publications could be in metric units. Even education could handle the shift in ten years, starting at the lowest grade where weights and measures are taught.

The metric system has advantages of simplicity, ease of calculation, and interrelationship between measure and weight. The disadvantages to the U. S. are the cost of conversion, confusion during the switch, and loss of something habitual or customary. There is no bar to Congressional authority, and the Constitutional Convention thought Congress would address the problem without delay. Nor is there great specific opposition. The main opponents in Congressional hearings have been those who have devised new systems. All others recognize, albeit reluctantly, that advantages of converting seem to outweigh disadvantages. Yet Congress had not by 1968 even authorized a study of the problem of conversion.

The reluctance to change weights and measures has been compared to changes in the calendar. There are still many calendars in use in the world. In some areas, there are calendars for trade with the rest of the world and calendars for use in the home, family, and religion. Time, length, and weight are basic ingredients of technology but they are very close to things that mankind does not want to change for any reason.

Conclusions

1. Conversion to the metric system would nullify a socially embodied reference system. It has been ignored at best and resisted at worst.

2. The reluctance to convert is reinforced by the expectation of immediate costs, unknown in amount, which would accompany the change.

3. No champions for conversion have developed. Changing to the metric system is a form of technical change that would require such a champion.

FOOTNOTES

[1] U.S. House, Committee on Science and Astronautics, *Notes on Conversion to the Metric System*, 89th Cong., 1st Sess. (Washington, D.C.: U.S. Government Printing Office, 1965), pp. 23-39; and U.S. Senate, *Increasing the Use of the Metric System*, Hearings before the Committee on Commerce on S. 441 and S. 2356, Nov. 15, 1967, 90th Cong., 1st Sess. (Washington, D.C.: U.S. Government Printing Office, 1967), *passim*. These two references were used in developing the chronology for this example.

APPENDIX F-12

TITANIUM METAL

Basic Research and Investigation

1789. Gregor discovered titanium, the fourth most abundant metal in the earth's crust and widely distributed. It has steel's strength with only 56 percent of its weight. Titanium also resists corrosion and maintains its strength at higher temperatures than other metals. It can be alloyed to produce widely varied materials. New uses and new alloys are still being developed.

Inventing Period

1910. M. A. Hunter isolated metallic titanium by reducing titanium tetrachloride with molten sodium. Titanium production, however, was considered economically impossible.

1928. William A. Kroll, owner of a private lab in Luxembourg, made metallic titanium while looking for a substitute for beryllium in copper-beryllium alloys.

Informing

1936. Kroll developed and patented a production process that involved dry, high temperature reduction under inert gases of titanium tetrachloride with molten magnesium. He found no commercial interest in titanium either in Europe or America.

1938. The Bureau of Mines became interested in titanium and in 1940, after Kroll fled from Luxembourg and published articles on the Kroll process, the Bureau of Mines began working to improve the process. Kroll was employed by the Bureau of Mines but worked on zirconium.

Innovating

1944-46. The Bureau of Mines perfected the Kroll process, making two tons of sponge metallic titanium in a pilot plant. A. S. Wartmen headed the development.

1948. Commercial production began at 20 tons per year.

Integrating

1950. Titanium Metals Corporation was formed by Allegheny Ludlum Steel Company and the National Lead Company, and commercial titanium production expanded. Commercial use began in jet aircraft applications because of the material's strength and light weight. In 1951, about 500 tons were produced.

1951. Imperial Chemicals Industries built a plant using the sodium reduction process which could produce 1,500 tons annually.

1952. The Office of Defense Mobilization fostered the titanium industry with construction loans, fast writeoffs, and purchase of output for strategic stockpiles.

1955. DOD established a titanium research lab and control facility for collection and dissemination of information on titanium characteristics, applications, and engineering. Uses then were primarily in jet propulsion components and in airframes. The information was made widely available.[1]

1957. The government stopped stockpiling titanium when DOD decided to base deterrent force on missiles instead of planes, causing some producers to withdraw from the field. Total production for 1957 was 17,500 tons, and 98 percent was used for defense.

1958. Sponge titanium fell from $5 per pound to $1.62 per pound and mill product prices fell from $15.25 to $7.59 per pound. At these prices titanium could compete with other metals.

1959. Titanium in nine years had achieved industrial production quantities that had taken lead, copper, and zinc 40 to 80 years, aluminum 28 years, and magnesium 26 years.

1962. Shipments of titanium exceeded previous peak volumes (in 1957), with the metal used in civilian and military aircraft, missiles, and some petro-chemical processing equipment.

1964. The newest military jet, the A-11, used many titanium parts. 7,500 tons of titanium were produced, with 93 percent used in the aerospace industry.

1965. The proposed design of a Mach 3 supersonic transport required extensive use of titanium to withstand high temperatures generated by air flows.

1966. Titanium uses diffused into production of valves, pumps, heat-transfer units, and lines. In electronics, because the metal absorbs gases and has a coefficient of expansion similar to ceramics, it has found several uses. It continues to be used in missiles, airframes, and nuclear reactors.

1968. The Tariff Commission held a hearing on June 4 on the allegation that the Soviet Union was selling titanium sponge in the U. S. below fair values.

Comments

Titanium can be compared with magnesium and aluminum in its diffusion. It reached .01 percent of GNP in 4 years, compared to 24 for magnesium and 10 for aluminum. It reached .02 percent of GNP in 6 years compared to 25 for magnesium and 14 for aluminum. In 1964, aluminum output was $1.21 billion versus $57 million for magnesium and $20.8 million for titanium. The U. S. has several producers of aluminum, four producers of magnesium, and three producers of titanium. All these metals respond to changes in military requirements.[1]

Conclusions

1.   Highly useful technology may be developed and made available by private enterprises in complex engineering fields, but these can lie unused.

2.   Information transfer about new technology may be accomplished by the patent system, movement of knowledgeable individuals, publication in the technical press, and personal salesmanship.   In the titanium example, personal salesmanship failed, but a combination of the other three succeeded.

3. The Bureau of Mines, the Office of Defense Mobilization, and the DOD each helped diffuse titanium use.   By 1957, the production industry was self-sustaining.   Government was active in applied research, making the information on the metal widely available through an information center, encouraging innovation, and inducing integration through use of the metal in military applications.   The defense aerospace industry continues to furnish a market and to standardize through specifications.

FOOTNOTES

[1] J. Wade Rice, "Recent Technical Developments—Titanium," *Technical Aids for Small Business* (Washington, D.C.: Small Business Administration, 1956), pp. 218-227.

[2] National Commission on Automation, Technology, and Economic Progress, *op. cit.*, pp. II 62-II 67.   Part of the chronology was also developed from this reference.

APPENDIX F-13

NUMERICAL CONTROL

The three types of manufacturing are mass production, continuous process, and job shop production. The last is historically the oldest, and still accounts for about 75 percent of production in the metal-working industries. It is found to a lesser extent in other industries, particularly those of high technology and specialized uses. Numerical control tools support production in these latter industries. During WW II, aircraft production became standardized. After the war, USAF studied its future aircraft requirements and concluded that it would not again need the number of planes then being mass produced. In searching for a way to produce the fewer, but more complex, planes that it would need, USAF concluded that the answer lay in highly flexible versatile production machines, especially machine tools, which could perform many tasks and could convert quickly from one task to another. If such tools could be developed, they would extend the economies of mass production to post-war aircraft.

Basic Research and Investigation

1725. A French inventor, Falcon, patented a knitting machine controlled by a perforated card.

1804. Another French inventor, Jacquard, patented a knitting and weaving machine controlled by a punched card.

1916. An American inventor, Scheyer, patented a continuous path machine for cutting cloth in the garment industry. It was controlled by perforations in a roll of paper similar to that used in a player piano.

Inventing and Informing

1930. A patent was issued to Max Schenker for a method of controlling the operation of machine tools by punched cards.

1946. John Parsons proposed to the USAF the development of a numerically controlled jig-boring machine to manufacture inspection templates for helicopter blades.

1948. USAF awarded a contract to Parsons Corporation to investigate the feasibility of numerically controlled milling machines.

1949. MIT was issued a contract by Parsons Corporation to develop a prototype of a numerically controlled milling machine. The scope of this development enlarged after USAF completed study of its future aircraft requirements.

1951. USAF awarded MIT the prime contract to continue developing a numerically controlled milling machine.

1952. MIT demonstrated the first protoype of the machine, a modified vertical milling machine.

1953. MIT supplied R&D on numerically controlled machine tools free to all interested companies.

Innovating

1954. USAF awarded a contract to Giddings and Lewis Company to develop a commercial numerical control system for machine tools.

1955. The first commercial numerically controlled machine tools were exhibited at the National Machine Tool Show. USAF first ordered numerically controlled machine tools.

1957. USAF placed the tools as government furnished equipment at various contractors' manufacturing plants around the country.

1960. Five percent of machine tools displayed at the National Machine Show were numerically controlled.

Integrating

1962. The development of cheap point-to-point numerical control positioning systems expanded application of numerical control.

1963. New solid-state electronic controls with modular circuit construction increased reliability of numerical control systems. 194 tools had been shipped to the motor vehicle and equipment industry. 68 were in the instruments industry. 335 had been shipped to the electrical machinery industry, half after mid-1962.

1964. Sales amounted to $206 million, 22 percent of the total metal-cutting machine tool sales. In addition, numerical control was diffusing into other uses such as flame cutting, hole piercing, steel cutting, producing engineering drawings, wiring panel boards for computers, and assembling electronic components.

1965. Most machine tool manufacturers exhibited numerically controlled tools at the National Machine Tool Show.

1967. Numerical control tools continued to diffuse as part of industrial automation.[1]

Comments

Numerically controlled machine tools have a specialized market, about $874 million in 1964. The spread of numerical control into other fields and its diffusion as a component of automation have been slow. Numerical control may be compared with computers, which have a wider market. Numerical control reached .02 percent of GNP in nine years while the computer took only six. Gross sales for the computer have already exceeded .2 percent of GNP, greater than the whole machine tool industry sales.[2] USAF's concern in 1948 for establishing its industrial base derived from experience during WW II mobilization. Similar concerns included dispersal of industry, stockpiling of strategic raw materials and critical tools, and civil defense.[3] Furnishing government equipment to dispersed locations (numerical control tools in contractors' factories) in 1957 was in accordance with national mobilization plans.

Conclusions

1. Numerical control technology diffused directly into industry through USAF market support of invention, information dissemination, innovation, and integration.

2. USAF supported this technology diffusion because it was part of mobilization plans for national survival.

3. No special arrangements or organizational mechanisms were necessary within DOD to support this diffusion. Congressional support for funding was a prerequisite.

FOOTNOTES

[1] "From Design to Finished Product," *Business Week*, December 30, 1967, pp. 88-90.

[2] National Commission on Automation, Technology, and Economic Progress, *op. cit.*, pp. II 86-II 91. Part of the chronology was developed from this reference.

[3] U.S. Congress, Senate, *Machine Tool Programs: Report of the Select Committee on Small Business on Machine Tools: Mobilization Planning, Reserve, and Replacement Programs*, 84th Cong., 2d Sess., Report No. 2229 (Washington, D.C.: U.S. Government Printing Office, 1956), pp. 30-32.

APPENDIX F-14

FOOD PRESERVATION: FREEZE-DRYING

DOD has long investigated cheap ways to handle food during war. The problem of preservation has been partly solved through canning, drying, and freezing. Nuclear radiation has been used in cold sterilization for preserving certain food forms. Food bulk causes shipping, storing, and handling problems which are not solved by freezing, canning, or cold sterilizing; however, bulk decreases with drying and a new process called freeze-drying. Water is restored during cooking, and no refrigeration is required for storage. All food processing changes the food's form, taste, or appearance. Cultural habits in eating determine acceptability of changed food forms. These habits change slowly, but they are influenced by economics and education.

Four related problems of DOD are to reduce bulk, stop bacterial action, kill insects, and stop or suspend enzymatic actions which change taste or form. Drying or dehydration is the only way to reduce bulk, and it also slows or suspends bacterial and enzymatic actions as well as reduces attacks of insects. Canning with heat process stops enzymatic actions but not organisms such as botulisms, nor does it reduce bulk. Freezing suspends most enzymatic, bacterial, and insect activity; but it requires special handling. Cold sterilization kills insects, stops sprouting, and kills botulisms and other bacteria; but it only retards enzymatic actions since it does not completely change the food form. Combinations of canning, dehydrating, freezing, and cold sterilizing can simplify handling of any given food; however, the food may not seem edible to consumers. During WW II and the Korean War, DOD sponsored research in all these processes. NASA has supported research on specialized food for eating during space travel.

Basic Research and Investigation

Before 1930. Conventional drying methods were the oldest form of food preservation.

1940's. Medical technologists developed freeze-drying to preserve blood.

Freeze-drying eased food transport in wartime because it eliminated water.

1955. A commercially promising method of freeze-drying foods was developed.

1958. Processes were developed to such an extent that the Army Quartermaster Corps could serve entire meals of freeze-dried, conventionally dried, and irradiated foods which had all the nutritional content of fresh food and a small proportion of its bulk. These were reconstituted using water and slightly changed cooking procedures.[1]

Informing and Innovation

1961. Freeze-dried foods were introduced to the commercial market.

1965. Several manufacturers introduced cereals that incorporated freeze-dried fruits in packages. The estimated value of freeze-dried outputs was $50 million. 2.3 million pounds of products, 40 percent of them meat, were produced by 1,250 people. Processing costs exceeded savings on transportation and handling.

1966. About 21 freeze-drying plants were operating in North America, with others under construction. The foods were specialty items such as mushrooms, food for campers, and products for military research and experimentation.[2]

Comments

Freeze-drying has been adopted rapidly but it has not reached integration into normal food processing. Freeze-drying is a parallel to frozen foods; while it took frozen foods 10 years to reach the $50 million volume of sales, it took freeze-dried foods only four years to reach this volume.[3]

Freeze-drying has encountered the problems of taste and preference. Instant coffee is preferred to freeze-dried coffee. Still others reject both forms of reconstituted coffee. Some even go to the expense of grinding their own beans to capture the flavor they like.

Food processing industries are diverse, with both small and large enterprises, both public and private research, and both local and national firms. The choice of food is so wide that only overriding advantages will cause rapid acceptance of a new product or process. There does not appear to be any overriding advantage in the U.S. for freeze-dried foods except for special applications such as camping. This process may have greater potential in other areas of the world which lack ample power and refrigeration facilities.

Conclusions

1. Under sponsorship of DOD, freeze-drying has been developed. Though this technology gives storage and health advantages, the public is accepting it quite slowly.

2. The Federal government is not overpowering in the food industries as it is in aerospace; hence, its influence and needs make less impact.

3. Technical information on freeze-drying has been readily available through government contract channels as well as in technical literature.

4. Technologies which tend to change taste and cultural preferences are diffused slower than those which improve the status quo.

FOOTNOTES

[1] The author was served an entire meal of these food forms while a student at the Command and General Staff College, Fort Leavenworth, Kansas, in 1958.

[2] National Commission on Technology, Automation, and Economic Progress, *op. cit.*, pp. II 73-II 76. Part of the chronology for this example is from this reference.

[3] Kermit Bird, *The Awakening Freeze-Drying Industry*, USDA Economic Research Service, January, 1965.

APPENDIX F-15

FOOD PRESERVATION: IRRADIATION

Basic Research and Investigation

1930. Otto Wüst of France took out the first patent on irradiated foods.

1946. Radioisotopes became available from the Oak Ridge National Laboratory.

1947. Serious research began in the government on food irradiation.

Inventing and Informing

1958. The Army Quartermaster Corps could serve irradiated food but the law did not allow its sale.

1960. Canada's Directorate of Food ruled that potatoes irradiated to prevent sprouting were safe to eat.

1961. Techniques for irradiation without adverse effects were not reliable; yet irradiation definitely killed parasites and insects, stopped sprouting, and postponed spoilage.[1]

1963. On February 8, the Food and Drug Administration (FDA) ruled that bacon preserved by irradiation was fit for consumption.

1964. In August the FDA ruled that nine irradiated packaging materials were safe to use with irradiated food.

1966. The Army began using irradiated bacon in its regular rations. The AEC program was concentrated on preserving fish and other seafood.[2]

1968. Fifteen commercial facilities were prepared to irradiate food. Others were prepared to furnish supporting engineering and materials.[3]

FDA investigators turned up evidence of adverse effects of irradiated food on laboratory animals.[4] FDA withdrew its previous approval of irradiated bacon and other products.

Comments

The food irradiation program reached a stalemate in 1968 until the FDA received more test results. AEC, DOD, and private industry regrouped and re-evaluated their activities; in effect, they continued to invent and investigate. During 1968 FDA was accused of over-cautiousness and its director resigned. The doubt raised, however, by the FDA must be resolved before irradiated food can be generally adopted. This whole technology was evaluated for adoption and temporarily rejected.

FOOTNOTES

[1] U.S. Department of Agriculture, *The First 100 Years, op. cit., passim.*

[2] U.S. Congress, Joint Committee on Atomic Energy, *Review of the Food Irradiation Program,* Hearing before the Subcommittee on Research, Development, and Radiation, September 12, 1966, 89th Cong., 2d sess. (Washington, D.C.: U.S. Government Printing Office, 1966), *passim.*

[3] "The Commercial Prospects for Selected Irradiated Foods," U.S. Department of Commerce, Business and Defense Services Administration, March, 1968.

[4] "Irradiated Foods Go Sour," *Business Week,* May 25, 1968, p. 160.

APPENDIX F-16

SYNTHETIC RUBBER

The rubber industry can use the products of the commercial rubber tree, guayule rubber, synthetic natural rubber (since 1965), or synthetic rubber, the type which became of great significance during and after WW II.

Basic Research and Investigation

1826. Faraday first chemically analyzed natural rubber.

1860. Williams isolated isoprene as rubber's basic component.

1887. Wallach produced crude synthetic rubber in the laboratory.

1908. A British firm, Strang and Graham, Ltd., started research to develop a commercial process for producing natural rubber.

Inventing and Informing

1910. A process for producing synthetic rubber was patented in England and Germany.

1911. Two American firms started research to develop a commercial synthetic rubber.

1915. The British blockade forced Germany to develop and manufacture a synthetic rubber; which was, however, unsatisfactory as a replacement for natural rubber.

1922. Patrick developed a specialized form of synthetic rubber called Thiokol.

1926. The German government instituted a program of synthetic rubber development so as to be independent of natural rubber supplies.

1928. The emulsion process for producing synthetic rubber from butadiene was perfected.

1932. Du Pont announced development of a new special-purpose synthetic rubber called Neoprene.

1933. The first truly commercial synthetic rubbers (Buna S and Buna N) were developed and patented in Germany.

Innovating

1934. Pilot plant production of synthetic rubber began in Germany and Russia. The automobile industry created a market that caused a rapid rise in natural rubber prices.

1939. Standard Oil obtained rights to the German patents, started pilot plant production of synthetic rubber in America, and announced construction of a full scale production plant. During the year, 1,739 tons of two special purpose synthetic rubbers were produced in the U. S.

1940. Standard Oil of New Jersey announced development of a butyl synthetic rubber. The government created the Rubber Reserve Company to manufacture synthetic rubber and coordinate its use for military and commercial purposes.

1941-44. The government invested $40 million for synthetic rubber process and product development and $700 million for plants and facilities. Four plants were constructed.

Integrating

1942. 22,000 tons of synthetic rubber were produced worth $156 million.

1944. 764,000 tons of synthetic rubber were produced worth $354 million.

1945. 950,000 tons of synthetic rubber were produced.

1946. The Interagency Committee on Rubber issued a report outlining a national policy concerning the government's ownership of synthetic rubber plants.

1948. The Rubber Act of 1948 extended the government's ownership of the plants and facilities.

1949. 470,000 tons of synthetic rubber were produced, which reflected the conversion from a wartime to a peacetime economy and renewed availability of natural rubber.

1955. Government-owned plants were sold to private industry. 900,000 tons of synthetic rubber had been produced that year. The development of "true" synthetic natural rubbers (polyisoprene and polybutadiene) was announced.

1964. Synthetic rubber production accounted for 60 percent of total consumption in the U. S. with a tonnage of 1,310,000. Synthetic rubber was 75 percent of new rubber, up from 51 percent in 1954.

1965. Production of new synthetic natural rubbers began. These do not require addition of natural rubber.

1967. Synthetic rubber and synthetic natural rubber accounted for over 75 percent of U. S. consumption.

Comments

Synthetic rubber was a defense-related, WW II development of large scope; however, synthetic rubber was known and commercially feasible years before wartime shortages of natural rubber forced its development. Information was available in patent disclosures and production processes were known. Government assumed all risk of innovation in 1941, furnished all the market for the first five years, and continued to support the market through government purchases until 1955 when the plants were sold.

Synthetic rubber development was compared by the National Commission on Automation, Technology, and Economic Progress to the development of plastics (synthetic resins), synthetic fibers, and synthetic leather, all done in the private sector. Synthetic leather research began at Du Pont in 1938, but output has not yet reached significant proportions in terms of GNP. Synthetic resins were slow in development and acceptance; however, both synthetic fibers and synthetic rubber reached .02 percent of GNP in one year, both affected by shortages of natural materials. Synthetic rubber reached .25 percent of GNP in less than four years, synthetic fibers in twenty-four years, and synthetic resins in forty-two years; however, synthetic rubber lost this ratio after WW II and has not yet regained it.

Differences in products also affect diffusion rates. Plastics diffused very slowly into industrial applications, and did not make rapid gains until they were adapted to commercial application. Synthetic fibers went directly into consumer application and steadily diffused into many fields. Synthetic rubber competes with both natural rubber and other materials. It gained most rapidly during WW II and the Korean War when other materials were scarce. The current market for all rubber is less than that of either plastics or synthetic fibers.[1]

Conclusions

1. The government can create effective organizations for innovating and integrating new technology into the economy. For synthetic rubber, the government created a defense-related agency to do mop-up development, production, and marketing. The time of innovation and integration was extremely short compared to almost any other new technology.

2. The diffusion depended more on market support than on R&D support. All the information to do the work was readily accessible in patent disclosures and in the knowledge of production processes. Only a little development ($40 million) was required compared to production support ($700 million). The effort could not have succeeded without the demand and ready market from the government.

3. Once public ownership of production for an item of technology is gained, it is difficult to transfer it back to the private sector. In this case it took ten years.

FOOTNOTES

[1] National Commission on Technology, Automation, and Economic Progress, *op. cit.,* pp. II 53–II 61.

APPENDIX F-17

INTEGRATED CIRCUITS

A great electronic advance of the 1960's has been microminiaturized circuits. These are tiny, more reliable than other circuits, faster and increasingly cost competitive. Using photoetching and photographic methods of production, these circuits can now be mass produced with semi-skilled labor. (Some firms ship materials to Hong Kong where they are assembled and shipped back.) Automation also applies to some production processes. Integrated circuits are revolutionizing electronics by changing design, construction, and assembly of products.[1]

Basic Research and Investigation

1916. Langmuir proposed the first theory of thin-film phenomena.

1948. Bell Telephone developed the transistor.

1956. Varo Corporation began research on integrated circuits.

1957. Brunetti of General Mills and Stone of Bell Telephone Laboratories presented papers on basic concepts of integrated circuits. IBM initiated research for the Army Signal Corps on thin-film circuit concepts.

Inventing and Informing

1958. The Army's Harry Diamond Laboratories developed simple integrated circuit devices and fabrication techniques for thin-film circuits. Varo Corporation was contracted by the Office of Naval Research to accelerate investigation of integrated circuits.

1959. Texas Instruments announced an integrated circuit device for computers.

USAF Air Research and Development Command awarded a major contract to Westinghouse to develop integrated circuit devices.

Lincoln Laboratories developed the first thin-film computer memory.

1960. Westinghouse revealed the results of its USAF contract on integrated circuit development.

Innovating

1960. USAF awarded Texas Instruments a contract to build a computer employing integrated circuits for military use.

1961. Fairchild Camera and Instrument Corp. introduced the first integrated circuit device for commercial applications.

Texas Instruments produced the first integrated circuit computer for the USAF.

Integrating

1962. The Bureau of Naval Weapons initiated a program to increase the use of integrated circuits in its equipment. The price of the circuits was about $150 per unit.

1963. Westinghouse announced completion of a $5 million facility for producing integrating circuits. RCA announced a major new technique for producing them. In June the price had dropped to $90 per unit. Total sales for the year were $18 million.

1964. Total sales for the year were $40 million. End-of-year prices were $14 per unit. Ninety-two percent of sales were to the government.

1965. Fairchild developed new manufacturing techniques which enabled it to sell commercial units at $1 each. Sixty percent of national sales were for military and space applications.

1966. Production rates were 20 million units per year. Twenty firms are producing significant quantities, but the top four are Texas Instruments, Fairchild, Motorola, and Westinghouse.

1968. Special purpose computers designed with integrated circuits were displayed at one-fifth former costs at the Spring Joint Computer Conference at Atlantic City.[2] New calculators also dropped in price as integrated circuits replaced mechanical parts.[3]

Comments

Integrated circuits are third-generation electronic developments, following vacuum tubes and separate parts and then semiconductors. The vacuum tube industry was developed privately, without great Federal contribution. Semiconductors were developed in the private sector but innovation and integration were supported by the government. Integrated circuits were developed under government sponsorship for aerospace application. Innovation and integration were supported by NASA and DOD.

Technical information was available to government contractors working on integrated circuits; whereas, some patent restrictions limited access to vacuum tube electronics. These same restrictions were also applied by Bell Telephone Laboratories to semiconductors until government antitrust action against BTL in 1956.

The most interesting feature of integrated circuits is the short time between the first circuit in 1958 and the first product using them in 1961. The increase as a percent of the GNP has been faster than for vacuum tubes but about the same as for semi-conductors. The drastic price drops in integrated circuits have increased their use, but the GNP ratio has been smaller.[4]

Conclusions

1. The integrated circuit technology was diffused into the economy

through DOD and NASA support of invention, information dissemination, innovation, and integration.

2. The military and space agencies supported the diffusion of this technology because of its promise in increasing reliability and performance for critical weapons and space systems.

3. No special arrangements have been necessary within DOD or NASA to support this diffusion.

4. Information was made available to contractors through the agency information handling systems. Much information was transferred through conferences, specifications, and company exchanges of knowledgeable people.

FOOTNOTES

[1] "Burning Up the Circuits," *Barron's,* August 9, 1965, pp. 3, 13-17.

[2] "Tiny Computers Lead a Price Decline," *Business Week,* May 11, 1968, pp. 108-114.

[3] "The Calculator Goes Electronic," *Business Week,* May 18, 1968, pp. 149-52.

[4] National Commission on Technology, Automation, and Economic Progress, *op. cit.,* pp. II 46-II 52. The chronology was partly derived from this reference.

APPENDIX F-18

HIGHWAY GROOVING

Skidding and spinout are the most frequent causes of single vehicle accidents and contribute from a third to half of multiple vehicle accidents. It is frequently identified as a factor in chain reaction or pile-up accidents. The components of skidding include the type of tire, tire pressure, tire tread, pavement surface, tendency of pavement surface materials to wear smooth, the weather or amount of water on the surface, the engineering of the roadway, the way pressure is applied to brakes or wheels, and the speed of the vehicle.

One of the ways an automobile skids is through hydroplaning, first identified by the English and later explained through tests by NASA. Water builds up in front of the tire until the tire does not contact the pavement. This is called dynamic hydroplaning and is the usual form on highways. Other forms of hydroplaning occur on airport runways during plane landing and takeoff. The road problem can be alleviated in a number of ways including resurfacing, reengineering the road, improving the tires, balancing the braking system, or simply decreasing speed.

One way to change the surface of concrete roadways is to place $\frac{1}{8}$ by $\frac{1}{8}$ inch grooves every $\frac{5}{8}$ inches in the direction of the highway lane. This method is generally applicable to the national highway system surfaces and may be used selectively at places of low surface friction or high accident rates. Equipment for measuring surface friction has been somewhat standardized in the past years and is available in most states.

Basic Research and Investigation

1945. Virginia studied pavement slipperiness and has since developed skid-resistant surface mixes. Other states became interested.

1946. Concut, Inc., was organized to manufacture concrete-cutting equipment.

1953-58. Skidding occurred in about 40 percent of accidents in the Virginia rural highway system. In 1958, the Indiana rates were almost half again that high. In England the incidence of skidding increased each year between 1951 and 1958.

1958. The First International Conference on Skid Prevention met at the University of Virginia. This began concerted effort to prevent skidding.

Concut developed a diamond headed cutter for removing bumps on airport runways.

Inventing and Informing

1960. In June the California Division of Highways began its first grooving experiment.

1960's. NASA conducted hydroplaning studies at Langley Research Center.

1961. Concut adapted one of its bump cutters to cut grooves for the California highway system antiskid experiments.[1]   In October, Route 99 in Kern County, California, was grooved for 28 miles in the northbound lane.   In 14 months previous to grooving, there were eight skidding accidents.   For 4½ years after the grooving, there were no skidding accidents.

1963. Kinsey reported the work in California on grooving in "Skidproofing Deck Roughening Carried Out at Night to Minimize Delays," **California Highways and Public Works,** Vol. 42, Nos. 1-2, 1963.

In November NASA published results of its test on pneumatic tire hydroplaning and some of the relationships among tire type and tread, surface irregularities, tire pressure, fluid depth, and speed.

1964. NASA developed a film of the hydoplaning studies and showed it to automobile tire manufacturers, car manufacturers, government agencies concerned with traffic safety, and a group of traffic engineers of the California Department of Highway Safety.

Innovating

1962. From July to September, St. Mary's Underpass, San Antonio, Texas, was grooved, and no accidents occurred in the next rainy period. Nearby underpasses did have accidents.

1963. In January a half-mile stretch was grooved on the Golden State Expressway.   Accident rates were reduced 80 percent.

In April a half-mile stretch was grooved on Highway 99 in Fresno County, California.   In three years before grooving, there were five skidding accidents.   In three years after grooving, there were two.

1964. On March 23, the President urged the Secretary of Commerce to give special attention to highways with high accident rates.

Csathy reviewed world literature on skidding and skid resistance for the Province of Ontario, Canada, and listed 432 publications on various aspects of the problems.   Grooving was mentioned as a California method of roughing concrete decks of bridges.

1965. In January, Horne and Joyner presented their hydroplaning research to the Society of Automotive Engineers and stated that tire tread design and pavement surface treatment would alleviate hydroplaning when the pavement was wet or slightly flooded but the best designs of neither would prevent hydroplaning when the pavements were deeply flooded.

In August the Federal Highway Administrator urged regional and division engineers to encourage states to give a substantial proportion of ABC funds to Federal-aid projects at hazardous points and sections.

In November a paper presented at the AIAA Aircraft Design and Technology meeting, "Recent Research on Ways to Improve Tire Traction on Water, Slush, and Ice," proposed grooving as a means of alleviating loss of tire traction on runways.

1966. The Committee on Public Works of the Senate recommended to the Bureau of Public Roads the use of longitudinal grooving to prevent skidding and hydroplaning, based on the California experience. The Committee encouraged other states to explore this method of surface treatment.

1967. Early in the year the Highway Planning and Research Program of the Federal Highway Administration was being conducted on slippery pavements in 23 states. Australia, England, Canada, Italy, and Germany were also studying the problem. However, only one U. S. state required a minimum coefficient of friction for new pavement. On June 27, Highway Safety Program Standards issued by the National Highway Safety Bureau, Federal Highway Administration, called for each state to develop a program for correcting sections of roads with surfaces showing high or potentially high accident rates or having low skid resistance.

1968. On April 29, Federal aid was authorized for states to apply to skidproofing spot improvement safety projects for highways with Federal fund participation. Two types of improvements were authorized: (1) adding a layer of thin bituminous material less than 1½ inches thick to any surface; and (2) grooving in the surfaces of concrete. Corrections were to be not less than 500 feet long. Records of the corrected section before and after grooving were required for continued study and evaluation. In May, one state, California, had adopted grooving. Six states had demonstration projects prepared by Concut. Two commercial and three military runways had been grooved. Virginia planned to groove several high accident locations during the year. 48 lane miles had been grooved in California at 54 locations and more work was planned. All California grooving was still considered to be effective.[2]

Comments

Technology diffusion for highway grooving is still in the innovation stage. The State of California accepted the technology before the Bureau of Public Roads. NASA has made information available through public releases, film, various reports, and testimony to Congressional committees. The Bureau of Public Roads did not specifically sponsor grooving until 1968 and then only as an alternative to resurfacing. NASA has claimed the grooving of highways as a successful transfer of technology in its publications and testimony to Congress. The California Division of Highways had apparently begun using grooving two or three years before NASA's publicity. The Highway engineers who saw the NASA film were interested in the explanation of hydroplaning and skidding, not the grooving.[3]

Grooving is only one of several ways to reduce hydroplaning, and the other ways also have advocates. These advocates sell non-skid surfacing materials in each state and frequently have influence there. The grooving machines are sold or licensed under patent from a single manufacturer, so far as can be determined. It may be significant that the grooving was adopted in the state where the grooving machine manufacturer was located.

This particular example was drawn from aeronautics research in NASA and would have been a logical development had there been no space activity. However, even though directly applicable to runways and highways, it has had a relatively cool reception. Though publicized by NASA as a technology transfer item, the record makes this quite doubtful.

Conclusions

1. Widespread publicity does not assure that a new and logical technology will be readily adopted, particularly if the developing and publicizing agency is not a normal supplier.

2. If the new item of technology has not been thoroughly tested, including life and side-effect tests, publishing and encouraging it will be considered premature by professionals.

3. Adoption and integration of a new technology by a Federal agency may be very slow if the technology was not developed in that agency.

4. A Federal agency may be slower to adopt those inventions which change relationships among its customers and suppliers.

5. Verbal encouragement by Federal agencies to use new technology has less effect than the tying of Federal funds to acceptable minimum standards.

6. State agencies are more innovative than Federal agencies and are more apt to investigate solutions using within-state materials and resources.

FOOTNOTES

[1] Personal communication with Mr. Glen E. Simms, President, Concut, Inc., El Monte, California, May 3, 1968. All the information on Concut was from this source.

[2] G. L. Russell, "Evaluation of Minor Improvements—Pavement Serration," Mimeographed Report, State of California Division of Highways, November, 1967.

[3] Personal Communication with Mr. A. C. Estep, Engineer of Design, California Division of Highways, May 17, 1968.

APPENDIX F-19

ERIC USE OF MICROFICHE

The michrofiche, developed in France, is a 4" x 6" film card which can carry images of sixty pages of print. When expanded on a viewer, print shows up larger than on the printed page. Viewers cost about $150. Each fiche costs from ten to twenty-five cents. The title tab for the fiche is a white surface which describes in normal print its contents. Machines have been developed to record microimages on fiche and reproduce 100,000 fiche in one day. Faced with its rapid buildup of R&D information after 1959, NASA pioneered use of microfiche as a rapid and economical method of making results of R&D available to workers in the field. An ordinary technical report can be placed on a few microfiche and air-mailed to users anywhere in the country.

In 1956 the Office of Education of D/HEW (OE) sponsored two million dollars of research. That year the Cooperative Research Act was passed and research efforts began to increase, reaching one hundred million dollars by FY 1968. New methods had to be used to disseminate the research to people who could use it. In 1964, the Committee on Scientific and Technical Information (COSATI) standardized the size, shape, and number of pages to be imaged on microfiche and agreed that microfiche would be used for distributing technical reports for Federal Aerospace-defense agencies. The COSATI action encouraged OE to use the microfiche approach.

The Educational Resources Information Center (ERIC) was created in May 1964 to "facilitate and coordinate information storage and retrieval efforts in all areas of educational research." ERIC's first big job was supporting the Elementary and Secondary Education Act of 1965, providing program descriptions and resumes of research on education of the disadvantaged, migrants, and poverty-stricken. Customers required over 200 million printed pages. ERIC adopted microfiche to transfer information to offices which could use it. In the first mailing of August, 1965, 330,000 individual microfiche were dispatched, replacing nearly twenty million printed pages.[1]

As the eighteen ERIC Clearinghouses were established from 1965 to 1968, each was provided with a package of all past OE and related research results; the package fitted into one small filing cabinet with space for several years of additions. The cost of the fiche, cabinet, and viewer was less than $1,000. The same research package has also been provided to OE Regional Educational Laboratories, state teachers' colleges, state boards of education, and other interested institutions and individuals.[2] In 1967, ERIC distributed 630,000 microfiche internally, and its contractor sold 560,000 copies. NASA used 8,000,000 copies, AEC 3,000,000, DDC 800,000, and CFSTI 1,500,000.[3] Only these five agencies had adopted microfiche for general use.

In 1968 National Cash Register Company of Dayton, Ohio, won the contract to handle microfiche operations for OE. National Cash expanded this government base into commercial applications for the technique by contracting with Merrill, Lynch, Pierce, Fenner, & Smith to put that securities firm's research files on microfiche for quick access by analysts and traders.[4] If this proves successful, competition may force other stock brokers into microfiche or other quick access microforms.

Conclusions

1. Microfiche technologies were successfully adopted and adapted by NASA and then imitated by OE in its ERIC. The transfer was expedited by Federal standardization, by NASA publication of its methods, and by availability to ERIC organizers of firms supporting NASA.

2. Economics of the microfiche technologies, when compared to alternative microforms, stimulated adoption. Most adoption units could afford a $150 reader, but few could afford the expensive equipment designed for other microforms. Fewer still could afford all the original documents.

3. Integration of microfiche technologies has been encouraged by their adoption by five large Federal agencies and by the increasing costs of full copy and library space to accommodate full copy. Use of microfiche in commercial operations has begun.

FOOTNOTES

[1] Lee G. Burchinal and Harold A. Haswell, "How to Put Two and a Half Tons of Research Into One Handy Little Box," Reprint from *American Education* (Washington, D.C.: U.S. Government Printing Office, 1966), pp. 1-3.

[2] Interview with Mr. Adam Woyna, ERIC Director, Center for Applied Linguistics, Washington, D.C., February 7, 1968.

[3] U.S. Department of Commerce, Business and Defense Services Administration, *Microforms: A Growth Industry* (Washington, D.C.: U.S. Government Printing Office, 1969), p. 18.

[4] "New Products . . . ," *Business Week, op. cit.*, pp. 150-154.

APPENDIX F-20

NUCLEAR POWER GENERATION

Man's quest for sources of cheap, reliable power has caused him to use natural forces of ocean tides, wind, sun, falling water, steam, and, more recently, nuclear power. First generation, watercooled, thermal, non-breeder, and heterogeneous reactors, similar to the naval vessel reactors, were used in 1969. Second generation breeder reactors were in a late stage of development in 1969.

Basic Research and Investigation

1896. Becquerel observed radiation from uranium.

1898. The Curies further investigated radioactive elements.

1932. The "cascade" gaseous diffusion principle for separation of isotopes was discovered.

1936. Bohr formulated the theory of neutron capture and nuclear disintegration.

1938. Atomic disintegration of uranium (fission) was discovered by Hahn and Strassman.

Inventing and Informing

1942. The first practical demonstration of controlled nuclear chain reaction took place at the University of Chicago.

1943. The Manhattan Project was well underway. The Oak Ridge reactor for producing plutonium was placed in operation. Reactors at Hanford for producing uranium were put into production. A gaseous diffusion plant to separate U235 from U238 was constructed.

1945. The first nuclear weapon was exploded.

1946. The Atomic Energy Act of 1946 (the civilian control bill) was passed. This established government monopoly with no private patents.

1948-56. Experimental nuclear reactors for naval application were developed and tested.

1950. AEC terminated breeder reactor work because of technical problems but resumed it later.

1951. On January 28 the industry participation program to encourage development of power reactors was established.

1951-53. AEC began constructing its first series of experimental reactors.

Innovating

1954. AEC and Duquesne Light Company of Pittsburgh announced building of the Shippingport, Pennsylvania, 60,000 kilowatt unit. Congress passed the Atomic Energy Act of 1954, which strongly encouraged the development of nuclear power generation. A joint government-industry five-year Reactor Development Program was established.

1955. Commonwealth Edison, Consolidated Edison, and Yankee Electric announced plans to build nuclear power generation plants.

1957. The Shippingport plant began to produce electricity at a cost of 60 mills per kilowatt hour.

1960. Electricity was first generated by the 210,000 kilowatt Dresden nuclear generating plant of Commonwealth Edison. The 185,000 kilowatt Yankee plant was placed in operation.

1962. The 275,000 kilowatt Indian Point nuclear power plant owned by Consolidated Edison opened.

1963. A 495,000 kilowatt plant was announced by Connecticut-Yankee for completion in 1967.

1964. The Private Ownership Act was passed to permit individuals (or corporations) to own special nuclear materials.

Integrating

1965. Six percent of the power generated was from nuclear plants. An 800,000 kilowatt Dresden II plant to be completed in 1969 was announced. A second plant for 1 million kilowatts to be in operation by 1969 was announced by Consolidated Edison.[1]

1966. Eleven plants were operating with total power capacity of 1,250,000 kilowatts.

1967. Half of all new power plants booked for construction were nuclear. The Oyster Creek Plant of Jersey Central Power and Light Company began generating electricity at about 4 mills per kilowatt hour.

1968. The Atomics International Division of North American Rockwell Corporation, General Public Utilities Corporation, Baltimore Gas and Electric Company, Duke Power Company, and South Carolina Electric and Gas Company joined forces to develop at Canoga Park, California, a fast breeder reactor suitable for installation by 1970.[2]

1968. Fuel reprocessing plants were opened by private industry and the AEC began withdrawing from this business.

Comments

In areas where hydroelectric and steam-produced power are expensive, even first-generation nuclear power plants have become competitive. Moreover, the government support of industry developments has helped produce many improvements. During the same period, the problems of coal have become more acute. Mining spoils land and pollutes streams. Burning coal for steam produces smog over industrialized areas. The lowest cost for conventional power is 3 or 4 mills, whereas large nuclear plants may be able to produce at 2 mills per kilowatt-hour.

James W. Kuhn studied the transition to nuclear power from the viewpoint of scientists and technologists who took part in it and concluded that Federal government played a strategic role in developing the new technologies, supporting research, making grants and furnishing government equipment, and in supporting the training of specialists from the participating companies. He concluded that companies were more reluctant to invest in employee training than in capital equipment.[3]

Conclusions

1. Generation of power from nuclear sources was an example of straightforward, mission-oriented, government development. The decision to develop was taken as a matter of national prestige.

2. Most patents and information in development and application were owned by the AEC. This information was made available to participating industry through the AEC Informing Program. Information was adequate for application.

3. Decisions to adopt nuclear power plants have not been generally based on economic criteria, but on social and prestige considerations. Plants now under construction may be economically competitive with coal.

4. Integration of nuclear power has considered the advantages of the new technology more than the disadvantages for coal producers, or its own disadvantages.

FOOTNOTES

[1] National Commission for Technology, Automation, and Economic Progress, *op. cit.*, pp. II 86–II 91. Most of the chronology was taken from this reference.

[2] "More Fuel for New-Reactor Race," *Business Week*, January 13, 1968, pp. 46–50.

[3] James W. Kuhn, *op. cit., passim.*

APPENDIX F-21

RADIOISOTOPES

In 1946 uses of radioisotopes in industry and science could be visualized, but mechanisms for such use had not been perfected. Nor did extensive use of isotopes develop rapidly. It was a slow, gradual process as procedures were developed, safety regulations perfected, and use of the materials integrated into educational programs.

Basic Research and Investigation

1907. Isotopes were identified; that is, samples of material with the same chemical composition had differing radioactivity.

1934. Scientists learned how to induce radioactivity in normally stable elements with cyclotrons.

1940's. Scientists with nuclear reactors were able to produce large quantities of radioactive materials.

1967. The gas centrifuge was proposed as a cheaper method of isolating isotopes.

Inventing

1934-46. Radioisotopes were manufactured on a limited scale and used in many research problems.

1946. AEC began developing Oak Ridge National Laboratory as the supplier of radioisotopes. Other laboratories began supplying radioisotopes later.

1958. In December AEC established an Office of Isotopes Development with a $5 million budget to supplement private efforts in development and application.

1934-68. Techniques for using radioisotopes have been developed in agriculture (plant, insect, biosynthesis, farm animal, and soil condition studies); medical diagnosis and therapy; physical and chemical research; life science research; and industry (process and quality control, correction of field problems, and research and development).

Informing (Information Transfer and Dissemination)

1945. The Army Corps of Engineers announced the availability of radioisotopes in the June 14, 1946, issue of **Science.**

1951. The Industrial Participation Program of AEC was established.

1956. SBA encouraged use of radioisotopes in quality control and non-destructive testing.

1963. SBA listed 75 typical uses of radioisotopes in R&D, and encouraged small businesses to use them in process control, plant, and field problems.[1]

Innovating (Application and Adoption)

1949. A. D. Little studied isotope application and found in the fourth semi-annual AEC report that only three percent of radioactive materials were being used by industry.[2]

1956. Zuckert, former AEC commissioner, estimated that process control using radioisotopes saved American industry $100 million yearly. In radiography, cobalt 60, cesium 137, and irradium were most used. Thickness gauging, position indication, and tracing were other uses. In agricultural uses (pest eradication, fertilizer studies, genetics, food handling, etc.), radioisotopes were estimated to save $210 million yearly.[3]

1957-58. During a 12-month period, 595 companies calculated $39 million savings from industrial use of isotopes.

1968. In April AEC began selling plutonium 238 at $1000 per gram. Neptunium 237 was reduced to $225 a gram and americum 231 went to $1000 per gram in January 1969.

Integrating

1946-58. Total sales of radioisotopes from Oak Ridge were $16,387,-361. In calendar year 1959, sales were $2,003,753. Oak Ridge sales stabilized as private firms began significant sales in 1959.[4]

1952-64. The increase of industrial users of radioisotopes was about 170 per year.

1962. Oak Ridge and private firm sales were about equal, to give a total domestic supply worth $3.5 million.

1964. American industry had invested $100 million in isotopes gauging systems. Ninety-five percent of automobile tires and 80 percent of cigarettes produced are controlled by radioisotope gauges. These two applications have reached full integration. Two hundred twenty of 1500 paper machines are equipped with radioactive gauges and two-thirds of the 220 are coupled with automatic control.[5]

1966. The number of industrial users exceeded all other users (one-third of 8000), followed by medical institutions and physicians, then Federal and state labs, then colleges and universities, then all others.

1967. During the fiscal year, AEC shipments were valued at $4,117,168.

1968. In March, AEC withdrew from production and distribution of cobalt 60 sources of 45 curies per gram specific activity or less. General Electric and Neutron Products, Inc., with an estimated capacity of 3 million curies annually, supplied the U. S. market. Atomic Energy Canada, Ltd., also marketed cobalt 60 in the U. S.

In May, AEC began consideration of relaxing restrictions on smaller users of radioisotopes so that they could be more flexible in their application.

The National Bureau of Standards formed a Center for Radiation

Research to conduct programs concerned with uses of radiation and nuclear science.

Comments

Dollar value of sales of isotopes and the number of users have risen at a steady rate as each new application was adopted and integrated as standard practice. Costs of licensing, regulation, and safety precautions have prevented many small businesses from using radioisotopes. One company reported its 1965 licensing and recordkeeping costs at $50,000. AEC patent policy also forces companies to give up their commercial rights to AEC, and some believe this slows down development of new isotope technology.[6]

Diffusion of radioisotopes has been carefully controlled and the safety record is excellent. This may be contrasted with use of pesticides by private and public agencies.

Conclusions

1. Radioisotopes have diffused into hundreds of uses, each requiring some adaptation and special information. Technical information and assistance have been available in AEC and professional channels.

2. Innovation and integration do not show the S-shaped adopter curve found in other diffusion, partly because of the large numbers of types of application. Within specific applications (e.g., automobile tire or cigarette gauging), the adopter curve may be found. The arithmetic rise in numbers of users reflects new applications more than new adoptions.

3. Government requirements for control and licensing restrain unlimited adoption.

4. AEC policy for patents may prevent some commercial research on new isotopes technology.

FOOTNOTES

[1] Small Business Administration, "Small Business Applications of Radioisotopes" (Washington, D.C.: SBA, September–October, 1963), p. 2.

[2] *A Selected Bibliography on the Industrial Use of Radioactive Materials* (Cambridge, Mass: Arthur D. Little, Inc., 1949).

[3] *Peaceful Uses of Atomic Energy*, Report of the Panel on the Impact of the Peaceful Uses of Atomic Energy to the Joint Committee on Atomic Energy (Washington, D.C.: U.S. Government Printing Office, 1956), vols. I and II.

[4] *Radioisotopes in Science and Industry: A Special Report of the United States Atomic Energy Commission* (Washington, D.C.: Atomic Energy Commission, 1960), *passim*.

[5] E. E. Fowler, "Radioisotopes and Radiation Utilization by United States Industry—Growth and Trends," a paper presented at the Opening Session of the Sixth Japan Conference on Radioisotopes, Tokyo, Japan, November 16–19, 1964 (Washington, D.C.: AEC, 1964), p. 10. Part of the chronology was also taken from this source.

[6] "Industry's Evaluation of Isotopes and Radiation," Mimeographed Report to the AEC by the Chairman, Advisory Committee on Isotopes and Radiation Development, April 19, 1965.

APPENDIX F-22

NUCLEAR-POWERED MERCHANT SHIPS

Successes of nuclear-powered submarines and other naval craft encouraged application of this technology to merchant ships. The two first ships to be powered with nuclear reactors were the Soviet icebreaker **Lenin** and the American **N.S. Savannah.** In contrast to **Lenin,** which had three reactors, the **N.S. Savannah** had only one, a pressure-vessel, pressurized water reactor capable of delivering through power conversion equipment 22,000 shaft horsepower to the screws. The **Savannah,** a sheltered deck ship with a modified mariner hull, was capable of carrying 60 passengers and 10,000 tons of dry cargo. It displaced 23,000 tons, was 1,596 feet long and 78 feet in beam, was manned by a crew of 66, and had a normal cruising speed of 20 knots. It was operated by the First Atomic Ship Transport Inc., a subsidiary of American Export Isbrandtsen Lines, Inc., for AEC and the Maritime Administration. The ship cost $55 million, and it was to determine the practicability of applying nuclear energy to commercial cargo and passenger vessels. Through 1967, the **Savannah** program cost $106 million.

Informing and Innovating

1953. In May, Nautilus Mark I went operational as the first pressurized water reactor for a ship.

1958. On May 22 the hull was laid for the **N.S. Savannah.**

1959. On July 21 the ship was launched.

1961. In December the reactor achieved criticality.

1962. Sea trials began for the **Savannah** in the spring. Full power operation was reached in April. It took sixteen hours for the reactor to reach power from a cold start and 3½ hours to get the reactor back on line after a scram. It could go from 20 percent to 100 percent power in thirty seconds. It took three minutes to go from full ahead to full astern, one minute to go from full astern to full ahead, and five seconds to go from full to zero power.[1]

1962-65. The **Savannah,** as a U.S testament for peaceful use of nuclear energy, travelled 90,000 miles, visited 64 ports in 39 countries or states, and received 1,390,000 visitors.

1966-67. Operating costs to the government were $853,480 beyond revenues of $2,614,421.[2]

1967. Because of operating losses, the administration proposed to lay up the **N.S. Savannah** after the end of the second year of commercial operations. Because of Congressional opposition, she was kept in operation.

1968. Germany launched the **Otto Hahn,** a $14 million nuclear merchant ship displacing 16,000 tons.

The Administration's speaker to Congress did not mention nuclear-powered merchant ships as part of the proposed five-year program.[3]

1971. The **N.S. Savannah** was mothballed.

Conclusions

1. The **N.S. Savannah** was a technical success exploiting technology available from the U. S. naval reactor programs.

2. The ship was an economic failure in that her operating subsidy was more than twice that of her class of conventional powered ships.[4] The technology has been temporarily rejected.

3. The ship operated for political and prestige reasons. Congressional and public support for her operation developed beyond the control of the Administration.

FOOTNOTES

[1] Robert L. Loftness, *Nuclear Power Plants* (New York: D. Van Nostrand Company, Inc., 1964), pp. 138–43.

[2] "Technical, Operational, and Economic Report on the *N.S. Savannah* for the Second Year of Commercial Operation: August 1966-1967," Office of R&D, Maritime Administration, U.S. Department of Commerce, 1967, pp. VI 1-VI 5.

[3] Statement of Alan S. Boyd, Secretary of Transportation, before the Senate Commerce Committee, Subcommittee on Merchant Marine and Fisheries, May 20, 1968.

[4] U.S. Senate, Committee on Commerce, *The Nuclear Ship Savannah,* Hearings before the Subcommittee on Merchant Marine and Fisheries, June 12, 1967, 90th Cong., 1st Sess. (Washington, D.C.: U.S. Government Printing Office, 1967), p. 7.

APPENDIX G

Comparisons Of Federal Agency Technology Diffusion Activities

APPENDIX G-1 — COMPARISON OF AGENCY INVENTING ACTIVITIES

	Agency inputs	Processing	Outputs	Feedback
USDA	Gov't. facilities. Civil service. $187 million FY 71 funding.[1] Clear mission. Needs by priority. National Agricultural Library.	Focused toward agricultural sector. Direct contact with potential users. Freedom to exploit breakthroughs. Sequential checking of results.	Public service patents. New or improved crops, equipment or techniques. Technical papers. Trained people.	Trials in state experiment stations. County agent interface to users. Decentralized control. Needs outlive usefulness. Formal program review at department level.
PHS	Gov't. & private facilities. Civil service & contractors. $882 million FY 71 funding. Clear mission. Previous work files & National Library of Medicine. Contractor proposals.	Focused on disease prevention. Fragmented to 19,000 projects. Peer selection of contractors. Freedom to exploit breakthroughs. Progression from known to unknown.	Public service patents. New medical reports, products, equipment & techniques. Trained people and unrecorded experience.	Careful testing of items. Environmental control not yet accomplished. Scarcity of medical professionals. Formal program review recently established.
DOD	Gov't. & private facilities. Contractors & civil service. $7,247 million FY 71 funding. Clear problem statement. Procedure to develop requirements. Defense Documentation Center. Contractor expertise.	Focused towards weapons & war materials. PPB & weapons systems management procedures. Selection during conceptual phase. Development & testing during definition and acquisition phases. Highly controlled environment. Work from known to related area.	Privately held patents. Weapons systems. Byproducts. Trained contractors & individuals.	Formal sequential testing of items. Incentive & penalty clauses. Economic concentration into favored areas & firms. Congressional committees influence program review.
Commerce	Gov't. facilities. Civil service. $102 million FY 71 funding. Internal requirements only. General economy support.	Focused toward service functions to support external inventing.	Private patents for general economy. Standards for general application.	Limited feedback. Minimal internal systems review. Minimal Congressional support.

[1]Funding includes applied research plus development, as shown in Appendices B-1 through B-7.

APPENDIX G-1 (continued)

	Agency inputs	Processing	Outputs	Feedback
NASA	Gov't. & private facilities. Contractors & civil service. Needs influenced by prestige and visibility. $2,577 million FY 71 funding.	Focused toward space missions. Facilities limited. PPB & project management procedures. Conceptual, definition, & acquisition phases. Some freedom to exploit breakthroughs.	Government patents. Space systems & technologies. Trained people & contractors. Byproducts.	Formal sequential testing of items. Economic concentration into favored areas & firms. Program review internally & at Presidential Office level.
AEC	Gov't. facilities. Contractors with civil service management. $1,026 FY 71 funding. Needs influenced by prestige & visibility.	Focused on nuclear industries, particularly nuclear power & radioisotopes. Contractor evaluates & selects projects.	Government patents (4500 now available). Trained contractor groups. Nuclear & non-nuclear technologies.	Formal & careful testing. Support concentrated into small number of firms & facilities. Program review internally & in Congressional committees.
SBA	Relies on other agencies for inventive work.			

APPENDIX G-2 — COMPARISON OF AGENCY INFORMING ACTIVITIES

	Agency inputs	Processing	Outputs	Feedback
USDA	Specific mission. Defined agricultural audience. R&D feedforward. Innovating feedback. National Agricultural Library (NAL). $10 million S&T information.[1]	Traditional procedures focused on agricultural user. County agents & land grant colleges in processing. USDA distribution system.	Trained people. Updated library. Awareness programs. Focused technical information.	Feedback from user through county agent & college channels as well as direct. Dispersed program. NAL lags. Systems review in total program context.
PHS	Specific mission. Generally defined medical audience. Feedforward from medical R&D. Innovating feedback. National Library of Medicine (NLM). $49 million S&T information.	Modern processing focused on medical industries & practitioners. Medical colleges in processing. PHS distribution system.	Trained people. Updated library & working files. New library techniques. Awareness programs. Focused technical information.	Internal evaluation on use & movements of facilities & people. Formal systems review by committees on information.
DOD	Internal feedforward. Specific internal but vague external audience. Defense Documentation Center. $141 million S&T information.	Traditional & modern processing focused on internal audience plus defense contractors. Intensive training programs. DOD distribution system.	Training in 1,500 specialties. Trained contractor & service groups. 20,000 documents to NTIS annually.	Expensive training & informing. Much informing through movements of trained people. Systems review in context of total programs.
Commerce	General mission but vague audience. Patent files & NTIS. $69 million S&T information.	Traditional processing focused on general audiences. Commerce distribution system.	45,000 Federal R&D reports & 70,000 patents annually. Awareness programs. Economic & social statistics.	"Near hits" for patents not processed. NTIS reports not evaluated. Patents not readily accessible to all. No formal systems review.

[1]Funds are for FY 71 in all agencies.

APPENDIX G-2 (continued)

	Agency inputs	Processing	Outputs	Feedback
NASA	Statutory mission. Specific internal, vague external audience. Internal R&D feedforward. S&T Information Div. $27 million S&T Information.	Modern processing focused on NASA & aerospace contractors. Training programs for industry. NASA distribution system.	Trained contractors & individuals. 1,000 technical briefs annually. 70,000 aerospace documents annually. 8,000 documents to Clearinghouse annually.	External activities not self-sustaining. Much external informing through movement of trained contractor groups. Internal systems review in context of total programs.
AEC	Statutory mission. Specific internal audiences. Internal feedforward. Div. of Public Infor. $5 million S&T information.	Modern processing focused on both internal & nuclear industry audiences. Training programs for industry. AEC distribution system.	Trained contractors & individuals. 5,000 documents to Clearinghouse annually. Updated files. Focused technical information. Awareness programs.	Much informing through movements of trained people. Systems review in context of total programs.
SBA	Office of Public Information. Limited information funds, under $1 million.	Traditional processing focused on small business audiences. Gov't. Printing does duplicating.	Selected technical items, aids, & advice. Trained people.	Response to items & training activities. Systems review at agency level.

APPENDIX G-3

COMPARISON OF AGENCY INNOVATING ACTIVITIES

	Agency inputs	Processing	Outputs	Feedback
USDA	Direct innovating mission. Public service patents. Well-defined customers. Strong support in county agent system, USDA agencies, and agricultural groups.	Information use identified. Potential market identified. Provides loans & subsidies. Adoption units go through AIETA.	New foods, fiber, & agricultural facilities. Trained people.	Market basic requirement for success. Support based on specific goals. Commercial farmers more prone to adopt. Small farmer squeezed to stay up.
PHS	Direct innovating mission. Public service patents. Customers fairly well defined. Strong support in national health institutes & consumer protection.	Information use identified. Provides public assistance, loans, & subsidies. Public & private health units go through AIETA.	New medical techniques, facilities, & equipment. Trained people.	Very rapid expansion, causing inflation and scarcity. Support for specific health groups. States & communities more prone to adopt.
DOD	Innovates indirectly. No specific mission beyond internal uses. Minimal support for external advocacy. General public customer.	Internal—Multiple-source procurement, small business set-asides, progress payments. Highly structured, decision processes in PPB & Weapons Systems Management.	Internal—Adopt new systems. Trained people.	Support based on specific goals. Government provides market support. Very expensive failures preclude other economic activities.
		External—Contractors exploit patents from DOD work & individuals apply DOD techniques.	External—Whole systems transferred to commercial use. Trained people moved to general economy. Commercial use of patents.	

APPENDIX G-3 (continued)

	Agency inputs	Processing	Outputs	Feedback
Commerce	Precluded from advocating specific patents. Private patents & proprietary information. General public customer. Limited support.	Provides general information and advice. Public or private units negotiate for proprietary rights in AIETA sequence.	New products & processes throughout the economy. Individuals with rights to exploit patents. General support information.	No direct gov't. support beyond patent rights. Dept. receives limited resource support.
NASA	External mission limited to advocacy. Marginal support for external work. General public customer.	Internal—Highly structured decision processes in PPBS & project management. External—Advocacy and limited creative adaptation.	Internal—adopted projects & trained people. External—Systems & items transfers to commercial use. Publication of patents and proprietary information.	Gov't. provides or supports market. Support based on specific goals. Constant high level systems review.
AEC	Limited innovating mission. Customer somewhat defined by law.	Internal—Changing contractors. External—Providing materials & training. AIETA sequence.	Internal—Adopted projects. Trained people. External—New processes or equipment applied.	Gov't. provides or supports market.
SBA	Direct innovating mission. Customer defined by law.	Provides technical, business, and management information. Information use is identified. Market is pinpointed. AIETA sequence.	New businesses. Businesses using new technology. Repaid loans.	Opportunities exceed funds.

APPENDIX G-4

COMPARISON OF AGENCY INTEGRATING ACTIVITIES

	Agency inputs	Processing	Outputs	Feedback
USDA	New technology. Existing regulation. Institutional support. $8,559 million FY 71 funding.[1]	Focused on agricultural sector. Adoption units follow AIETA & USDA offices support.	Increased production. Conservation. Community support. Displaced labor. Changed relationships. New regulations.	Labor saving, capital using, farm concentrating. Suboptimized to agriculture. Dept. level reviews. Congress & farmer groups overview.
PHS	New medical technology & training. 3 million clients. $2,160 million FY 71 funding. Rising deaths from technology.	Focused on disease prevention in public health. State, local, & medical units follow AIETA & PHS offices support.	Increased facilities & services to more citizens. Successful new medical practices. Cleaner environment. New regulations.	Environment not yet controlled. Maldistribution of doctors & health professionals. Labor & capital using. Service & dept. reviews. Health industry overview.
DOD	New technologies. National power & prestige goals. No specific non-mission goals. Partisan support. $75,921 million FY 71 funds.	Focused on defense sector. Centralized decisions to adopt. Highly structured in total system procurement.	Market support for new technology. New weapons systems. Trained contractors. Trained individuals.	Labor & capital using. Total effort precludes other national efforts. Control suboptimizes on defense needs. Main program review in Congress.
Commerce	All new technology. Clear goals, minimal support. $1,188 million FY 71 funding. Mainly EDA.	Focused on past integration. Private initiative. General statistical data provided.	Basic standards... General statistics. Few jobs in backward areas.	Job creating is costly. Little effect on overall integration. No overall systems review.

[1] Total agency or departmental funding is shown as best indicator of integrating effects.

APPENDIX G-4 (continued)

	Agency inputs	Processing	Outputs	Feedback
NASA	New technologies. National prestige goals. Minimal non-mission effort. Fading political support. $3,380 million FY 71 funding.	Focused on aerospace sector requirements. Centralized decisions to adopt. R&D procedures for almost entire budget.	Market support for space technology. New space systems & techniques. Trained contractors & individuals.	Labor and capital using. Total effort precludes other national activities. Neglect of aeronautics. Systems review of agency work is external.
AEC	New nuclear technologies. Clear internal goals to use advances. External goals in specific fields. $2,274 million FY 71 funding. Director of Regulation to control integrating.	Focused on nuclear-associated sectors. Imitative AIETA for adopting units. AEC changes contractors and transfers responsibilities to state and industrial offices.	New industries. New standards & regulation. Better quality goods. Trained contractors & individuals.	Labor saving, capital using. Some undesirable side effects. Costly to use nuclear processes. Congressional as well as internal reviews.
SBA	New technology from Federal & private R&D. Business opportunities. Clear agency mission. Direct & indirect funding support, $333 million direct.	Focused on small business. Imitative AIETA for small business adopters. SBA offices support with management, business, & technical information, advice, & loans.	New businesses. Reduced economic concentration by firm size. Local employment.	Repaid loans. Most loans are to areas of economic concentration. Agency and Congressional agency review.

INDEX

Name Index*

* f indicates footnote

Subject Index